Studies in Contemporary Economics

Ben C. J. van Velthoven

The Endogenization of Government Behaviour in Macroeconomic Models

Springer-Verlag
Berlin Heidelberg New York
London Paris Tokyo

Editorial Board

D. Bös G. Bombach B. Gahlen K. W. Rothschild

Author

Dr. Ben C. J. van Velthoven
Associate Professor
Department of Economics, Faculty of Law, Leiden University
P.O. Box 9521, NL-2300 RA Leiden, The Netherlands

ISBN 3-540-50925-9 Springer-Verlag Berlin Heidelberg New York
ISBN 0-387-50925-9 Springer-Verlag New York Berlin Heidelberg

This work is subject to copyright. All rights are reserved, whether the whole or part of the material is concerned, specifically the rights of translation, reprinting, re-use of illustrations, recitation, broadcasting, reproduction on microfilms or in other ways, and storage in data banks. Duplication of this publication or parts thereof is only permitted under the provisions of the German Copyright Law of September 9, 1965, in its version of June 24, 1985, and a copyright fee must always be paid. Violations fall under the prosecution act of the German Copyright Law.

© Springer-Verlag Berlin Heidelberg 1989
Printed in Germany

Printing and Binding: Weihert-Druck GmbH, Darmstadt.
2142/3140-543210

*to the memory
of my father*

CONTENTS

0	WHAT THIS BOOK IS ALL ABOUT	1
1	THE TRADITIONAL THEORY OF ECONOMIC POLICY	7
1.1	The theory of economic policy	7
1.2	Empirical reaction function studies	11
1.3	Targets and instruments	13
1.4	Macroeconometric modelbuilding	16
1.4.1	A historical sketch	16
1.4.2	Critique	18
1.5	The preference function of the policy maker	23
1.5.1	Establishing the preference function	23
1.5.2	Optimizing or satisficing	31
1.6	Conclusions	33
2	THE IMPACT OF POLITICS, A SURVEY OF THE LITERATURE	35
2.1	Introduction	35
2.2	The median voter model	36
2.3	Voting and popularity functions	42
2.3.1	Introduction	42
2.3.2	Theoretical foundation	43
2.3.3	Discussion and empirical findings	45
2.3.4	Summary	52
2.4	Government behaviour	53
2.4.1	Introduction	53
2.4.2	The political business cycle	54
2.4.3	Political parties and (macro)economic policy	59

2.4.4	The Frey-Schneider approach and related models	63
2.4.5	Two other models: crisis management and the permanent income hypothesis	73
2.4.6	Conclusion	77
2.5	The influence of the bureaucracy	78
2.5.1	Introduction	78
2.5.2	Bureaucrats as voters	79
2.5.3	Bureaucrats versus politicians within the public sector decision making process	81
2.5.4	Summary	87
2.6	Interest groups	88
2.6.1	Introduction	88
2.6.2	The logic of collective action	88
2.6.3	The influence of interest groups on public sector decision making	89
2.6.4	Summary	93
2.7	The Marxist approach	94
2.8	Conclusions	97
3.	**THE INTEREST FUNCTION APPROACH**	**101**
3.1	Introduction	101
3.2	Outline of the interest function approach	101
3.3	Discussion	113
3.4	Summary and conclusions	126
4.	**THE ENDOGENIZATION OF STATE EXPENDITURE AND TAXATION IN A SIMPLE KEYNESIAN MODEL**	**129**
4.1	Introduction	129
4.2	The behaviour of the state	132
4.3	A static Keynesian politico-economic model	142
4.4	Some dynamic aspects of the model	148
4.5	Summary	153

5.	**AN APPLICATION TO THE NETHERLANDS**	**155**
5.1	Introduction	155
5.2	Data and empirical application	158
5.2.1	The data	158
5.2.2	State expenditure and tax receipts	159
5.2.3	The power coefficient δ	161
5.2.4	The power coefficient δ; a transformation	173
5.3	Conclusions	178
Appendix	More on the data	180
6.	**A DYNAMIC VERSION OF THE MODEL WITH AN ENDOGENOUS SOCIAL POWER STRUCTURE**	**185**
6.1	Introduction	185
6.2	General dynamics	186
6.3	A special case	194
6.4	Conclusion	201
7.	**TOWARDS A POLITICO-ECONOMIC THEORY OF SOCIAL SECURITY**	**203**
7.1	Introduction	203
7.2	The behaviour of the state; social security policies	206
7.2.1	Social classes and interests	206
7.2.2	The behaviour of the state	208
7.2.3	Endogenization of the unemployment benefit level	214
7.2.4	Some additional remarks	217
7.3	Social security in a complete politico-economic model	218
7.3.1	The model	218
7.3.2	The effects of social security on production and employment	222
7.3.3	The effect of social security on the stability of the economy	225
7.3.4	Some first conclusions	227
7.3.5	Demographic developments	228

7.3.6	Changes in the effective interest structure Δ	229
7.4	Empirical application	230
7.4.1	Introduction	230
7.4.2	Regression results	231
7.4.3	An exercise in revealed preference	238
7.5	Conclusion	241
Appendix	Data for application of the model including the social security system	243

8.	**TOWARDS A BEHAVIOURAL-THEORETIC ANALYSIS OF BUDGET DEFICITS**	**249**
8.1	Introduction	249
8.2	The model	253
8.2.1	Introduction	253
8.2.2	The model	258
8.2.3	Alternative formulations	262
8.3	Discussion	264
8.3.1	Introduction	264
8.3.2	Impact of the preferences for private and public goods	265
8.3.3	Impact of the time preferences and time horizons	268
8.3.4	Income versus profit taxes	273
8.3.5	Impact of the level of state debt and the rate of interest	275
8.3.6	Impact of the size and the growth rate of the tax base	277
8.3.7	Impact of the time horizon	280
8.3.8	Conclusions	282
8.4	The budget deficit over time; some preliminary results	283
8.4.1	Introduction	283
8.4.2	The budget deficit along a steady growth path	284
8.4.3	The budget deficit along the business cycle	286
8.5	Conclusion	290

9.	**EPILOGUE**	**293**

NOTES	303
REFERENCES	339
AUTHOR INDEX	359
SUBJECT INDEX	363

ACKNOWLEDGEMENTS

The research on which this book is reporting was started in the months preceding the Dutch 1981 parliamentary election, at the time Frans van Winden had finished his PhD-thesis. He suggested that we should write an article for the Dutch professional economics weekly ESB, applying the interest function approach that he presented in that thesis to the analysis of politico-economic interaction in the Netherlands. The article should appear in may 1981 in the week of the election when presumably the readers would be most susceptible to the subject. The article indeed did come out, but only in november 1982. However, the result then proved to be a nicely handable description of public sector decision making on expenditure and taxation, fit for inclusion in macroeconomic modelling and for empirical application, and apt for further elaboration. This book is, for the time being, the end product of the subsequent research.

Accounting for my indebtedness to all kinds of persons, I wish to thank first of all Frans van Winden for giving me the impulse to enter into the field of research, for having been the co-author of several papers underlying this book, and for the inspiring discussions and comments during the final stage of writing this monograph. I am also grateful to all those who contributed in one way or another to the publications on which a number of chapters of this book are based. Paul Renaud should be named explicitly for offering some useful suggestions; Eitel Homan, Cees-Jan de Wolff, Frank Ottenhoff, Rogier Simonse and Ton Timman for computational assistance at some time or other during the past years; and Hedy Braun, Saskia ten Asbroek and Joyce Hillebrand for secretarial assistance. I further wish to thank Nelie Westra-van den Berg, who is employed at the department "centrale tekstverwerking" of the Faculty of Law of Leyden University, for carefully typing the manuscript of this book. Finally, I wish to acknowledge the mental support by W. Eizenga who never stopped asking me, in his well-known gentle manner, when the book would be ready.

CHAPTER 0. WHAT THIS BOOK IS ALL ABOUT

In the past decades the public sector has been growing steadily and considerably. In all Western countries the government plays a central role in the economy, due to its own expenditure, the redistribution of resources within the economy, and the regulation of the private sector.

As an illustration table 0.1 presents some figures for the Dutch economy. This table shows that by now two thirds of national income in one way or another passes through the public sector. In 1950 this share only amounted to somewhat above 30%. Of the different kinds of outlays, especially transfers have been booming. The growth of the public sector's own expenditure has been substantial too, but considerably less relative to national income. In recent years interest payments on government debt have been rising rapidly due to high interest rates and increases in budget deficits. As to the public sector's receipts, social security premiums have increased, parallel to the building up of the social security system. Non-tax receipts have also shown a rapid growth recently, due especially to profits from the exploitation of Dutch natural gas reserves. Finally, the considerable budget deficits of the past years should be noticed. In other OECD-countries the pattern of public sector outlays and of financing them may differ, and the share of the public sector on average may be lower, nevertheless this share (relative to GDP) ranges from a low 35% in Japan and the US, a medium 50% in France, Germany and the UK, to a high 65% in the Netherlands and Sweden. For a recent survey, see Saunders and Klau (1985).

This huge share of the public sector and its concomitant large influence on the economy with respect to issues of allocation, redistribution as well as stability, makes the public sector - or maybe we should say more accurately, the central government - the single most important agent in the economy. But then, of course, economists could - or better, should - be asked what theories they have to offer on the activities of this agent, both with respect to the consequences of these activities on the economy and, more specifically, with respect to the decision making processes within the public sector from which these activities originate. This study will deal with the latter issue. However,

Table O.1. Public sector outlays and receipts in the Netherlands, 1955-1986

	National income (net, market prices)	Public sector outlays	Public sector outlays[a] total	expenditure	transfers	Interest on government debt	Public sector receipts[b] total	taxes	social security premiums
	in billions of guilders		in % of national income				in % of national income		
1955	27.3	10.2	37.4	18.7	13.4	2.6	(31.5)	24.8	5.1
60	38.4	14.8	38.7	18.4	14.5	3.0	(36.3)	25.2	9.0
65	62.6	28.2	45.1	21.2	17.7	2.6	40.9	26.2	12.4
70	111.5	53.3	47.8	21.1	21.1	3.2	44.3	26.9	15.0
71	125.1	62.7	50.2	22.1	22.0	3.2	46.2	28.0	15.9
72	141.7	71.6	50.5	21.2	23.3	3.0	47.3	28.8	16.1
73	162.6	81.4	50.0	20.3	24.1	3.0	48.2	28.4	17.4
74	184.2	95.9	52.1	20.9	25.9	3.2	50.0	28.8	18.4
75	199.9	115.2	57.6	22.7	29.5	3.4	52.2	29.1	19.3
76	229.6	132.3	57.6	22.3	29.9	3.3	52.7	29.3	18.8
77	251.2	144.7	57.6	22.0	30.4	3.3	53.5	29.9	18.7
78	269.7	159.3	59.1	22.3	31.9	3.4	53.4	29.8	19.1
79	285.9	175.3	61.3	22.7	33.5	3.6	55.3	30.6	19.7
80	303.6	194.8	64.2	22.7	35.3	4.1	57.0	31.0	20.2
81	316.3	212.6	67.2	22.5	37.3	4.9	58.1	30.0	20.9
82	330.6	228.1	69.0	22.3	38.9	5.7	58.4	29.1	21.9
83	342.4	237.3	69.3	21.8	39.6	6.3	60.0	28.4	24.3
84	356.9	244.1	68.4	21.0	39.1	6.7	59.3	28.2	23.2
85	373.4	250.2	67.0	20.3	38.0	7.1	59.0	28.2	22.7
1986	380.7	254.3	66.8	19.9	37.9	7.3	57.8	28.9	22.2

Sources: - Miljoenennota 1987, Bijlage 15 (data for public sector outlays)
- Centraal Planbureau, Centraal Economisch Plan 1987 and 1979, Bijlage B.1 (national income data) and C.1 (data for public sector receipts; the data within brackets were calculated by the author from the National Accounts).

a) The column transfers includes income and capital transfers to households and firms and subsidies to firms.
   That part of total outlays which is not covered in the three separate columns, refers to the issuing of loans by the public to the private sector.
b) That part of total receipts which is not covered in the two separate columns, refers to non-tax receipts, especially income from investments and participations.

for the sake of manageability and exposition, we shall restrict ourselves, as the title of this book indicates, to macroeconomic aspects and to economic and political aggregates. That is, we study the determination of the levels of government expenditure, social security outlays, taxation, the budget deficit, public sector employment and the like, without going into the details of their composition. When economists would have a coherent theory of public sector decision making at their disposal, they would be in a position to fully endogenize the respective components of government activity in their macroeconomic models. As will be discussed in the sequel, this would help to avoid certain errors in the specification and estimation of these models and to produce better forecasts, while, more generally, it would give rise to a more realistic vision on the potentialities and limitations of (macroeconomic) policy advising.

We start our analysis with a review of the literature on macroeconomic policy making. Generally speaking, two trains of thought can be distinguished. On the one hand, the so-called theory of economic policy, which has a normative tendency (how to determine an optimal economic policy), and which points economists - once they take the aims and preferences of the political authorities for granted - the way to macroeconomic policy advising. On the other hand, the public choice approach, which - at least those parts of it which are most relevant to our subject - studies the decision making processes within and the behaviour of the public sector from a positive point of view. That is, it tries to explain what is actually going on. The two approaches will be surveyed critically in the first two chapters of this book, respectively. Chapter 1 reviews the traditional theory of economic policy. This theory of economic policy shows deficiencies once one tries to turn it into a positive theory, as it lacks a theory of the political and economic forces determining the targets and preferences of the policy makers. The public choice approach tries to fill in this gap, by studying voting behaviour, the behaviour of politicians and political parties, the behaviour of the bureaucracy, and of pressure groups. But this literature, as will be discussed in chapter 2, lacks internal coherency, while moreover the empirical support is neither unanimous nor very convincing. Because of the many bits and pieces of this literature and the plethora of publications in recent years, we have thought it desirable and useful to reserve some space to bring its development, as far as it may be of relevance for macroeconomic modelling, in focus. Those readers who are already familiar with the literature can be advised to skip directly to the summary and conclusions in section 2.8.

From chapter 3 onwards we then shall present our own approach to the analysis of public sector behaviour with regard to the macroeconomic functioning of society. Our analysis will be based on the so-called interest function approach that has been developed by Van Winden (1983, 1987). In this approach individual as well as collective actions are supposed to be related to individual interests. However, as purely individualistic interests typically do not count in political processes, attention is focused on the interests of individuals as occupants of certain basic or elementary economic positions. For research-strategic reasons, four such elementary economic positions are distinguished, to wit: state sector worker (politician or bureaucrat), private sector worker, capital owner, and dependant. The group of people in each elementary economic position is referred to as a social class. Connected with this distinction between social classes, the approach emphasizes the importance of the power structure of society; to which extent do the members of the different social classes ultimately - i.e. through all the available means combined - succeed in getting their interests promoted in the public sector decision making process. The interest function approach leads to the observation that the behaviour of the public sector (or state) can be explained as acting in accordance with the - constrained - maximization of a state interest function; this state interest function is a weighted representation of the interest functions of the representative individuals of the social classes, the weights being determined by the power structure of society. The interest function approach thus offers a coherent, yet condensed picture of the influence of the social classes on public sector behaviour. It is presented and criticized in some detail in chapter 3.

Chapter 4 presents our basic model to be used in subsequent chapters. Employing the interest function approach to analyze the decision making process with regard to public expenditure and taxation, behavioural equations are derived for state expenditure, state employment, and the tax rate. These behavioural equations are then used to transform the textbook Keynesian income-expenditure model, which can serve as an easy point of reference, into a politico-economic model. The comparative-static and dynamic properties of this politico-economic model are analyzed at some length.

To illustrate the potentialities of our yet simple model as well as to discuss the problems involved, the basic model of state behaviour is applied to Dutch data (period 1952-1984) in chapter 5. This empirical application - which, it should be stressed, is only intended to be of an exploratory nature - provides some support for the hypothesis that the relative influence on public sector decision making of the (economically active) social classes is related to and can be proxied by their relative numerical strength.

The latter finding can be inserted in the basic model of chapter 4, turning it into a fully dynamic, closed politico-economic model. The analysis of that model in chapter 6 suggests that the politico-economic system might at any rate be globally stable if the state would not run into budget deficits.

In the chapters 7 and 8 we return to the basic model of chapter 4 and extend it in two different directions, respectively. In chapter 7 the model is elaborated to cope with transfer payments. A distinction is made between labour market related social security programs (unemployment benefits) and labour market unrelated income transfers (such as to pensioners, widows and disabled persons). From this extended model we can, e.g., deduce the impact of changes in preferences and in the power structure of society on the social security benefit rates, and on the level of state employment and the number of social security beneficiaries. Inserting the behavioural equations for the state in the benchmark Keynesian income-expenditure model shows, among other things, that it is precluded that both the labour market related and labour market unrelated social security programs have a stabilizing impact on the economy at the same time; it remains possible that they simultaneously have a negative impact on stability.

In chapter 8 the setting of the basic model is transformed into one of multi-period planning in order to study public sector decision making on the size of the budget deficit/surplus, in addition to public expenditure and taxation. Budget deficits are assumed to be fully covered by the issuing of bonds; financing through money creation is not taken into consideration. From the behavioural equations for the state, it follows, e.g. , that the budget deficit will tend to be larger the more the time horizon of the state surpasses the time horizons of the social classes, the higher are the rates of time preference of the social classes, the higher is the expected rate of growth of the economy, and the lower is the rate of interest. Changes in the social power structure will also affect the budget balance. Whether the budget balance reacts pro- or countercyclically to changes in the tax base appears to depend on how the public sector is actually forming expectations on the future course of the economy.

Chapter 9, lastly, summarizes the main features of the book and concludes with some final remarks.

We end this synopsis of our book, in which we will be mostly interested in the functioning of western representative democracies, with a terminological issue. Quite often, as in common parlance, we will be using the terms public sector, state and government interchangeably. Sometimes, however, it will prove necessary to give these terms a more precise meaning. Throughout, public sector and state will be used as substitutes, to denote the organization that successfully claims the monopoly of legitimate violence within a certain territory. The different institutions and apparatuses that the state organization consists of, can be subsumed under two headings, government and bureaucracy. Then, the term government is used to denote the "representative" bodies, forming the formal decision making centre; the government is made up by politicians, the bureaucracy by bureaucrats. Government thus comprises parliament and cabinet (in a parliamentary system), or congress and president (as in the US presidential system). In an even more restricted sense, especially relevant in the context of a multi-party system with coalition cabinets, government will be used as a substitute for cabinet, as opposed to parliament. The context in which the terms are used, will make clear which meaning is intended.

CHAPTER 1. THE TRADITIONAL THEORY OF ECONOMIC POLICY

1.1. The theory of economic policy

The theory of economic policy can be said to have its origin with the seminal contribution by Tinbergen (1952). In its broadest sense "economic policy" may stand for the acts of economic behaviour by any agent whichsoever; in its more specific sense, however, the expression refers to the behaviour of governments. Tinbergen distinguishes between two different kinds of economic policy, quantitative and qualitative policy. By qualitative economic policy is meant the changing of certain qualitative aspects of the economic structure, such as for instance the introduction of a customs union or the nationalisation of an industry. Interesting and important as this qualitative economic policy may be, it is - because of its nature and long term relevance - not very easy to investigate and to quantify its effects. The analysis of Tinbergen, and of the researchers following him, focusses almost entirely on quantitative economic policy. By this is meant the changing, within the qualitative framework of the given structure, of certain (political) parameters or instruments.

The basic ingredients of the analysis are the following:
- a set of <u>instrument variables</u>, which are subject to direct control by the policy maker;
- the set of other, noncontrolled variables. As far as the values of these variables are of interest to, or contribute to the "welfare" of, the policy maker, they are called <u>target variables</u>;
- a <u>quantitative empirical</u> (econometric) <u>model</u>, describing the economic relationships between (the values of) the target, instrument and other variables. Let x denote the column vector of values of the instrument variables, y the column vector of values of the target variables, and s the column vector of remaining variables, including lagged variables, noncontrolled exogenous variables and, possibly, disturbance terms. If R and Z are the appropriate matrices of reduced form coefficients, the economic model can be represented by the linear system:

(1.1) $y = Rx + Zs$;

- a criterion, preference or "welfare" function W, which evaluates the level of satisfaction the policy maker associates with the values of the target and instrument variables;
- and, possibly, a set of boundary conditions or constraints on the target, instrument and/or other variables.

According to the theory of economic policy, the policy maker now must make a choice among the alternative values of the instrument variables available to him, such that the result, given the prediction from the economic model of the future course of the noncontrolled variables, is "satisfactory" or even "best" according to his preferences.

In the original formulation by Tinbergen the stage of determining the welfare function W was passed over. Instead, relevant target values, say y^*, for the target variables are chosen directly. These y^* can be interpreted to be unique optimal levels for these variables, but can also indicate certain "aspiration levels" with which the policy maker would be satisfied in the given circumstances. Now, if the number of target variables equals that of the instrument variables, and if the matrix R is non-singular, it is possible to express x in terms of y. Hence, we can derive for each set of target values y^* the appropriate set of instrument values to attain these targets:

(1.2) $x = R^{-1}[y^* - Zs]$.

This vector x is the solution to the policy problem. But, in case the number of instruments is smaller than the number of targets, the targets cannot in general be realized simultaneously. The policy problem then has no solution. If the number of instruments is larger than the number of targets, degrees of freedom arise for the policy maker. Different sets of instrument values are available to reach the targets y^*. In this situation the original Tinbergen formulation offers no way of choosing between the alternatives.

For these latter cases Theil (1958) advocates the optimization approach, a more general formulation in which an explicit criterion function W = W(x,y) is used. In the resulting so-called flexible target model the instrument values are chosen to optimize the function W, subject to restrictions imposed by the working of the economy, as represented by the empirical model. To be more specific, Theil introduces a quadratic welfare function, according to which the preferences of the policy maker are represented by:

(1.3) $W = a'x + b'y + \frac{1}{2}[x'Ax + y'By + x'Cy + y'C'x]$,

where a, b, A, B and C are vectors and matrices of appropriate order with fixed elements and where A and B are symmetric. Theil then introduces the principle of certainty equivalence. If the additive term s in (1.1) is stochastic, but everything else is known with certainty, the optimal policy can be obtained by maximizing (1.3) under the restriction (1.1), with the random variable s simply replaced by its expected value E(s).

Frequently in the literature, see e.g. Friedlaender (1973), instead of the welfare function (1.3) a quadratic loss function is used which has to be minimized by the policy maker. A priori established desired values of the target and instrument variables are denoted by y^* and x^*. Furthermore, interactions between preferences for targets and instruments are neglected, i.e. C = 0, implying that the policy maker does not associate beforehand specific tools with specific goals. The policy problem then reads:

(1.4) minimize $W = a'\bar{x} + b'\bar{y} + \frac{1}{2}[\bar{x}'A\bar{x} + \bar{y}'B\bar{y}]$

subject to y = Rx + Zs,

where $\bar{x} := x - x^*$, $\bar{y} := y - y^*$, and s is the vector of expected values of the remaining variables. Substituting y = Rx + Zs into W, differentiating with respect to x, and deriving the usual first-order condition yields:

(1.5) $a + R'b + A\bar{x} + R'B\bar{y} = 0$.

Assuming that the second-order conditions are fulfilled the solution to the policy problem is then given by:

(1.6) $\quad x = (A + R'BR)^{-1}(-a - R'b + Ax^* + R'By^* - R'BZs)$.

In deriving this solution the excessively restrictive requirements of the Tinbergen solution noted above could be avoided. Note that in general the optimal values for the instrument and target variables will not be identical to the desired values, x^* and y^*, which underlie the criterion function (1.4). The policy makers' "reaction function" (1.6) shows how the government should react to changes in (the structure of) the economy or to changes in its preferences. In many empirical studies, to which we shall turn shortly, (1.6) is replaced by its analogon derived from (1.5):

(1.7) $\quad \bar{x} = - A^{-1}(a + R'b) - A^{-1}R'B\bar{y}$,

which is also often called a reaction function.

A further extension of the framework is a dynamic generalization to a multi-period planning horizon. But, as is noted by Theil (1958), the formulation above will suit that purpose well after a proper redefinition of all variables and matrices to their multi-period equivalents.

For our purpose, this much will do as an introduction to the theory of economic policy. For a thorough discussion of the more technical problems related to issues such as the estimation of the empirical model, the solution methods of control problems for dynamic and stochastic economic systems, and generalizations to non-linear models and to criterion functions which are not quadratic, the reader is referred to the specialized literature. See, among others, Fox, Sengupta and Thorbecke (1966), Chow (1975), Friedman (1975), Preston and Pagan (1982), Hughes Hallett and Rees (1983).

We now want to give attention to the applicability and actual application of the theory of economic policy. As indicated, the framework of the theory is formed by a set of targets, a set of instruments, a quantitative empirical model of the economy, and a criterion or welfare function of the policy maker, which is optimized over the set of alternatives. Before we start a more thorough discussion of these basic ingredients of the theory, one at a time, we first shall take a look, in section 1.2, at the empirical evidence contained in the reaction function literature, which suggests that the theory of economic policy has been put to practice, or at least that economic policy is being carried out in some systematic manner. Turning to the basic ingredients of the theory we shall in section 1.3 discuss which variables belong to the sets of targets and instruments, and how these sets are delimited. The historical development of macroeconometric modelbuilding, aimed at providing increasingly more reliable, and more specific, tools for the analysis of the effects of economic policy actions, is briefly sketched in section 1.4. Our primary interest in that section, however, will be directed to the problems connected with the proper specification, estimation and application of these models, that arise as soon as economic policy would indeed be following a path described by a reaction function like eq. (1.7). Most serious difficulties in applying the theory of economic policy, at least for outside observers, are presented by the policy maker's criterion function, or better, by the lack of knowledge of this function. In section 1.5, therefore, a review is given of the methods used by economists to determine this criterion function. In that context we shall also address ourselves to the suggestion put forward in the literature that in practice policy makers might not be optimizing but only just satisficing. Section 1.6 concludes.

1.2. Empirical reaction function studies

The presentation of the theory of economic policy in the previous section suggested that economic policy should follow a pattern described by a reaction function like (1.6) or (1.7). In that connection it is very interesting to take a look at the empirical evidence for the use of reaction functions by policy makers. As Cowart (1978a, p. 309) puts it: "Prescriptive policy theory, once it comes to enjoy widespread dissemination among policy makers, soon becomes empirical policy theory". In the literature, indeed, attempts have been undertaken to identify and test policy reaction functions. These studies focus mainly on the behaviour of the monetary authorities, much more than on fiscal policy, as probably monetary policy is more easily (technically, politically) adjusted in the short run to changing economic conditions. Beginning with Dewald and Johnson (1963) and Reuber (1964), a large number of empirical studies have been published. To mention just a few: Wood (1967), Fisher (1968), Friedlaender (1973), Froyen (1974), Fase and Den Butter (1977), Fair (1978a), Cowart (1978a), Abrams, Froyen and Waud (1980). A striking characteristic of these studies is the variety of dependent variables representing the instruments of monetary policy. If we take the US as an example[1], we encounter the money supply (Dewald and Johnson), open market operations (Friedlaender), the monetary base (Froyen), the treasury bill rate (Fair) and the federal funds rate (Abrams c.s.). Furthermore, although the authors agree that the monetary authorities are reacting in a systematic way to the major macroeconomic target variables, no agreement exists as to the targets which are found to have a significant influence. Dewald and Johnson as well as Froyen find significant effects for targets concerning unemployment and the growth of national income, Wood for the balance of payments position and unemployment, Friedlaender for national income growth and inflation. It should be added that several authors have (re)estimated their equations for several subperiods, e.g. Friedlaender, Froyen, Abrams c.s. It appears that the reaction functions are not very stable over time.

Similar conclusions have been reached for the Netherlands. Fase and Den Butter (1977) estimate monetary reaction functions for discount rate policy and credit restrictions. They conclude that the rate of unemployment and the movements of interest rates in the domestic and foreign money market were the main determinants of Dutch discount rate policy over the period 1958-1975. For credit control policy the main determinants appear to be the balance of payments and the rate of unemployment. Dividing the sample periode into three subperiods shows that the reaction functions are not very stable. These results are corroborated by Cowart (1978a) who studies, among other things, Dutch discount rate policy over the periode 1959-1975:I and finds a significant influence for the unemployment variable.

Although the monetary reaction function studies are far outnumbering the studies on fiscal policy, the latter do exist. Friedlaender (1973) considers reaction functions for government expenditures, personal tax rates and corporate tax rates, and obtains, for the US, good fits and several significant effects for unemployment, the rate of growth, and the balance of trade. Cowart (1978b), on the other hand, in his analysis of the budget surplus/deficit for several European countries finds no significant influence from unemployment and inflation. However, making allowance for partisan differences in fiscal policy making, he finds evidence for Germany and some indication for the Netherlands that politically left governments have been more willing to pursue activist fiscal policies than right ones.

The latter result points to a more general finding, namely that politics matter. Friedlaender (1973) and Froyen (1974) obtain for the US different reaction functions for different administrations. Cowart (1978a) finds for a series of European countries important differences among types of government.[2] In Dutch monetary policy, e.g., the officially set discount rates are higher - ceteris paribus - under Labour/Catholic coalitions than under majority Catholic rule without Labour participation. According to his results, governments of the left also have exhibited a level of responsiveness to changes in unemployment and inflation which far exceeds that for their conservative counterparts. As we shall address the political issue in greater detail later on in this book, we content ourselves for the moment with this making mention of it only.

1.3. Targets and instruments

There is thus empirical evidence that economic policy is characterized by some sort of regular pattern, which need not be stable over time. In that context it seems useful to review the basic ingredients of the theory of economic policy more thoroughly.

The first issue then is what the <u>targets</u> are of economic policy. As the framework's formulation is very general, these targets can, in principle, be in the fields of stabilization, allocation, as well as redistribution policy. In the Netherlands for instance, the empirical point of reference for this study, the Social Economic Council (a tripartite advisory body to the government, made up by an equal number of representatives of trade union federations, employers associations, and government appointed independent experts) formulated in the early fifties five general goals for economic policy, which have been generally advocated subsequently. These, sometimes rather indefinite, goals are: full employment, price stability, balance of payments equilibrium, economic growth, and a fair income distribution. In the seventies this set has been extended with the objective of environmental protection and pollution control. See De Wolff and Driehuis (1980) for more details. As a matter of fact, this set of stated objectives is not specific to the Dutch situation, but appears to meet a rather general acceptance across countries. Some other objectives which might be added to the list are improvement in the allocation of production factors and the satisfaction of collective needs. A full account of the targets of economic policy is contained in Kirschen et al. (1964).

When discussing the <u>instruments</u> of economic policy the first to think of concern the field of public finance: the level and composition of government expenditure; the level and composition of taxation; the extensiveness, the level of benefits and the premiums of the social security system. Furthermore, the policy maker may have at its disposal instruments of monetary policy and the exchange rate, instruments of wage and price policy, and other forms of regulation and deregulation. For an extensive discussion the reader is again referred to Kirschen et al. (1964).

At this point some reservations should be made:
<u>a</u>. What goes under the heading of targets, does not always seem to belong there. From the usual formulation of (individual) utility functions one would expect to see as the objectives of economic policy the level (and the distribution) of the provision of private and public goods and services (including leisure time). From this perspective objectives such as balance of payments equilibrium and price stability are no more than constraints, not targets in themselves. However, for practical purposes given the actual importance of these constraints, they are usually reckoned among the targets.

More generally, the theory of economic policy takes the target variables, the aims of the policy maker for granted. These aims of economic policy need not be constant over time, for, as can be deduced from the empirical results in section 1.2, politics may intervene here. The political justification of the choice of targets, and of their weighing in the criterion function, thus needs further study. This is not the proper place to do so; but see chapter 2.

b. The border line between objectives and instruments of economic policy is fluent. For instance, the level of government expenditure is both an instrument (controllable by the government) and an objective (the provision of public goods). This problem is taken account of in the theory by allowing that both targets and instruments enter the criterion function and by letting the border line between targets and instruments coincide with that between endogenous and exogenous variables.

Connected with this point, it should be stressed that the instrument variables have to be properly defined. The tax rates rather than tax revenue are an instrument of economic policy, as the latter also depends on the level of economic activity, (probably) an endogenous variable. In the same vein are the discount rate and the minimum required reserve ratio rather than the interest rate or the money supply instruments of monetary policy. And so on.

Finally, anticipating the ensuing discussion of macroeconom(etr)ic model building, it may be noticed that the use of reaction functions by governments would blur the distinction between endogenous (target) and exogenous (instrument) variables, at least for an outside observer. For the policy maker and the policy adviser this problem does not arise (although they too should take care that the model they use is not subject to specification errors; see further on).

c. Instruments differ in the timing and the extent of their effects. The quantitative empirical model is designed and used to offer answers to this sort of questions. Apart from the gestation period, time interests us here for two other, related reasons. First, time may elapse between a change in the economy which would necessitate the policy maker to take measures, and the actual execution of such measures, as several lags may occur in the process of policy making itself. Kirschen et al. (1964) list the stages of this process, and the possible time lags involved, as follows: 1. recognition, 2. analysis and 3. designing of measures, 4. consultation of e.g. political parties and interest groups, 5. parliamentary discussion, and 6. execution.

Secondly, institutional and other factors may bring about that not all instrument variables can be varied to the same extent and within the same time span. For example, civil servants cannot be hired and fired at will; projects once instituted are protected by vested interests. On the other hand, central bank discount rates can in general be adjusted very rapidly. Incidentally, this may be one of the main reasons why the reaction functions literature originated with and centred around monetary policy.

1.4. Macroeconometric modelbuilding

1.4.1. A historical sketch

Our next point of attention is the quantitative, empirical model. While the use of macroeconom(etr)ic models is now widespread over the world, its cradle presumably stood in the Netherlands. For already in 1936 the first (crude) econometric model of the Dutch economy was constructed; see Tinbergen (1936). We shall lift out some elements from the Dutch history of model building to outline more general developments.

Immediately after World War II, an institute was set up in the Netherlands, the Centraal Planbureau (Central Planning Bureau, CPB), to assist the government with technical advice in the process of policy making and especially the preparation of the annual budget. It was instructed to give "a balanced system of forecasts and directives in relation to the economy". Apart from directly advising the government, the CPB twice a year makes public forecasts based on (intended) government policy. Underlying the work of the CPB are quantitative macroeconomic models. The first CPB-model to be published, after the year of publication known as model-1955, consisted of 27 equations including 11 reaction functions.[3] Notable characteristics: it was an annual model of a truly Keynesian nature, fully linear, without lags, and with coefficients not estimated but chosen a priori. This model has in several steps (models 1961, 63-D, 69-C)[4] been perfected by estimating the coefficients, making allowance for lagged effects, introducing non-linearities and taking some notice of the influence of monetary factors. In the seventies, these annual models - destined for the formulation of stabilization policies - were replaced by quarterly models.[5] For medium term forecasting and structural policy analysis other models were developed[6], in which the effects of investments and of real wage developments on the economy's production capacity were taken into consideration. In the most recent generation of CPB-models[7], these two lines of modelling have been integrated, while also a full monetary section has been added. One quarterly model - containing a few hundred equations - is now being used for both short-term forecasting and medium-term analysis.

From the earliest models on, it has been recognized that at least some of the variables related to government activity have an endogenous nature. Already in model-1955 it is modelled - in what are called "institutional equations" - how the tax receipts and the outlays for unemployment insurance depend on the level of economic activity, given the tax rates and the dole rate. In the more recent models this "endogenization" of the government sector by institutional relations has been extended to: the public sector wage rate and social security benefits which in principle have been coupled to the private sector wage or consumption price indices; the determination of social security premiums as social security is financed by a pay-as-you-go-system; and the issuance of government debt which follows from the government budget constraint once the stance of monetary policy is set.

In the course of time the models have grown such as to give more, and more precise, entries for the simulation of the impact of different kinds of instruments, specified in greater detail. At the same time, however, the original almost universal acceptance of the CPB-forecasts - attributed to the scientific reputation of its directors and its monopoly position in econometric modelling - diminished. First, of course, violent economic-theoretical discussions have been running in the international literature on the usefulness of (the current) large macroeconometric models. More specifically for the Netherlands, some experiences have led especially the trade unions to question the accuracy and the unprejudiced nature of the CPB-forecasts, while also the formulation of the CPB-models - especially VINTAF - has not gone unquestioned. Furthermore, the monopoly position of the CPB had to give way to a number of alternative models and competing forecasts by the central bank and several universities.

For several reasons then, optimal control exercises with CPB-models in Dutch policy practice are hard to imagine. The models are very large and highly non-linear, the forecasts are not accurate enough to command general acceptance, and politicians/governments do not seem prepared to let their preferences systematically be recorded. Therefore the CPB contents itself with forecasting in the form of 'datum alternatives' and 'policy alternatives'.[8)]

1.4.2. Critique

After this introductory sketch of the history and current state of affairs with respect to the development and use of macroeconom(etr)ic models, it is time to discuss the critique on macroeconomic modelling as far as it is related to and relevant for the process of the formulation of economic policy.

<u>a</u>. We already pointed above to the problem of the border line between targets and instruments, between endogenous and exogenous variables. For instance, is the money supply an exogenous variable, an instrument to be controlled by the monetary authorities, or is it an endogenous variable which can only to some extent be steered by the monetary authorities when they properly use instruments such as the discount rate and open market operations.

Once economic policy would indeed be following a path laid down by a reaction function like (1.6) or (1.7), the problem of the distinction of endogenous and exogenous variables is also becoming highly relevant in the context of a <u>correct specification</u> and econometric <u>estimation</u> of the macroeconomic model. In eq. (1.1) (the reduced form of) the economic model was hypothesized to be

(1.1) $y = Rx + Zs.$

Now assume that the policy maker is at the same time manipulating its instruments according to the reaction function (1.7). With c a vector of constants we then have:

(1.8) $x = c - A^{-1}R'By$.

The estimation of eq. (1.1) when ignoring the existence of the policy reaction function (1.8) - and thus ignoring the preference function underlying government policy - may lead to substantial specification errors. See Crotty (1973), and also Blinder and Solow (1974). For, due to the policy reaction function, the x and the error term in (1.1) are no longer statistically independent. Blinder and Solow drive the point home by discussing the extreme: If the use and timing of the instruments of economic policy was perfect, such as to completely offset exogenous disturbances in s, then a regression of (1.1) would give zero coefficients for the instruments.

<u>b</u>. If economic policy is conducted according to a reaction function, this may also have consequences for the process of <u>making forecasts</u> with the macroeconomic model.

Let us for the sake of exposition have recourse to the most simple textbook Keynesian income-expenditure model: $Y = C + I + G$, $C = c(Y-T) + C_o$, $I = I_o$, $G = G_o$, $T = T_o$, with: Y = national income, C = consumption, I = investment, G = government expenditure and T = tax receipts, while the suffix o denotes autonomous elements. Of course, the national income multiplier with respect to investment and government expenditure equals $[1 - c]^{-1}$. As noted earlier, it is generally agreed that at least some of the variables related to government activities are of an endogenous nature; given a marginal tax rate t tax receipts will depend on the level of economic activity. For that reason the "institutional relation" $T = tY + T_o$ is typically inserted into the model, with the result that the national income multipliers for investment and government expenditure change into $[1 - c(1-t)]^{-1}$. However, that is not the end of it. For, what happens if the policy maker sets the value of its instrument variable G according to a reaction function, for instance in the form $G = g(Y-Y^*) + G_o$, $g < 0$. The multiplier $[1 - c(1-t)]^{-1}$ above may remain of use for those involved in the process of policy making, to make forecasts regarding the effect of a one dollar change in G or I. However, for the outside observer who has to accept the economic policy just as it is carried out, the above multiplier for government expenditure loses its meaning. For him government expenditure has become an endogenous element of the system. For the same reason, accounting for this endogeneity of government expenditure, the national income multiplier with regard to investment changes into $[1 - c(1-t) - g]^{-1}$.

This point has also been stressed by Mosley and Cracknell (1984). They analyze what happens to the predictions and the estimated multiplier effects of an existing macro-model, notably the so-called Spartan-model of the UK-economy, if policy reaction functions are inserted into it. They conclude that their "modified" model which contains policy reaction functions, predicts better than the "raw" model which excludes them, in the case of six out of eight key target variables. The "modified" model in general exhibits lower multipliers for those variables or policy instruments which remain exogenous, than the "raw" model.[9]

Thus far we distinguished policy makers from outside observers with respect to the policy making process. The same topic can also be looked at from a somewhat different angle, by taking account of the fact that within the public sector more than one policy making centre may be active and more than one policy making process may take place. Think alone of fiscal and monetary policy. If these policy makers are relatively autonomous, and if one of them is behaving in a systematic manner according to a policy reaction function, then the other cannot just ignore this behaviour. Fair (1978a) demonstrates for the case of the US that the performance of the fiscal authority with respect to maximizing some objective function will depend significantly on the behaviour of the FED. The FED is found to "lean against the wind", with regard to the treasury bill rate. From a simulation of his macroeconometric model Fair derives that the fiscal authority does not do as well when the FED behaves endogenously, as when the FED behaves by keeping the bill rate unchanged. The fiscal policy maker does not do as well in terms of lowering the value of the loss function, and the optimal policy calls for about twice as much fiscal stimulus to offset the increases in the bill rate by the FED.

c. In relation to the endogenous nature of government behaviour, there is yet another important problem with regard to macroeconometric models, the so-called Lucas' critique. The discussion above under point a. may have given the impression that by properly taking account of the reaction function (1.7) when estimating the economic model (1.1), simultaneity biases can be avoided, such that the true structure of the economy y = Rx + Zs is obtained. Lucas (1976) argues that the coefficients of this model describing the behaviour of the private sector agents will in part reflect the economic policy during the period over which they are estimated, and thus need not be stable. As he states it: "Given that the structure of an econometric model consists of optimal decision rules of economic agents, and that optimal decision rules vary systematically with changes in the structure of series relevant to the decision maker, it follows that any change in policy will systematically alter the structure of econometric models" (Lucas (1976, p. 41)).[10] A change in the monetary policy rule, e.g., will change future inflationary expectations, and for that reason influence current price setting behaviour. To give another example, a commitment of the government to full employment changes the bargaining power of trade unions in, and thus influences the outcome of, wage negotiations. Consequently, the assumption made in the derivation of the policy reaction function (1.7) that the coefficients of the economic model are invariant to the choice of this policy rule, is inappropriate. Simulations using the current macroeconomic models can then, in principle, provide no useful information as to the actual consequences of alternative economic policies.

The problem is neatly summarized by Sargent and Wallace (1976, p. 183): "In order for a model to have normative implications, it must contain some parameters whose values can be chosen by the policy maker. But if these can be chosen, rational agents will not view them as fixed and will make use of schemes for predicting their values. If the economist models the economy taking these schemes into account, then those parameters become endogenous variables and no longer appear in the reduced-form equations for the other endogenous variables. If he models the economy without taking the schemes into account, he is not imposing rationality".[11]

Let us pursue the theme of the (in)variance of the coefficients of the macroeconomic model to the economic policy rule being followed, somewhat further. If it is true that private sector behaviour is in part determined by the policy rule, and if - as has been touched upon in section 1.2 - policy reaction functions may vary according to the political colour of the administration, then private sector behaviour may in part depend on political variables. This idea has already been present for some time in the international relations literature. In several studies of international investment flows variables have been introduced measuring the political (in)stability and the international political alignment of the recipient countries (cf. the survey in Frey (1984, ch. 4)). Recently, the idea has been taken up in the context of macroeconomic modelling. Aubin et al. (1985) observe that "if private agents form their expectations in a relatively rational way, they also take into account the expected economic measures that a specific political climate may generate". They formalize this in a model for the French economy, by allowing the possibility of private expenditure to vary according to political uncertainty, generated by intermittent elections. They find that pre-election periods, creating uncertainty about future economic policy, have a very significant restrictive impact on private investment. Aubin and Goyeau (1986), elaborating the analysis somewhat further, conclude that it is especially the (expected) political colour of the future government which is of relevance. Gärtner (1981) also picked up the idea, when studying the specification of wage equations. He notes that socialist parties rate the goal of full employment relatively higher than the goal of price stability, whereas conservative parties place clear priority on obtaining price stability.[12] When indeed left-wing governments would apply the instruments such as to realize a more ambitious, lower unemployment rate than right-wing governments do, this would lead to higher inflationary expectations and, thus, an upward shift in the Phillips-curve trade-off, compared to the situation under a right-wing government.

Gärtner takes yet one step further by suggesting that trade unions may also pursue political goals (a more even distribution of income, equal educational opportunities for working-class children, extended industrial codetermination), and will not be indifferent between the ideological stands of the incumbency and the opposition. Now, the popularity and (re)election prospects of politicians are, as empirical studies suggest (cf. chapter 2), a function of macroeconomic variables, in particular the rates of unemployment and inflation. Combination of these two elements would give trade unions a motive and an opportunity to follow specific wage bargaining strategies to enhance the election chances of either the ruling parties or the opposition, depending on which of them they prefer. Gärtner's politico-economic hypotheses are supported by empirical results for West-Germany, for the period 1960-1976. He concludes that trade unions quite markedly supported the re-election prospects of the socialist-dominated governments in 1972 and 1976.

Summarizing the discussion: the coefficients of macroeconomic models may not only be unstable because rational private sector agents will react to the economic policy chosen or expected - which reactions by the way might follow a predictable pattern -, but also because private sector agents may play games with the government themselves.

1.5. The preference function of the policy maker

1.5.1. Establishing the preference function

Continuing our discussion of the basic ingredients of the theory of economic policy, we now come to the welfare or preference function W. The question how this "social welfare function" is related to the preference orderings of the individuals in society is highly interesting, but need not detain us here. At this stage we are only interested in the ordering which represents the policy maker's preferences over the set of conceivable states of the economy, however it comes about. Thus, W is conceived of as a social welfare function in the Bergsonian sense; cf. Sen (1970).

Johansen (1974) extensively discusses how these preference functions for macroeconomic decision models might be obtained. He distinguishes several approaches, notably: a. direct specification, b. imaginary interviews, or inference from planning documents, c. interview methods, and d. revealed preference functions. We shall present a short survey of the applicability of these approaches.

a. The most direct approach of course is to invite the policy maker himself to write down the function in mathematical terms. This approach does not seem to have ever been followed, or to be very useful, as policy makers - even if prepared to do so - probably would not be able to write them down in this way.

b. The alternative is that the policy adviser and/or economic expert formulates the function. If the expert has received enough information, e.g. deduced from planning documents, or disclosed during deliberations before policy decisions, he may feel confident enough to fit the pieces introspectively together to write down the function.[13] This is the imaginary interview approach adopted by Van Eijk and Sandee (1959), at that time both at the Dutch Central Planning Bureau. They note that: "for the time being, however, a genuine interviewing of policy-makers is impossible. This means that interviews must be imaginary. All available knowledge of private and public utterances of members of the government or its advisers must be used. Furthermore, one must interpret the political relations in parliament and in the Social Economic Council. In short, the presumable outcome of a real interview must be forecast."

Van Eijk and Sandee proceeded with the construction of a welfare function for the Netherlands, pertaining to the period 1956/57. It is perceived that the welfare function, although it will in general not be linear, can always be represented by a linear approximation, at least within a reasonable, well-defined interval. That is, the continuously curved surface is replaced by a set of contiguous bits of hyperplanes, called facets. Their result looks like:

$$(1.9) \quad W = (E-M) + 0.25\, G + 0.20\, I + 0.05\, w - 0.075\, p_c + 0.20\, a + 0.50\, S_G,$$

where $(E-M)$, G, I and S_G denote, respectively, the changes in the balance of payments surplus, government expenditure, investment and the government surplus, all measured in billions of guilders, while w, p_c and a denote, respectively, the percentage increases in real wages, consumer prices and employment. Connected with this function are well-defined boundaries for the instrument and target variables, within which it is valid.[14]

c. The former method will be open to those who directly take part in the deliberations during the policy making process, as it seems that only in that way adequate information may be acquired for the construction of the preference function. For that reason the construct can not easily be subjected to external validation, and will therefore remain rather subjective in nature. For outsiders other methods of establishing preference functions are available, however. The first one of these is the <u>direct interview</u> method.

The policy maker is asked to answer a systematically composed set of hypothetical questions concerning preference comparisons between alternative states of the economy. The preference function is then established by the expert on the basis of these answers. Cf. the exposition in Johansen (1974).

In the Netherlands several attempts have been undertaken with the direct interview method to construct preference functions for political parties, interest groups, and opinion leaders. Merkies (1973) put a simple question to the larger political parties in parliament, asking them after their marginal rate of substitution between an increase in employment and five other economic variables, with two additional questions pertaining to the possible omission of variables and to the linearity of the preference relation. Only two political parties - the social-democrats (PvdA) and one of the christian-democratic parties (ARP) - answered in such a manner that their preference relation could be formalized. Using the symbols introduced in eq. (1.9), these functions for the year 1972 read:

$$W = (E-M) + 2 G + I + w - 0.67 p_c + 4 a \quad \text{(PvdA)}$$
(1.10)
$$W = (E-M) + 0.33 G + 0.5 I + 0.1 w - 0.1 p_c + 2 a \quad \text{(ARP)}$$

Next it can be mentioned that Van der Geest (1977) presented three preference functions, obtained with the interview method, which he deems are in a way representative for the left, centre and right positions along the political scale. For completeness sake we reproduce his equations (the coefficients sum to 100 for each equation):

$$W = -6.3 U - 12.7 p_c + 3.3 y - 64.9 \text{ NIR} + 12.8 \text{ EPE} \quad \text{(left)}$$
$$W = -2.2 U - 55.3 p_c + 19.4 y + 13.4 \text{ NIR} + 9.7 \text{ EPE} \quad \text{(right)}$$
(1.11)
$$W = \begin{cases} -0.8 U - 25.4 p_c + 44.0 y - 23.6 \text{ NIR} + 6.2 \text{ EPE}, \\ \quad \text{if NIR} > 4 \\ \\ -0.9 U - 28.7 p_c + 50.0 y + 13.4 \text{ NIR} + 7.0 \text{ EPE}, \\ \quad \text{if NIR} < 4 \end{cases} \quad \text{(centre)}$$

where: U is the level of unemployment (in thousands of persons); p_c, y and EPE denote the percentage changes in consumer prices, real GNP and real environmental protection outlays, respectively; and NIR is the quotient of the average net income of the top 3% of the personal income distribution and the net minimum wage. These equations suggest that, indeed, the political left attaches more importance to the reduction of unemployment and income inequality and less to the combat of inflation than the political right. The preference function for the centre is linear, but asymmetric.[15] Reduction of income inequality is valued positively, until a certain level of inequality has been reached (NIR = 4); after that further reduction of income inequality is valued negatively.

Merkies and Vermaat (1981) examined the preference functions more thoroughly. They first asked political parties about their political aims. This led to the selection of five economic variables, generally felt to be the key variables. Subsequently they asked the political parties to evaluate 16 alternative sets of values of these five variables on a 0-100 scale. They then fitted linear equations to these answers. If that gave unsatisfactory results, the analysis was extended to asymmetric linear or even quadratic forms. We present their results for the three most important Dutch political parties, the social-democrats (PvdA), the christian-democrats (CDA)[16] and the liberal-conservatives (VVD):

$$W = -10.65\ u - 4.46\ p_c - 3.46\ \text{LIS} - 3.99\ \text{WCU} + 10.18\ \text{CBY} \quad \text{(PvdA)},$$

(1.12)
$$W = -10.13\ u - 5.17\ p_c - 1.62\ \text{LIS} - 17.34\ \text{WCU} - 7.60\ \text{CBY}^+ + 7.39\ \text{CBY}^- \quad \text{(CDA)},$$

$$W = -14.19\ u - 17.19\ u^2 - 11.00\ p_c - 12.08\ \text{LIS}^+ - 0.36\ \text{LIS}^- - 15.04\ \text{WCU} - 7.84\ \text{CBY} \quad \text{(VVD)},$$

with u the percentage rate of unemployment, p_c the percentage rate of increase of consumer prices, LIS the share of labour in national income, WCU the percentage rate of increase of real labour costs per unit of production, and CBY the collective burden of taxes and social premiums as a percentage of net national income, all measured in deviations from their 1977-levels. Two of the preference functions contain asymmetric terms, i.e. the coefficients differ if the variables go up (CBY^+, LIS^+) or down (CBY^-, LIS^-). The preference function for the VVD is quadratic in the unemployment term. From these preference functions it can be derived that the political left is prepared to pay a somewhat higher price for the reduction of unemployment in terms of increasing inflation than the political centre, and the centre at its turn is prepared to pay a higher price than the political right.

Overlooking the results obtained with the direct interview method we can draw the conclusion that in principle it is possible to quantify preference relations, but also that it poses a series of problems, such that the usefulness of the results can be seriously questioned.

- Care should be taken that the answers to the questions only have regard to preferences, and have nothing to do with considerations of economic or political feasibility, or with economic relationships between instruments and targets. That in practice making this distinction poses serious difficulties to the interviewed politicians, can be learned from Van der Geest (1977), and Merkies and Vermaat (1981).
- Political parties and politicians are prepared to answer questions pertaining to their preferences, but, as Merkies and Vermaat note, that willingness will diminish quickly if the number of questions grows. But then, if a preference function is to be established over an infinite set of possibilities by means of a small set of responses to interview questions, some a priori restriction on the form of the preferences must be brought in. This will be done by the economist by restricting the class of mathematical forms permitted for the welfare function, notably by using a linear approximation locally. (Even then, 16 answers to fit equations like (1.12) is still a rather poor base).

In that connection it should be noted that the reported preference relations are not very stable. Variables contributing to welfare appear and disappear. And the marginal rates of substitution seem to change drastically over time. The price, e.g., that the PvdA seems prepared to pay for a reduction of unemployment with 1% of the dependent labour force in terms of increasing inflation amounts to some 6% according to (1.10), 20% according to (1.11), and 2½% according to (1.12). Even if the results would be locally correct, in that (1.10), (1.11) and (1.12) are different facets of the same non-linear welfare function, the global usefulness of these results would not be enhanced as long as the full curvature of the function is unknown.[17)]

- An interesting element of the results is that they show marked differences in the weighing of the relevant variables along the political spectrum. However, the question of how to aggregate these preference functions for different political parties into the welfare function pertinent to public sector decision making, is left unanswered. And the chance that a prime-minister or a cabinet council will be prepared to cooperate with a direct interview is probably not very large, let alone informative.

<u>d</u>. There is yet another method to determine the social welfare function W necessary for the outlining of the optimal economic policy. The <u>revealed preference</u> method tries to draw inferences about the preference function of the policy maker from observed behaviour. What is revealed through actual decisions may be expected to reflect the preferences - and indeed those of the policy maker - more truly than answers to interview questions. Now it has to be recognized in this context that actual policy behaviour is a function of preferences and constraints. This can directly be seen from our reaction function (1.7):

$$(1.7) \quad \bar{x} = - A^{-1}(a+R'b) - A^{-1}R'B\bar{y} \;,$$

where the coefficients relating target and instrument variables represent the <u>combined</u> influence of the effect of the instruments on the target variables (the matrix R), and the weights of the target and instrument variables in the objective function (matrices A and B, vectors a and b). The question then is whether it is possible to disentangle the preference weights from estimation of equation (1.7). Suppose, we have obtained the following regression estimates:

$$(1.13) \quad \bar{x} = d + D\bar{y} + u,$$

with d a vector of constants, D a matrix of coefficients and u a vector of residuals. Remembering that the matrix B is symmetric, letting m and n, respectively, denote the number of instrument and target variables, and assuming - as is generally done in reaction function studies - that matrix A is diagonal, it easily follows from the comparison of eqs. (1.7) and (1.13) that for the regression coefficients it holds:

$$
\begin{aligned}
d_j &= -\frac{1}{A_{jj}} \cdot [a_j + \sum_{i=1}^{n} R_{ij} b_i], & j=1, \ldots, m, \\
D_{ji} &= -\frac{1}{A_{jj}} \cdot [\sum_{h=1}^{n} R_{hj} B_{hi}], & j=1, \ldots, m; \; i=1, \ldots, n.
\end{aligned}
\tag{1.14}
$$

If we could have the reduced form coefficients R_{hj}, relating instruments to targets, at our command, we might be able to identify the preference weights a_j, b_i, A_{jj}, B_{hi}. Makin (1976) enumerates under which conditions unique solutions for the preference weights can be obtained. With regard to equation (1.14), note that for identification the number of equations, $m(n+1)$, should equal the number of preference weights, which, choosing one of them as numéraire, equals

$$2m + n + \sum_{i=0}^{n} (n-i) - 1.$$

Friedlaender (1973) follows this procedure. Introducing exogenous information from the MIT-FRB-model with respect to the reduced form coefficients R_{hj}, and after having dropped the linear terms from the preference function because of insignificance, she is able to calculate the preference weights for the case $m=4$, $n=6$. Her results show that the Republican Eisenhower administrations valued price stability, relative to full employment, more than the Democratic administration of Kennedy-Johnson. Furthermore she notes that increasing weight was given to the balance of trade as the balance of payments situation deteriorated in the period considered.

Although the revealed preference method thus seems to work, several observations are in place here.

The method assumes that the policy maker reckons with the impact of each of his policy instruments on each of the target variables, the matrix R. If the reduced form coefficients which the investigator uses in the derivation of the revealed preference weights, differ from those the policy maker used when he made his policy decisions, then incorrect inferences regarding the preferences of the policy maker will be drawn. Whether the investigator's R conforms to the policy maker's R does not seem to be an easy task to find out. Moreover, the coefficients which the investigator adopts from equation (1.13) and from estimates of R, may be be biased, if no proper account has been taken of the simultaneity present there. Cf. the discussion in section 1.4.

In the analysis above we mentioned the (possible) existence of certain patterns of delay in the policy making process. In the formalization and the derivation of the reaction function (1.7), however, we did not take explicit account of such lags. If their occurrence and their length is not known with certainty, these lags have to be estimated too, further aggravating the identification problem.

Note, furthermore, that in order to be able to derive results, some a priori restrictions have to be imposed on the mathematical form of the objective function;[18] see our earlier discussion of the same topic when the direct interview method was evaluated.

Then there is the issue whether the policy maker (person, party, coalition, and so on) has been long enough in office to produce a sufficient number of observations for allowing estimation of his preference weights. For, as we already concluded at several instances, another policy maker may bring along other preferences. This problem may be less serious in the case of monetary policy than in the case of fiscal policy. With monetary policy, quarterly or even monthly observations make sense, as the instrument variables can be and are changed rather rapidly and frequently, as opposed to fiscal policy where the budget is settled in principle once a year. Besides, the monetary authorities generally possess a more permanent position than the authorities in the political sphere.

Finally, we have the important question whether policy makers are optimizing their objective function. If they are not, then the interpretation of eq. (1.13) in terms of preference weights and reduced-form coefficients becomes highly problematic.

All these observations together point out that, although comparatively the revealed preference method is the most readily available method and presumably can yield the most reliable information on the social welfare function used by the policy maker, certain rather stringent conditions have to be fulfilled before it can give us that information.

1.5.2. Optimizing or satisficing

At this point it seems proper to dwell still somewhat longer on the last issue that was raised in the previous subsection. According to the theory of economic policy policy makers would be optimizing. From a normative point of view the issue is settled with that. But from the positive point of view, the question remains: Are policy makers indeed maximizing? Frey and Schneider (1978a), e.g., who would like to assume that a government maximizes its own utility function subject to a series of economic, administrative and re-election constraints[19], state: "The dynamic maximization problem (or even differential game) as set up would, of course, be much too complex for any government to solve. Rather, it is assumed that a satisficing strategy is followed".

Mosley (1976, 1984) attacked the optimization-proposition most thoroughly. (Admittedly scarce) evidence on British government decision making processes "does suggest that desired values of targets are seldom formulated in explicit quantitative terms, and that so far from being continuously manipulated ex ante so as to optimize a function of these targets, the instruments have rather been periodically manipulated, all together, as an ex post response to crises resulting from unacceptable values of those targets". In Mosley's view the policy maker has no objective function in the sense of a consistent set of preferences between alternative states of the world. Instead, the policy maker has acceptable-level goals or aspiration levels, and things are good or not good enough depending on whether these aspiration levels have been reached or not. The policy maker is satisficing, i.e. only if things are not good enough policy action is undertaken. First, by applying rules of thumb. Only in case of major, nonroutine crises search behaviour starts, ending with the invention of new policy instruments or, at its worst, with the jettison of targets. As to the "satisfactory" levels of targets: they are seen as compromises between groups in the policy-making circle pushing in opposite directions, and, most importantly, they are "not rigid, but are revised in an upward or downward direction according as performance exceeds or falls short of aspiration". This satisficing approach is given more concrete shape with the following equation, in our usual symbols:

$$(1.15) \quad \Delta x_t = \begin{cases} \alpha + \beta(y-y^*)_{t-k}, & \text{if } y > y^* \text{ for three successive periods} \\ 0, & \text{otherwise} \end{cases}$$

with the "satisfactory" level of the target variable y^* in any period (quarter) modelled as the average value of that target over the previous twelve periods. That is, only if the target variable remains above its satisfactory level for three periods or more, provoking a "crisis" in the policy authorities' minds, action is taken and instrument values are changed.

Evaluating the approach, it should be noted first that the empirical results Mosley (1984) presents for the UK and the US, are not at all convincing, and sometimes even contradictory.[20] Equation (1.15) with different segments applied to crisis and non-crisis periods does not seem to perform better than a single reaction function $\Delta x = \alpha + \beta(y-y^*)$ applied to the period as a whole. But, with a single reaction function we would be back where we started. And then we have not even mentioned the rather ambiguous nature of the choice of the target variables and of their satisficing levels y^*, and the fact that according to (1.15) instrument values apparently only change in one direction. Remarkable in the theory itself is the absence of any kind of weighing of targets and of instruments, and the absence of any reference to the use of macroeconomic models. Remarkable indeed, in view of Mosley's own detailed description of the systematic process of preparation and weighing of the policy alternatives.[21] This description could also be interpreted as supporting the working hypothesis of optimizing behaviour by the policy maker.

Of course, the above evaluation is no proof that policy makers are optimizing. Also, it does not seem that the hypothesis can ever be shown to be true. But as an "as if" approximation - recall Machlup's automobile driver - it may suffice.

1.6. Conclusions

We summarize the main lines of argument of this chapter in a few points.

<u>a</u>. The public sector has assumed a major role in economic affairs. Even if it were only for that reason, it should be given great attention in formal model building. In present-day macroeconomic models only some variables related to the economic activities of the public sector have been endogenized, in what are called institutional equations. The coefficients in these equations and the other parts of public sector behaviour - including real government expenditure, public sector employment, tax rates, the central bank discount rate - are considered to be exogenous to the model.

<u>b</u>. According to the traditional theory of economic policy we need a set of target and a set of instrument variables, an empirical model, and a social welfare function to be able to derive the optimal economic policy. In the course of time macroeconomic modelbuilding has passed through a substantial development, improving the applicability and the usefulness of the models for the simulation of all kinds of economic policy (but see point c). Apart from potential technical problems with optimization procedures, the practical use of the theory of economic policy seems to have come quite a few steps nearer; at least for the policy maker, who knows his preference function. For the outside observer, however, the prospects for the practicability of calculating and checking the optimal economic policy are bad, for there seems to be no readily available manner to establish the relevant social welfare function.

<u>c</u>. The normative theory of economic policy, once it is being actively used by policy makers (either in its full-fledged form or in some more pedestrian version), can be turned into a positive, empirical theory, by estimating which reaction functions are actually being used by policy makers. Granted that it is behaving in a systematic manner, we have some very good reasons why we should give more attention to the public sector in macroeconomic modelling, apart from the intrincic value of studying

public sector behaviour:
- If an endogenous variable is treated as if it were exogenous, the model estimation may be seriously misspecified; simultaneity bias may be present, and the coefficients need not be invariant to the economic policy that is being pursued.
- Taking account of the endogenous nature of some (or all) economic policy instruments may help to improve forecasting, and to produce more accurate multipliers for the remaining exogenous variables (among which possibly other economic policy instruments).

These latter issues may first of all seem to be of relevance for purely scientific research, when one is setting out to develop an explanatory model of the macroeconomic functioning of society. But note that the argument is of equal importance to the policy-adviser, if he wants his policy-model to yield reliable forecasts of the effects of the policy measures which are taken into consideration. Then, he should give heed, in estimating the model and in forecasting policy effects, to the simultaneity bias referred to above and to the possible variance of the coefficients of the model to the economic policy that has been and is going to be pursued.[22]

<u>d</u>. At several instances it has become apparent that the use of simple reaction functions like eq. (1.7) is not the end of the story. Politics intervene, such as in the choice of target variables and in their weighing in the preference function. The theory of economic policy cannot help us any further here, as it takes political elements for granted. In the following chapters we will give due attention to the role of politics. Chapter 2 starts with a review of the literature.

CHAPTER 2. THE IMPACT OF POLITICS, A SURVEY OF THE LITERATURE

2.1. Introduction

In chapter 1 we concluded that public sector decision making may well have certain regularities, but that in order to get a better insight into these regularities political processes should explicitly be taken into account. In this chapter we present a critical review of the wide-ranging theoretical approaches and the - mostly rather scattered - empirical findings, that figure in the literature on the impact of politics, political processes and institutions on (macro)economic policy. This literature belongs to the research fields of public choice - mainly - and Marxian economics. The literature is rather novel, with much incoherence still, and with mostly ambiguous empirical results up till now. At this moment, it is not evident which ideas, approaches, hypotheses should be rejected, and in favour of which alternatives. For these reasons, it seems very useful to give the literature involved a more or less full treatment. Those readers who are already familiar with the literature, may prefer to skip to section 2.8 where the main lines of argument are summarized and the conclusions are drawn.

At the outset it should be memorized that we shall restrict our attention to Western democracies, where decisions are in principle made by the method of majority decision. In section 2.2 we shall study whether the criterion function W can be a representation of the prefences of (the majority of) the individual members of society. In that context we shall take a look at the median voter model. In section 2.3 we follow a different approach, taking account of the fact that voters in general are not well informed, and that elections are only held with intervals of a number of years, giving the elected politicians some monopolistic power in the meantime. In that context we review the literature on voting and popularity functions. How politicians might react to the voting and popularity signals when setting out economic policies, will be discussed in section 2.4. We shall especially review the political business cycle studies emanating from Nordhaus' original contribution, the approach inspired by Hibbs stating that governments with a different party-composition might pursue different economic policies due to differences in objective economic interests and subjective preferences of their class-based core constituencies, and the Frey-Schneider model. The theoretical and empirical contributions in the literature pertaining to the special role of the bureaucracy and of (organized) interest groups in the public sector decision making process will be the subject of sections 2.5 and 2.6, respectively. In section 2.7 we shall pay separate attention to the Marxist approach. Section 2.8 concludes.

2.2. The median voter model

In this section we shall discuss whether W may be taken to reflect the preferences of the individuals of society, in the sense that a collective choice rule - and more specifically the method of majority decision - specifies the preference ordering for society. Then, we are not talking about a Bergsonian social welfare function any more, but of a social welfare function in the sense of Arrow. Characteristic of Arrow's social welfare function is that it is based on individual orderings, and that it specifies an ordering[1] of preferences for society. Arrow proved that no such social welfare function exists which satisfies simultaneously a set of four mild looking and very reasonable conditions. Cf. Sen (1970).

As it has been proved that no social welfare function can satisfy these conditions at the same time, this must also hold in case of the collective choice rule of majority voting. Majority voting, indeed, does not yield a preference ordering for society for every logically possible set of individual preferences, as is shown by the well-known paradox of voting. Consider three individuals 1, 2 and 3, and three alternatives x, y and z. Let individual 1 prefer x to y and y to z, individual 2 prefer y to z and z to x, and individual 3 prefer z to x and x to y. It is easily seen that in a vote x defeats y by two to one; similarly, y defeats z, and z defeats x. Thus, while the preference ordering for each individual is well-defined, no well-defined preference ordering for society results. The method of majority voting may give rise to intransitivities (x defeats y and y defeats z does not imply that x defeats z), and can lead to cycling in the voting process, without the resulting of an equilibrium.

Arrow's theorem only tells us that there is <u>some</u> configuration of individual preferences which can yield an intransitive social ordering. It does not tell us the likelihood with which we can expect such a situation to arise, nor does it tell us the seriousness of the intransitivities when they occur. Let us address the issue under which conditions with respect to individual preferences a voting equilibrium and a preference ordering for society may exist.

It is most simple and instructive to start with the case of a <u>one-dimensional issue</u>, e.g. the amount of public sector expenditure. The alternatives can be arranged on, say, the horizontal axis in a two-dimensional figure, while the voters' preferences in the sense of an ordinal evaluation are measured on the vertical axis. A voter's ordering can be represented by a curve connecting the voter's evaluations of the alternatives. Furthermore it is assumed, as before, that voters act rationally; they cast their votes for the alternative which best serves their self-interest and which is accordingly evaluated most favourably. There is no abstention. Black (1948) showed that if an ordering of the alternatives on the horizontal axis exists such that all voters' preference curves are single-peaked, then a voting equilibrium exists in the sense that one alternative can beat or tie the others. For each voter the ideal point is defined as his most preferred alternative among all feasible alternatives. Define a median ideal point to be any alternative such that no more than one half of the voters have ideal points below it in the ordering and no more than one half of the voters have ideal points above it. It follows that in a simple majority vote between a median ideal point and any other alternative, the median ideal point will never lose (although it may tie). This discussion thus has brought us to the result that - under certain conditions - <u>the median voter</u> is decisive.[2] A similar line of reasoning underlies Downs' (1957) proposition that in a two-party democracy vote-maximizing parties will change their platforms so that they converge to the position of the median voter. According to this theory, then, public sector decision making would reflect, either directly or indirectly, the preferences of the median voter.

Alternatively, one may leave open the possibility of individual preference patterns leading to social intransitivity and inquire into the probability that the voting paradox will occur; see, e.g., Gehrlein and Fishburn (1976) and DeMeyer and Plott (1970). These studies compute the probability that a simple majority winning alternative exists, assuming that all possible orderings of alternatives are equally likely and are distributed randomly among voters. The probability diminishes if the number of voters grows and especially if the number of possible alternatives increases. For instance, with 3 alternatives the probability of obtaining a voting equilibrium decreases from 0.94 in case of 3 voters to 0.91 when the number of voters is infinite; with 6 alternatives the probability decreases from 0.80 in case of 3 voters to 0.68 in case of an infinite number of voters; and with 15 alternatives the probability starts at only 0.58 in case of 3 voters. In reality not all possible orderings of alternatives are equally likely. To a certain extent voters have the same or similar preferences. It has been shown that with increasing social homogeneity the likelihood of avoiding the paradox increases; see, e.g., Berg (1985).

As the requirement to bring down political disputes to one dimension seems very restrictive, an appropriate next step is to search for equilibria in a multi-dimensional issue space; see, e.g., Riker (1980), Enelow and Hinich (1984). An equilibrium is said to exist if there is an alternative, which is called the dominant point, which no other proposal will beat in a majority contest. An alternative is a dominant point if it is a median in all directions, that is: every line (plane) passing through this point must divide the ideal points of the members of society so that at least half are on either side of it (the line itself included on each side). The general impression is that this (kind of) symmetry condition required for the existence of equilibria is "so restrictive as to render equilibria virtually non-existent" (Riker (1980, p. 442)). Notice that even if an equilibrium would exist, its existence and identity would be sensitive to slight changes in even one voter's preferences. Furthermore, when equilibrium breaks down, it breaks down completely. McKelvey (1979) proved that "for majority voting over multidimensional spaces of alternatives, the majority rule intransitivities can generally be expected to extend to the whole space of alternatives in such a way that virtually all points are in the same cycle set" (p. 1085). In other words, given almost any two alternatives it is possible to construct a majority path which starts at the first and ends at the second point.

Although the median voter model, from a theoretical point of view, may not have much in it to recommend it for <u>empirical application</u>, attempts to test the model have been undertaken in several directions.

One approach is to study individual preferences (voter attitudes) from <u>survey data</u>. Courant c.s. (1980) report on a survey to analyze the voting pattern for or against various tax limitation proposals in Michigan in 1978. The median respondent seems to desire no change in public spending or at most only a modest change, implying that the state is more or less in median voter equilibrium. Kristensen (1982), on the other hand, analyzing Danish survey data for the year 1979, concludes that data on item-by-item public spending preferences "constitute a hard blow to the median voter proposition".[3]

In the context of our study it is also of interest to quote some Dutch survey data, published by the Sociaal en Cultureel Planbureau (1986). Data obtained in 1967, 1975 and 1979 indicate that at the time the median respondent was satisfied with the level of total public spending; from 1980 onwards (according to data obtained in 1980, 1981, 1983, 1985) a majority of the respondents was favouring a cut-back in public spending. Indeed, the Cabinet-Lubbers, governing since 1982, declared its policy to be a curtailment of (the growth of) public spending. On the other hand, looking at disaggregated data with respect to some specific public provisions, it appears that only a small minority of respondents is of the opinion that the social security benefit levels are too high, while at the same time the government has been cutting back these benefits. All in all then, this evidence is rather inconclusive with respect to the median voter proposition.

Romer and Rosenthal (1979) review the empirical <u>cross-section</u> studies applying the median voter model to expenditures of local governments. They point out that methodological problems make the testing of the hypothesis extremely difficult, and conclude that the studies under review "fail to indicate that actual expenditures correspond in general to these desired by the median voter" (p. 143). The study by Pommerehne (1978) on public expenditure in 110 Swiss municipalities around 1970, while subject to at least part of the methodological critique of Romer and Rosenthal, has some elements in it which are of special relevance to us here. For, interestingly enough, the municipalities dealt with were characterized by considerable differences in their political institutional set-up; 48 were <u>direct</u> democracies and 62 <u>representative</u> democracies. The results show that for direct democracies the demand-oriented median voter model may be adequate. For representative democracies it is not, and this suggests, as is noticed by Pommerehne, that other models should be developed which account for the government's re-election constraint and bureaucracy's direct influence, and where time-series analysis is more suitable.

Such a <u>time-series analysis</u> has been undertaken by Pommerehne and Schneider (1983), who study the use of fiscal policy instruments in Australia in the period 1971.1-1977.9, confronting two types of models. They report the empirical support for the Downsian-type model, in which the government <u>always</u> uses its instruments in accordance with the preferences of the majority of voters, to be not very convincing.

Separate attention, finally, should be given to the rational theory of the size of the government, presented by <u>Meltzer and Richard</u> (1981). Their theory analyzes the position of and the decision making by the median voter within the context of a general equilibrium model of a labour economy. The analysis concentrates on the demand for redistribution, neglecting any public goods provided by the public sector. The voters are rational, fully informed, and take account of the disincentive effects of taxation on the labour-leisure choice of their fellow citizens. If individuals differ only with respect to productivity, and if a linear tax is levied against earned income financing a lump-sum redistribution to all citizens, it can be shown that the individual choices of the tax vote can be ordered by productivity (or income); the higher an individual's productivity, the lower is his most preferred tax rate. Accordingly, under majority rule the voter with median productivity (income) is decisive. At this point it should be pointed out that the programming problem for the decisive voter is so complex, that no explicit solution for the most preferred tax rate can be deduced. Nevertheless, some interesting theoretical results are derived. First, changes in the franchise up or down the productivity distribution change the decisive voter and the tax rate. Secondly the size of government also changes if there are changes in relative income (productivity); the tax rate is expected to rise as mean income rises relative to the income of the median voter.[4) 5)]

An empirical test of the model on US annual data (1937-1940 plus 1946-1976) is given by Meltzer and Richard (1983), using a linear approximation to derive an explicit solution of the optimal tax rate for the decisive voter. For publicly supplied private goods the model does not work well. With respect to redistribution in cash the results generally support the hypothesis; however, of the two crucial coefficients one has the correct sign but is much below the theoretically expected value - which by the way may be due to the linearization - while also doubts arise as to the adequacy of the median income concept used.[6)] The authors themselves also point to the possibility of simultaneous equation bias.

We draw some <u>conclusions</u>. It must be questioned, both theoretically and empirically, that public sector decision making is purely demand determined, in the sense of being a pure representation of voters' preferences.

Theoretical problems, as we have seen above, are related to intransitivities and cycling. The requirements underlying the median voter model to avoid the paradox of voting are rather stringent; cf. the series of assumptions which had to be made by Meltzer and Richard, to ensure the existence of a voting equilibrium. Meltzer and Richard also make us aware of the informational requirements on the part of the voters; they must acquire all relevant information and process it in a suitable way to reach their decision. Furthermore, if the voter starts calculating rationally, he might well conclude that the benefits to him of his single vote in a large community do not outweigh the costs of gathering and processing the relevant information and of voting itself. But if voters abstain, the median voter model may be undermined.

The empirical evidence quoted above is inconclusive, either because the various results are contradictory and inconsistent or subject to methodological criticism. The results of Pommerehne and Schneider - see also the study by Pommerehne - suggest that models in which the supply side of the political market is taken account of, perform better. This brings us to the conclusion of, among others, Romer and Rosenthal (1979) that institutional details are important. Voting in practice takes place every 4 or 5 years, with regard to candidates and not on a multitude of issues, creating room in the time between elections for monopolistic pursuance of the own preferences by politicians, and by the bureaucracy.

2.3. Voting and popularity functions

2.3.1. Introduction

When elections in general are only held with intervals of a few years and voters in general do not take the trouble to be fully informed, politicians, political parties and the public bureaucracy will have some monopoly power in the time between elections to pursue their own preferences. In this perception the criterion function of the policy maker, W, is not a pure representation of the voters' preferences. Accordingly we must distinguish between (the preferences of) voters and policy makers in the public sector, and treat these as separate agents.

Figure 2.1, cf. Frey and Schneider (1975), presents a picture of the ensuing interaction between voters and policy makers, and between the economic and the political sphere of society. In the lower loop of the figure voters evaluate the economic situation (policies, prospects). On the basis of this evaluation they elect the politicians. In the time between elections voters only can send signals to the politicians through opinion polls informing them on their popularity and their re-election chances. Next we come to the upper loop. The election outcome determines or co-determines the composition of the government, depending on whether we have to do with a two-party system or with a multi-party system and coalition formation. The political colour of the government and its re-election chances affect the objective function relevant for public sector decision making. This objective function in its turn is decisive for which economic policy actions will be undertaken. And so on. In this section we will focus on voting and popularity functions. The analysis of the economic policy actions will be postponed till section 2.4.

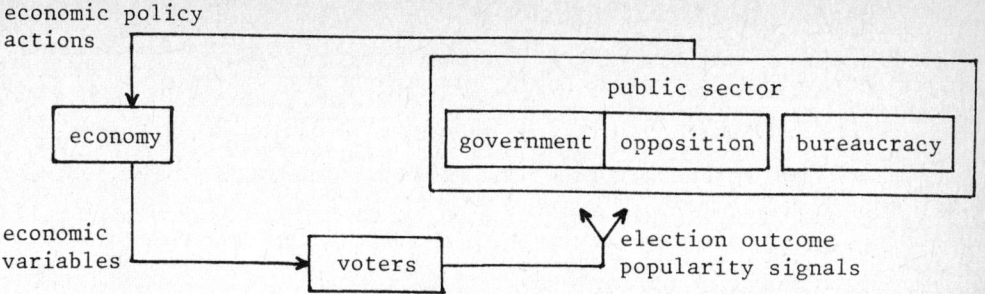

Figure 2.1. Politico-economic interdependence.

2.3.2. Theoretical foundation

Over the last 15 years, since the seminal papers by Kramer (1971), Mueller (1970) and Goodhart and Bhansali (1970), an enormous amount of studies has been published, analyzing the influence of economic variables on election outcomes and on the popularity of the government. The economic variables most frequently inserted in voting and popularity functions are the level of and/or changes in the unemployment rate, the level of and/or changes in the inflation rate, and the growth rate of real per capita disposable income. In addition to typical political variables (e.g., the electoral cycle – the regular movement of popularity indices between elections – in Britain, or the Vietnam War and Watergate in the US), one sometimes also comes across other economic variables such as the balance of payments deficit and the development of the exchange rate. Recent surveys of the literature are given by Paldam (1981), Schneider (1984), Kiewiet and Rivers (1984).

First of all, it should be noticed that voting and popularity functions differ – despite their many similarities – in some important respects. Voting functions describe and predict election outcomes, which are directly relevant for the composition of government. As long as the political colour of the government affects the content of economic policy, the importance of introducing these voting functions in macroeconomic modelling is obvious. The relevance of popularity functions depends on whether the incumbent politicians take account of the effects on their re-election chances when deciding on economic policy actions. Secondly, voters presumably will have taken more time to gather the appropriate information when actually voting than when just answering some opinion poll questions. Voters may also be more sincere. That is, opinion polls can be used to signal discontent with certain policy measures taken at the time, without respondents having the actual desire to change government. Thirdly, as elections only take place with certain intervals long observation periods are needed to gather enough data for the estimation of a voting function. But the longer the period under consideration, the more likely it is that voters' preferences and general economic conditions will have changed, making it less probable to find a stable relationship. Popularity functions do not suffer from a lack of data, as observations are available with a monthly or quarterly interval. Being aware of these differences between voting and popularity functions, we shall ignore them in the sequel, and turn our attention to the common theoretical foundation.

Although many empirical studies on voting and popularity are not very explicit on their theoretical underpinning, a theoretical basis has been provided in the literature. See, e.g., Downs (1957), Fair (1978b), Fiorina (1981). It is most concisely called retrospective voting. Inspired by the economic theory of voting of Downs it is hypothesized that citizens act rationally and maximize their utility. The individual voter evaluates the positions of the different parties (or candidates), by predicting the expected utility if these positions are realized. If expected utilities differ significantly, the individual decides to vote, and he votes for the party (candidate) whose position maximizes his expected utility.

It is generally taken for granted that individual voters will not take the trouble to evaluate party platforms and specific policy proposals in order to construct a record of expected future utility for the different parties. To gather and process all information required for the construction of such a hypothetical record is an impractical – if not impossible – and costly procedure. Moreover, platforms are no binding commitments, so the voter should have to estimate what the parties would actually do were they in power. This kind of calculations becomes even more cumbersome in a multi-party system, when no party is endowed with a majority of votes or seats and a coalition has to be formed in order to get a majority government.

It is also generally assumed (for exceptions, see later on) that voters for reasons of information costs do not have enough incentive to try to evaluate the adequacy of the use of policy instruments as such by past and current governments. Instead, they will use those indicators for which information is readily available. Economic indicators which fulfil this condition are related to the prevailing economic situation, such as the rate of unemployment, the rate of inflation, the growth of disposable income, and so on. Data on these economic indicators are regularly published and extensively discussed in the media. The voters will also have some personal experience with this kind of issues. It, further, stands to reason that it is the incumbent government which should be held responsible for the prevailing economic conditions, not the opposition. By taking the current and a series of past election periods, and using a proper time discounting mechanism to give recent periods more weight than remote periods, one can construct for each party a record of how well it handled its job of managing the economy. These records can be interpreted as giving an indication of what is to be expected in the future from each party.[7]

In short, it is hypothesized that the vote share (or popularity) of a party will be a function of its accumulated past discounted economic performance.[8]

2.3.3. Discussion and empirical findings

In this section we shall discuss some important aspects of the voting and popularity function literature and render an account of the empirical findings.

<u>a</u>. The presentation above primarily applies to short-term shifts in voting patterns, to so-called floating or <u>swing voters</u>. Apart from swing voters each party also has a core of partisan voters. Their <u>party identification</u> will be based on specific class, occupational, regional or religious characteristics, and will be subject to change only in the

longer run. In studies on vote and popularity functions this pattern of party identification is generally taken for granted, and taken along in the constant term or at the most in a simple time trend. But see Fiorina (1981).

b. An important issue is whether voters react to the economic situation in general nation-wide terms[9], or more specifically to how they are personally affected by economic conditions. From a theoretical point of view it can be argued that the specific personal economic fortunes of voters can usually be readily attributed to personal, situation specific factors, for which the government cannot be held responsible. As far as the government's responsibility is concerned, it is the general economic development that counts. The empirical evidence for the effects of personal financial conditions on voting is, indeed, rather weak. See Kinder and Kiewiet (1979), Fiorina (1981), Kiewiet and Rivers (1984).[10]

c. A related question is precisely which economic variables should be inserted in the voting and popularity functions. Mosley (1984) argues that it would be rational for utility maximizing people to look at the growth of real disposable income. But, "why should changes in the inflation rate and in unemployment affect a voter's behaviour independently of their effect on real income?" (p. 21). Hibbs (1979) would be surprised if the public is sensitive to inflation, as "what matters most from an economic point of view are real quantities such as output and employment, not the nominal price level." "Since neither the income, wealth, nor tax effects of inflation appear large enough to explain widespread public aversion to rising prices, less tangible subjective and psychological factors are probably more important than objective costs" (pp. 710, 712). Kirchgässner (1985) notes that the relation from unemployment to popularity would not be consistent with the Lucas-Sargent policy-ineffectiveness proposition. Rational voters who are aware of government's inability to influence unemployment in a systematic manner, should not punish the government for high unemployment rates.[11] More generally, it might be sensible to distinguish between the anticipated and unanticipated parts of economic conditions.

One step further, it might be argued (cf. Stigler (1973)) that general economic conditions as such will have no effect at all. Between parties there will be consensus on the desirability of the pursuit of low inflation, high employment and steady growth of real income. Moreover, it is very likely that the major parties will in general be equally well equiped (internal skills, the intellectual support from the bureaucracy) to deal with macroeconomic policy. And if there are differences in the proposed policies, all of them supported by professional economists who apparently cannot agree on which is right, why should voters be able and try to evaluate which party should govern? According to Stigler the economic basis for party affiliation must be sought in redistributional issues where parties do take different positions and where it is in the direct interest of the voter to decide which party benefits him most.

After having enumerated all sorts of objections to insert certain (kinds of) economic variables in voting and popularity functions, it seems wise to let the facts speak. With only a very few exceptions then (cf. Stigler (1973)) the empirical studies do find (among other issues of a political nature, which are not our primary interest here) a statistically significant and quantitatively important impact of the economic situation in a country on the popularity of the president or government and on election outcomes. The better (worse) the economic conditions, the more the government's popularity or re-election chances increase (decrease). However, how strong this influence is, and which economic variables are of most interest, varies considerably among countries and over time. That is, the voting/popularity function manages to be at the same time highly significant and unstable.[12)]

Several reasons for the observed instability can be advanced. The specific mathematical form used (mostly a linear equation) may be only locally valid and too restrictive to encompass changing economic conditions. Relatedly, public attitudes on economic issues may shift over time, depending on which issues are perceived to be important at a certain time, and to what extent. Think of the role of opinion leaders and mass media. Thirdly, external factors may have interfered, recognized by anybody, for certain economic developments, so that it would have been unreasonable to hold the government responsible. Fourthly, there may be aggregation difficulties, as the electorate is not homogeneous as to the weighing of the relative importance of, e.g., full employment and price stability. We shall turn to this issue shortly.

d. Another important issue is the <u>time discount rate</u> of voters. Many studies just assume that voters are myopic and take account of the most recent economic experiences only. Some studies, however, explicitly investigate this topic. According to Fair (1978b) the discount rate is very large, probably infinite. In the popularity functions by Frey and Schneider (1978b, 1981b), Pissarides (1980), Borooah and Van der Ploeg (1983), the coefficient of the lagged dependent variable suggests too that the voters' memory horizon is very short; i.e. not much longer than 1, maybe 2 years. However, Hibbs (1982a,b) has argued that relying on the coefficient of the lagged popularity variable to capture distributed lag effects may be improper, as it implies that support for the incumbent government is influenced by its own (past) performance ánd the performance of previous governments formed by the current opposition in the <u>same</u> way. Hibbs developed an alternative formulation in which voters' choice depends on the difference between the cumulative discounted past performance of the current incumbent party and the cumulative discounted past performance of the present opposition party. His results (cf. Hibbs (1982a,b); see also Hibbs and Vasilatos (1981), Chappell (1983), Chappell and Keech (1985a,b)) imply that the adjustment of voters' memories is slow, with time horizons of 4 to 6 years.

e. The results discussed so far, seem to indicate that voters are myopic and naive, in that they only look at the (fairly) recent economic performance of the government as measured by the state of the economy. Only a few studies investigate hypotheses that the voters might behave somewhat more "<u>rational</u>", "<u>sophisticated</u>" or "<u>strategic</u>". Such voters would have some knowledge of the working of the economy. They will be aware of the interaction between government behaviour and the economy, and of the fact that short-run policy choices are subject to constraints (e.g. to points on a short-run Phillips-curve). One possibility is that voters are forward-looking, and reward or punish the government according to whether the chosen policy promotes movement toward desired long-run outcomes. Alternatively, voters are still backward-looking, but form their economic expectations in a more or less rational manner, in the sense that they distinguish between anticipated and unanticipated economic developments, take account of the differential effects of both, and of the extent to which the government can be held responsible. Anticipated and unanticipated inflation, e.g., may have quite different effects on the distribution of income, and may for that reason be evaluated quite differently by voters.

The empirical results obtained thus far can not be said to give firm support to these alternative hypotheses. MacRae (1977, 1981) presents only some very indirect evidence that for several (not all) US presidential election periods the strategic hypothesis might do a better job than the myopic hypothesis. Minford and Peel (1982) state that their findings would not exclude that voters use rational expectations; however, their procedure is heavily criticized by Kirchgässner (1985). Kirchgässner concludes from his own analysis that at least a large part of the electorate does not seem to use rational expectations. Finally, the results reported by Michaels (1986), Chappell (1983), Chappell and Keech (1985a,b) are inconclusive.

<u>f</u>. The discussion of the influence of economic conditions on popularity and voting thus far has treated the electorate as if it were a homogeneous group. As noted before, not much evidence was found for the direct influence of personal economic grievances on voting. That is not to say that the perception and the evaluation of the general economic situation may not be coloured by the voters' own social and economic positions and experiences. Voters' responses to economic conditions are likely to vary considerably because of differences in the objective, concrete interests at stake. <u>Different groups of voters</u> can be expected to be differently affected by changes in the economy. Accordingly, changes in political support generated by, for instance, changes in inflation or unemployment, need not be uniform within the electorate.

Several studies have presented empirical evidence on this issue. Hibbs (1979) found from US survey data (for the UK, see Hibbs (1982b)) that lower status, blue-collar occupational groups are less averse to inflation and more averse to unemployment than upper status, white-collar groups. It is quite understandable that low-income, blue-collar workers are relatively more concerned about unemployment as they have a greater chance of being dismissed and having to incur the cost of finding a new job. As to inflation, nominal wage rates may be expected to reflect inflationary movements quite closely and automatically; and as the lower-income groups have little property to be concerned about, they do not need to attach as much importance to price stability. Schneider (1984) presents estimates of separate popularity functions for six different income classes (US presidents, period 1969-1976). Indeed, the unemployment coefficient appears to fall continuously as we move from low- to high-income groups, while the inflation coefficient moves in the opposite direction. See also Hibbs (1982a,b) for similar results. Thus, it turns out that the political responses to macroeconomic performance vary across occupational groups, as will the politically acceptable short-run macroeconomic policy trade-offs.

g. The discussion until now implicitly referred to a two-party (or candidate) choice situation in which only one party is governing and will presumably be held responsible, and in which the popularity of the one party is the unpopularity of the other. Such a two-party system is essentially found in the US and, to a certain degree, in the UK. Things are somewhat different in multi-party systems with coalition governments, as, e.g., in Germany and the Netherlands. There it is no longer obvious which of the (coalition) parties is to be held responsible for government actions and economic performance. Secondly, when estimating separate popularity functions for the different parties, one must take account of cross-equation restrictions because of the adding up-restraint.

Frey and Schneider (1979), studying the case of Germany, succeed in skipping the problems by just estimating a popularity function for the government as a whole, introducing dummy variables to account for the specific party composition and basic popularity level of each kind of coalition. The popularity level of the government automatically indicates the inpopularity of the opposition (parties). Kirchgässner (1985), on the contrary, estimates separate popularity functions for the (major) German parties (period 1971-1982), taking properly account of cross-equation restrictions. Voters' assignment of responsibility for economic performance, indeed, appears to follow a somewhat peculiar pattern. When the economic situation deteriorates the government parties together lose votes; however, the major coalition party loses more votes than the opposition party wins, showing that within the coalition the minor party wins. Similarly, Renaud and Van Winden (1987b), applying the multinomial logit model presented by Van Winden (1983) and Borooah and Van der Ploeg (1983), conclude for the Netherlands (period 1970.1-1981.12) that the popularity of the parties that form a government are not equally affected by the economic situation; apparently, a coalition government cannot be handled as a homogeneous entity.

Finally, let us have a look at the Netherlands. Peeperkorn and Steenkamp (1986) estimate a popularity function for the government, with quarterly data (1968:I - 1982:III). With respect to the economic variables, only the coefficient of the unemployment rate is found to be significantly different from zero, but it seems to diminish in the course of time. The other available studies analyze popularity data for the three main Dutch political parties, to wit liberal-conservatives (VVD), christian-democrats (CDA) and social-democrats (PvdA). Keizer and Van Veen (1984) estimate popularity functions on yearly data (1964-1978). They report insignificant results for the unemployment and inflation rates in case of PvdA and CDA; only in case of the VVD unemployment and (the change in) inflation are affecting popularity. From a follow-up study, based on monthly data for the period 1970.1-1980.12, Keizer and Van Veen (1986) even conclude that inflation and unemployment have no significant effect at all on the popularity of the political parties. Renaud and Van Winden (1987b) analyze monthly popularity data for the three parties (period 1970.1-1981.12) with a multinomial logit model. Estimation of lead functions entering the economic variables in a linear way, shows that neither inflation nor unemployment has a significant effect on the popularity of the different parties; the growth of real disposable income only turns out to have a significant positive effect on the popularity of the PvdA. To allow for interaction effects, as, for example, voters may take account of an unemployment-inflation trade-off, the product term of inflation and unemployment is added to the formulation. It, then, appears that the coefficients of unemployment, inflation and the product term are all significant, but different for the three parties.

All in all, the above empirical evidence for the Netherlands, with the exception of the last-mentioned - rather ad-hoc - estimate, does not really point at a marked effect of the general economic situation on the popularity of the political parties.

2.3.4. Summary

We summarize the most important findings from our review of the literature on voting and popularity functions.
- There is ample evidence for a significant influence of economic conditions on voting outcomes and on the popularity of the government, political parties and politicians. Apparently, the latter are held responsible for economic policy and economic developments. At the same time it is found that the relationships involved are very unstable.
- The economic variables which particularly seem to play a role, pertain to general economic conditions, not to the personal financial situation of voters.
- Most studies indicate that the evaluation of economic performance by voters is retrospective and myopic. However, the short memory horizon of the electorate has been called into question, with some success. Also the naive nature of the behaviour of voters - only looking at current and past macroeconomic developments, instead of forming forward looking expectations and evaluating the adequacy of the use of policy instruments - has been questioned; here the empirical results are until now rather ambiguous.
- The assignment of responsibility for economic conditions to the coalition parties in a multi-party system does not seem to follow a clear-cut pattern.
- The literature which has been reviewed, primarily deals with swing voters and with short-term fluctuations in voting and popularity patterns. However, longer-term developments should also be taken account of, for instance changes in party identification by core voters. In that context it is of interest to recognize that the electorate is not homogeneous. Disaggregated studies show marked differences in the evaluation of inflation and unemployment between different income and occupational groups. This could point at group-related constituencies of political parties.

2.4. Government behaviour

2.4.1. Introduction

In figure 2.1 we sketched the interaction between the economy and the polity. The lower loop of the figure, as we have seen in the preceding section, can be described by voting and popularity functions. Now we come to the upper loop of the figure, where the public sector's economic policy actions are decided on, and influence the course of the economy. For the moment we shall let the bureaucracy's influence rest (see section 2.5), and turn our attention to the decision making by political parties and politicians.

Related to the voting and popularity studies, two very different approaches to the subject can be discerned. On the one hand we have the hypothesis originating from Nordhaus (1975), that it might be rational for incumbent politicians to generate a "political business cycle", in order to enlarge their political support at election date from myopic, backward-looking swing voters (see section 2.4.2.). On the other hand, we have the proposition emanating from Hibbs (1977) that in class-based electoral systems it might be rational for a political party to keep the promises to its core constituency, and thus to pursue its own ideology, once it is in government (see section 2.4.3.). A third approach then is to combine the preceding two alternatives in one model. In principle the government is assumed to follow a specific ideological course, but as soon as its re-election prospects are endangered, it takes actions to enlarge its popularity. The model of Frey and Schneider (1978a,b, 1979) is in this line (see section 2.4.4.). Finally, it should be mentioned that there are also authors who conclude from the voting and popularity studies that these cannot form an appropriate base for the foundation of economic policy actions. Arguing along this line are Alt and Chrystal (1983) who end up with a permanent income model, or Mosley (1976, 1984) according to whom macroeconomic policy making boils down to crisis management by a satisficing organization (see section 2.4.5.).

2.4.2. The political business cycle

Nordhaus (1975) started a lively debate when he suggested that incumbent politicians interested in re-election might have an incentive to engineer cyclical economic activity. See also MacRae (1977, 1981) and Lindbeck (1975, 1976) for similar reasoning.

The essential elements of the Nordhaus model can be stated as follows.

<u>a</u>. (Floating) voters dislike both inflation and unemployment. Furthermore they are backward looking; in particular they do not consider the consequences of government policy actions for periods following the election.

<u>b</u>. Government is chosen in periodic, competitive elections. The incumbents are interested in securing re-election, and for that reason maximize the (expected) number of votes at the forthcoming election. Politicians are myopic, in that they do not look further ahead than the next election.

<u>c</u>. The economic system has some exploitable dynamic characteristics, and the government has sufficient economic control and sophistication to steer the economy in the desired direction. More concretely, the economy is characterized by a Phillips-curve trade-off between unemployment and inflation, the trade-off being steeper in the long-run than in the short-run (because of lags in the inflation process and/or because of slow adjustment of inflationary expectations); unemployment is assumed to be the control variable which the policy makers can set at any level they wish.

The basic logic behind the Nordhaus proposition is simple. It all centers around the question how the incumbents can secure for themselves a higher vote-share at the forthcoming election. First of all, after the election the unemployment rate should be raised, inducing a deflationary shift along the momentary short-run Phillips-curve. In the course of the incumbency period the inflationary expectations in the economy will then gradually be revised, shifting the short-run Phillips curve downward. When the next election is drawing near, the economy should be inflated again. With sufficient control, the economy could end up with lower inflation and unemployment at election day, delivering the incumbents a higher level of political support, than would have been obtained otherwise.[13]. Note that the stimulation of the economy will after some time lead to a revision of inflationary expectations, shifting the Phillips-curve upward again. As this latter development takes some time, while voters are only backward looking, this allows the government to escape at election day the penalty for the inflation which is to occur in the near future. In the next incumbency period the whole process will repeat itself.

This theory of the political business cycle thus predicts a clockwise movement around the long-run Phillips-curve, with unemployment and deflation in the early years of an incumbency period followed by an inflationary boom as the next election approaches. The exact timing and dosage of deflationary and inflationary measures can be obtained from solving the corresponding optimal control problems.

Let us now have a look at the empirical evidence for the occurrence of a political business cycle of the above kind. Nordhaus (1975), Tufte (1978) and Soh (1986), tabulating data for large series of democratic countries, report that in several cases they can find political-business-cycle-like patterns in unemployment, inflation and/or real income growth figures. However, in view of the procedures used the inferences drawn do not seem to be justified by the data.[14] Paldam (1979) dealing only with "stable" governments (i.e. majority governments which ruled throughout the normal election period) on average did find an election cycle in aggregate data, but one which is quite different from the Nordhaus cycle.

Amacher and Boyes (1982) regress US unemployment rates on time, for pre- and post-election periods separately. They can only find a significant coefficient for those pre-election periods, in which case the incumbent won. This might suggest that only when the incumbent was successful in manipulating the economy, he was re-elected. See also Allen, Sulock and Sabo (1986). MacRae (1977, 1981), Beck (1982a) and Thompson and Zuk (1983), on the other hand, can find little or no support for an American political business cycle.

The results reported hitherto do not give strong support to the political business cycle hypothesis. However, the hypothesis was tested only indirectly as the data pertained to the outcomes of the economic process. Of course, there are serious identification problems here. On the one hand, the functioning of the economy has not only been subject to political manipulation, but also to all kinds of external influences; on the other hand, political interventions may not be perceived, if they have been undertaken without success. For those reasons it is of interest to see whether the use of economic policy <u>instruments</u> has been subject to some kind of election cycle. This approach is the more useful in the context of this book, as it could produce results which are more easily integrated in macroeconomic models than the Nordhaus prediction itself.

Several authors have estimated reaction functions - describing to which extent fiscal and/or monetary policy is affected by varying economic and political conditions (cf. chapter 1) - with the addition of certain variables intended to capture the effect of an election cycle.[15] In this context it should be noted that Laney and Willett (1983) report the (cyclically adjusted) US federal deficit to be significantly higher in pre-election than in post-election periods. However, their finding is contradicted by Lowery (1985), while Golden and Poterba (1980) and Beck (1982b) too cannot find evidence that the timing of elections has had an impact on US economic policy. See also Mosley (1984) for some mixed results.

The rather negative empirical evidence as to the existence of a Nordhaus-like political business cycle or the corresponding use of policy instruments should not be read as to imply that governments never would engage in re-election activities. When governments do, they just do not do it in the Nordhaus-fashion. This questions the robustness of the Nordhaus-proposition. Let us review the validity of and the effect of changes in the various assumptions.

<u>a</u>. The analysis concentrated on <u>voters</u> disliking both inflation and unemployment. However, our survey of empirical voting and popularity functions in section 2.3.3 must lead to a series of critical observations. Firstly, we have concluded that voting and popularity functions are unstable. If the relation between popularity, unemployment and inflation is, indeed, unstable, and thus unpredictable, it cannot act as a menu for policy choice. Even if it were desirable, it just becomes impossible for the government to control its popularity level. Secondly, the particular

structure of the Nordhaus cycle depends on the phenomenon that voters dislike both inflation and unemployment. If, for instance, the electorate does not care about inflation at all, there would be no reason for the government to generate a cycle in order to maximize votes (cf. Van der Ploeg (1984)). The empirical results on voting and popularity have further shown that also other (economic) variables may play a role, such as the development of the exchange rate, or the balance of payments. Van der Ploeg (1984) points out that an overwhelming concern of the voters with the balance of payments could very well swamp the political business cycle.

Still more fundamental is the question whether voters are really backward looking, and whether they would remain so if incumbent politicians systematically followed a Nordhaus-like re-election strategy. A rational electorate would (learn to) penalize any undesirable actions occurring after the forthcoming election. Once the electorate is forward looking and fully informed as to the macroeconomic structure, it could devise an optimal plan over the entire horizon, and vote strategically by penalizing the incumbent politicians for any deliberate policy deviation from that plan. The conclusion is that the cycle would vanish.[16] Of course, it should be recalled from section 2.3.3 that the empirical evidence for rational (strategic, sophisticated) voting until now is not quite convincing.

Finally, it can be remarked that the aggregate relationship between unemployment, inflation and popularity is only part of the voting story. Ideological and class-based differences between political parties and the concern for core voters may be important other elements in explaining the determination of government behaviour.

b. The next element in our discussion of the political business cycle will be the <u>government</u> itself. The analysis assumed that elections occur at fixed, foreseeable intervals. In general there exists an institutionally defined upper limit on the length of the electoral period, but, as Lächler (1982) points out, most constitutions also contain provisions for dissolving legislative bodies before this limit is reached. A first alternative is that the election date is controlled by the government. This will tend to impart greater regularity to the political business cycle. Cf. Lächler (1982). Secondly, the election date may not be controlled by and not known with certainty to the government. In case of a coalition government, for instance, not all partners may be equally affected by the development of unemployment and inflation (cf. section 2.3.3). There is a chance then that coalition parties will defect to the opposition and support a vote of no-confidence, at times which suit them better than the institutionally defined election day. Lächler (1982) and Ginsburgh and Michel (1983) investigate the case that the election date is treated by the government as a random variable. The result is a less pronounced political business cycle, both in amplitude as well as in regularity. Moreover, if the election is called before the legal term there may be no or even an inversion of the cycle.

Our next point of attention is whether governments would really be striving after re-election, and whether they would be interested in the maximization of votes in order to secure this re-election. It is not sure that parties in the opposition are powerless, as from that position they can compete with the government by mobilizing political support for alternative policy plans (cf. Stigler (1972)). Further, when in power parties might first of all be interested in carrying their ideology into effect. Kirchgässner (1984) demonstrates that the political business cycle may vanish, or that even its structure can change, if governments follow an ideological policy subject to the constraint of preserving at least a minimal vote share. Finally, even if politicians are only interested in retaining their seats, it is not quite clear why their time horizon should be no longer than one electoral period. Why not maximize the uninterrupted length of time in office, as Frey and Ramser (1976) suggest? Such an objective may yield an optimal strategy without political business cycles. See also Van der Ploeg (1984).

c. The final element in our critical review of the Nordhaus proposition, is the modelling of the economy. Nordhaus modelled the economy by way of an expectations-augmented Phillips-curve, being in the long-run steeper than in the short-run. The dynamics of the political business cycle is very sensitive to this specific economic model. See, e.g., Lächler (1978). Also, as with the voting and popularity functions, the question should be raised whether it is really adequate to assume adaptive formation of expectations. If a political business cycle is being generated, the formulation would imply that economic agents are constantly in error due to mistaken inflationary expectations. But, economic agents might learn and adjust their procedure of forming expectations. With rational expectations, the political business cycle will vanish (cf. Kirchgässner (1984); see also Borooah and Van der Ploeg (1983)).

If we stick to the original formulation with adaptive expectations, the other issue is whether we can expect the government to have a perfect control of the business cycle. Lindbeck (1976) enumerates several reasons for this control to be imperfect: "(1) the high frequency of exogenous shocks that continuously hit the economy, for instance from international sources; (2) the limited understanding among politicians and their advisers of the functioning of the very complex macroeconomic system; (3) the 'imperfections' in the political-administrative system, including the celebrated 'policy lags' - recognition lags, decision lags and effect lags; and (4) the delicate balancing of the interests and opinions of various organizations which challenge the authority of the national government". "All this puts obvious limits on the possibilities of a successful fine tuning of the mixed economic and political business cycle" (p. 14).

From our discussion of the various underlying assumptions it has become clear that the actual structure of the political business cycle depends on specific assumptions concerning the preferences of voters, the objectives of government, the expectation formation procedure, and so on. Furthermore, the empirical research has not yielded much evidence for the existence of the cycle. All in all we are tempted to conclude that it has not become very likely that a political business cycle exists. Nevertheless, it may well be possible that governments undertake re-election activities on a more ad-hoc base.

2.4.3. Political parties and (macro)economic policy

Manipulating swing voters through an adequate use of the electoral calendar may set the timing of (certain) economic policy actions. The substance of economic policy is yet another question. Here the influence of the core constituency and the ideology of political parties and politicians may enter.

Already in chapter 1 we saw that political parties (politicians) differ on what they consider to be desirable economic policy. Recall the preferences of political groupings in 8 western countries presented by Kirschen et al. (1964), and the estimates of preference functions for Dutch political parties reported in section 1.5.1.

It is natural to try to relate the divergent economic policy preferences of different political parties to differences in their membership. In section 2.3.3 economic policy preferences within the electorate were seen to be at least partially class-based. Lower income, lower status, blue-collar workers are relatively more in favour of efforts to reduce unemployment, while high income, upper status, white-collar citizens are more interested in efforts to reduce inflation. These different economic priorities can serve to attract different constituencies to each party (candidate). Indeed, party allegiances may have a clear class-oriented base, as Hibbs (1982b) confirms for the UK.

In the most simple Downsian two-party model with a unimodal distribution of voters' preferences, incentives operate in a direction that encourages parties to blur the differences between their platforms and to move toward identical ideological positions (the position of the median voter; cf. section 2.2). However, Downs (1957) also notes that whenever the distribution of voters is polymodal, a multi-party system - with three or more major parties - is likely to occur. For parties in a multi-party system no incentive is present to move toward each other ideologically; they will strive to distinguish themselves from each other and to maintain the purity of their position.

As parties are composed of or at least responsive to differing sets of individuals, and as these subgroups have differing interests and valuations of economic policy, it should in general make a difference for economic policy whether a left-wing or a right-wing party is in power. Economic policy of the incumbent parties should broadly be in agreement with the economic interests of their class-defined core constituencies.

This premise is still somewhat further elaborated in Alt (1985a), where it is suggested that this partisan effect may be of a transitory rather than a sustained nature. A sustained reduction of unemployment, e.g., requires repeated interventions, such that after some time the instruments may become blunt, and other economic problems may arise (inflation, balance of payments deficits). Also, voters may become accustomed to low levels of unemployment, ceasing to give the government credit for it and turning attention to other issues, such that the political agenda changes. Finally, the core class of support may not be large enough to provide an electoral majority, necessitating the government to bid for the support of other groups by pursuing some different policies.[17]

Let us review the empirical evidence for partisan effects on economic policy. Cross-section data for industrialized countries have been presented by Hibbs (1977), Tufte (1978), Cameron (1978). For the period 1945-1969 Hibbs finds that nations in which Social-Democratic and Labour parties have governed for most or much of the time have on average experienced comparatively high rates of inflation and relatively low rates of unemployment. Tufte adds some material suggesting that income equalization through direct taxation has been greatest in countries where the left has governed the longest. As to the size of the public sector, Tufte asserts that "from 1945 to 1969, each additional decade of left-wing control meant an additional 10 percentage point increase in government receipts" (p. 97), while Cameron adds that during the period 1960-1974 the expansion of the public sector was greater, the longer the period of control by the left.

Next, we turn to the findings from time-series studies. Hibbs (1977) investigated the hypothesis of the occurrence of a gradual rise in unemployment levels under right-wing and a gradual decline under left-wing governments. For the UK his findings imply a noticeable difference between the unemployment levels associated with Labour and Conservative governments. As to the US, the results of both Hibbs (1977) and Beck (1982c) are consistent with the notion that Democratic administrations suffer less unemployment, but the party differences found by Beck are considerably smaller (by about half) than those by Hibbs. According to Beck, interadministration differences even tend to explain significantly more of unemployment than interparty differences. In that case the hypothesis of relatively stable, class-based core constituencies of the parties should be questioned, at least for the US. Alt (1985a) investigates for both the

US and UK whether partisan effects on unemployment are sustained or only transitory (see above). For the UK the transitory-impact model confirms the expectations; for the US, it is the sustained-impact model which is in exact accord with the party-change hypothesis (even though administrations are considered separately). In a follow-up study, Alt (1985b) considers 13 other western industrial nations for the period 1960-1983. For 8 countries partisan effects are revealed; changes in the party composition of government had at least once a significant effect on unemployment in the predicted direction. In four of these countries the transitory-impact model turns out to give the best fit, in the other four the sustained-impact model prevails. Most notably, the Netherlands is the country which presents the best evidence for the partisan effect hypothesis. At the occasion of four - out of 6 - changes in party composition of government significant partisan effects are detected; the sustained-impact model performs best.[18]

It can be concluded that there are clear indications of party differences in the ultimate economic outcomes like unemployment; the evidence for a choice between the sustained- and transitory-impact models is not yet conclusive. The need arises to find similar partisan differences in the governments' use of economic policy <u>instruments</u>. As to the US, Friedlaender (1973) and Golden and Poterba (1980) indeed report to have found some significant partisan differences in their policy reaction function estimates. The results of Froyen (1974) and Lowery (1985), on the other hand, do not support the partisan diffence hypothesis. Cowart (1978a,b), looking for partisan effects on the use of instruments of fiscal and monetary policy in seven European countries, only finds significant results for Germany (in both monetary and fiscal policy) and the Netherlands (in monetary policy only). These results, moreover, are not consistent with the party effects hypothesized above, as governments of the left exhibit a far greater responsiveness to both unemployment and inflation, than their conservative counterparts; the left is simply much more interventionist. As to the UK, Minford and Peel (1982) report to have found strong support for the party change effect proposition, while Alt and Chrystal (1983) could only find a partisan effect on transfers for the 1964-1970 Labour government.

With Alt (1985a) we must conclude that as yet no consistent significant party differences in the use of economic policy instruments have been found. Clearly, the result of finding party differences in the ultimate economic outcomes but not in the use of instruments is unsatisfactory. It points to some sort of misspecification. As the outcome effects have been found to be rather robust, we first of all should turn to more elaborated models of the use of instruments. For that reason we discuss in the next subsection models, which are so ambitious as to integrate political business cycle and ideological considerations in one model.

2.4.4. The Frey-Schneider approach and related models

Most notable in the class of models which try to explain government behaviour as a combination of re-election and ideologically motivated efforts, is the politico-economic model of Frey and Schneider, which builds on the theoretical lines that were presented originally by Frey and Lau (1968). See, especially, Frey and Schneider (1978a,b; 1979; 1981a; 1982) and Schneider and Frey (1983).

The model consists of two kinds of relations, a popularity function and one or more reaction functions, corresponding with the lower and the upper loop of figure 2.1, respectively. The popularity function follows the traditional patterns in dealing with the influence of economic variables - notably the rate of unemployment, the rate of inflation and the rate of growth of real disposable income - on government popularity. Frey and Schneider (1978a,b; 1979) report for the US as well as the UK and Germany that all three economic variables mentioned have a significant impact on government popularity, and that it is only the current or slightly lagged state of the economy that counts. Moreover, they claim to have found for all countries and all periods considered (with the exception of Switzerland) that a one percentage point change in the rate of unemployment has a larger marginal effect than a one percentage point change in inflation; a change in the growth of real disposable income always has the smallest effect (cf. Frey and Schneider (1981a)). The results suggest that in the countries and periods considered an expansionary policy lowering unemployment (and raising income growth) would have been the most effective policy for raising popularity. Its positive effect is not only greater, but also more immediate than the negative effect resulting from any subsequent inflation.

The other part of the model describes how the government sets the values of its economic policy instrument(s). The government is hypothesized to maximize it own utility, which it derives from pursuing its own - ideological - goals.[19] In pursuing its goals, the government is subject to a series of political, economic and administrative constraints. The dynamic, constrained optimization problem faced by the government is considered to be so complex, and to require such an amount of information, that in general it will be impossible to derive an exact, analytical solution. Therefore, the government is assumed to resort to a satisficing strategy, and to use some simplified behavioural rule. According to Frey and Schneider the main features of this behavioural rule are represented by the following <u>reaction function</u>:

(2.1) $$INSTR_{t+1} = a_o + [a_1(POP^* - POP)_t^2 + a_2 TBE_t] D_t$$
$$+ (\sum_i a_3^i I_{it})(POP - POP^*)_t^2 (1-D_t) + a_4 GR_t + a_5 INSTR_t ,$$

with:
$$D_t = \begin{cases} 1 & \text{if } POP_t < POP_t^* , \\ 0 & \text{if } POP_t \geq POP_t^* , \end{cases}$$

where INSTR refers to the value of the economic policy instrument concerned; POP is the current popularity level of the government, while POP^* is the minimum popularity level which is deemed necessary to be certain of re-election; D is a dummy variable equal to one in case of a popularity deficit (POP < POP^*) and equal to zero in case of a popularity surplus (POP $\geq$ POP^*); TBE indicates how much time is still available for the government before the next election; the I_i's are dummy variables, one for each (kind of) government or president, being equal to one when kind i of government or president is in power and otherwise equal to zero; GR, finally, denotes government receipts.

Most interesting about reaction function (2.1) is the clear distinction made between periods of popularity deficit (D = 1) and popularity surplus (D = 0). It is taken for granted that politicians can only pursue their goals if they are and remain in office. Popularity is a convenient and widely observed indicator of the probable election outcome. A government can only be confident of re-election if a certain minimum popularity level is reached or surpassed. If so, the government meets no political constraint to put its ideological views into practice. It is assumed that it will increasingly seize this opportunity as the popularity surplus becomes larger. As to the content of the ideological views, it is presumed that left-wing governments will, ceteris paribus, tend to increase public expenditure, while right-wing governments will have a lower target share for the size of government.

On the other hand, if current popularity is below the minimum target level, the government probably will not be re-elected if conditions remain unchanged. It is, therefore, urged to react to induce such changes in the state of the economy as will increase its popularity. According to the estimates of the popularity function reported above, an expansionary policy should be undertaken. It is, furthermore, reasonable to assume that the reaction will be stronger the larger the popularity deficit, and the closer the election date.

There are two kinds of economic constraints. The budget constraint is modelled by inserting last year's government receipts into the equation. For the UK, Frey and Schneider introduce instead the general wage level as it is (in combination with below average productivity increases) responsible for the rise in relative cost of government activity. The other economic constraint is given by the structure of the economy, which specifies how economic policy instruments influence the state of the economy. The specific structure of the economy is - implicitly - reflected in the parameters of the reaction function. However, it may be necessary to add additional elements to eq. (2.1), when certain constraints are not yet properly accounted for. The state of the balance of payments in the UK offers an example of this.

Administrative constraints are due to all kinds of perception, decision and execution lags, including legal obligations and the impact of the public bureaucracy trying to maximize its own utility. In the literature it has been argued (cf. section 2.5) that the members of the public bureaucracy are only interested in expansion of expenditure and jobs as this increases income, status and influence; and they will tend to resist changes in the structure of expenditure as this threatens to destroy their current positions. This administrative constraint is modelled by Frey and Schneider by assuming that adjustment of instrument values takes place only gradually. For that reason the lagged endogenous variable has been added to eq. (2.1).

It should be added that with respect to the details, the model is differentiated when applied to different countries.

It is time to take a look at the <u>empirical results</u> for the Frey-Schneider reaction function.[20] The model has been applied by the authors to US federal government decision making (Frey and Schneider (1978a), Schneider and Frey (1983)), to the UK (Frey and Schneider (1978b, 1981b, 1982)), and to Germany (Frey and Schneider (1979, 1981c)). The results reported for these three countries are very similar, and are interpreted to substantiate the theory as the coefficients in most cases obtain the expected signs. With respect to re-election efforts the popularity deficit variable nearly always has a significant coefficient, indicating that governments indeed undertake an expansionary policy in times of a popularity deficit. The coefficients related to the time-before-election and the ideological goal variables are significantly different from zero in only part of the cases. Moreover, the ideology parameters for different kinds of governments and administrations are generally not found to be significantly different from each other. For the US and Germany the dependent variable, lagged one year, receives a coefficient ranging from 0.64 to 1.09, which points to a rather slow adjustment of instrument values. For the UK the dependent variable, lagged one quarter, has a coefficient between 0.6 and 0.8, suggesting that here the adjustment speed is substantial. In the latter case it was further found that the past instrument value has a smaller weight in case of a popularity deficit than with a popularity surplus; apparently, governments may perceive the re-election requirements to be more pressing than the pursuit of ideological goals.[21] Finally, the economic constraint variables inserted mostly appear to have a statistically significant effect.

The Frey-Schneider model has also been estimated by others, however with remarkably less success than by the authors themselves. Ahmad (1983) re-estimates their original model for the US for a prolonged period and reports that of the three instruments considered it only performs reasonably well for transfer payments. Neck (1982), analysing real public consumption for Austria does not find an ideological difference between left-wing and right-wing governments, nor an effect of the time-before-election variable, while the popularity deficit gets the wrong sign. Renaud and Van Winden (1987b) report similar results from an application of the model to the Netherlands.

We presented the Frey-Schneider model[22] in some detail as it is - in the words of two vehement critics - "certainly the most ambitious empirical politico-economic model in the literature".[23] For that same reason we shall also discuss the critique of the model in some detail, as it can help us in our search for other, better ways of modelling politico-economic interdependence.

a. The first series of critical remarks is of a more or less technical nature.
- Frey and Schneider do not maintain the same specification in their different empirical studies. The lag structure is changed, the popularity deficit is squared or not, variables representing the economic constraints are sometimes omitted, the operationalization of ideology differs, and so on. Undoubtedly, these differences can - at least to some extent - be justified by referring to peculiarities regarding the institutional setting or the economic situation in different countries and periods. But as to how and how much of the differences can be explained in this way, comments on the part of the authors would have been welcome.
- What is striking, is the variety in the instruments considered and in the units of measurement of these instruments. One comes across (categories of) government expenditure and government revenues, in nominal amounts, in real amounts and as a share of national income; government jobs, both as a number and as an employment rate; and the government wage rate. Most of these measures of fiscal manipulation are flawed, as such and/or in the context of eq. (2.1). See also Golden and

Poterba (1980). First, why use nominal or real <u>amounts</u>, not adjusted for the rate of inflation and/or the size of the economy, while the re-election effort and ideology variables (with the exception of ideology in the UK) are expressed in terms of a popularity <u>rate</u>? Secondly, variables are assigned to be instruments which are not really within the control of the government. In the case of taxes, e.g., a government can vary the tax rates but it cannot control tax revenues. Similarly with transfers, it can vary the benefit rates but not the amount that is paid on, e.g., unemployment benefits (cf. Borooah and Van der Ploeg (1983, p. 142)).

- In chapter 1 it was already discussed in general that simultaneity biases may be present in the estimation of policy reaction functions. This problem may also arise with the Frey-Schneider kind of models, as the relation between targets and instruments has been replaced by a relation from targets via popularity to instruments. Frey and Schneider circumvent the problem by the imposition of a specific lag structure on the model (cf. eq. (2.1)).

- With regard to eq. (2.1), relating government's use of economic policy instruments, e.g. expenditure, to last year's (or quarter's) government receipts only does not seem a very sensible way of modelling the budget constraint. Ahmad (1983) remarks that it would make more sense to relate it to (expected) current receipts. Notice further that government revenue, or at least the tax rate, is itself an instrument of economic policy.

- Arguing along the same line, it should be acknowledged that the instruments of economic policy are not all independent. Through the budget constraint and through the working of the economic system they are all mutually constrained and constraining. Thus, instruments should not be considered separately (cf. Ahmad (1983, p. 174); see also Frey and Schneider (1981c)).

- One step further yet, Ahmad argues that it is not only fiscal manipulation the government can take recourse to; it may also try to manipulate monetary policy. This calls in question the relative autonomy of the central bank as a policy making unit, an important question which is still open to further empirical research. See, e.g., Frey and Schneider (1981c), Beck (1982b), Laney and Willett (1983).

b. With the last remark we have come to the <u>roles of the actors</u> in the political process.

- Although the bureaucracy is hypothesized to try to maximize its own utility, its role according to eq. (2.1) only amounts to retarding the adjustment of government policy. There is no sign of a specific, independent influence of the bureaucracy on public sector decision making; cf. section 2.5.
- A central assumption of the Frey-Schneider model is that politicians only can pursue their goals if they are in office. The opposition is without influence. Furthermore, government coalitions are treated as a homogeneous entity, with a dominating will to get re-elected. This view of the political process is rather simplistic, especially in a multi-party system, for it ignores the existence of cabinet crises, the conditions under which a coalition can be continued after an election, and the like.
- A related question is raised by Golden and Poterba (1980) who doubt whether a popular government would not engage in economic manipulation, even if it would be unnecessary for electoral victory. First, they argue, governments might be vote-maximizers, as a landslide victory brings substantial political benefits. Secondly, an unforeseen event could dramatically cut even the most popular government's victory margin. The use of expansionary policies could perhaps provide insurance to risk-averse politicians.

c. Another important issue in the interpretation of the Frey-Schneider model is the <u>connection between the popularity and the policy reaction functions</u>.

- Frey and Schneider contend that re-election efforts should be expected to be expansionary, as the marginal contribution to popularity of lower unemployment is found by them to be (much) more important and direct than that of inflation. However, we have learned in section 2.3 that popularity functions are rather unstable. But, if the Frey-Schneider popularity function is not robust, then the formulation and interpretation of their policy reaction function is seriously called in question. Why would governments engage in a re-election effort, when they do not know whether and to what extent it contributes to their popularity level?

- Next, as Ahmad (1983), observes the inclusion of the popularity deficit and surplus variables implies that economic policy is largely determined by political considerations, which would give a rather narrow view of economic policy determination. Of course, the existence and extent of a popularity deficit or surplus itself is a function of the economic situation. But note that through this formulation the approach neglects the fact that each kind of government may have its idiosyncratic weighing of the importance of each of the targets of economic policy.
- Finally, the government is always assumed to react to a popularity crisis with its instruments in the same manner regardless of the origin of the crisis. According to Borooah and Van der Ploeg (1983) this is, for instance, at variance with British government behaviour over the past two decades, "which have for example imposed incomes policies when they regarded inflation as the source of crisis and reflated when they regarded unemployment as being too high" (p. 142).

d. Another critique of the model pertains to the specification of <u>ideology</u> and ideological differences.
- A general critique is formulated by Borooah and Van der Ploeg (1983, p. 142). By considering broad aggregates the approach misses the ideological differences between political parties with respect to (re)distributional issues. For example, when both right-wing and left-wing governments (are forced to) cut public expenditure, they will emphasize different items.
- Ideological differences are only relevant in the case of a popularity surplus. Furthermore, it is assumed that ideology can be modelled in terms of a preference for a reduction or an extension of government activity; that is, as a target share of government expenditure in national income.[24] However, it can be seriously questioned whether that is the only (macroeconomic) issue on which ideological differences exist. As was already referred to above, there may also exist ideological differences between parties and governments on the point of sensitivity to unemployment and inflation.
- Relatedly, it is not altogether clear why ideological differences could not extend to re-election policies, such that right-wing governments would spend less than left-wing governments, but more than when electorally safe. Why should governments have a target share of national

income when electorally unconstrained, and not when they are constrained? See Chrystal and Alt (1981). To a large degree, the above critique on the specification of the ideological variables originates from the fact that Frey and Schneider do not have a theory to offer, which explains the ideological differences between parties.

- In the empirical results there is not much sign of statistically significant interparty ideological differences. For the UK, Chrystal and Alt (1981, p. 733) note that "without the inter-party differences, whether what is left is ideology is open to doubt, as the variable contains the product of popularity deficit and national income." They suggest that the apparent significance of ideology is really just the significance of the income term; in no case they were able to find a significant effect of popularity deficits on government expenditure, once national income was included in the equation as well.[25)]

e. A final remark must be made regarding the suggestion, e.g. in Frey and Schneider (1981a), that their model is a <u>closed model</u> of interdependence between the economy and polity. Certainly, an important feedback loop can be introduced into macroeconomic modelling through the combined popularity and policy reaction functions. The claim that this loop is closed is not always warranted, at any rate not for their estimates with respect to the US and Germany. Popularity was modelled as a function of the economic situation, to which a series of dummies was added to capture the specific popularity level of each president (US) or each kind of government (Germany). Similarly, in the policy reaction functions ideology was entered through dummy variables, again one for each president and for each kind of government. However, a function stipulating which kind of coalition government will be formed after each election, or which person will be elected president, with his specific popularity level and ideology, is yet missing. As to the UK, the model can for practical purposes be considered to be closed, as there are only two (main) parties alternating in government. Here, the estimate, produced by the popularity function, of the popularity lead of the government at the date of the election can give a useful indication of which of the two main parties will be in power during the next election period; and so on.

Apart from the Frey-Schneider model there have also been some <u>other attempts</u> to take account of both political business cycle and partisan effects on economic policy. Pommerehne and Schneider (1983) estimate fiscal policy reaction functions for Australia, which are in line with eq. (2.1) except for the multiplication of the re-election constraint and the ideological variables with the dummies D and 1 - D. Thus, they do without the sharp distinction between periods of popularity deficit and surplus. Golden and Poterba (1980) and Ahmad (1983) include the targets of economic policy (unemployment, inflation, income growth) directly in their reaction functions, in addition to popularity, electoral cycle and ideological variables. As these alternative models have a rather ad-hoc specification, missing a clear logic of reasoning, while moreover the empirical results are not very conclusive, we will not dwell on them here.

The most interesting alternative formulation comes from Aubin c.s. (1985). Instead of the dummy D and the corresponding dichotomy between periods of popularity deficits and surpluses, they introduce a continuous index ρ. If popularity is below a threshold level POP^{*-}, such that the government is certain to be defeated at the next election, $\rho = 1$; if popularity is above a second threshold level POP^{*+}, such that re-election is ensured, $\rho = 0$; in between the two thresholds ρ is assumed to decrease linearly. Furthermore, Aubin c.s. explicitly introduce the target variables of economic policy. Their reaction function integrates political and economic considerations in the following manner:

$$(2.2) \quad INSTR = a_0 + \sum_k [a_1^k \rho + a_2^k (1-\rho)] Y_k + a_3 TBE + \sum_j a_4^j Z_j ,$$

where Y_k stands for target k of economic policy, TBE denotes the time before the next election, and the Z_j represent other variables, e.g. technical constraints. The use of the index ρ allows a differentiation in economic policy reactions, depending on whether political support is deemed too low (a_1^k), high enough (a_2^k), or somewhere in between (a weighted average of a_1^k and a_2^k). Aubin c.s., applying (2.2) to French data, come up with some interesting initial results. These suggest that government reacts to rising unemployment by increasing expenditure, only in case popularity is insufficient; and that it reacts to inflation by increasing taxes, only in case popularity is high. The electoral cycle has a quite significant influence too; the prospect of national elections leads to a relative decline in direct taxes, to a faster growth of social transfers, and to an increase of public consumption.

Coming to conclusions, it is evident that Frey and Schneider did an important work when they tried to combine re-election efforts and ideological activities by politicians into one model. They accomplished this by making a strict division between periods of popularity deficit and of popularity surplus. The resulting formulation of the policy reaction function, well interpretable and useful as it is, has in its turn been subject to a series of more or less important criticisms. Popularity function estimates, for instance, tend to be unstable; the operationalization of the ideological goal variables is rather unsatisfactory; the influence of the bureaucracy is poorly integrated, let alone of organized interest groups; and the model is hardly, if at all, applicable to multiparty systems with coalition cabinets. Examining the empirical evidence presented by Frey and Schneider and others, it must be concluded that these findings are not quite satisfactory, certainly not with regard to the ideological activities. Certain variations on the Frey-Schneider model did not yield remarkably better empirical results, while missing the clear logic of reasoning behind the model.

2.4.5. Two other models: crisis management and the permanent income hypothesis

At the end of this section we discuss two approaches which cannot be easily fitted in elsewhere in this chapter, but which are nevertheless interesting enough to make mention of them. It concerns the "crisis management" model of Mosley (1984), and the permanent income hypothesis of Alt and Chrystal (cf. Chrystal and Alt (1981), Alt and Chrystal (1981, 1983)).

Mosley first points out that even though the economy may be the most important issue facing the government, the response of government popularity to the state of the economy is anything but steady and

reliable. It is concluded that the popularity function is just too unstable to act as a menu for policy choice. With regard to economic policy, Mosley puts forward the hypothesis that governments behave as satisficing instead of optimizing organizations (see also section 1.6), and that the political purpose of economic policy is to steer the economy out of crisis zones. The latter because the electorate only displays concern about the economy when things are going sufficiently bad. His model has the following features (cf. Mosley (1984, p. 76)):
- the policy maker does not have a criterion function, in the shape of a consistent set of preferences between alternative states of the world; rather, manipulation of instruments is a response to whether the state of the economy is 'satisfactory' or not;
- if the economy is operating on a satisfactory level and there is no crisis, no macroeconomic action of any sort will be taken; however, if the economic target variables stray outside the satisfactory zone, instruments are manipulated, initially according to standard rules of thumb;
- if these standard rules of thumb do not have the desired result, a search process starts for new policy instruments;
- the satisfactory levels of the targets (and the occasional replacement of one target by another) are determined as result of conflict between the actors in the policy-making process;
- the acceptable levels of the targets are sensitive to the discrepancy between these aspiration levels and actual performance;
- finally, in an election year, regardless of the state of the economy, economic policy will be more expansionary in order to reflate personal disposable incomes.

The Mosley-model is formalized in the following reaction function:

$$(2.3) \quad \Delta x_t = \begin{cases} \alpha + \beta(y-y^*)_{t-k} + \gamma E, & \text{if } y > y^*, \\ 0, & \text{if } y \leq y^*, \end{cases}$$

where x is an economic policy instrument, y a target variable and E an election year dummy. The satisfactory target level y^* is determined as a moving average of y over time.[26]

The Mosley-model can be criticized on several grounds. Firstly, according to the model economic policy instruments apparently are only subject to change in one direction (unless crises of different kinds are alternating). Secondly, in view of Mosley's own popularity function estimates there seems to be no theoretical justification for the inclusion of the re-election variable E in eq. (2.3). Thirdly, there is hardly any theoretical underpinning for the (changes in the) choice of the target variables, nor for the identification of their satisfactory levels. Rather arbitrary, the major targets for the UK are assumed to be unemployment and the balance of payments for the period 1945-1973, and inflation for the period 1974-1982. Still more arbitrary, the satisfactory level of a target variable in any quarter is modelled as the average value of that target over the previous twelve quarters, while a crisis is assumed to exist if the target variable remains above its satisfactory level for three quarters or more. All in all, the model is hardly political in nature. It is not made clear what is the content of the conflict between the different actors in the policy-making process resulting in the determination of the satisfactory levels, and what determines the relative bargaining strength of the actors in the conflict. Note also that the political colour of the government does not play any role.

The empirical application of the model to the UK and US in Mosley (1984) does not look convincing either. Correlation coefficients and Durbin-Watson statistics are either very low or not reported at all. The coefficient β is significantly different from zero in crisis periods in two out of every three cases considered, but in no case is it significantly different from the coefficient for non-crisis periods. Finally, with regard to the election year dummy: for the period 1945-1973 the coefficient only appears to be significant for the UK, for the period 1974-1982 it is only significant for the US.[27]

Contrary to Mosley's crisis management, <u>Alt and Chrystal</u> base their model upon the view that government expenditure is extremely 'sticky', that is, exhibiting a high level of inertia in response to short-term changes in the political or economic environment. This stability is due to the behaviour of the institutions which determine public expenditure. Institutional procedures adopted for medium-term expenditure planning in some western countries – Alt and Chrystal refer to the UK and Germany – deliberately target expenditure growth on expected national income growth.[28] Thus, expenditure is planned in relation to levels of national income experienced over some time. "The institutional rigidities of any national political and administrative system make it impossible for policy-makers to hire and fire civil servants, cancel and instigate projects, and raise and lower pensions and taxes in response to their transient fortune in the opinion polls, at least on a scale large enough to appear in aggregate expenditure figures".[29] The hypothesis then is that expenditure responds mainly to the trend or permanent level of national income. This is easily modelled by relating government expenditure to its own lagged value and the current level of national income. However, it is granted by Alt and Chrystal that some other factors, such as a deliberate Keynesian-type stabilization policy or the growth of transfer payments due to an increase of unemployment, may cause cycles about the trend.

Alt and Chrystal (1981, 1983) report empirical results for the UK and the US which are said to support the permanent income hypothesis. In all cases considered, both the national income term and the lagged dependent variable have a significant impact. There is also some evidence for the presence of stabilization policy actions; in the UK, government consumption was found to react to the rate of unemployment. Now, it should be observed that in this case of UK government consumption, for instance, the coefficient of the lagged dependent variable ranges between 0.546 and 0.718, based on quarterly data. That is, the average time lag between national income and expenditure growth is only some one till three <u>quarters</u>, which can hardly be interpreted as support for the extreme 'stickiness' and stability of government expenditure.

Furthermore, it is easy enough to criticize the model on theoretical grounds (cf. Frey and Schneider (1983)). For, while Alt and Chrystal refer to institutional behaviour and procedures as the basis of their model, no analysis of such government behaviour can be found in their publications cited. No analysis is presented of what motivates and constrains the politicians and the bureaucracy. No reason is given why the policy-makers want to keep expenditure a stable share of expected national income. Similarly for the stabilization part of the model: to refer to the task of counter-cyclical policy is normative, but does not explain how governments actually behave.

Concluding: even though the principal characteristic of expenditure might be a close relationship to trend national income, as Alt and Chrystal suggest, a theoretical underpinning is still needed.

2.4.6. Conclusion

In this section we reviewed the literature pertaining to the ways in which politicians and political parties react to voting and popularity signals in the formation of economic policy. That review yielded a series of approaches to the formulation of policy reaction functions, which are very different with regard to the size and timing of the impact of politics. With the exception of the Hibbs-approach, the theoretical underpinning of the models is rather shaky. The empirical results were found to be rather mixed and inconclusive. The impact of the bureaucracy on public sector decision making, let alone the influence of interest groups, is not at all or only in a rudimentary fashion integrated in these models. For those reasons it would be unwise to opt for any of the approaches at the moment. First, we shall survey, in the next two sections, the literature addressing the influence of the bureaucracy and of interest groups on economic policy.

For the sake of clarity, we yet summarize the empirical findings for the Netherlands, a multi-party system with coalition governments. No signs were found for the existence of a political business cycle in the outcomes of the economic process; cf. Tufte (1978), Soh (1986). As to the partisan effects in economic policy making, Alt (1985b) presented evidence for the existence of such effects on the course of unemployment. However, no clear partisan effects could be detected in the use of economic policy instruments (cf. Cowart (1978a,b); see also Renaud and Van Winden (1987a)). Finally, application of the Frey-Schneider model by Renaud and Van Winden (1987b) yielded negative results.

2.5. The influence of the bureaucracy

2.5.1. Introduction

To discuss the influence of the bureaucracy on public sector decision making, we start with its main characteristics. First, the bureaucracy is a group of agents within the public sector, which assist the politicians in the preparation of public sector decisions, in the implementation of the decisions, and in the production of public provisions. Bureaucrats, however, are distinct from politicians in that their position is mostly not (directly) related to election outcomes. Secondly, they benefit from the public provision of goods and services not only in their role of consumers – as do all members of the population – but also from the provision itself as it is the source of their jobs, income, prestige, and so on.

After this short characterization, sufficient to delineate the specific social position of the bureaucracy, we take a look at the different channels through which the bureaucracy can exert influence on the public sector decision making process.
- The role of the bureaucrats within the public sector enables them to directly influence the outcome of the decision making process, both in the preparatory phase (through the provision and processing of information, or through agenda control) and in the implementing phase. Public bureaucracy has a certain discretionary leeway in putting into action laws promulgated by the legislature. Moreover, only part of bureaucratic activity is based directly on legal statutes, such that they have to some extent a law-making function (cf. Frey and Pommerehne (1982)).

Apart from this direct impact, bureaucrats can also influence the decision making process of the public sector indirectly, in the same manners as other parts of the population:
- By voting. It is often presumed that bureaucrats have a higher participation rate in elections, and tend to vote for larger public expenditures, than the electorate as a whole.
- By becoming a member of parliament. This opportunity is exploited in many countries to a considerable extent, such that their share of seats

in parliament far exceeds their share of the population; see, e.g. Frey
and Pommerehne (1982), and Van den Berg (1981). Compared to their
colleagues in the private sector, public employees receive a series of
special facilities when residing in parliament.
- By organizing or participating in <u>interest groups</u>. Indeed, public
employees are traditionally well organized in labour unions and other
interest groups, allowing them to exert labour market as well as
political pressure.

In the next two subsections we shall pay attention to the first two of
these channels of influence, as they have been discussed in the literature
in a way that - at least potentially - might be of use in the context of
macroeconomic modelling.[30] The influence of interest groups will be
discussed in section 2.6.

2.5.2. Bureaucrats as voters

Bush and Denzau (1977) argue that bureaucrats can influence the
election outcome and, hence, public sector decision making through their
voting behaviour. First, it is likely that public employees will show a
higher preference for public expenditure, ceteris paribus, than other
voters. For, in addition to benefiting from the public provision of goods
and services as consumers, like all other voters, they also benefit from
(an extension of) the provision itself as it may result in higher
salaries, increased prestige, job security and fringe benefits. Secondly,
it is likely that public officials have a higher turnout at the polls than
other (occupational) groups. As the first point suggests, their
(potential) benefit from the election outcome may be (relatively) high.
Furthermore, bureaucrats are more likely to have better information about
political issues and are better able to determine which candidates are
more likely to affect their well-being, while also their direct costs of
voting are typically low (cf. Bennett and Orzechowski (1983)). Thus, there
are good reasons to believe that bureaucrats derive larger expected net
benefits from voting than others, leading to a greater participation in
elections.

Bush and Denzau suggest that, in the context of the median voter
model, the two elements of a higher preference for public expenditure and

a higher voting participation of public bureaucrats might result in a process yielding an excessive (growth of the) public sector. A larger quantity of public goods means more bureaucrats, who will favour a larger quantity of the public good than they did when they were not yet public employees; as a consequence the provision of public goods will be enlarged, and so on.

The empirical findings almost unanimously report a greater than average voting participation by bureaucrats, also when factors such as education, income, age, race and sex have been controlled for (cf. Wolfinger and Rosenstone (1980), Bennett and Orzechowski (1983) and the review by Frey and Pommerehne (1982)). It should be noted, however, that the results found by Jaarsma, Schram and Van Winden (1986) studying voter turnout for five Dutch national elections between 1971 and 1982, are somewhat less definite. In only one election, the difference in turnout between public employees and private-sector workers is significantly different from zero. Pooling the data, allowing for specific year-effects, improves the results; the public bureaucracy indeed shows a significantly higher voting participation rate than the private sector. Even then, the marginal effect on voter turnout of being employed in the public sector instead of the private sector is not more than some 3.5%.

Let us turn to the second hypothesis, that public employees - ceteris paribus - are more favourably disposed towards public sector activities than are voters employed in the private sector. This hypothesis has received some empirical support in the literature, especially in Courant c.s. (1980). This study of Courant c.s., as well as Aberbach and Rockmann (1976), further suggests that considerable differences in outlook exist <u>within</u> the bureaucracy. The findings argue for a positive agency effect upon bureaucrats, in the sense that those working in a certain government branch attach more value and importance to its activities than those working at other bureaus.

Summarizing, the above material suggests that the voter turnout of the public bureaucracy may indeed be (somewhat) higher than for other parts of the electorate. Also, it seems to be the case that preferences for public spending are shaped, at least in part, by the environment.

However, it is still an open question whether the latter finding on preferences is not an effect of a selection bias when people opt for public vs. private employment. In principle, then, the voting power aspect of the public bureaucracy may be of some - but rather limited - importance.[31]

2.5.3. Bureaucrats versus politicians within the public sector decision making process

The economic modelling of the interaction between the politicians (government, parliament) and the bureaucracy in the provision of goods and services by the public sector got its real start with the seminal contribution of Niskanen (1971). He characterizes the relation between the politicians and the bureaucracy as a bilateral monopoly. The bureaucracy is the monopolistic supplier of the public provision, selling its production in one package to a single buyer, the government. Niskanen summarizes government's preferences in a budget-output function, which renders the maximum budget B the government is willing to pay for each specified output level Q:

(2.4) $\quad B = aQ - bQ^2 \quad , \; a, b > 0.$

The (minimal) cost C of producing each level of output is given by

(2.5) $\quad C = cQ + dQ^2 \quad , \; c, d > 0.$

The analysis is couched within the utility maximization framework.[32]

For the government (or legislature) the optimum point is reached when marginal (social) benefits are equal to marginal (social) costs; or, stated otherwise, when the social surplus B - C is maximized. This optimum point - the social optimum if the government can be assumed to perfectly represent the electorate's preferences - is given by

(2.6) $\quad Q = \dfrac{a-c}{2(b+d)} \; .$

As to the bureaucracy, Niskanen originally introduced budget maximization as the central objective bureaucrats strive for.[33] Migué and Bélanger (1974) suggested, alternatively, that the bureaucracy's objective may be defined in terms of the level of output and the discretionary budget. Following Niskanen (1975), consider an individual bureaucrat with a utility function

$$(2.7) \quad U = \alpha_1 Y^{\beta_1} P^{\gamma_1},$$

where Y is the (present value of the) bureaucrat's income from his position, and P is the set of non-monetary amenities of his position. The conditions valued by the bureaucrat, such as salary, perquisites of the office, power, public reputation, will be related to the performance of his bureau, for instance through the reward structure of the institution as established by the government. Let it be given that:

$$(2.8) \quad \begin{aligned} Y &= \alpha_2 Q^{\beta_2} (B-C)^{\gamma_2}, \\ P &= \alpha_3 Q^{\beta_3} (B-C)^{\gamma_3}, \end{aligned}$$

with $B - C$ the "discretionary budget" of the bureau (the difference between the total available budget B and the minimum cost C of producing the output). Substituting (2.8) in (2.7) and maximizing with respect to Q given that the bureaucracy knows the maximum willingness to pay function (2.4), yields the optimum level of output from the point of view of the bureaucracy:

$$(2.9) \quad Q = \frac{\beta+\gamma}{\beta+2\gamma} \cdot \frac{a-c}{b+d}, \text{ with } \beta = \beta_1\beta_2 + \gamma_1\beta_3, \; \gamma = \beta_1\gamma_2 + \gamma_1\gamma_3.$$

As long as the relation between government and bureaucracy is one of pure bilateral monopoly, the actual level of public provisions will lie somewhere on an interval for which the end-points - (2.6) and (2.9) - were just derived from the demand- and the supply-side, respectively. It can, however, be argued that the relative incentives and available information give the bureaucracy the dominant monopoly power. If the government is not informed on the minimum budget which is necessary to supply a provision, this leaves the government no other room to affect the final output of the bureaucracy than setting the budget constraint; the bureaucracy is free to choose its utility maximizing level of output, and to charge the government for the maximum budget it is willing to pay for that output-level.

Comparing the actual outcome under these circumstances, i.e. the bureaucracy's optimum (2.9), with the government's or social optimum (2.6), it is easily seen that the public sector will be larger than socially optimal, if $\beta, \gamma > 0$. Furthermore, the discretionary budget is positive; the bureaucracy's budget is too large, connected with a technically inefficient mode of operation.

The assumption of a passive government, leaving the bureaucracy with the - informational - monopoly to steer decision making on the level of output and the budget in any direction it desires, should be questioned on several grounds. As Breton and Wintrobe (1975) have noted, the bargaining power of the bureaucracy in this set-up depends on its ability to distort information or conceal it from its sponsor. However, in view of the fact that the electorate would welcome a reduction of public provisions (and the amount of taxes it pays), politicians seeking for re-election would have incentive enough to attempt to exploit their position as monopsonistic buyers of the bureaucracy's output. Be it for this reason or another, it is likely then that governing politicians being aware of the bureaucracy's propensity to distort or withhold information, will use techniques to hold or gain control, such as by direct monitoring, overlapping bureaus, duplication of services, and the purchase and acquisition of information from alternative sources, including sources at lower levels in the bureau itself. Of course, these control devices are costly, and will be used only up to some point. Besides, monitoring the operation of the bureaucracy is a public good for politicians, which may create a free-rider problem among them and a tendency for monitoring activities to be undersupplied (cf. Niskanen (1975); see also Fiorina and Noll (1978)). But the view that the sponsor is completely dominated by the bureaucracy is difficult to swallow.

In addition, it can be doubted that the budgetary process necessarily reveals more information to the bureaucracy than to its sponsor. For, government's demand for public provisions changes over time (due to changes in the electorate's preferences, election outcomes, and coalition formation), probably more so than the cost functions and the maximand of the bureaucracy. Then, it could be easier for the government to know what the bureaucracy is maximizing, than the other way round (cf. Miller and Moe (1983)).

Finally, the budgetary process is characterized by a fundamental asymmetry; it is the government which has the authority to impose any structure it wants on the decision making process, and which makes the final decisions. In view of these considerations there is no reason to believe that the bargaining game between bureaucracy and politicians is inherently stacked against the latter.

This leaves us with the question on the exact point between the two extremes (2.6) and (2.9) where the actual outcome will appear. The answer depends on the specific institutional arrangements: Who decides on what (e.g., do the bureaucrats determine the level of output within the budget forwarded by the politicians, or do the politicians establish both the budget and the output level); how is the organization of the exchange of information (e.g., who goes first, and in what terms); how is the organization of the decision making process among politicians (e.g., is there a committee system in the legislature); what is the structure of the bureaucracy (e.g., how strongly are bureaus consolidated within departments); and so on. Miller (1977), Miller and Moe (1983), Moene (1985) analyze a series of variations on the Niskanen-theme. The result is a taxonomy of solutions, the level of output varying between (or even beyond) the two extremes, depending on the premises started out with. Under certain circumstances the public sector can even be too small, that is smaller than the social optimum (2.6), while remaining technically inefficient.[34]

Let us turn to the _empirical_ applications. The theory clearly indicates that public production will be technically inefficient. Orzechowski (1977) reviews a series of empirical studies, which indicate that, indeed, private suppliers are more efficient than public ones, suggesting that considerable slack exists in public agencies. See also Niskanen (1975). The results by Le Pen (1985) and Brosio and Manzini (1986) are somewhat less definite.

As to the result of oversupply - the public sector being too large - the theory is more ambiguous. Moreover, referring to the taxonomy of solutions, it shows up that these solutions have a very similar structure for quite different information, decision and power configurations. On a time series basis, then, it is hardly possible to distinguish between the alternative set-ups, unless certain clearly discernable unidirectional shifts in the structure of information exchange, the decision making procedures, or the distribution of power have taken place. Niskanen (1975) has a try at it. He analyzes the effect on US federal government outlays for some specific services due to a major structural change in the organization of the federal bureaucracy, namely the consolidation of bureaus supplying related services in new departments. The pattern of results is not inconsistent with the hypothesis that the establishment of the new departments increased spending.

When it comes to a more general empirical application such that incorporation within macroeconomic modelling would become possible, presumably the only workable hypothesis as yet is that the relative power of the bureaucracy vs. the politicians might be positively related to its relative size (the larger the bureaucracy, the greater the opportunity of concealing and distorting information, the greater the pressure from the lower ranks on the top to increase budgets, and so on). The (relative) size of the public sector then might be positively affected by its (relative) level of employment. Notice that the testing of the hypothesis in this sense is problematical. First, due to the method of construction of the national accounts, the value of the output of the public sector cannot be distinguished from the value of the inputs. Secondly, the hypothesis formulated in this way can hardly be distinguished from the hypothesis discussed in section 2.5.2 with respect to the influence of bureaucrats as voters. Lybeck (1986) tests the hypothesis in a study on the growth of government, where he distinguishes the factors working on the demand and on the supply side within an explicit disequilibrium setting. For 12 OECD-countries (estimation period 1960-1982) he finds that on the supply side the share of public employment frequently - i.e. in half of the cases – exerts the expected influence separate from that of relative prices. However, the effect disappears when the data are pooled. It may be added that the effect is also absent in the Netherlands. Further, Fratianni and Spinelli (1982) report some evidence that the bureaucracy contributed to the growth of government in Italy in the period 1926-1956, but not in the more recent period 1952-1976. Mueller and Murrell (1986), finally, report a lack of significance of the bureaucratic strength variable in their cross-section study on the size of government.

Another hypothesis was encountered above in the context of the Frey-Schneider model. Bureaucrats, interested in expansion of expenditures and jobs, would tend to resist changes in the structure of expenditure. Accordingly, the adjustment of economic policy instrument values is assumed to take place only gradually. Indeed, the coefficient of the lagged endogenous variable in eq. (2.1) turns out to be of a considerable size and highly significant. However, it remains a quite open question whether the effect found is due to deliberate, self-interested behaviour (or inactivity) of the bureaucracy. Political decision making itself may be subject to a series of recognition, consultation, decision and implementation lags (including legal obligations). Thus, attention is directed to the fact that "the data on which any tests of these hypotheses must be based reflect conditions that are _jointly_ determined by bureaucracy and representative government" (Niskanen (1975, p. 629)).

A possible solution would be to analyze the budgetary process as such, without troubling about the precise information, decision and power structure underlying it, and hoping that the latter structure did not appreciably change over the period that is being considered. The reader is referred to the permanent income model of Alt and Chrystal already discussed in section 2.4.5, and the incremental budgeting approach of Wildavsky c.s. As to the latter, Davis, Dempster and Wildavsky (1966) model the interaction between the agencies' requests for funds and the appropriations passed by the legislature. Because of the huge number of items to be considered and the extraordinary complexity of the calculations involved, it is argued that budgets are almost never actively reviewed as a whole in the sense of considering at once the value of all existing programs as compared to all possible alternatives. Decision makers use incremental calculations, starting from the existing base, and concentrating on a narrow range of increases or decreases, expressed in terms of percentages. Accordingly, the budgetary process in essence can be modelled in two linear equations, one stating agency requests as a function of previous year's appropriations, the other stating appropriations as a function of agency requests. Estimating the model for 56 US non-defence agencies (period 1947-1963) appears to give a reasonably good fit. A closer look, however, reveals that for a substantial majority of the cases the equations are not temporally stable. The model is not predictive then. As there is no theory underlying the precise form and the value of the coefficients in the two equations used, we have not got any further, after all.

2.5.4. Summary

In this section we discussed the influence of the bureaucracy on public sector decision making. The theoretical suppositions, combined with the empirical findings, suggest the following conclusions:
- Bureaucrats should be considered as a separate social group, with special interests of their own. These interests, however, are not uniform over the bureaucracy; differences in and conflicts of interests exist between agencies, and within agencies between the top and the lower echelons;
- The theoretical analyses indicated - although not uniformly - that the influence of the bureaucracy works in the direction of a larger (too large) size of the public sector, both in the sense of an oversupply of public provisions and of inefficiencies in producing them. This supposition receives some, yet rather weak, support from the still relatively scarce empirical studies on these matters;
- A somewhat related hypothesis on the influence of the bureaucracy states that the bureaucrats, interested in budgets, jobs et cetera, will resist changes in the structure of public expenditure. Their influence would lead to only gradual, or incremental, changes in expenditure, public sector size, and so on. Although the empirical evidence does seem to support such an incremental view of the development of the public sector a satisfactory theoretical underpinning is still missing.

2.6. Interest groups

2.6.1. Introduction

It is widely acknowledged that interest groups affect public sector decision making. For our purpose, an interest group can be defined as a group of people who share some common interest and engage in some sort of collective action to further this interest. The element of collectivity in the interests and in the activities makes it compelling to give separate attention to the behaviour and influence of interest groups, in addition to the mere influence of the members as voters (cf. sections 2.2 and 2.3).

Two issues are at stake here. First, under which circumstances is it to be expected that people sharing some interest will organize themselves and undertake some kind of collective action. Secondly, how can interest groups influence the public sector decision making process; to what extent and in which direction is the decision outcome affected. In section 2.6.2 we shall address the first of these issues, and in section 2.6.3 the second. Section 2.6.4 will summarize the main conclusions.

2.6.2. The logic of collective action

The conditions under which it can be expected that individuals sharing some common interest will organize themselves and act to further this interest, have been discussed extensively by Olson (1965). Given that furthering the common interest has the characteristic of a collective good, the incentive for the individuals to engage in political activities will generally be relatively low. For the individual who is rationally comparing costs and benefits, an additional spending of energy, time and resources on political action in general will only lead to relatively small additional benefits. On the other hand, the individual can consider to become a free-rider, profiting from the amount of the collective good the group as a whole - i.e. the others - have been able to obtain. The larger the group, the greater are the incentives for the individual members to try to withhold their contribution, and the greater are the costs of communication among the group members, of any bargaining between them, and of creating, staffing and maintaining any formal group organization. These factors then tend to keep larger groups from furthering their own interests in an organized manner. To get a large group organizing itself, either requires coercion or the introduction of "selective incentives" which are rewards only given to those who contribute to the group effort.

Olson (1982) discusses some important implications from this theory. First, the incentives for political involvement - and the resources for political action - are unevenly distributed over society. The implication is that no symmetrical organization of all groups with a common interest will be attained. Small groups with specific, specialized interests will get more easily organized and engaged in collective action to further these interests, than large groups with general, diffuse interests.

The second implication relates to the emergence of organizations for collective action over time. As it takes some hurdles to overcome, favourable circumstances and time are needed for organized interest groups to develop. "The other side of the matter is that those organizations that have secured selective incentives to maintain themselves will often survive as organizations even if the collective good they once provided is no longer needed" (p. 40). The more time that passes, then, the larger the number of organized interest groups that will be accumulated in society. The latter implication has received empirical support from cross-section studies by Murrell (1984) and Mueller and Murrell (1986). It appears that the length of time since modern political and economic development began, is a significant determinant of interest group formation, in addition to the size of the population and the degree of decentralization of government.[35]

2.6.3. The influence of interest groups on public sector decision making

The next question is how the different groups may succeed in translating their interests in actual public sector decision making. At least three channels can be distinguished, through which interest groups might exert influence.
- Interest groups could directly influence the economic situation in the country; think of strikes, blockades, investment stops and the like.

This would probably have a negative impact on the government budget constraint through lowering tax revenue, while at the same time voter attitudes toward government performance might be affected. Reasoning along this line, Gärtner (1981) suggests that trade unions pursuing political goals might vary the power they utilize in wage bargaining, pressing for higher-than-usual wage increases towards election date under conservative rule in order to boost inflation and enhance the chance of an electoral victory for the opposition.

- In a world of imperfect and costly information politicians are typically dependent on outside information and help. As the restriction on available time for each topic is quite severe, a high premium is placed on readily accessible information sources. Through their lobbying efforts, then, well-organized interest groups can seize the opportunity to get politicians better informed on their problems, needs and interests, and better provided with technical assistance to solve these problems, than will be the case with regard to the more diffuse, general interests of the electorate.
- In a world of imperfect information[36] interest groups can also provide assistance to politicians to influence the election outcome in their favour. Interest groups may keep their members informed of government actions and of proposals that will affect them. Interest groups may endorse specific parties or candidates running for political office, in order to (or at least trying to) supply them with the votes of their members. And they can supply politicians with campaign assistance, to persuade the general voter to support the candidate.

Will interest groups, using one or more of the above channels, actually succeed in affecting the outcome of the public sector decision making process? Several attempts have been undertaken in the literature to model the interaction among interest groups and between interest groups and politicians (cf. Peltzman (1976, 1980), Becker (1983), Denzau and Munger (1986)).

This literature corroborates the presumption that interest groups can influence public sector decision making. This influence has been recorded to depend, among other things, on the possibilities and costs for groups to organize and their effectiveness in producing pressure, on the dead weight costs of the policies involved, and on the preferences and the level of information of the electorate.[37] However, when it comes to the identification, possibly even formalization, of the more precise impact of interest group activities on the outcome of public sector decision making, and more specifically macroeconomic policy, the above theories prove much less helpful.

Of course, interest groups try to obtain policies which benefit them. That is, in general they will strive for specific expenditures, for specific subsidies or tax exemptions, for specific regulatory measures, to serve their special interests. In this sense, the impact of interest groups should first of all be studied from case studies. As far as the impact of interest groups is considered at the macro level, the general presumption seems to be that interest group activities tend to enlarge the size of the public sector. Several caveats are in order, though. Some of the favours interest groups seek do not seem to have a direct impact on the size of the public sector as traditionally measured (regulation), while another part of interest group striving may actually tend to reduce it (tax exemptions). In many instances just a transfer of wealth is sought for, without any aggregate effect being involved, or at least intended. Further, interest groups are regularly found to oppose each others intentions, cancelling each others influence, at least to a certain degree. Moreover, interest group systems may have an upper-class bias, because of the tendency for upper-status individuals to be more active group participants, and the importance of resources such as money, expertise and political skills which tend to reside in upper-class groups. To the degree that upper-status groups oppose government activism, strong interest group systems may tend toward the conservative side (cf. Nice (1984)). Notwithstanding these caveats, many interest groups strive for the installment or the extension of government expenditures and programs. Moreover, the increasingly complex regulations resulting from lobbying and related processes have to be administered, thereby increasing the scale of the bureaucracy and the public sector.

It is time to review the __empirical evidence__. Case-studies are offered by: Nice (1984), on child allowances and consumer protection legislation across US states; Salamon and Siegfried (1977), on the distribution of effective tax rates across industries in the US; Esty and Caves (1983), on political activity and success of manufacturing industry in the US Congress; and Frey (1984), summarizing the evidence on the degree of protection against foreign competition across industries. On the whole, these studies appear to, or can be interpreted to, give empirical support for the influence of interest groups on public sector decision making.

Schneider and Naumann (1982) consider for Switzerland the impact of the activities[38] of the four most important interest groups (i.e. the associations of small- and middle-sized business, industry and trade, farmers, and the central trade unions) on nine categories of government spending (period 1951-1978). With the exception of the expenditures for courts and police at least one pressure group has a significant and quantitatively important influence on each category of government spending. In the case of welfare and of agriculture the coefficients of all four interest groups are statistically significant. The associations of small- and middle-sized business and of industry and trade tend to dampen the increase of these spending items, ceteris paribus, while the other two tend to further an increase of these items; the net effect of these counteracting influences for welfare payments is a reduction of 4.5 percent, and for agricultural expenditures an increase of 3.6 percent.

Turning to a macro context, the reader can be referred to three studies which try to give explicit attention to the influence of interest groups on the size of the public sector. In their study on the growth of government in Italy, Fratianni and Spinelli (1982) try to assess the impact of specialized- versus diffuse-interest groups. As a suitable proxy for the size of the specialized-interest groups, benefiting from government activity, they chose the labour force in agriculture as a fraction of the total labour force, and the salaried civil servants as a fraction of the total population; as a proxy for the diffuse-interest groups, representing those who pay for government growth, they took the resident population from age 20 to age 59 as a fraction of the total population. The empirical results are not quite convincing. There is evidence in favour of a push for a larger government emanating from those working in the public sector in the first period considered (1926-1956)[39], and from those working in agriculture in the second period. However, while the effect of the diffuse-interest group variable is negative albeit insignificant in the first period - as hypothesized -, it is significant and positive in the second period. Mueller and Murrell (1986) test the effect of interest groups on the size of government in a cross-section study (data for 1970), by simply including in the regressions the <u>number</u> of interest groups in society (proxied by the number of trade associations). A consistent positive relationship is found between this number-of-interest-groups variable and the size of government. The latter result is corroborated by Lybeck (1986). He reports for Sweden (period 1950-1982) a significant positive effect on government size of the number of employees in interest organizations. Turning to a series of 12 OECD-countries (period 1960-1982), the degree of unionization of the labour force obtains a significant positive coefficient in only 6 out of 36 possible cases when separate regressions are run for each country; but pooling the data once again yields a significant positive coefficient. It may be added that the effect is absent in the Netherlands.

Altogether, the studies reported above give empirical support for - at least do not contradict - the influence of organized interest groups on public sector policies. However, it still remains an open question how and to what extent macroeconomic policy is exactly affected.

2.6.4. <u>Summary</u>

In this section we analyzed the influence of interest groups on public sector decision making. The main conclusions can be readily summarized.
- It can be expected that small groups with specific, specialized interests will get more easily organized and engaged in collective action, than large groups with general, diffuse interests.
- The number of interest groups in society tends to accumulate over time.
- The theoretical literature gives a clear indication that interest groups can influence public sector decision making. This influence has been recorded to depend on the possibilities and costs for groups sharing a common interest to organize and on their effectiveness in producing pressure, on the deadweight costs of the policies involved, and on the

preferences and the level of information of the electorate. The case-studies mentioned in this section give empirical support to the hypothesis that interest groups influence public sector decision making.
- In a macro context, the pressure of interest groups presumably leads to a larger size of the public sector. The available empirical evidence does not contradict this presumption. Other, more precise, hypotheses on the influence of interest groups on macroeconomic policy could not be found in the literature.

2.7. The Marxist approach

The theories that have been presented in this chapter until now can be said to fall within the public choice tradition. This tradition is rooted within neoclassical economic theory, and is characterized by an individualistic approach. The behaviour of the public sector and other organizations like private interest groups is related to the behaviour of their individual members. The basic behavioural postulate is that every individual acts rationally, is self-interested, and maximizes utility.

Quite differently, the Marxist tradition considers class struggle as the motor of history. Modern society is not just a collection of individuals, it consists of classes and class fractions. The relations between the agents in society are class relations, classes being social groupings that are principally defined by their position in the production process, more specifically by their economic control of the means of production. In a capitalist economy the main classes are the bourgeoisie (the exploiting, dominant, owning class), and the working class or proletariat (the exploited, dominated class). In addition, there are the so-called middle-classes. Classes involve class antagonisms and class struggles that not only take place on the economic level, but also on the political and ideological level; the class interests follow the positions in the economic process.

In a Marxist perspective, the state has to be understood first of all in relation to the class relations between capitalists and workers, and more specifically in relation to the interests of the dominating, capitalist class. The basic function of the state is considered to be to (help) (re)produce the conditions for the reproduction and accumulation of capital.

In the instrumentalist version of the theory the state is acting predictably in defence of the interests of capitalists because it is manned by capitalists or like-capitalists. Miliband (1973, p. 61), e.g., states "that in terms of social origin, education and class situation, the men who have manned <u>all</u> command positions in the state system have largely, and in many cases overwhelmingly, been drawn from the world of business and property, or from the professional middle classes". Alternatively, the structural-functionalist version of the theory accepts that the state may be relatively autonomous from particularistic interests of capitalists. It explains particular relations in capitalist society by showing that these relations meet a "need" of the system as a whole. Apparently, if it can be shown that a certain action helps to reproduce capitalist social relationships, then we have a good explanation for why the action did in fact occur (cf. Poulantzas (1973)). Both versions of the theory do not seem to be satisfactory, the first because it is hard to reconcile with the facts as far as capitalists themselves are concerned, while further it is not made clear why the professional middle classes would represent their interests, the second because it does not account for why and how conflicts among specific groups result in the state performing its function. Both also tend to obscure the contradictions and clashes of interests between the various fractions of the capitalist class, and among and within the various state apparatuses.

An alternative point of view is put forward by Przeworski and Wallerstein (1982). Within a theory of class conflict, they show that the continuing existence of capitalist relationships could be due to a (tacit) compromise between capitalists and workers. The function of the state then would be to do what appears necessary to reproduce capitalism because this is the choice of the workers as well as the capitalists.

Whatever may be the further assessment of the theoretical points of view touched upon, quite striking is their lack of specificity. Foley (1978, p. 233) notes that "at point after point, clear models of the mechanisms through which relations of production influence other aspects of economic life (clear models of the operation of money, labor markets, price formation, political influence, for example) are lacking". Of course, this lack of specificity seriously hampers the application and testing of Marxian ideas in empirical research, such as in the context of macroeconomic modelling.

From the literature only a limited number of hypotheses can be distilled, which might be useful within the context of this book.

For the growing size of the public sector the Marxist analysis suggest two explanations; cf. Foley (1978). The first locates the growth of the state in relation to the concentration and centralization of capital. It is observed that capital accumulates unevenly, with large and small capitals coexisting at a time. For large capitals certain necessary conditions of production, like labour supply, market for output, supplies of raw materials, and financing of working capital emerge as strategic problems which state policies can help to manage. Thus, large capital may support state expenditures to regulate the labour supply (including education, welfare, unemployment compensation), to ensure stable political and social environments for foreign investment, and to secure markets and access to raw materials. The second explanation links the growth of the state to the economic crises of the capitalist system. As these crises became more and more severe (the Great Depression, World War II), the state has come under pressure to prevent or alleviate collapses of market demand by expanding its own expenditure. The argument suggests that those contradictions, like an imbalance between capital accumulation and the growth of labour supply, or an overly competitive structure of capital, which produced depressions without state intervention now produce pressures and conflicts over state economic policy.

From this latter explanation of the growth of the public sector it takes just one further step to arrive at the Marxian hypotheses on the political business cycle as put forward by Kalecki (1943) and Boddy and Crotty (1975). For, there is a contradiction inherent in the policy of managing aggregate demand resulting in the maintenance of low levels of unemployment, if long periods of low unemployment strengthen labour's bargaining position and lead to an erosion of profits. According to Kalecki: "Under a regime of permanent full employment 'the sack' would cease to play its role as a disciplinary measure. The social position of the boss would be undermined and the self-assurance and class consciousness of the working class would grow. Strikes for wage increases and improvements in conditions of work would create political tension" (p. 326). In addition, it is argued by Boddy and Crotty that the ratio of profits to wages starts a pronounced decline halfway through the typical expansion of the economy. Thus, capitalists would press the state to deliberately deflate the economy, once full employment is approached, to restore discipline among the labour force, and as a necessary stage for attaining the highly profitable first phase of the (next) expansion.

Interesting as these Marxian hypotheses may be, in an empirical test they seem to be hardly if at all distinguishable from non-Marxian ones. The explanation for the growing size of the state in terms of crisis management coupled with the Kaleckian political business cycle suggestion, for instance, would result in a normal Keynesian-type stabilization policy. Furthermore we are not aware of any rigorous empirical tests of the Marxian hypotheses cited above.[40]

Concluding, for our purpose the major contribution of the Marxian approach seems to be its emphasis on the necessity to distinguish within society different groups with conflicting interests, principally based on their position in the production process of the economy. As such it is complementary to, and reinforcing, suggestions presented earlier in sections 2.3 and 2.4.3. The lack of specificity of the Marxian analysis of the functioning of the public sector is, however, striking and hampers empirical research in that direction. Only the Kaleckian political business cycle stands out in this respect, but this hypothesis cannot be distinguished it seems from a Keynesian-type stabilization policy.

2.8. Conclusions

In chapter 1 it was ascertained that there are some very good reasons to give more attention to the public sector in macroeconomic modelling. Furthermore, it appeared that politics, political processes and institutions, matter when it comes to the analysis of economic policy. In this chapter we reviewed the relevant literature on public sector decision making processes.

We now summarize the main line of argument and draw our conclusions.

<u>a</u>. The idea that public sector decision making is purely demand determined, a pure representation of the voters' preferences, has been shown to be unsatisfactory, both theoretically and empirically.

<u>b</u>. As elections are only held with certain intervals and as moreover voters do not take the trouble to be fully informed, politicians and the public bureaucracy have some leeway to pursue their own preferences.

Voters' preferences have been summarized in voting and popularity functions, in which the general economic conditions appear to exert both a significant and an unstable influence. Whether voters are really so ill-informed that they evaluate the state of the economy retrospectively and myopically, is still open to debate. Disaggregated studies have shown marked differences in the evaluation of the economic situation between different income and occupational groups.

Dependent on their objectives (securing re-election, maximizing length of time in office, or, more ideologically, bringing the platform into practice), politicians may react in quite different manners to these voting and popularity signals. On the one hand it has been suggested in the literature that governments might manipulate the economy and retrospective voters into a political business cycle. On the other hand, the government might decide to perform an economic policy which follows the interests and preferences of its own - perhaps class-based - core constituency. The economic policy chosen might also combine elements of these two options, or even might have no relation at all to popularity signals because informational requirements, the poor controllability of the economy, and rigidities in the political and administrative decision making processes prevent the government from taking account of the signals. Both theoretically and empirically these various entries to the understanding of economic policy making, and to the formulation of policy reaction functions, have been shown to be defective. At any rate, the evidence was inconclusive.

Apart still from the problem that several approaches could not cope with multi-party systems and coalition governments, we have further established that the influence of the bureaucracy and interest groups on economic policy making has until now hardly been integrated in the analysis of policy reaction functions.

Bureaucrats, which should be considered as a separate social group with special interests of their own, may promote these interests through the ballot-box, where they were found to have a higher turn-out than other social groups. They may also exert their influence within the public sector decision making process, as politicians will not be fully informed on all aspects (e.g., productivity, costs) of public sector activities. It has been conjectured that this influence operates in the direction of a large and inefficient public sector.

Turning more generally to groups of people sharing some common interests, it is to be expected that small groups with specific, specialized interests will get more easily organized than large groups with general, diffuse interests. In a world of imperfect information these interest groups can provide politicians with information and technical assistance for direct use, and with campaign assistance to mobilize the electorate. Through these channels and in still other ways (e.g., strikes), interest groups can try to exert influence on politicians and public sector decision making, to further their special interests. On the macro level, it has been suggested that the overall effect could be to enlarge the size of the public sector. The Marxist approach, finally, would add that the most important interests to take account of are those of the workers and the capitalists in the economy, as their position and relationship vis-à-vis each other and with regard to the state is most fundamental to the development of the latter.

c. Inspecting the literature, we thus have found a multitude of theories, approaches and suggestions, as to the objectives and behaviour of voters, politicians, parties and government, bureaucrats, and interest groups. The empirical support for these various theories, insightful as they may be in themselves, is only limited, however. Most importantly for us, the different approaches are rather incoherent. No general, comprehensive theory exists which combines and confronts the influence of voters, political parties, bureaucrats and interest groups on public sector decision making in a multi-party system, and which can be used for the delimitation of the political and economic factors underlying economic policy. Of course, we could try to develop such a full-fledged, coherent theory of. In view of the complexity of the interrelationships involved, and taking account of the state of the art, this would be an enormous and ambitious task. It remains to be seen whether that task can be accomplished, and whether it yields solutions that might be used for a better specification of policy reaction functions. For the moment, it seems much wiser to adopt the research strategy followed by researchers in the field of industrial organization.[41] In their structure-conduct-performance framework of analysis of markets and industries, market conduct represents a necessary and logical link between structure and performance. For several reasons, however, researchers started for purposes of empirical study with "attempts to establish links between market structure and performance, leaving the question of just how conduct forms the bridge between structure and performance to the realm of abstract theorizing".[42]

A somewhat similar approach could help us a great deal further, when it comes to the endogenization of public sector behaviour in macroeconomic modelling. Here, the interest function approach developed by Van Winden (1983) enters the field. Based on an essentially Marxian distinction of economic positions in society with concomitant interests, the approach analyzes public sector behaviour as a whole without bothering about the intricate relationships between voters, political parties, bureaucrats and interest groups. This approach, which will be presented in chapter 3, will indeed prove to be useful for our purposes, and will be applied, both theoretically and empirically, to the analysis of economic policy making in the remaining chapters of this book.

CHAPTER 3. THE INTEREST FUNCTION APPROACH

3.1. Introduction

In chapter 2 we concluded that the present public choice and marxist approaches to the study of political processes, as far as relevant for the analysis of economic policy making, are unsatisfactory, for reasons of incoherency, insufficient empirical support, and lack of specificity. It was suggested that a different approach to the subject might be fruitful. To that purpose, we now turn our attention to the so-called interest function approach to the study of politico-economic phenomena, that has been developed by Van Winden (1983). See also Van Winden (1987), Van Velthoven and Van Winden (1986).

Without paying too much attention to the specific conduct of and intricate relationships between voters, politicians, bureaucrats and interest groups, the interest function approach intends to combine valuable elements of the marxist and public choice analyses. According to Van Winden (1983, p. 12) "this means that in studying the interaction between state and private sector, attention should be paid to:
- social <u>classes</u>, and the impact of class/power relationships on political and economic processes;
- the way that social <u>power structures</u> (involving the real control over state activities) are maintained or altered;
- the <u>relative autonomy</u> of political processes (involving the state) and its consequences for, as well as its dependence on economic processes;
- individual <u>motivations</u>;
- the possibility of mathematical <u>formalization</u>."

Section 3.2. will give a general introduction to the concepts and the line of argument of the interest function approach. Some more specific aspects will be addressed in section 3.3.

3.2. <u>Outline of the interest function approach</u>[1]

In the interest function approach it is assumed that agents - both individual and collective decision making units, in the private and public sector of the economy - <u>represent interests</u>. That is, they have preferences with respect to the outcomes of political and economic processes. The promotion and realization of these interests is subject to <u>contraints</u>. Van Winden distinguishes between constraints that are due to <u>structural coercion</u>, and constraints that are due to <u>pressure</u>. Pressure stands for influence attempts directed at an agent by other agents (individual, collective) in the environment. Structural coercion stands for all other, "anonymous", restrictions that stem from the nature (structure) of the environment in which an agent operates. As regards the public sector, structural coercion might refer to constraints implied by decentralized decision making in the private sector (e.g. incentive effects, or the operation of the Phillips-curve), by the existing body of technological know-how, or by the budget restraint. With respect to pressure, one should think of influence attempts by interest groups accompanied by positive and negative sanctions (information, campaign assistance, threats to strike).

Activities of agents, thus, are related to three determinants: representation of interests, structural coercion and pressure. The first determinant has to do with the internal environment of an agent, i.e. the nature of the interests represented by that agent; the other two have to do with the character of the agent's external environment. We shall first have a look at the representation of interests.

Individual as well as collective actions (activities by collectivities) are, ultimately, supposed to be related to <u>individual interests</u>. Because of the apparently extreme complexity and pluriformity of the interests of individuals involved in politico-economic processes, however, Van Winden does not occupy himself directly with purely individualistic interests. Instead, attention is focused upon the interests of individuals as occupants of certain economic positions. Apart from research-strategic reasons, this approach is inspired by the knowledge that individualistic interests typically (corruption aside) do not count in political processes. Think alone of the information required to public sector decision makers, and the influence required for individual agents to make their demands effective. Only the interests of - representative individuals of - social groups appear to play a role.

In Van Winden's model production is divided into non-market goods produced by the public sector, and market goods produced by the private sector. People are assumed to be interested in (to derive utility from) their control over market and non-market goods and, thus, in the bundles of public and private goods they can acquire. The opportunities, action space or power of people in this respect, and the particular forms in which their basic interests will manifest themselves, are shaped by the position that they have with regard to the production process of the economy. Given the distinction between an interest in market goods, for which an income is required, and an interest in non-market goods, provided by the public sector and financed out of taxes, it is possible to delineate a small number of social groups that seem to be particularly important here. To that purpose, attention is focused at the different ways in which people acquire an income, which are directly related to the position of people in the production process in society.

Four <u>elementary economic positions</u> are distinguished in a capitalist economy:
1. worker in the state[2] sector (politician or bureaucrat);
2. worker in the private sector;
3. capital owner (capitalist);
4. dependant ("unemployed", in a wide sense).

Capitalists and workers differ from each other in their control over means of production, while their basic interest in market goods takes the particular form of an interest in profits and wages, respectively. An important distinction between state sector workers and private sector workers is that taxes (forced payments) instead of proceeds of sales are the characteristic source of the wages of the former. There are also some other differences in the positions of these groupings in the economy that should not be neglected.[3] The dependants are not directly involved in production, and are for that reason dependent on transfers from those who are, which gives them - in this respect - the weakest position in the economy. Only their numerical strength may be a factor of importance.

The set of agents in each elementary economic position is referred to as a <u>social class</u>. In the sequel, the four classes that have been distinguished will be indicated by an index k; k = 1,2,3,4, respectively. It is noted that Van Winden does not preclude that for the analysis of concrete social phenomena it may be necessary to make further divisions into social groupings.[4]

The next issue is, what interests precisely play a role and should be taken account of in the field of study. Above, it has already been noted that the interests of people regard the goods and services that can be obtained both in and outside the market. The bundle of goods and services that can be obtained in the market is reflected by <u>real disposable income</u>. As regards the goods that can not be obtained inside the market, attention goes to the <u>amount of goods and services supplied by the public sector</u>. Beside these two kinds of interests, Van Winden (1983, p. 92) singles out a third, to wit the <u>relative numerical strength of the social classes</u>. He argues that the extent to which agents are able to realize their (class) interests, and the security of their position, may be related to the numerical share of their class in the population. He refers to the importance of number in the context of elections, political movements, etc. It is, therefore, assumed that people may not only, basically, be interested in their direct control over market and non-market goods, but also in the relative number of people that are in the same economic position (the relative size of their class), as this, generally, will facilitate an indirect control over these goods.

The three interests for - the <u>representative member</u> of - a social class are represented by a so-called <u>elementary interest function</u>[5] P_k,

(3.1) $\quad P_k = P_k(w_k, e_k, x_{sk}), \quad k = 1,2,3,4,$

where w_k = the real disposable income of the representative member of social class k;

e_k = the relative numerical strength of social class k;

x_{sk} = the bundle of (non-marketed) goods and services provided by the state sector to the representative member of social class k.

Van Winden (1983, p. 93) specifies the functional form of the elementary interest functions to be of the Cobb-Douglas variety:

(3.2) $P_k = w_k^{\varepsilon_{k1}} \cdot e_k^{\varepsilon_{k2}} \cdot x_{sk}^{\varepsilon_{k3}}$, $\varepsilon_{kg} \geq 0$, $g = 1,2,3$, $\Sigma_g \varepsilon_{kg} = 1$, $\forall k$.

The symbols ε_{k1}, ε_{k2}, ε_{k3} denote the relative weight that is attached to each of the three interests in social class k. It is assumed that the members of a social class would like to see the interest function maximized that is supposed to hold for them, and will act accordingly.[6]

With Ten Raa (1984) it can be questioned whether the numerical strength variable is properly included in function (3.1) on a par with the other two. It might be surmised that the basic interests (the goods and services that are directly relevant for the utility level of the individual agent) are mixed up with the structure or means (such as elections) through which they are promoted. Presumably, the presence of "class mates" is a positive externality, and/or the elementary interest function should be taken as a kind of indirect utility function. We shall return to this issue later on.

When it comes to the determination of the behaviour of an individual or collective agent, more than one elementary interest function may be relevant. Van Winden (1983, p. 93) distinguishes four reasons why an agent by itself, that is without any external pressure, may take account of more than one elementary interest function:
- ideology;
- mobility;
- multiple positions;
- heterogeneous membership, in case of collectivities.

As regards <u>ideology</u>, one should think of the effect of innate altruism or jealousy.[7] <u>Mobility</u> refers to the fact that agents may move from one elementary economic position to another, voluntary or compulsory. For instance, workers may perceive a chance to become unemployed; people know they will get older and retire on pension one day. In view of these eventualities, people will orientate themselves in advance with respect to the new position concerned, and that is where other elementary interest functions come in. <u>Multiple positions</u> refers to the phenomenon that agents may occupy more than one position in the economic process. For instance, bureaucrats may hold shares in joint-stock companies, "captains of industry" have positions in the public sector as minister or adviser, and so on. An unemployed person, who is also a shareholder, will not only be interested in public policy with respect to the dole rate, but also in the development of corporate profit taxes. Finally, <u>collectivities</u> may be made up by agents having similar interests, but also by agents with dissimilar, conflicting interests. The latter situation will be the most common for the collectivities that we are interested in here; think of political parties, the public sector. Van Winden[8] observes that in case of conflicting interests between agents it might be appropriate for a given organizational context to introduce quite complicated assumptions about the possibilities of coalition formation, and that this might lead to a proliferation of special theories with a large element of descriptive detail. See also our conclusions in section 2.8. As this is not a very attractive prospect, Van Winden proposes - as a provisional way out - to follow the idea that a collectivity can be considered as a coalition of interests in which class relationships express themselves. This would bring us back to the elementary interest functions.

For the aforementioned cases in which more than one elementary interest function plays a part, the concept of a <u>complex interest function</u>, P_c, is introduced. It is a weighted representation of elementary interest functions:

(3.3) $\qquad P_c = \Pi_k P_k^{\lambda_{kc}} \quad , \quad \lambda_{kc} \geq 0 \;\; \forall k, \; \Sigma_k \lambda_{kc} = 1,$

where λ_{kc} indicates the weight attached to P_k, the elementary interest function connected with economic position k.

Summarizing: a complex interest function may hold for an individual agent, in case of an ideologically affected or altruistic attitude, (anticipated) mobility, and the occupation of multiple positions. The weights that are being attached to the different P_k's will depend on the relative importance of the various economic positions. In case of mobility, e.g., the perceived probabilities of getting into the various positions may serve as weights; in case of multiple positions, the weights will be related to the relative contribution from the different positions to the total control over goods and services. The complex interest function may also hold for a collectivity, in case of heterogeneous membership. It is assumed that the collectivities act in accordance with the maximization of the complex interest function that is supposed to hold for them. The weights denote the relative importance assigned within the collectivity to the interests of agents in economic position k.

We have proceeded a good deal with the exposition of the interest function approach. However, before we can arrive at the presentation of the interest function which is assumed to hold for the public sector (cf. the function W of chapter 1), two other concepts must be introduced, namely nested complex interest functions and augmented interest functions.[9]

The first of these concepts has to do with the fact that collectivities in general, and the public sector in particular, consist of factions, departments, and interest units on different decision making levels. The occurrence of these <u>interest blocs</u>, as they are called, gives rise to a complex of decisions and non-decisions within the collectivity, and of conflicts and compromises between the interest blocs. To deal with this phenomenon Van Winden (1983, p. 98) introduces the notion of a <u>nested complex interest function</u>. A nested complex interest function is a function of complex interest functions (which themselves may be nested again) referring to interest blocs of a collectivity.

Distinguishing between different decision-making and interest structure levels within a collectivity, there are two types of interest blocs: <u>level-specific blocs</u> and <u>representative blocs</u>. The former are specific for a decision-making level under scrutiny, while the latter somehow aggregate and represent the interests of lower level blocs. The interests of each bloc will be portrayed by a - complex or nested complex - interest function P_{hi}, where hi denotes interest bloc i at decision-making level h (with h = 1 as top level).[10] For the nested complex interest function of a representative bloc - say, interest bloc n at decision-making level m - it is now assumed that:

(3.4) $\quad P_{mn} = \Pi_{hi} P_{hi}^{\lambda_{hi}^{mn}}, \quad \lambda_{hi}^{mn} \geq 0 \; \forall hi, \quad \Sigma_{hi} \lambda_{hi}^{mn} = 1,$

where λ_{hi}^{mn} denotes the relative strength with which the interests of hi are represented by mn. For level-specific blocs, which do not represent the interests of other blocs within the collectivity, a complex interest function of the form (3.3) may be assumed to hold.

In this set-up, some specific attention should be paid to the representative agents that make up the representative interest blocs. Of course these agents (individuals or collectivities) have their own - say, internal - interests. Those internal interests of the representative agents should be considered as level-specific interests, i.e. of the variety (3.3). It then remains to be seen why and how they represent the (external) interests of other agents, of other interest blocs. According to Van Winden (1983, p. 100), this depends upon structural coercion and the pressure that is exerted on them by these agents. Because of the, generally, intimate structural relationship between representatives and represented it is assumed that this sort of structural coercion and pressure can be dealt with in the same multiplicative way as the interests of the agents themselves. One might say that the lower level interests have been internalized on the decision-making level under consideration. (For a more general discussion of pressure, see further on).

In the light of the discussion until now, we can take a first look at the decision-making structure of the <u>public sector</u>. It is represented by the interest tree in figure 3.1. (Cf. Van Winden (1983, p. 169)). For reasons of exposition, only two hierarchical levels have been depicted. The top-level is where the politicians (government, parliament) reside, and where - at least formally - decision-making takes place. The second level is the executive level, where the departments, the bureaucracy, can be found. Let us consider the position of the politicians more closely. They have to cope with: 1. the level-specific interests of themselves; 2. the representation of the interests of the bureaucracy; and 3. the representation of the interests of their political parties and the electorate.[11]

P_{11} denotes the level-specific interests of the politicians, which are shaped by their position in the public sector. Politicians are state sector workers just like bureaucrats; the main difference is that the position of politicians is, generally, less secure than that of

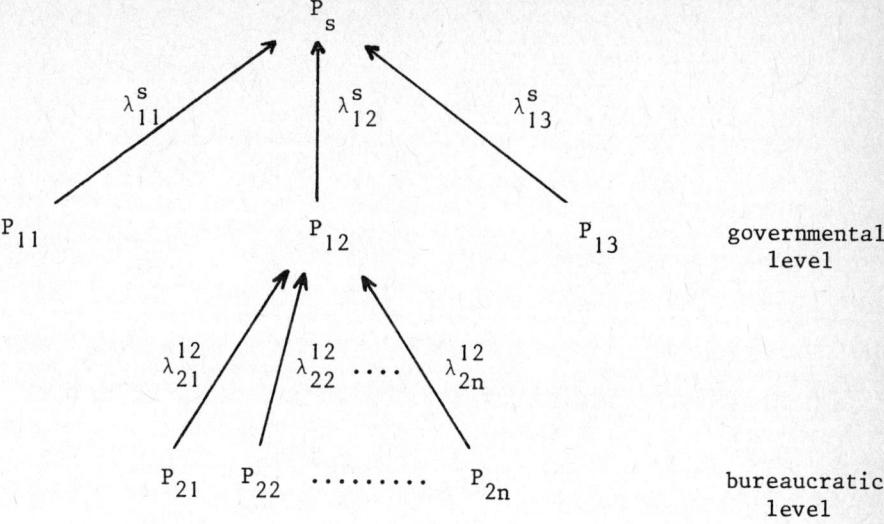

Figure 3.1. The public sector interest tree.

bureaucrats due to the system of elections. Elected politicians do not only take account of their own interests, in case of ministers they also represent (as the result of internal pressure) the interests of bureaucrats. P_{12} indicates the representative interest bloc of the bureaucrats, made up by the ministers as formal heads of the bureaucratic apparatuses. P_{12} is a nested complex interest function, comprising the interest functions P_{21}, ..., P_{2n} of the level-specific interest blocs of the bureaucrats (think of the departments). Each of the latter functions may in itself be a complex interest function, as bureaucrats, e.g., may have multiple positions in the economy, or even a nested complex interest function, if certain agencies and hierarchical levels within a department should be distinguished.[12] Thirdly, politicians represent - to a certain extent - the interests of political parties (as the result of external pressure, see below). To account for the latter aspect, the interest function P_{13} is inserted, which stands for the interests of the politicians as party representatives. P_{13} itself is again a nested complex interest function, related to the heterogeneous membership and organizational structure of the parties determining the political platforms and nominations, in combination with the impact of the electorate on the party composition of parliament and cabinet.

The different interest blocs P_{11}, P_{12} and P_{13} are compromised by the politicians (under internal and external pressure) into the nested complex interest function P_s, which denotes the interest function holding for the public sector decision-making process as a whole. The function P_s underlies the determination of the distribution of national income between the public budget and private sector disposable income, and the distribution of the public budget across departments.

If we leave, for the moment, ideology, mobility, and multiple positions out of consideration, as well as a particularization of interests within the bureaucracy, the above analysis of the decision-making structure of the public sector would suggest the following formulation:

(3.5) $\quad P_s = \Pi_i P_{1i}^{\lambda_{1i}^s}$,

with:

$P_{11} = P_1$,

$P_{12} = \Pi_j P_{2j}^{\lambda_{2j}^{12}}$, where $P_{2j} = P_1 \; \forall j$,

$P_{13} = \Pi_k P_k^{\lambda_k^{13}}$,

where λ_k^{13} denotes the relative strength with which the interests of social class k are represented through the party and election system (see also further on). Substituting the functions P_{11}, P_{12} and P_{13} into P_s yields the following result:

(3.6)[13] $\quad P_s = \Pi_k P_k^{\lambda_k}$, $\lambda_k \geq 0 \; \forall k$, $\Sigma_k \lambda_k = 1$, with λ_k denoting the relative strength with which the interests related to elementary economic position k are represented in the public sector decision making process, through all the various channels combined. Note that the structure of the interest functions in (3.5) might have been different, if we had allowed for ideology, mobility and multiple positions; P_{11} and P_{2j}, e.g., might have been complex interest functions of the form (3.3). Still, substituting into P_s would have yielded the same form of solution as eq. (3.6), with only the weights λ_k differing in substance and - perhaps - size.

Till here, the exposition primarily paid attention to the internal functioning of the public sector decision-making process. However, the analysis of political processes in advanced capitalist economies should also take heed of the fact that (apart from political parties, which already have been taken care of) collectivities and organizations have developed outside the public sector, that cannot be considered as insignificant and anonymous to the state. Collectivities that have the capacity to threaten and to bargain, can be expected to use this capacity, when it is perceived to further the realization of the interests they represent. Collectivities that try to influence the behaviour of the public sector will be labelled interest or <u>pressure groups</u>.[14]

The approach Van Winden (1983) presents does not explicitly deal with the pressure activities of the pressure groups, or with the processes of bargaining. "For the development of general politico-economic models, the direct inclusion of bargaining processes, instead of treating them as a black box, would seem to lead to a too great complexity" (p. 219). Rather, the approach models the consequences that can be expected to arise from the (many-sided) interaction between pressure groups and the public sector. In case of a pressure group that is able to noticeably and structurally (enduringly) affect the interests and behaviour of the public sector due to its pressure activities, it is suggested that a fair approximation of public sector behaviour can be arrived at by substituting for the public sector interest function a so-called <u>augmented interest function</u>. This augmented interest function is a weighted representation of the interest functions of the public sector itself and the pressure group. More specifically, let the complex interest function of the pressure group that we will focus upon - say, c - be denoted by P_c (cf. eq. (3.3)), and the nested complex interest function of the public sector by P_s (cf. eq. (3.5)). It is then assumed that the public sector will act in accordance with the (constrained) maximization of the augmented interest function $\bar{P}_s$, where

$$(3.7) \quad \bar{P}_s = P_s^{(1-\lambda_c^s)} \cdot P_c^{\lambda_c^s}, \quad 0 \leq \lambda_c^s \leq 1.$$

The weight λ_c^s indicates the strength with which the interests of pressure group c are furthered by the state. This weight is supposed to reflect the "acknowledged power" of c, or one might say, the extent to which the interests of c are "vested". Such a vested interest can be thought of as being produced by accumulated pressure, a kind of capital good; the persistence of pressure activities, then, is necessary to keep this capital good from decaying.

Let us now return to the structure and process of public sector decision making - cf. figure 3.1 - for a second and final look. Adding pressure group impact to figure 3.1 amounts to the same thing as combining eq. (3.5) with eq. (3.7). If it is taken for granted that the complex interest function(s) of the pressure group(s) can be described by eq. (3.3), substituting into (3.7) and rearranging terms directly yields:

$$(3.8) \quad \bar{P}_s = \Pi_k P_k^{\bar{\lambda}_k}, \quad \bar{\lambda}_k \geq 0 \; \forall k, \; \Sigma_k \bar{\lambda}_k = 1,$$

with $\bar{\lambda}_k$ denoting the relative strength with which the interests connected to elementary economic position k are represented in the public sector decision making process through all available channels and by all available means (political parties, voting, pressure group activities, the bureaucracy etc.). Of course, due to the multiplicative structure of the interest functions, the solution in eq. (3.8) has the same structure as that in eq. (3.6); only the interpretation and size of the weights may differ because of the inclusion of external pressure.

In the sequel, whenever P_s and eq. (3.8) are being referred to, the bars will be omitted for notational simplicity.

At the beginning of the exposition of the interest function approach it was noted that the promotion and realization of interests is subject to two kinds of constraints: constraints due to structural coercion and due to pressure. The (augmented) interest function for the public sector in eq. (3.8) was derived as encompassing all constraints which are due to pressure. Then, an important point emerges. According to Van Winden "it stands to reason to base the <u>constraints</u> subject to which (3.8) is supposed to be maximized, on the assumption that the activities of the public sector will be taken as given by the pressure groups; after all, the public sector is assumed to pay heed to the "acknowledged" power of the pressure groups. Thus, <u>for the sake of modelling</u>, the approach roughly suggests ... to specify the constraints <u>as if</u> there is no pressure".[15] Stated otherwise, the only constraints which remain to be taken account of in modelling, are those due to structural coercion.

We end the presentation of the interest function approach with the following conclusion. Hypothesizing that in the end - through the intermediation of complex, nested complex and augmented interest functions - all interests can be reduced to interests connected with elementary economic positions - abstracting from a further particularization of interests -, the interest function approach leads to the observation that the public sector should be considered as a coalition of interests in which the class relations express themselves. Public sector behaviour can be explained from (acting in accordance with) the maximization of some weighted representation of elementary interest functions P_k, subject to constraints which are due to structural coercion.[16]

3.3. <u>Discussion</u>

Several aspects of the interest function approach that has been unfolded in the previous subjection, deserve further attention. Some elements have already been criticized in the literature, others give rise to qualifications in the interpretation and application of the interest function approach.

<u>a</u>. To start our discussion we address two specific issues on which Van Winden's (1983) exposition is not always as lucid as we would like it to be. Firstly, it has not become clear to us what is the real difference between the <u>nested complex</u> and the <u>augmented</u> interest functions. For, with both concepts it is intended to model the impact on the behaviour and interest representation of one collectivity (organization), which results from pressure by other collectivities (organizations). The two concepts would be prevented from coinciding, if the first would refer to internal pressure within an organization, while the other would refer to external pressure from collectivities outside the organization. However, this distinction is not the one used by Van Winden in his analysis of public sector behaviour. Cf. the nested complex interest function for the state in eq. (3.5), which is also said to encompass the influence of political parties and the electorate. Indeed, Van Winden (1983, p. 221), at the introduction of the augmented interest function concept, acknowledges that his analysis of the decision structure of a collectivity three chapters earlier (cf. our figure 3.1 and eq. (3.5)) "already employed the construct of an augmented interest function". But then it would be natural and logical to let the two concepts coincide, in order to economize on concepts and terminology.

Note that the above interpretation problem has no consequence whatsoever for the derivation of eq. (3.8).

<u>b</u>. A second ambiguity in Van Winden's exposition bears upon the relation between <u>bureaucrats</u> and <u>politicians</u>.

Bureaucrats and politicians are regarded to form one social class. This sounds reasonable, as they share in a basic sense the same position towards the process of production in society: they both derive their income from forced payments (taxes). Yet, their positions within the public sector in a democratic political system also show some marked differences. For politicians, holding their seats is rather more insecure than for bureaucrats, as it is subject to the outcomes of - regularly held - elections. For this reason (anticipated) mobility may be greater under politicians than under bureaucrats, which could affect the (complex) interest functions that describe their (level-specific) interests. However, in practice this latter problem will be less severe than it may seem at first sight, as the (great) majority of politicians appears to be recruited from and returns to positions in the public sector (cf. section 2.5). Their personal orientation will primarily be directed towards the public sector.

Another important difference between bureaucrats and politicians has to do with their (relative) power. After all, it is the politicians who are - at least formally - vested with the decision making power. It must be noticed that Van Winden (1983) remains somewhat ambiguous on the matter, presumably due to the gradual development of the approach in the course of his book. At one place[17] it is suggested that public sector behaviour can be analyzed using a complex interest function, which would imply that the public sector can be considered as a collectivity with heterogeneous membership, in which (representatives of) the social classes directly bargain with each other. At another place[18] the state is depicted as an organization with (at least) two hierarchical levels, with the politicians residing at the top-level, being responsible for formal decision making, and the bureaucrats operating at the lower levels. Still further[19], Van Winden notes that the public sector is "supposed to behave in accordance with the maximization of an interest function - a weighted representation of the interests of bureaucrats and politicians - subject to a number of (in)equality constraints". This latter quotation suggests that the decisions in the public sector are taken by politicians <u>and</u> bureaucrats. The above ambiguity once again points at the fact that the relations in the public sector decision making process between politicians and bureaucrats are often inextricably interwoven (see also section 2.5), which does not make it an easy task to model or summarize them in a succint way. All in all, Van Winden (1987) appears to prefer the interpretation of the state as a hierarchical organization; we have followed this view in our exposition in the previous subsection. This view also fits in best with the introduction and interpretation of the nested complex and augmented interest function concepts. However, such a point of view would yield a good motive for the distinction of bureaucrats and politicians as separate social groups, operating as they are on different levels of decision making. First, note that distinguishing separate social groups of politicians and bureaucrats does not lead to a different formulation of eq. (3.8), as long as it is recognized that both groups basically share the same (level-specific) interests (see the discussion above). Secondly, even if one would prefer a complete disaggregation of the two groups, the interest function approach would still yield a solution of the same structure as eq. (3.8), then with the inclusion of the elementary interest functions of five instead of four social classes. In that context the reader can be referred to Borooah and Van der Ploeg (1983), who apply the interest function approach disaggregating the class of state sector workers into civil servants, i.e. workers employed by the state and only interested in real disposable income, and bureaucrats, the top civil servants who are primarily interested in the size of the public sector. Note that this specific particularization is not of much help to our analysis, as the politicians seem to have disappeared, while the two kinds of interests mentioned already both appear in our elementary interest functions (3.1) and (3.2).

<u>c</u>. With the last remark we have come to the role and the specification of the <u>elementary interest functions</u>.

First, observe that the derivation of the state interest function P_s in eq. (3.8) does not presuppose any specific functional form of the elementary interest functions P_k. Nor does it prescribe which arguments – kinds of interests – should be inserted, or excluded. In this sense, Van Winden's specification of the elementary interest function in eq. (3.1), and the functional form chosen in eq. (3.2), should be taken as no more than a – albeit serious – suggestion. The reader will remember that we already put some question marks at the insertion of the numerical strength variable e_k in the elementary interest functions P_k.

With regard to this freedom in the specification of the P_k's, reference can be made to Borooah and Van der Ploeg (1983). They come up with a formulation which differs considerably from that contained in eqs. (3.1) and (3.2). Private sector agents as well as civil servants (see above) are supposed to be interested in the total real disposable income of their social group – implying perfect substitutability between the real disposable income of the representative member of the group, w_k, and the numerical strength of the group, e_k. Further it is assumed that rentiers take an interest in (a decrease of) the rate of inflation, unemployed in (a decrease of) the rate of unemployment, and bureaucrats in the size of the public sector. Unfortunately, Borooah and Van der Ploeg do not present empirical support for their specification, which seems to be of a less general and less structural nature than the specification advanced in eq. (3.1).[20]

While the freedom in the specification of the P_k's may be substantial, it is not without limit. The formulation of the state interest function P_s implies that the (elementary) interest functions should be measured along a cardinal scale, in the sense that they should be unique up to a positive proportional transformation. As can be easily seen from eq. (3.8), such a proportional transformation would leave the maximization problem unaffected. A more general positive monotonic or even a simple additive transformation would - given the weigths λ_k, as far as they are positive - affect the relative valuation of the P_k's and consequently change the solution to the maximization problem (see also below, at point g).

<u>d</u>. Next we must pay some attention to the assumption that public sector behaviour is in accordance with the <u>maximization</u> of the state interest function P_s over the <u>set of feasible alternatives</u>. This feasible set is defined by the (in)equality constraints that are due to structural coercion. Both Borooah and Van der Ploeg (1983) and Ten Raa (1984) claim that the maximization procedure results in a Pareto optimal outcome for the economy. Following that claim, Ten Raa heavily criticizes the interest function approach, for "the incapability to describe inefficiencies in the interaction between state and private sector is a serious shortcoming of a theoretical analysis that pretends to be nonnormative" (p. 490).

Now, what is the matter? In figure 3.2 we have reduced the maximization problem for graphical reasons to a two-dimensional one. The problem is to maximize

$$P_s = P_1^{\lambda_1} \cdot P_2^{\lambda_2}, \quad \lambda_1, \lambda_2 \geq 0, \lambda_1 + \lambda_2 = 1,$$

over the feasible set. Let the set of feasible P_1, P_2 - combinations be convex, as given by the shaded area OAB. It is obvious, then, that the solution point will lie on the frontier AB; which point will actually be arrived at is dependent on the distribution of the weights λ_k. The frontier AB might be called the Pareto-frontier of the problem at hand; for each point on this frontier it is impossible to find another point in the feasible set such that the interests of (at least) one group are furthered to a greater extent without damaging the interests of at least one other group. It seems very sensible that the outcome of the public sector decision making process lies on this frontier. For, why should the politicians compromising the perceived interests from all kinds of organizations and groups that exert pressure on them, not use some of the possibilities which they regard to be attainable?

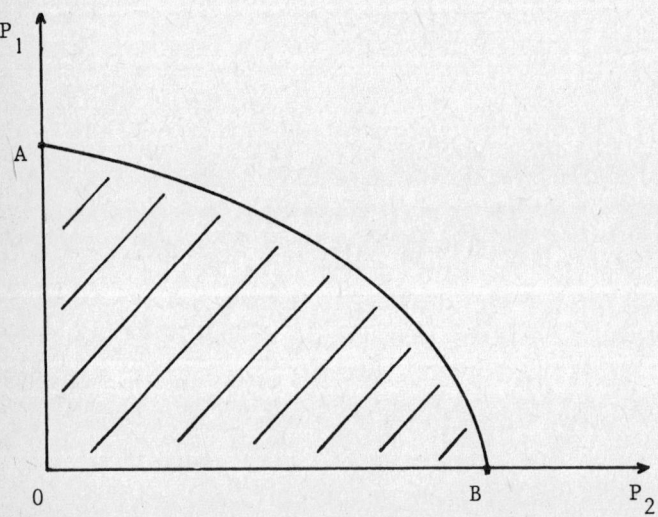

Figure 3.2. The set of feasible alternatives

The assumption that politicians, given the vested interests and acknowledged power of the various interest groups in society, try to make the best out of their situation, is fully in line with the orthodox assumption of utility maximizing individuals. In case of such a utility maximizing individual no one would associate the optimal consumption bundle on the frontier of the feasible consumption set as such with a Pareto efficient allocation in the economy. Similarly, optimal public sector behaviour does not - at least not necessarily - entail a Pareto efficient allocation of the resources in society among the interest groups. It all depends on what the feasible set stands for. There is no reason to assume a priori that the constraints taken into consideration by the public sector coincide with the production possibility frontier of the economy. The public sector will in general lack full information on the behaviour and the reaction patterns of the private sector. Nor may it have enough instruments to steer that behaviour and prevent distortions. The critique of Ten Raa thus seems to be misplaced.

To the discussion above we should like to add that in our view the issue <u>whether</u> the Pareto-frontier is actually reached (as noted, why should the state not use the opportunities discerned to be available to it), is much less interesting than the problem of <u>which point</u> will be arrived at.

<u>e</u>. This brings us to the issue of the distribution of the <u>power weights</u> λ_k. It will have become apparent from the exposition in section 3.2 that, generally speaking, the interest function approach does not offer us much help for a further analysis of the factors and processes determining the distribution of the λ's. The approach essentially treats the public sector as a "black box".[21] The actual conduct of the various participants in and around the public sector decision making process (including voting, the functioning of political parties, cabinet coalition formation, the operating characteristics of the hierarchically structured bureaucracy, pressure activities, threats, bargaining processes, and so on) is not explicitly taken along in the process of modelling. All these activities and all the interrelationships are regarded to be compressed into and represented by the weights λ. By thus refraining from modelling actual conduct and treating the public sector as a black box, the interest function approach resembles the structure - performance approach in industrial economics; cf. the discussion at the end of chapter 2. However, this is not the end of the story.

First of all, it should be noted that it might be possible to determine the values of the power weights, treating them as parameters, in an empirical way. Van Winden (1983, pp. 188ff) shows how the revealed preference method may be of help here, provided that sufficient information on the preferences of the social classes is available from other sources.

However, just treating the power weights as parameters which are constant over time, would seem to be rather simplistic. In the previous section it was argued that acknowledged power, a vested interest, can be thought of as being produced by accumulated pressure, a kind of capital good. Such a point of view clearly suggests that vested interests can alter over time, affecting the distribution of the power weights λ_k. In other words, the λ's should be treated as variables. Van Winden (1983) takes a first step towards tackling the problem, albeit only partially. He considers the interrelation between voting and party behaviour and its consequences for the power weights in the state interest function. It is assumed that voters evaluate the (factual or hypothetical) performance of political parties, using the elementary interest functions as yardstick. Note that by using these interest functions not only the influence of inflation, unemployment and real disposable income can be allowed for, but that also distributional aspects and the impact of the consumption of state goods are taken into account. Party choice is thus suggested to be class interest orientated. The behaviour of the respective political parties, in turn, is assumed to be determined by the class structure of each party's constituency (which comprises all who voted for the party). A party is thus not treated as a unitary actor, but as an amalgam of different interests and factions. From the class interests represented by a party's constituency it follows which interests will be promoted by that party. Assuming, finally, some lags in the interaction between voters and parties as sketched above, results in a dynamic model of interactive voting and party behaviour. For a two-party system this model could readily predict which party will receive the majority of votes. Supposing that the opposition party is powerless, it then could be derived from the class constituency of the dominant party which interests will be represented in the public sector decision making process by the politicians in their role of party representatives.[22] It must be clear that the above analysis of voter-party interaction, useful as it is, can only give us an indication as to the value of the power weights in the interest function P_{13} of the interest tree in figure 3.1. The roles of pressure groups, the bureaucracy, and the level-specific interests of the politicians themselves with regard to the distribution of the power weights in the state interest function P_s have not yet been taken into consideration. Thus, while we have good reasons to expect that the power weights will vary over time, we do not have a theory to explain and predict the development of the λ's. The black box is still with us.

This state of the art will necessitate us in forthcoming chapters to make a search for a suitable proxy which might capture the dynamics of the power relations.[23]

f. Above, we argued that the interest function approach in its present form essentially treats the public sector as a black box. An analysis of the actual conduct of the participants, including e.g. party behaviour, pressure activities and processes of bargaining, is lacking. That is not to say that it is impossible to model behavioural aspects of the public sector decision making process. The whole of chapter 2 was devoted to a discussion of the efforts to model the behaviour of voters, politicians, bureaucrats and pressure groups; the analysis of voter-party interaction under the previous point offers another example. The problem with these modelling efforts, as we noted in chapter 2 as well as above, is that they do not offer anything near a complete and coherent picture of the public sector decision making process. The interest function approach offers a way out there. But we certainly do not want to claim that it is the only one. In the context of our study it is of interest to note that two alternative formulations have been proposed in the literature in substitution for the derivation in section 3.2, which nevertheless lead to solutions that can be shown to be in conformity with the public sector interest function P_s of eq. (3.8). These alternative formulations might be regarded as substitutes for the interest function approach, but also - our interpretation - as strenghtening support for the use of the interest function P_s in the analysis of public sector policy making.

One alternative formulation is brought forward by Ten Raa (1984). He suggests that the power weights are just <u>Lagrangean multipliers</u>. Let us for expositional reasons restrict attention to the two-dimensional case of figure 3.2, and assume that the Pareto-frontier AB can be described by the differentiable function $P_1 = f(P_2)$. Consider, then, the following maximization problem: maximize (log) P_1, subject to the constraint that (log) P_2 is (at least) equal to some minimum value (log) P_2^o, given the set of feasible P_1, P_2 - combinations. Ten Raa states that this formulation gives a precise representation of the pressure exercised by interest group 2 onto group 1 (say, the politicians, or, more generally, the state sector workers). Letting μ denote the Lagrangean multiplier, the problem can be solved by maximizing

(3.9) $\qquad \log P_1 + \mu \cdot (\log P_2 - \log P_2^o)$

over the feasible set. The solution P_1^*, P_2^* is given by:

(3.10) $\qquad P_2^* = P_2^o$,

$\qquad P_1^* = f(P_2^o)$,

$\qquad \mu = -\dfrac{P_2^*}{P_1^*} \cdot f'(P_2^*)$.

The programming problem for the state, emanating from the interest function approach (cf. eq. (3.8)), was to maximize

$$P_s = P_1^{\lambda_1} \cdot P_2^{\lambda_2}$$

over the set of feasible outcomes. Taking logarithms an equivalent objective function is (assuming $\lambda_1 > 0$)

(3.11) $\qquad \log P_1 + \dfrac{\lambda_2}{\lambda_1} \cdot \log P_2$.

Comparing the maximands (3.9) and (3.11), it is evident that the programming problem based on the interest function approach yields the same solution as Ten Raa's alternative formulation, provided that

$\lambda_2/\lambda_1 = \mu$, with μ defined as in eq. (3.10). Note that the Lagrangean multiplier could rightly be termed a power weight too, as it brings out to which extent group 2 is able to put pressure on group 1, i.e. is able to further its own interests at the cost of the pursuit of interests by group 1. When it comes to a comparative evaluation, the interest function approach seems to be preferable, as an empirical determination of the minimum value P_2^o would be very difficult, if not impossible; the prospects for the empirical determination of the power weights λ are less gloomy (see above).

g. The other alternative formulation to the interest function approach to be considered here, is based on game-theoretical considerations. In Van Winden (1983, p. 256) it is pointed out that there is a correspondence between his interest function approach and the Nash bargaining solution for cooperative games.

Prima facie, it is appealing to apply game theory to political processes, to study the context of our black box. How, is just another matter. For, within public sector decision making several kinds of processes can be distinguished: competitive processes (between political parties courting the favour of the electorate), hierarchically structured decision processes (bureaucracy versus politicians), and processes of bargaining (e.g., coalition formation, logrolling) alternate and complement one another. Moreover, these processes are generally characterized by incomplete information, be it by the nature of things, because participants rationally decide to remain uninformed, or because information has purposely been distorted. Shubik (1982) surveys the application of game theory to political processes, and observes that both cooperative and non-cooperative solution concepts merit examination. On the overall level, which we take interest in, presumably the best approach is to consider public sector decision making as a cooperative game. The social classes are colliding and colluding with one another through the various channels and with the various means available, and it is by way of the political process, through the intermediation of the politicians, that their interests are weighted, negotiated, and compromised into binding agreements. Conceiving of the public sector decision making process as a pure bargaining game, could yield us the specific one-point Nash bargaining solution.[24]

In this bargaining game, the participants are faced with a set of feasible alternatives, any one of which will be the outcome if it is specified by the unanimous agreement of all participants. In the event that no unanimous agreement is reached, a given disagreement outcome, often called the threat point, is the result. The outcome for the respective participants in case of disagreement will be denoted by P_k^T, $k = 1,2,\ldots$ It has been shown that under reasonable assumptions the unique (Nash bargaining) solution to the game P_k^*, $k = 1,2,\ldots$, is obtained at the point which maximizes the Nash-product $\Pi_k (P_k - P_k^T)$ over the feasible set.[25] Let us for expositional reasons further address the two-dimensional case of figure 3.2, and assume that the Pareto-frontier AB can be described by the differentiable function $P_1 = f(P_2)$. The first-order condition for the maximization of the Nash-product over the feasible set, i.e. over the Pareto-frontier, then reads:

$$(3.12) \qquad f' = -\frac{P_1 - P_1^T}{P_2 - P_2^T} .$$

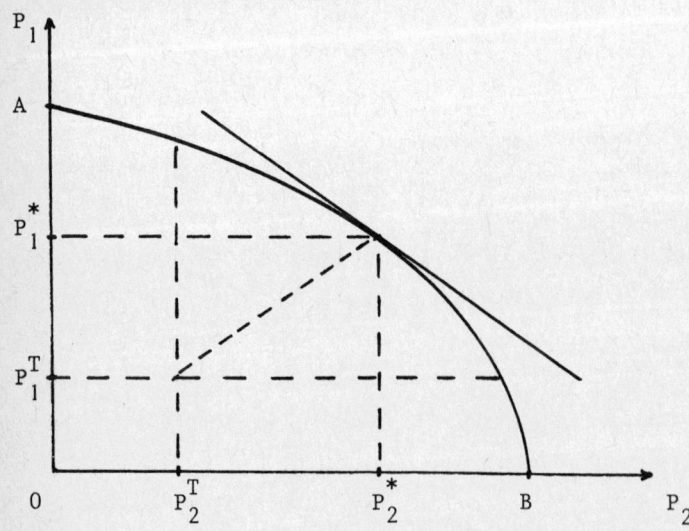

Figure 3.3. The Nash bargaining solution

This immediately brings out that in the solution point (P_1^*, P_2^*) the slope of the frontier of the feasible set is of opposite sign to the slope of the straight line through the threat point (P_1^T, P_2^T) and the solution point; cf. figure 3.3. Note, furthermore, that a linear transformation of any one of the interest functions P_k - i.e. a transformation of P_k into $aP_k + b$, $a > 0$ - will leave the solution (in the sense of the behaviour behind the pay-offs P_k, $k = 1,2,..$) unaffected.

We now return to the optimization problem for the public sector which is based on the interest function approach: maximize

$$P_s = P_1^{\lambda_1} \cdot P_2^{\lambda_2}$$

over the set of feasible alternatives. The first-order condition for this problem reads:

(3.13) $$f' = -\frac{\lambda_2}{\lambda_1} \cdot \frac{P_1}{P_2} .$$

Confronting (3.13) with (3.12) it turns out that the present maximization problem will yield the same solution P_1^*, P_2^* as the Nash bargaining game, if the power weights λ meet the condition

(3.14) $$\frac{\lambda_1}{\lambda_2} = \frac{P_1^*}{P_2^*} \cdot \frac{P_2^* - P_2^T}{P_1^* - P_1^T} .$$

The position of the threat point in the bargaining game and the distribution of the power weights λ in the corresponding interest function formulation are directly related. If the threat point would shift to the north-west in figure 3.3, improving the position of group 1 in case of no agreement and deteriorating the position of group 2, it can be deduced from eq. (3.12) that the solution point will shift in the same direction, where the slope at the contour will become flatter. From eq. (3.13) it follows that λ_1/λ_2 goes up, as could be expected.[26]

We want to add two specific observations. Firstly, while the Nash bargaining solution is not affected by linear transformations of the interest functions P_k, this does not hold for the corresponding interest function formulation, as is evident from eq. (3.14). While a proportional transformation of (any one of) the P_k's leaves λ_1/λ_2 unchanged, this is not true for an additive transformation. Note that this observation links up with a remark made earlier under point c. Secondly, what counts, here as well as in the case of Ten Raa, is the ratio of the power weights, λ_1/λ_2, not their absolute level. This holds for eq. (3.8) generally; it is just a matter of normalization to have the power weights sum to 1.

When it comes to a comparison of the Nash bargaining and interest function approach, we prefer the interest function approach. The direct empirical determination of the threat point in case of public sector decision making will be very difficult, if not impossible; the prospects for giving empirical content to the weights λ are less gloomy. Besides, notice that given the values of the power weights λ it is possible to turn eq. (3.14) round and derive the locus of the threat point. At least, if the underlying relationships and processes are properly described by a Nash bargaining game.

In section 3.2 we derived that the public sector interest function P_s of eq. (3.8) neatly summarizes the decision making process with regard to public policy, according to Van Winden's interest function approach. It now has turned out that the same function, with proper choices of the power weights λ, can also serve as a representation of both the Nash bargaining game and Ten Raa's Lagrange multiplier model. We conclude from this that the hypothesis that the public sector acts in accordance with the maximization of P_s over the set of feasible alternatives, gives us, from a theoretical point of view, an interesting tool for the analysis of public policy making.[27]

3.4. Summary and conclusions

At the end of chapter 2 we had to conclude that the present public choice and marxist approaches to the study of political processes, as far as relevant for the analysis of economic policy making, are unsatisfactory for reasons of incoherency, lack of empirical support, and lack of specificity. For that reason we presented in this chapter an alternative approach, the interest function approach to the study of politico-economic phenomena developed by Van Winden. It combines elements from the marxist and public choice traditions, yet refrains from modelling the specific conduct of and the intricate relationships between voters, politicians, bureaucrats, and pressure groups. It is assumed that the interests of people are shaped by the economic position they are in. All interests are, in the end, reduced to the interests of representative individuals in four elementary economic positions. These four positions are: 1. state sector worker (bureaucrat and politician), 2. private sector worker, 3. capital owner, 4. dependant. The set of agents in each elementary economic position is referred to as a social class.

Through the intermediation of the concepts of complex, nested complex and augmented interest functions, the interest function approach leads to the observation that the public sector should be considered as a coalition of interests in which the relations between the social classes find expression. Public sector behaviour should be explained from (acting in accordance with) the (constrained) maximization of the state interest function P_s. This state interest function is a weighted representation of the (elementary) interest functions of the four social classes; $P_s = \Pi_k P_k^{\lambda_k}$.

In section 3.3 we submitted the various elements of the interest function approach to a critical examination. We discussed: the relation between nested complex and augmented interest functions; the differences between bureaucrats and politicians within the one class of state sector workers; the degrees of freedom in the specification of the elementary interest functions P_k; and the possibility of a Pareto optimal outcome of the public sector decision making process. We further saw that the power weights λ may be determined empirically, if they are treated as parameters; however, power relations presumably change over time. Finally, we examined two alternatives for the assumed maximization of the state interest function P_s: the Nash bargaining solution for the case of a cooperative game, and the Lagrange multiplier solution for the case in which one class has full discretion within the minimum constraints imposed by the other classes. It turns out that both alternatives lead to solutions that would also follow from a maximization of P_s, given a proper set of λ's.

Some conclusions. By refraining from modelling actual conduct, the interest function approach in its present form largely treats the public sector as a black box. In this it resembles the structure-performance approach employed in industrial economics. Because of this characteristic the interest function approach can offer us a coherent, yet condensed picture of the impact of the social classes, through all available channels and means combined, on (economic) policy making. Due to the explicit attention for power relations - cf. the power weights λ - the approach is truly politico-economic in nature. The fact that the (constrained) maximization of P_s not only fits in with the interest function approach, but might also be used to represent other ways of looking at the public sector decision making process, makes the case for using this approach in the analysis of economic policy making even stronger.

CHAPTER 4. THE ENDOGENIZATION OF STATE EXPENDITURE
AND TAXATION IN A SIMPLE KEYNESIAN MODEL

4.1. Introduction[1]

The Keynesian income-expenditure model is, on an introductory level, a most instructive model in macroeconomics. It is widely used in textbooks - see, e.g., Samuelson (1980), Lipsey, Steiner and Purvis (1987) - to give a feeling for the complexity and internal coherence of an economy, and to show in a simple way how decentralized decision making can lead to results (unemployment) that are not aimed at. For expositional reasons we link up with this tradition and use the Keynesian model as a starting point for our analysis. This will enable us to focus attention on the modelling of public sector behaviour, and on its consequences, without being distracted by the present controversies on the proper formulation of the model that best represents the functioning of the economy.

Let us start from the most simple textbook version that deals with a closed economy without a monetary sector.[2] Investment as well as state expenditure are taken to be exogenously determined; tax receipts are acknowledged to depend on the level of economic activity, given the - again, exogenously determined - marginal tax rate. Usually, it is noted that investment is only "for the time being" supposed to be an exogenous variable. Indeed, when dynamics are introduced into the model, or a monetary sector, investment is related to changes in national income or consumption, or to the rate of interest. However, no attempts are made to explain and to endogenize state expenditure and the rate of taxation.[3] Instead, the textbook authors extensively discuss how these latter (and other) variables could be used as instruments of economic policy, in order to attain targets of full employment, price stability, balance of payments equilibrium, and the like. What the textbooks fail to perceive is that the instruments of economic policy such as state expenditure and the rate of taxation will follow well-defined, predictable time paths, once the textbook (or other) recipes are put in practice. At this point the reader will recall the discussion of chapter 1.

The question now arises how the weak spot of the exogeneity of public sector behaviour can be removed from the model, under the retention, as much as possible, of its attractive simplicity. The simplest surgical operation would follow if it could plausibly be assumed that state expenditure is linearly related to national income. Assuming that the public sector is pursuing an anti-cyclic stabilization policy, the behavioural equation for state expenditure could read:

(4.1) $\quad G = g(Y-Y_{fe}) + G_o, \; g < 0,$

with Y_{fe} = full employment national income. This formulation is in line with the policy reaction functions from chapter 1, eq. (1.7); see also Mosley's crisis management model, eq. (2.3). However, as we saw before, this kind of policy reaction functions is found to be rather unstable in empirical research, which may be due, among other things, to the fact that no proper account is taken of political factors and processes.

Alternatively, we could postulate a positive linear relationship between G en Y:

(4.2) $\quad G = gY + G_0, \; g > 0 \; .$

Note that eq. (4.2) implies that governments would not really try to stabilize the economy; indeed, the endogenization of state expenditure by inserting eq. (4.2) into the Keynesian model would add a factor that may cause instability.[4] As a matter of fact, there appears to be empirical as well as theoretical support for such a relationship. It would be obtained, for example, from Peacock and Wiseman's (1961) "displacement effects" theory, which says that outside periods of major social disturbance (such as wars) tax rates can hardly be changed; in that case $G = T = \tau Y$ would seem to hold, with τ fixed (in "normal" times). We could also invoke Alt and Chrystal's permanent income theory, or the (empirical) studies that seem to support Wagner's Law. Nevertheless, on the basis of the foregoing alone, we would not like to propose to enrich the Keynesian model with eq. (4.2) for state expenditure. The reason is that this behavioural equation is as non-political as the original one. The almost endless series of empirical studies concerning Wagner's Law, for instance, shows that it is of the utmost importance to have an explanatory model; facts do not speak for themselves (cf. Wagner and Weber (1977)). See also the critical evaluation of Alt and Chrystal's permanent income hypothesis in section 2.4.5.

To fill the gap, we could turn to the theories of the political processes underlying public sector decision making, which were reviewed in chapter 2. It was observed there that these theories do not offer clear-cut suggestions on how to model the influence of the bureaucracy and pressure groups in a macroeconomic context. When it comes to an endogenization of the role of politicians and political parties, in the line of Nordhaus' political business cycle, Hibbs' partisan effects or the Frey-Schneider popularity surplus/deficit dichotomy, it would be necessary to study a dynamic version of the Keynesian model, add the electoral agenda, and model the ideological differences between the political parties. In principle this would be possible, although not as simple to carry out as the mere insertion of eq. (4.1) or (4.2). Still, we would not recommend such an approach, for reasons of theoretical weaknesses and insufficient empirical support, discussed at length in chapter 2.

The theoretical and empirical results assembled in chapters 1 and 2 support the point of view that we should take account of political factors, the dynamics of the social power structure, in explaining public sector decision making. At the same time it is necessary to study these political factors in a coherent and consistent fashion, not just singling out one of the many channels and means through which social groups can exert influence on the outcome of the public sector decision making process, but taking into consideration all the channels and means which are available to the different groups in society. Here, the interest function approach to the study of politico-economic phenomena provides a suitable alternative as we have seen in chapter 3. In the present chapter we undertake a first attempt to employ the interest function approach in the context of macroeconomic modelling. To that purpose we focus on the determination of state expenditure and taxation, leaving the analysis of social security transfer payments and the decision making on budget surpluses and deficits for later chapters. In section 4.2 we model public sector decision making and derive behavioural equations for state expenditure, state employment, and the rate of taxation. It will appear that these behavioural equations can be used to transform the textbook

Keynesian model in a relatively simple manner into a politico-economic model. In section 4.3 the comparative static properties of this politico-economic model will be analyzed; section 4.4 pays attention to some dynamical properties. Section 4.5 concludes this chapter, which paves the way for the empirical application in chapter 5, and a fully dynamic analysis of the social power structure in chapter 6.

4.2. The behaviour of the state

In chapter 3 we extensively discussed the logic behind the interest function approach. We saw that the analysis starts from the assumption that individual as well as collective actions are, ultimately, related to individual interests. These interests regard goods and services that can be obtained either in or outside the market. The particular form in which the basic economic interests of people will manifest themselves, as well as their action space or control over marketed and non-marketed goods, are shaped by the position they have with respect to the production process in society. Attention is, therefore, focused upon the interests of individuals as occupants of certain economic positions. Four elementary economic positions are distinguished:

1. state sector worker;
2. private sector worker;
3. capital owner; and
4. dependant.

The set of agents in each elementary economic position is referred to as a social class (index $k = 1,2,3,4$, respectively).

In a macroeconomic model, the interest in market goods is reflected in an interest in real disposable income. As regards the goods that cannot be obtained inside the market, attention is restricted to the goods and services supplied by the state, and the relative numerical strength of the social classes. The numerical strength of a social class is considered to be an indication of the positional security of the average member of that class. The extent to which agents are able to realize their interests and to safeguard their position may be expected to be somehow related to this strength. The goods and services supplied by the state will be taken to be purely collective in nature. This approach is followed for simplicity, and

with an eye on the empirical application of the model as in general sufficient data on the incidence of state provided goods across social groups are lacking. Resuming, the representative member of social class k has three basic interests:
1. his real disposable income, w_k;
2. the relative numerical strength of his social class, e_k; and
3. the bundle of collective goods and services supplied by the state, x_s.

For the elementary interest functions P_k the following Cobb-Douglas specification is chosen:[5]

$$(4.3) \quad P_k = w_k^{\varepsilon_{k1}} \cdot e_k^{\varepsilon_{k2}} \cdot x_s^{\varepsilon_{k3}}, \quad \varepsilon_{kg} \geq 0 \; \forall g, \; \Sigma_g \varepsilon_{kg} = 1.$$

Next, we come to the state. According to the interest function approach, its behaviour can be assumed to be in accordance with the maximization - within certain constraints - of the state interest function P_s, which is a weighted representation of the elementary interest functions P_k:

$$(4.4) \quad P_s = \Pi_k P_k^{\lambda_k}, \quad \lambda_k \geq 0 \; \forall k, \; \Sigma_k \lambda_k = 1.$$

The (power) weight λ_k denotes the (relative) strength with which social class k, through all available channels and by all available means, gets its specific interests promoted by the state.

In this chapter we will focus on state expenditure, employment and taxation. The income transfers via the social security programs are not taken into account, as far as state behaviour is concerned; they will be considered to be taking place within the private sector. Accordingly, then, the class of dependants has in that respect no <u>specific</u> interests to be guarded by the state. To this it can be added that the dependants are not directly involved in the production process, and for that reason have the weakest position in politico-economic affairs. For both reasons, and for simplicity, the class of dependants will not be distinguished separately in this first attempt to model and endogenize state behaviour;

i.e., it will be assumed that $\lambda_4 = 0$.[6]

We are now ready to derive more specific results concerning state behaviour. As indicated above, we focus on public sector activity with respect to the provision of goods and services; transfers are for the moment considered to take place within the private sector. The (real) value of the state supplied goods and services, which are taken to be purely collective in nature, is measured by (exhaustive) state expenditure G.[7] In conformity with the definition in the national accounts, state expenditure equals the sum of the public sector wages W_s and non-wage (material) expenditure G_m. The wage sum W_s is given by the public sector wage rate w_s times the number of state sector workers E_s. Non-wage expenditure G_m is taken to bear a constant proportion γ to the public sector wage sum; one could think, e.g., of a technical complementarity between labour and material inputs.[8]

Next, we have to consider how state expenditure is being financed. Firstly, it is assumed that a fraction θ of state expenditure has to be covered by tax receipts; the remaining fraction $1-\theta$ will define the budget deficit (or surplus, for that matter). In the present analysis θ will be taken to be fixed; in chapter 8 we shall address the decision making process on the size of budget deficits and surpluses in greater detail. Taxes T are taken to (ultimately) fall on business profits Π. This assumption is introduced in view of the empirical application in the next chapter as it has been a general opinion in the Netherlands that taxes and social security contributions on wages have been shifted, possibly even fully, in the past.[9] However, we shall also consider in a little while the case of a general income tax. Business profits Π are equal to the difference between labour productivity in the private sector α_p and the private wage rate w_p, times the number of private sector workers E_p. The tax rate will be indicated by τ.

In equation-form the above reads:

(4.5) $G = W_s + G_m = w_s E_s + G_m$,

(4.6) $G_m = \gamma w_s E_s$, $\gamma > 0$,

(4.7) $\quad \theta G = T, \theta > 0,$

(4.8) $\quad T = \tau \Pi,$

(4.9) $\quad \Pi = (\alpha_p - w_p) E_p.$

Using the model specification, the following can be substituted for the arguments of the elementary interest functions (4.3):

(4.10) $\quad w_1 = w_s, w_2 = w_p, w_3 = (1-\tau)\Pi/E_c,$

(4.11) $\quad e_1 = E_s/\Sigma_k E_k, e_2 = E_p/\Sigma_k E_k, e_3 = E_c/\Sigma_k E_k,$

(4.12) $\quad x_s = G = (1+\gamma) w_s E_s, \forall k,$

where E_c stands for the number of capital owners; the total number of people $\Sigma_k E_k$ is taken to be given.

The final step in modelling state behaviour bears upon the formulation of the constraints – arising from structural coercion; cf. chapter 3 – subject to which the state interest function P_s is being maximized. One important constraint has already been taken into consideration, i.e. the budget restraint (4.7). Further, it is assumed that the state has a short time horizon. Partly for that reason, partly because of lack of knowledge (for one thing, which economic model should be employed), the state takes the expected level of activities in the private sector as given. With regard to the public sector wage rate – although in principle an instrument of economic policy –, the functioning of the labour market obviously plays an important role. In the Netherlands, e.g., the wage rate in the public sector has during half the post-war period even been officially tied to the private wage rate. As modelling the labour market is not the aim of this study, the wage rates will be considered to be exogenous.

Using eqs. (4.3), (4.4), (4.10), (4.11), (4.12), we can rewrite P_s as a function of the state's instruments E_s (or G) and τ:

(4.13) $P_s = A \cdot E_s^{\delta_1} \cdot (1-\tau)^{\delta_2}$,

where A comprises all the – from the point of view of the state – exogenous variables, and

(4.14)
$$\delta_1 = (\varepsilon_{12}+\varepsilon_{13})\lambda_1 + \varepsilon_{23}\lambda_2 + \varepsilon_{33}\lambda_3,$$
$$\delta_2 = \varepsilon_{31}\lambda_3.$$

The budget constraint (4.7) can be rewritten as:

(4.15) $\theta(1+\gamma)w_s E_s + (1-\tau)\Pi = \Pi$.

Maximization by the state of P_s under this constraint then yields the following <u>behavioural equations</u>:

(4.16) $E_s = \delta \cdot \left[\dfrac{\alpha_p - w_p}{\theta(1+\gamma)w_s}\right] \cdot E_p$,

(4.17) $\tau = \delta$,

where the parameter δ, which will be called the <u>power coefficient</u> is given by:

(4.18) $\delta = \dfrac{\delta_1}{\delta_1+\delta_2}$, $0 \le \delta \le 1$.

Discussion

<u>a</u>. Apart from the profit margin $\alpha_p - w_p$ and the budget constraint parameter θ, the relative size of the public sector – E_s/E_p – appears to depend on the power coefficient δ. From eq. (4.17) it appears that the tax rate is even fully determined by this power coefficient. The coefficient δ can be said to summarize the <u>effective</u> interest structure of society. It is

determined by the preference weights ε_{kg} that the classes attach to their respective interests, weighted by the relative strengths λ_k with which the classes get their interests vested with and promoted by the state.

In view of this result with respect to the tax rate, we may bring to notice Goldscheid's point of view that tax struggle is the oldest form of class struggle (see Goldscheid (1967), p. 202).

Let us consider some special cases to bring out how the conflicts of interest and the struggle for political power between the social classes affects state behaviour. If, e.g., capitalist interests are not represented by the state, i.e. $\lambda_3 = 0$, it follows from eq. (4.14) that $\delta_2 = 0$. Consequently, $\tau = 1$; all profits are used for the financing of state expenditure. Through the shifting of taxes on to profits, the state and private sector workers succeed in enjoying the provision of public goods and services, without having to pay for it. Note that in this case the available room for expanding the size of the public sector is maximally exploited, irrespective of the distribution of power between the classes of state and private sector workers (λ_1 vs λ_2). The capitalist class also enjoys the public provision of goods and services, but to an extent which will exceed its own preferences.

This latter phenomenon will not occur if capitalist interests "rule" the state; that is, if $\lambda_3 = 1$, and $\lambda_1 = \lambda_2 = 0$. In that case, it follows that $\delta = \varepsilon_{33}/(\varepsilon_{31}+\varepsilon_{33})$; the tax rate and the size of the public sector depend on the relative interest that capitalists take in state goods (ε_{33}) vis-à-vis marketed, private goods (ε_{31}). Note that in this case state expenditure may well be too low from a welfare theoretic point of view, as the groups of state and private sector workers presumably set value on, but do not contribute financially to the provision of public goods and services.[10]

Finally, we can complete our picture by totally differentiating eq. (4.18) with respect to the power distribution λ:

$$(4.19) \quad d\delta = \frac{\varepsilon_{31}}{(\delta_1+\delta_2)^2} \cdot [(\varepsilon_{12}+\varepsilon_{13})\lambda_3 d\lambda_1 + \varepsilon_{23}\lambda_3 d\lambda_2 - ((\varepsilon_{12}+\varepsilon_{13})\lambda_1 + \varepsilon_{23}\lambda_2)d\lambda_3].$$

Remembering that $\lambda_1+\lambda_2+\lambda_3 = 1$, it follows that a shift of power from private and/or state sector workers to the class of capital owners will lower the power coefficient δ, and thus the tax rate and the size of the public sector. A shift of power from private sector workers to state sector workers (holding λ_3 constant) will lead to an increase in δ, and accordingly in the tax rate, if $\varepsilon_{12}+\varepsilon_{13} > \varepsilon_{23}$. This latter inequality will be the more probable to hold, the larger is ε_{12}, i.e. the larger is the preference weight given by state sector workers to their numerical strength, i.e. to the size of the bureaucracy (cf. section 2.5).

<u>b</u>. In view of the discussion in section 4.1 (cf. equations (4.1) and (4.2)) it is interesting to note that eq. (4.16), with the help of definitional equations $Y = w_s E_s + X_p$ and $X_p = \alpha_p E_p$, can be rewritten into the following linear relationship between state expenditure G and national income Y:

$$(4.20) \qquad G = [\frac{1}{1+\gamma} + \frac{\theta}{\delta(1-w_p/\alpha_p)}]^{-1} \cdot Y.$$

State expenditure and national income are positively related. The ratio between G and Y is negatively linked with θ (the fraction of state expenditure to be paid out of taxes), and positively related to γ (linking non-wage and wage expenditure in the state sector) and the before-tax profit share in private output $(1-w_p/\alpha_p)$. Moreover, it is positively related to the power coefficient δ in which – as indicated above – not only preferences regarding private goods and state goods play a part, but also the relative weight attached by social classes to their numerical strength, as well as the relative strength with which they get their interests promoted by the state; these latter factors seem to have been neglected in the studies reflecting on Wagner's Law with respect to the relation between G and Y.

The result (4.20) may also be read as to lend theoretical support to the permanent income approach of Alt and Chrystal. Notice, however, that the stability of the relationship depends on the stability of the parameters δ, γ, θ, and the profit share, determining the state's marginal propensity to spend.

c. Until now, we assumed that taxes (ultimately) fall on profits. This profit tax may have come about by political decisions, but it may also be thought of as the result of a full shifting of taxes on profits which has taken place in the product and labour markets, outside the political sphere.

As announced above, we shall also have a look at the case of a general <u>income tax</u>. After having adjusted the model equations, especially (4.8), (4.10), (4.14) and (4.15) to the situation of an income tax with a uniform tax rate τ', and assuming that the tax base Y is considered by the state to be an exogenous variable, the following behavioural equations for the state can be derived:

(4.16') $\quad E_s' = \dfrac{\delta'}{\theta(1+\gamma)w_s} \cdot Y,$

(4.17') $\quad \tau' = \delta'$, with

(4.18') $\quad \delta' = \delta_1'/(\delta_1'+\delta_2')$, where

(4.14') $\quad \begin{aligned} \delta_1' &= (\varepsilon_{12}+\varepsilon_{13})\lambda_1 + \varepsilon_{23}\lambda_2 + \varepsilon_{33}\lambda_3, \\ \delta_2' &= \varepsilon_{11}\lambda_1 + \varepsilon_{21}\lambda_2 + \varepsilon_{31}\lambda_3. \end{aligned}$

Whenever the definitions and values of variables and parameters differ from those introduced above, primes have been added for the sake of distinction. The general form of the solution does not deviate from that of the profit tax model. The tax rate is fully determined by the power coefficient δ'. Also, a linear relationship is obtained between state expenditure and national income, the stability of which depends on δ', θ.

However, there are also some differences. In general, the tax rate will be lower in the income tax model, ceteris paribus, than in the profit tax model. While the effective interest weight, i.e. the preference weights ε weighted with the relevant power weights λ, for publicly provided goods is the same ($\delta_1' = \delta_1$), the effective interest weight for real disposable income is greater ($\delta_2' > \delta_2$), as more social groups are carrying the tax burden and exert influence on this matter. Regarding the level of tax receipts and the size of the public sector no simple comparative statement can be made, due to counteracting forces: the tax rate is lower in the income tax model, but the taxable base larger.

Let us have a short look at two extremes. Firstly, the case that capitalist interests are not represented by the state ($\lambda_3 = 0$). In the profit tax model, the tax rate then is equal to 1. In the income tax model it is given by:

$$\tau' = \frac{(\varepsilon_{12}+\varepsilon_{13})\lambda_1 + \varepsilon_{23}\lambda_2}{(\varepsilon_{11}+\varepsilon_{12}+\varepsilon_{13})\lambda_1 + (\varepsilon_{21}+\varepsilon_{23})\lambda_2} ,$$

which is smaller than one, taking for granted that ε_{11}, $\varepsilon_{21} > 0$. Contrary to the profit tax model, the tax rate now depends on the power distribution between private and state sector workers. A shift in power from private to state sector workers will lead to an increasing tax rate if $(\varepsilon_{12}+\varepsilon_{13})/\varepsilon_{11} > \varepsilon_{23}/\varepsilon_{21}$. Further, tax receipts will be larger in the income tax case, if $\tau' > \Pi/Y$.

Secondly, if capitalist interests rule the state ($\lambda_3 = 1$), the tax rate is equal for both tax models: $\tau' = \tau = \varepsilon_{33}/(\varepsilon_{31}+\varepsilon_{33})$. But, because of the larger tax base, the tax receipts and the size of the public sector will be larger in the income tax model.

d. Both the profit and the income tax model discussed above could be considered as special cases of a more general model, in which <u>tax rates</u> can be <u>differentiated</u> across income sources and, thus, social classes.

Let τ_1 denote the tax rate on state sector wages, τ_2 that on private sector wages, and τ_3 the profit tax rate. Then the programming problem for the state is to maximize

$$(4.13'') \quad P_s'' = A.'' \, E_s''^{\delta_1''} . (1-\tau_1)^{\delta_2''} . (1-\tau_2)^{\delta_3''} . (1-\tau_3)^{\delta_4''}, \text{ with}$$

$$\begin{aligned}
\delta_1'' &= (\varepsilon_{12}+\varepsilon_{13})\lambda_1 + \varepsilon_{23}\lambda_2 + \varepsilon_{33}\lambda_3, \\
\delta_2'' &= \varepsilon_{11}\lambda_1, \\
(4.14'') \quad \delta_3'' &= \varepsilon_{21}\lambda_2, \\
\delta_4'' &= \varepsilon_{31}\lambda_3,
\end{aligned}$$

subject to the budget constraint. Again assuming that the state considers the tax base to be fixed when solving its programming problem[11], the following behavioural equations are obtained:

(4.16'') $$E''_s = \frac{\delta''_1}{\Sigma_j \delta''_j} \cdot \frac{1}{\theta(1+\gamma)w_s} \cdot Y, \quad Y = W_s + W_p + \Pi,$$

$$\tau_1 = 1 - \frac{\delta''_2}{\Sigma_j \delta''_j} \cdot \frac{Y}{W_s},$$

(4.17'') $$\tau_2 = 1 - \frac{\delta''_3}{\Sigma_j \delta''_j} \cdot \frac{Y}{W_p},$$

$$\tau_3 = 1 - \frac{\delta''_4}{\Sigma_j \delta''_j} \cdot \frac{Y}{\Pi}.$$

First of all, note that the general solution for state employment, state expenditure, and the <u>average</u> tax rate is equal to that of the income tax model; cf. eqs. (4.16'), (4.17'). These aggregate variables are unaffected by the distribution of income and taxation; for an aggregate analysis the uniform income tax model thus seems very well applicable. On a disaggregated level, eq. (4.17'') shows that the tax rates may well vary over the income sources. Tax rates will only be uniform if $\delta''_2/W_s = \delta''_3/W_p = \delta''_4/\Pi$, i.e. if the effective interests attached to the specific categories of (real disposable) income are equally proportional to the shares of those income categories in national income.

The model above would translate into the profit tax model, if both τ_1 and τ_2 would be equal to zero. That would be the case if

$$\frac{\delta''_2}{\Sigma_j \delta''_j} = \frac{W_s}{Y}, \quad \frac{\delta''_3}{\Sigma_j \delta''_j} = \frac{W_p}{Y};$$

that is, if both state and private sector workers succeed in exerting enough pressure on the state to guard their real disposable incomes (enough, in relation to the pressure of capitalists, and in relation to the effective interest attached to the provision of state goods). Thus, apart from the possibility that taxes are shifted on to profits in the labour and product markets, due to <u>market power</u>, a single profit tax may also arise due to <u>political power</u> of state and private sector workers vis-à-vis capital owners.

For the reason indicated earlier, we shall adhere in the sequel to the profit tax model. However, the above discussion has made clear that it can easily be replaced by an income tax model, without affecting the general structure of the solution.

4.3. A static Keynesian politico-economic model

The equations of state behaviour which were derived in the previous section will now be used to transform the textbook Keynesian model discussed in section 4.1 into a politico-economic model. Because of our distinction of social classes, some disaggregation is called for. We differentiate between private sector production X_p and the production of purely collective goods in the public sector, and between wage income $w_p E_p$ and profit income Π in the private sector. The production in the private sector is adapted to the demand for its output, consisting of private consumption C, private investment I, and non-wage state expenditure G_m.

Duplicating for the sake of clarity the relevant equations from the previous section, the complete model reads:

(4.21) $\quad X_p = C + I + G_m$,

(4.22) $\quad C = c_1(w_s E_s + w_p E_p) + c_2(1-\tau)\Pi + C_o, \quad 0 < c_2 \leq c_1 < 1$,

(4.23) $\quad I = I_o$,

(4.24) $\quad G_m = \gamma w_s E_s, \quad \gamma > 0$,

(4.25) $\quad X_p = \alpha_p E_p$,

(4.26) $\quad \Pi = X_p - w_p E_p$,

(4.27) $\quad E_s = \delta \dfrac{\alpha_p - w_p}{\theta(1+\gamma)w_s} E_p, \quad \theta > 0$,

(4.28) $\tau = \delta$,

(4.29) $\delta = \dfrac{\delta_1}{\delta_1 + \delta_2}$, with

$\delta_1 = (\varepsilon_{12} + \varepsilon_{13})\lambda_1 + \varepsilon_{23}\lambda_2 + \varepsilon_{33}\lambda_3$,

$\delta_2 = \varepsilon_{31}\lambda_3$,

where c_1 and c_2 denote the marginal propensities to consume out of wage and (disposable) profit income, respectively, C_o and I_o denote autonomous consumption and investment, respectively. Furthermore, it will be assumed that $\alpha_p > w_p > 0$ and $C_o + I_o > 0$. Because $Y = X_p + w_s E_s$ and $G = w_s E_s + G_m$, eq. (4.21) is equivalent to $Y = C + I + G$.

By solving the model the equilibrium values of the endogenous variables can be calculated. Note that the state has been assumed to have only limited information at its disposal and to be short-sighted when developing its policies; it does not take into account, <u>a priori</u>, the (expected) effects of its own behaviour on the production and employment levels in the private sector. However, as soon as its behaviour effectively influences private sector activities, such that the tax base is changing, then the state may well be presumed to start reconsidering its policies, <u>a posteriori</u>, probably with some delay. This latter process of the state adjusting its policies to actually changing conditions is taken full account of in deriving the following equilibrium solution of the model.

For the <u>equilibrium</u> level of <u>private output</u> the familiar result is obtained, i.e. the product of a multiplier and autonomous expenditure. The multiplier m equals

(4.30) $m = \{1 - [\dfrac{c_1 + \gamma}{\theta(1+\gamma)} \cdot \delta(1 - \dfrac{w_p}{\alpha_p}) + c_1 \cdot \dfrac{w_p}{\alpha_p} + c_2(1-\delta)(1 - \dfrac{w_p}{\alpha_p})]\}^{-1}$

The second term in the expression within hooked brackets is the marginal propensity to consume of private sector workers, the third term is the marginal propensity to consume of capital owners, while the first term denotes the marginal propensity to spend of state sector workers (as consumers) and the state, all weighted with the relevant income shares.

For the equilibrium level of <u>state sector employment</u>, it follows:

$$(4.31) \quad E_s = \frac{\delta(1-w_p/\alpha_p)}{\theta(1+\gamma)w_s} \cdot m \cdot (C_o + I_o) .$$

<u>Discussion</u>

<u>a</u>. Our first concern is whether an economically interpretable equilibrium exists, i.e. whether the <u>multiplier m</u> is <u>positive</u>. In general, for m > 0 to hold, a lower bound for θ can be derived which depends on the value of the power coefficient δ:

$$(4.32) \quad m \gtrless 0 \text{ if } \theta \gtrless \frac{(c_1+\gamma)(\alpha_p-w_p)\delta}{(1+\gamma)[\alpha_p-c_1 w_p-c_2(1-\delta)(\alpha_p-w_p)]} .$$

Figure 4.1 depicts the relevant parameter ranges

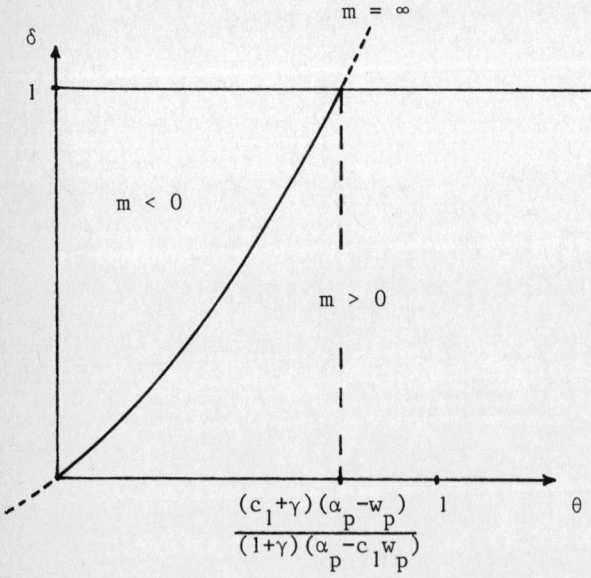

<u>Figure 4.1</u> The value of the multiplier m.

It is easily seen that $m > 0$ holds, if the state strives for a balanced budget ($\theta = 1$). In that case income is only redistributed from the private to the public sector and as $0 < c_2 \leq c_1 < 1$ an equilibrium is assured.

<u>b</u>. It can be shown that the multiplier value of our model with endogenous state behaviour is larger than that of the same model but with state behaviour exogenously determined.[12] This finding suggests that the politico-economic system may be <u>less stable</u> than can be calculated using pure economic models only.

However, from the literature on "automatic (fiscal) stabilizers", notably Smyth (1963, 1974), it can be learned that for drawing conclusions on stabilization and destabilization it is not enough to look at the value of the multiplier, but that one should study the dynamics of the model. In section 4.4 we shall take a look at the dynamic version of our politico-economic model.

<u>c</u>. The <u>sensitivity</u> of the equilibrium solution for parameter changes has been derived and summarized in table 4.1.
- Private sector output and employment are positively related to the value of the power coefficient δ, at least if θ is not too large[13]; it certainly holds for $\theta \leq 1$. An increase in δ will, ceteris paribus, increase taxation and, hence, state expenditure and employment. Each dollar of profit taxed away will decrease capital owners' consumption with c_2, but increase non-wage material expenditure by the state with $\gamma/[\theta(1+\gamma)]$ and wage payments with $1/[\theta(1+\gamma)]$ dollar, increasing consumption by state sector workers with $c_1/[\theta(1+\gamma)]$. Given that $c_2 \leq c_1$ and $\gamma > 0$, and if θ is not too large such that not too much purchasing power is leaking away from the circular flow of income through a budget surplus, effective demand for private output will be boosted, raising private output and employment.
- State sector employment is positively related to δ. An increase in the power coefficient directly leads to a rising tax rate; moreover, as we just saw, the tax base may be enlarged too.
State sector employment is further positively related to c_1, c_2, C_o and I_o, and negatively to w_s, w_p and θ. Its sensitivity with regard to γ appears to depend on the other parameter values.

Table 4.1. The signs of the first partial derivatives of the equilibrium solution with regard to a series of parameters

	γ	θ	α_p	w_p	w_s	δ, $\theta \leq 1$	δ, $\theta > 1$
X_p	+	−	±(±)	±(±)	0	+	±
E_p	+	−	±(−)	±(±)	0	+	±
E_s	±(−)	−	+	−	−	+	+
$E_p + E_s$	±(±)	−	±(±)	±(±)	−	+	±
E_s / E_p	−	−	+	−	−	+	+
G/Y	+	−	+	−	0	+	+
ξ	±(0)	−	±(0)	±(0)	0	+(0)	−

In some cases the direction of the influence of the parameters could not be ascertained; in those cases we have added between brackets which sign obtains in case the state budget balances ($\theta = 1$). ξ denotes the deficit in the state budget, expressed as a fraction of national income.

- Not amazingly, the various social classes are affected differently by a change in the power coefficient δ. If, e.g., δ_2 (= $\varepsilon_{31}\lambda_3$) decreases so that δ increases, state sector workers are affected positively as are private sector workers; both employment and the provision of collective goods and services grow (cf. eq. (4.3)). For the class of capitalists the result is most probably negative, for the growth in the provision of state goods will generally be outvalued by a loss in real disposable profit income.
- As to θ, however, note that <u>all</u> social classes profit from a loosening of the budget discipline (a decrease in θ). As in the present model formulation no heed is given to the (future) costs of present deficits-and-borrowing, the positive effects dominate; due to the increase in state expenditure, state and private sector employment, the provision of collective goods and services, and disposable profit income all grow.[14]
- The effect of an increase in labour productivity α_p on state sector

employment is invariably positive, because it increases the profit margin and the tax base. The effect on private sector employment is not necessarily negative, as the increase in state sector employment and, consequently, in material state expenditure and consumption by state sector workers, in addition to the increase in profits and, consequently, in consumption by capitalists may compensate for the initial loss in private sector employment and in the consumption by private sector workers. Private sector employment appears to be positively affected if

$$\theta < \frac{(c_1+\gamma)\delta}{(1+\gamma)[1-c_2(1-\delta)]} \; ;$$

it can be shown that the right-hand side of this inequality is less than one, implying that a deficit in the state's budget is required.
- The budget deficit is in our model given by

$$(1+\gamma)w_s E_s - \tau(\alpha_p - w_p)E_p \; ;$$

as a fraction of national income it is denoted by ξ. Remember that the parameter θ has been introduced to denote which part of state expenses has to be covered out of tax receipts. Thus, $\xi = 0$ if $\theta = 1$; the budget is balanced.

Loosening the budget constraint by decreasing θ has a stimulating, demand enlarging effect on the economy. However, the resulting growth of national income appears to be insufficient to prevent the budget deficit from rising as a fraction of national income; the fraction ξ is negatively related to θ.

Given that $\theta < 1$, ξ is positively related to the power coefficient δ. At an increase of δ, the state's budget and the budget deficit grow, just as national income, but faster.

- Note that the state sector wage rate w_s does not show up as a determinant of ξ, nor of X_p and E_p. This has to do with the fact that, due to the functional form of the interest functions, state sector employment is unitelastic with respect to its wage rate; cf. eqs. (4.16) and (4.31). An increase in w_s affects state employment negatively;

however, the state's wage sum as a whole remains unaffected and, consequently, all other variables.

<u>d</u>. For the sake of completeness, it is observed that the traditional textbook exercises of manipulating state expenditure and/or taxation in order to obtain full employment, cannot be practised with our politico-economic model, because state expenditure and taxation have become an endogenous part of it.

If economic agents are interested in a change in total employment, they should try to alter the value of the parameters. This might be established by changing the "conventional wisdom" on the desired value of θ (but see chapter 8), or, as regards δ, by structurally changing the internal and/or external pressure on the state, for instance through the formation of new pressure groups. At any rate, a simple policy advice to the state to change the level of expenditure and/or taxation will not work, if it neglects the determinants of state behaviour.

4.4. Some dynamic aspects of the model

The comparative-static analysis of our politico-economic model pointed out that its multiplier value is larger than that of the same model but with state behaviour exogenously determined. This finding might imply that the political-economic system is less stable than the analysis of purely economic models alone suggests. However, at the same time it was noted that for drawing proper conclusions on the matter of (in)stability, one should study the dynamics of the model.

The (static) model was given by eqs. (4.21) - (4.29). To be able to analyze its <u>dynamic</u> properties, we have to impose a particular lag structure. Plausibly, consumption will react with some lag to (disposable) income; furthermore, as noted earlier, the state's decision making on expenditure, employment and tax rates may be assumed to react with some delay to changes in economic conditions affecting the tax base. Non-wage state expenditure will - as material input - most probably be coupled to contemporary public sector employment and production. Neglecting for the present changes in prices and wages and shifts in the power structure of society (but see chapter 6), the dynamic model (with time index t) looks as follows:

(4.33) $X_{pt} = C_t + I_t + G_{mt}$,

(4.34) $C_t = c_1(w_s E_{st-1} + w_p E_{pt-1}) + c_2(1-\tau_{t-1})\Pi_{t-1} + C_o$,

(4.35) $I_t = I_o$,

(4.36) $G_{mt} = \gamma w_s E_{st}$,

(4.37) $X_{pt} = \alpha_p E_{pt}$,

(4.38) $\Pi_t = X_{pt} - w_p E_{pt}$,

(4.39) $E_{st} = \delta \cdot \dfrac{(\alpha_p - w_p)}{\theta(1+\gamma)w_s} \cdot E_{pt-1}$,

(4.40) $\tau_t = \delta$.

Solving the model yields a second-order difference equation in E_p:

(4.41) $\alpha_p E_{pt} = [c_1 w_p + c_2(1-\delta)(\alpha_p - w_p) + \dfrac{\gamma\delta(\alpha_p - w_p)}{\theta(1+\gamma)}] E_{pt-1}$

$+ \dfrac{c_1 \delta(\alpha_p - w_p)}{\theta(1+\gamma)} E_{pt-2} + C_o + I_o$.

The (steady state) equilibrium solution is given by eq. (4.30) in the previous section. To derive the conditions for the dynamic stability of this equilibrium, we must analyze the characteristic equation of (4.41):

$$\lambda^2 + a_1 \lambda + a_2 = 0,$$

where: $a_1 = -c_1 \dfrac{w_p}{\alpha_p} - [c_2(1-\delta) + \dfrac{\gamma\delta}{\theta(1+\gamma)}](1 - \dfrac{w_p}{\alpha_p})$, < 0;

$$a_2 = - \frac{c_1 \delta}{\theta(1+\gamma)} (1 - \frac{w_p}{\alpha_p}), < 0.$$

The stability conditions - cf. Gandolfo (1980, p. 59) - read:

$$1 + a_1 + a_2 > 0,$$
$$1 - a_2 > 0,$$
$$1 - a_1 + a_2 > 0.$$

It is easily checked that the second and the third condition impose no additional constraints on the parameter set once the first is satisfied, because $a_2 < 0$, $a_1 < 0$. The first condition just states that the multiplier m should be positive; cf. eq. (4.32) and figure 4.1.

Our conclusion thus can be that the politico-economic model given by eqs. (4.33) - (4.40) is stable, if the condition for m > 0 given by eq. (4.32) is fulfilled.[15]

For a comparison we now turn to the case of exogenous state behaviour. Considering E_s, G_m and τ to be autonomous variables, the solution of the dynamic model changes into:

$$\alpha_p E_{pt} = [c_1 w_p + c_2 (1-\delta)(\alpha_p - w_p)] E_{pt-1} + C_o + I_o + c_1 w_s E_s + G_m.$$

The stability condition for this model just holds that its static multiplier:

$$[1 - c_1 \frac{w_p}{\alpha_p} - c_2 (1-\delta)(1 - \frac{w_p}{\alpha_p})]^{-1}$$

should be positive and finite, which is satisfied for all relevant parameter values. Observe that the higher the tax rate (δ), the lower is the value of this multiplier, and the faster proceeds the dynamic adjustment towards equilibrium; taxation operates in this case as an automatic stabilizer.

Comparing the models with endogenous and exogenous state behaviour not only points out that the multiplier value is larger in the former model, but also that dynamic stability is not always guaranteed in the former model in contrast to the latter one. The politico-economic system, indeed, seems to be less stable than purely economic modelling suggests.

However, the literature on the possible destabilizing effects of automatic stabilizers - see, e.g., Smyth (1963, 1974) - has made us aware that the above kind of conclusion may be rather sensitive to the specification and dynamic structure of the model.

To get some insight into this phenomenon, we introduce a simple <u>accelerator</u>-mechanism in the investment equation (4.35). Henceforth:

$$I_t = I_o + v(X_{pt-1} - X_{pt-2}), \quad v > 0.$$

Solving the politico-economic model again yields a second-order difference equation in E_p:

$$\alpha_p E_{pt} = [c_1 w_p + c_2(1-\delta)(\alpha_p - w_p) + \frac{\gamma\delta(\alpha_p - w_p)}{\theta(1+\gamma)} + \alpha_p v] E_{pt-1}$$
$$+ [\frac{c_1\delta(\alpha_p - w_p)}{\theta(1+\gamma)} - \alpha_p v] E_{pt-2} + C_o + I_o.$$

The equilibrium solution is invariably being given by eq. (4.30). The dynamic stability condition, on the other hand, undergoes a change. To the condition that the multiplier m should be positive - cf. eq. (4.32) -, a second condition now is added, to wit:

$$v < 1 + \frac{c_1\delta(1 - w_p/\alpha_p)}{\theta(1+\gamma)}.$$

In contrast with the condition on the multiplier, this second condition will be more easily satisfied, the higher is the value of the power coefficient δ.

Considering the same model but with state behaviour exogenously determined, we just obtain the standard (Hicksian) multiplier- accelerator model. Its dynamic stability condition is simple and well-known:

$$v < 1.$$

Comparing the models with endogenous and exogenous state behaviour anew, the static multiplier is still larger in the politico-economic model. However, the dynamic stability conditions are overlapping now. For some parameter values the exogenous state model is stable, while the endogenous state model is not; but it may also be the other way round. The politico-economic model may be stable while the model with exogenous state behaviour is not.[16]

Summing up: in the first part of this section it was recalled that taxation acts as an automatic stabilizing force in a simple (dynamic) Keynesian model. Once it was recognized that not only tax receipts may vary, but state expenditure too, this conclusion could not be sustained. State activity as a whole, taxation plus expenditure, may well be destabilizing, in our simple model of reference.

In the same way, however, as the automatic stabilizing nature of taxation has been challenged in the literature, so may the destabilizing effect of state activity as a whole be disputed. Analyzing in the second part of this section a multiplier-accelerator version of the model, it appeared that the politico-economic system may after all be more stable than a system without state activity, or a system with built-in flexibility of taxes and autonomous state expenditure.

On a general theoretical level, then, no clear-cut conclusions can be drawn as to the (de)stabilizing influence of state activity; much depends on the particular specification and lag structure of the model. On the other hand, it has become clear that it makes a great difference for the issue at hand, whether one takes account of the endogenous nature of state activity in general and state expenditure in particular, or not.

4.5. Summary

In this chapter we made our first step towards the endogenization of state behaviour in a macroeconomic model, employing the interest function approach discussed in chapter 3. To have a simple and well-known point of reference, with which it is easy to compare, the politico-economic model is built up from an elementary Keynesian income-expenditure model. Public sector decision making has been modelled in such a manner that behavioural equations could be obtained for state expenditure, state employment and taxation. Subsequently, we analyzed the comparative static properties of the politico-economic model, as well as some of its dynamic aspects.

We mention a few interesting results.
- The rate of taxation is fully determined by the preferences and the relative influence on state behaviour of the different social classes.
- A linear relationship between state expenditure and national income is obtained; a relationship which has been put forward by some theoretical as well as empirical studies, albeit without a behavioural explanation as is offered by the present study. The stability of the relationship appears to depend, inter alia, on the power structure of society.
- The profit tax in the model, which may result from the political power of private and state sector workers, but may also be due to their market power to shift taxes on to profits, may be replaced by a uniform or differentiated income tax, without altering the general structure of the solution.
- The multiplier value of our (politico-economic) model with endogenous state behaviour appears to be larger than the multiplier of the same model but with state behaviour exogenously determined.
- The effect of an increase in private sector labour productivity on employment is not necessarily negative. The increase in state sector employment which results from the growing tax base, and the concomitant expenditure, may well compensate for the direct negative effect on private sector employment.
- No clear-cut conclusions can be drawn with respect to the (de)stabilizing impact of state activity. But it has become clear that it can make a great difference in matters of stability and instability, whether one takes the endogenous nature of state activity into

consideration, or not.

Of course, the analysis in this chapter was just a first step. The problem of balancing the state budget, the income transfers of the social security system, and the dynamics of the social power structure will be dealt with in later chapters. First, however, we shall apply our yet simple model to Dutch data, to illustrate its potentialities as well as to discuss the problems involved in its empirical application.

CHAPTER 5. AN APPLICATION TO THE NETHERLANDS

5.1. Introduction[1)]

The Netherlands can be characterized as a parliamentary democracy. General elections for parliament[2)] in principle take place every four years; however, provisions exist to dissolve parliament during the regular electoral period, and to hold early elections. The electoral system is marked by proportional representation.

Since World War II, the period to be considered here, the number of political parties elected to be represented in parliament varied between 7 and 14. Dutch politics is dominated by the christian-democratic, liberal-conservative and social-democratic parties. The vote share of the social-democratic party (PvdA) varied from 23 to 34%, with an average of 28%, while that of the liberal-conservatives (VVD) grew from some 8 to some 20%, averaging 12% over the period since WW II. The christian-democrats were until 1977 divided over three separate autonomous parties: one catholic party (KVP; the largest, with an average vote share of 28%), and two protestant parties (ARP and CHU, obtaining on average, respectively, 10 and 8% of the votes being cast). Over time, the combined vote share of KVP, ARP and CHU declined from somewhat above 50% during the fifties until 31% at the 1972-election. In 1977 the three parties merged into one christian-democratic party (CDA), which since then has succeeded in maintaining its share of the vote at around 30%. The vote shares of the remaining, minor parties, several of which had only a short-lived history, varied between 0.7% and 11%. For more details, cf. Parlement en Kiezer (1986).

As no single party ever received more than 34% of the vote, it goes without saying that governments in the Netherlands are formed by coalition cabinets. Since 1945 20 cabinets have been in power successively. After some broadly based coalitions including the political centre, left and right during the period of reconstruction immediately after the war, periods of centre-left and centre-right government have alternated. Only one party, that of the catholics, was included in all coalitions.

Of the total number of 20 cabinets, 4 were short-lived "intermezzo" cabinets, the main task being to prepare early elections. Interestingly enough, 10 of the remaining 16 "normal" governments included parties that were numerically unnecessary for the cabinet to obtain a majority support in parliament. De Swaan (1973) points out that there was an outspoken preference on the part of the catholic party for such "supercoalitions", even at the cost of losing some portfolio's to the additional partners. This is explained by the desire of this party to maintain its options; to extend its key position in parliament into the cabinet coalition. The desire to do so, in turn, would "spring from the urgent necessity to keep the internal factions of trade union, farming and entrepreneurial interests at bay by avoiding a clear commitment to one political side or another".[3] It should further be observed that only three cabinets survived the regular parliamentary period of four years without interruption.

For our purpose, this short characterization of the Dutch political system will suffice. For a more detailed account of the economy and politics of the Netherlands the reader may be referred to Griffiths (1980); see also De Swaan (1973), Parlement en Kiezer (1986).

In the light of the above sketch we can now return to the empirical results concerning politico-economic interaction in the Netherlands, cited in chapter 2, for an interpretation.

In the Dutch multi-party system with its inevitable coalition cabinets, it is for voters a difficult, if not unsolvable, problem to try to attribute responsibility for economic and political developments to one or other of the coalition parties.[4] Moreover, the election outcome normally leaves several options for the politicians to choose from, during the formation of the next cabinet; "loosers" may get in, "winners" may stay out, whether they are big or small.[5] In such a context it need not surprise if no stable voting and popularity functions, with a significant contribution of the macroeconomic development, can be detected; cf. the results reported in section 2.3. Of interest is also the conclusion of Andeweg (1982), obtained from survey data (period 1966-1977). While there is a clear association between socio-economic background and voting behaviour (see also Schram and Van Winden (1986a)), this is not the case for electoral change. "The growth of some social classes or other socio-economic categories of voters at the expense of others, has not contributed to the changes in the election results in a significant measure" (p. 122).

As to political parties, it then seems to be unrealistic to hypothesize that they - by themselves or as a coalition - head for, or guard, a more or less clear-cut minimal vote share in order to secure a prolonged participation in cabinet. Also, it may be surmised that parties do not want to govern at all costs.[6] For one thing, it may be wise in a multi-party system to maintain a consistent, ideologically pure position. And parties in opposition, presumably, are not without influence, given the heterogeneity of the coalition. Indeed, it was reported in sections 2.4.2. and 2.4.4. that with respect to the Netherlands as yet no empirical support has been found for the Nordhaus-type political business cycle, nor for the Frey-Schneider re-election efforts.

This is not to say that Dutch parties are not interested in votes; they are, but it appears to be more in line with reality to assume that votes are attracted on the basis of a given party programme determined by the structure of interests and influence within the party. Further, at cabinet formations, other factors than just vote shares seem to play an important role, such as "ideological nearness" of the partners and "closedness" of the coalition.[7] In section 1.5 some studies were cited to the effect that Dutch parties differ in their preferences with regard to various aspects of macro-economic developments. And in section 2.4.3. we could report some significant effects of the party composition of government on the course of unemployment, as found by Alt (1985b). However, the latter result stands alone, as De Grauwe (1985), Cowart (1978a,b) and Renaud and Van Winden (1987a) could not detect (consistent) partisan effects.

Apart from the influence of the various political parties, one could ask about the impact of the bureaucracy and interest groups on Dutch policy making. It was noticed above that public employees are grossly overrepresented in parliament (cf. section 2.5.1), and that they tend to have a higher voting turnout than other social groups (the difference being limited to some 3.5 percentage points; cf. section 2.5.2). The effect on macroeconomic policy, however, has hardly been a serious subject of research. The findings of Lybeck (1986) reported in sections 2.5.3 and

2.6.3 do not give much hold in this connection.

Taking into consideration the veritable multi-party structure of the Dutch democracy, the disappointing empirical results obtained thus far, and the present state of the art in general, it is interesting to apply our own model of state behaviour presented in chapter 4 to the analysis of politico-economic interaction in the Netherlands. However, while we engage in that operation, it is acknowledged at the outset that the empirical work in this chapter can only be of an exploratory and illustrative nature, bearing in mind the simplicity of the model that does not as yet, for example, explicitly deal with public sector decision making on income transfers and the level of budget deficits/surpluses.

The organization of the chapter is as follows. In section 5.2 we discuss the data that will be used, and present the results of a first attempt to estimate behavioural equations for tax receipts and state expenditure. It is concluded that the parameters in these equations have not been constant over time. We then turn to the estimation of - a linearized version of - the equation for the tax rate, while controlling for partisan effects and re-election efforts, which variables, however, do not come out significantly. Given these results we then show how, by using a transformation of the tax rate equation, at least in principle - taking the theory for granted - some information on the preference weights underlying the behavioural equations can be derived. Section 5.3 concludes.

5.2. Data and empirical application

5.2.1. The data

For the application of the model the period 1952-1984 has been chosen. In 1952 the reconstruction period after the war can be considered to be ended, while, moreover, all the data that are required are available on a regular base.

In general, the yearly data are taken from the national accounts, issued by the Dutch Central Bureau of Statistics (CBS).[8] A serious problem is posed by a major revision of the construction of the national accounts in 1977. This revision was carried through for a number of reasons, connected with changes in definitions and methods of registration, changes in estimation methods, and the availability of data from newly established statistical series.[9] According to the CBS, the national accounts data from before and after the revision are not comparable. Fortunately, the CBS has recently published national accounts data for the years 1969-1976 in compliance with the 1977-revision. Thus, we will have two overlapping time series at our disposal; one series for the period 1952-1977, and another (revised) one which can be used for estimation over the period 1970-1984.[10]

Some manipulations with the data have been carried out in order to fit them to the model structure, the most important of which had to do with the relegation of social security to the private sector, and the fact that taxes - or better, all public sector revenues net of transfers - are supposed to be borne by profits. It may be added here that the larger part of Dutch social security benefits are financed via a pay-as-you-go system, and that the general opinion is that taxes and premiums have been largely shifted towards profits in the period under consideration (in particular during the sixties and seventies).[11]

For more details and for the two data sets themselves the reader is referred to the Appendix.

5.2.2. State expenditure and tax receipts

The model that was developed in chapter 4 gives an explanation of public sector behaviour with respect to expenditure, employment and taxation. Building on eqs. (4.3) - (4.12), the analysis ended up with the behavioural equations (4.16) and (4.17). When it comes to an empirical application in order to be fitted in with macroeconomic modelling, the model of public sector behaviour can most readily be summed up in three equations for taxation and the wage and non-wage components of public expenditure. As dependent variables we then get the state wage sum W_s (= $w_s E_s$), non-wage (material) state expenditure G_m, and net (after transfers) state revenues T. From eqs. (4.8) and (4.16) it follows $T = \delta.\Pi$; from eq. (4.17) $W_s = [\delta/\theta(1+\gamma)].\Pi$; and from eq. (4.6) $G_m = \gamma.W_s$. Observe that the power coefficient δ, the material expenditure parameter γ, and the budget deficit parameter θ can be identified from the coefficients of the latter equations.

In line with section 4.4 we impose a particular lag structure on the three equations. The state's decision making on expenditure, employment and taxation is assumed to react with some delay to changes in economic conditions, affecting the taxable base Π; non-wage expenditure will - as material input - be considered to be coupled to the contemporary public sector employment and production levels. Adding error terms, with the assumption that these are independently, normally distributed (ε_{it} ~ $IN(0, \sigma_i^2)$, i = 1,2,3), we obtain regression equations which can be estimated using OLS.[12] Table 5.1 presents the results.

Table 5.1 The model of state behaviour applied to the Netherlands.[a]

1952 - 1977	1970 - 1984 (revised data)
$T = 0.51\ \Pi_{-1}$ $R^2 = 0.994$ $DW = 0.41$ $(62.93)^{**}$	$T = 0.43\ \Pi_{-1}$ $R^2 = 0.989$ $DW = 0.32$ $(35.88)^{**}$
$W_s = 0.30\ \Pi_{-1}$ $R^2 = 0.979$ $DW = 0.18$ $(33.84)^{**}$	$W_s = 0.30\ \Pi_{-1}$ $R^2 = 0.995$ $DW = 0.44$ $(54.35)^{**}$
$G_m = 0.70\ W_s$ $R^2 = 0.983$ $DW = 0.17$ $(38.86)^{**}$	$G_m = 0.65\ W_s$ $R^2 = 0.996$ $DW = 0.37$ $(59.41)^{**}$

a) Yearly data; OLS-estimates. Figures within parentheses denote t-ratios; R^2 denotes the coefficient of determination; DW is the Durbin-Watson statistic. Two asterisks denote in this book a statistical significance level of 1%, one asterisk a level of 5%.

These results look promising. The fit is good, the coefficients seem to be highly significant, and from the equations we can obtain two sets of parameter estimates:

1952-1977: $\delta = 0.51$, $\gamma = 0.70$, $\theta = 1.00$;
1970-1984: $\delta = 0.43$, $\gamma = 0.65$, $\theta = 0.88$.

However, it should be observed that all regressions show a serious measure of autocorrelation, which makes the significance level of the coefficients highly dubious. Of course, one should not really be surprised to run into problems with these regression equations. Yet apart from the potentiality of the occurrence of heteroscedasticity and the omission of variables, the assumption that the model parameters, and more specifically the power coefficient δ, have been constant, can be expected to have been mistaken.[13] The variability of δ could answer for the autocorrelation in the T- and W_s-regressions. The autocorrelation in the G_m-regression can be explained from variations of γ through time, for which in particular the changing ratio of the price level of private sector goods and the state wage rate could be responsible, assuming a more or less technical (production function) relationship between material and labour input in public sector production. For the latter some initial empirical support is given in Van Velthoven, Van Winden and Renaud (1984). As we want to retain a direct tie between our theoretical model and the empirical application, our attention here will be focussed on the power coefficient δ, for which the model - cf. eqs. (4.14) and (4.18) - gives a clear indication of how to explain its development.

5.2.3. The power coefficient δ

According to eqs. (4.14) and (4.18) the power coefficient is composed of the preference weights ε_{kg}, attached to the different interests of the social classes, and the relative strengths λ_k with which the interests of these classes are vested with, and consequently promoted by, the state. To simplify reference, we copy the relevant formula:

$$(5.1) \quad \delta = \frac{(\varepsilon_{12}+\varepsilon_{13})\lambda_1 + \varepsilon_{23}\lambda_2 + \varepsilon_{33}\lambda_3}{(\varepsilon_{12}+\varepsilon_{13})\lambda_1 + \varepsilon_{23}\lambda_2 + (\varepsilon_{31}+\varepsilon_{33})\lambda_3}.$$

Now, although there is no direct evidence for it, it may be plausible to assume that the preference weights have been more or less constant over the period under consideration. As regards the relative influence of the social classes on the behaviour of the state, however, such an assumption seems unwarranted.

(Relative) Influence is the result of pressure originating from within the state organization (internal pressure, by interest blocs such as state departments) and/or from agents in the private sector (external pressure, e.g. by political parties, pressure groups). Some interests may find support in this way from within as well as outside the state sector; think of the interests of state sector workers. A series of factors can be enumerated which may be expected to co-determine the power weights λ_k. We mention: the costs of obtaining and processing information, and of communication; the extent to which members of the different social classes have organized themselves, such as in unions or trade associations, and the character of their mutual relationships; the number of votes at the command of the different social classes; their financial means; the relative scarcity of the various factors of production and the control of the social classes over these production factors.[14] Because of the great complexity involved here - see chapter 2 -, and because of the lack of usable data, it is far beyond the scope of this book to strive for an appropriate modelling and measurement of the importance of these factors vis-à-vis one another. Instead, we must have recourse to proxy variables, which are measurable and related to our distinction between social classes, and give an indication of the relative strength of these social classes.[15]

Now, note that in case of a democracy with a perfect proportional political representation the relative influence of the social classes would be equal to their relative numerical strengths. But it is not to be expected that a real-life parliamentary democracy would function that way; think of the interference of political parties and coalition formation, and the influence of the bureaucracy and pressure groups, discussed above. On the other hand, the process of organization occurs among all the social classes which are actively involved in the production process, such that each of them after all may not have to give in much in terms of influence. For that reason a first, but admittedly deficient, approach would be to consider the <u>relative numerical strength</u> of the economically active social classes as an indicator for λ_k, $k = 1,2,3$. To obtain a measure of the number of private and public sector workers, E_p and E_s, does not pose any problem. Things are different with the number of capital owners, to be indicated with E_c. In the sequel, we shall approximate E_c by the number of self-employed, for which figures are published regularly. Apart from the latter, not unimportant, circumstance, our choice can also be justified by pointing at the fact that the self-employed are for their livelihood almost exclusively dependent on profits, in contrast to the average share-holder or director of a joint-stock company.[16]

A second factor of interest to be used as a proxy variable in the context of our class model would seem to be the tightness of the labour market. To that purpose the total <u>employment rate</u>, EMPR, will be used as an indicator; EMPR = $E/(E + U)$, where $E = E_s + E_p + E_c$, and U stands for the number of unemployed.

Totally differentiating eq. (5.1) with respect to the power distribution λ (cf. eq. (4.19)) yields

$$(5.2) \quad d\delta = \frac{\varepsilon_{31}}{(\delta_1+\delta_2)^2} \cdot [(\varepsilon_{12}+\varepsilon_{13})\lambda_3 \, d\lambda_1 + \varepsilon_{23}\lambda_3 \, d\lambda_2 - ((\varepsilon_{12}+\varepsilon_{13})\lambda_1 + \varepsilon_{23}\lambda_2) \, d\lambda_3] \, .$$

Remembering that $\lambda_1 + \lambda_2 + \lambda_3 = 1$, it follows that:
$d\delta/d\lambda_1 > 0$ when keeping λ_2 constant, while in case λ_3 is constant $d\delta/d\lambda_1 \gtreqless 0$ if $\varepsilon_{12} + \varepsilon_{13} \gtreqless \varepsilon_{23}$;
$d\delta/d\lambda_2 > 0$ when holding λ_1 constant, while in case λ_3 is constant $d\delta/d\lambda_2 \gtreqless 0$ if $\varepsilon_{12} + \varepsilon_{13} \lesseqgtr \varepsilon_{23}$;
$d\delta/d\lambda_3 < 0$, whether λ_1 or λ_2 is held constant.[17]

On account of this result it is expected that, at any rate, δ is inversely related to the relative numerical strength of the class of capital owners, E_c/E. Moreover, as one would expect $\varepsilon_{12} + \varepsilon_{13} > \varepsilon_{23}$ to hold, it is hypothesized that δ is positively related to E_s/E; the sign of the effect of changes in E_p/E seems indeterminate.

What about the impact of EMPR? An increase in the rate of employment might tend to reinforce the position of labour vis-à-vis capital; it might also change the balance of power between private and public sector workers, presumably in favour of the former.[18] But then, it is not a priori clear what the sign of the effect of EMPR on δ will be.

However, the inclusion and the direction of the impact of the EMPR-variable can also be rationalized in a more elaborated manner, by referring to the discussion in chapter 3 of the phenomenon of (anticipated) mobility between social classes.[19] It may be assumed that economic agents perceive a (subjective) probability of becoming unemployed; it seems plausible that these agents will be wise enough to take into account beforehand the position they might get in later. When getting unemployed, they will be interested in transfers (unemployment benefits) as their source of real disposable income, while state expenditure may be extra valued as it may entail specific public provisions for them. If anticipated social mobility really is an issue such that the eventual future position throws its shadow ahead, then - according to the logic of chapter 3 - the elementary interest function P_k which was used in chapter 4 to represent the preferences of the representative member of social class k, should be replaced by a complex interest function, say P_k^c. This function P_k^c would be a weighted representation of the elementary interest function corresponding to the present socio-economic position, P_k (k = 1,2,3), and the elementary interest function corresponding to the position of unemployment, P_4; the weights being given by the (subjective) probabilities of remaining employed, denoted by π_k (k = 1,2,3), and of becoming unemployed, $1 - \pi_k$:

(5.3) $\qquad P_k^c = P_k^{\pi_k} \cdot P_4^{1-\pi_k}$, k = 1,2,3,

$\qquad$ where: $P_k = w_k^{\varepsilon_{k1}} \cdot e_k^{\varepsilon_{k2}} \cdot x_s^{\varepsilon_{k3}}$, k = 1,2,3,4 ,

in accordance with eq. (4.3).[20] Sticking for the moment to the presupposition that social security is a private sector concern (but see chapter 7), w_4 and e_4 can be considered to be exogenous variables as far as state decision making is concerned. Deriving the behavioural equations for the state in this new set-up yields the familiar equations (4.16) - (4.18); the only difference lies in the definition of δ_1, δ_2. For the power coefficient δ it now holds:

(5.4) $\delta = \dfrac{\delta_1}{\delta_1 + \delta_2}$, with

$\delta_1 = [(\varepsilon_{12}+\varepsilon_{13})\pi_1 + \varepsilon_{43}(1-\pi_1)] \lambda_1 + [\varepsilon_{23}\pi_2 + \varepsilon_{43}(1-\pi_2)] \lambda_2$
$\quad\quad + [\varepsilon_{33}\pi_3 + \varepsilon_{43}(1-\pi_3)] \lambda_3$,

$\delta_2 = \varepsilon_{31}\pi_3\lambda_3$.

Let us now hypothesize that the probability π_k of retaining employment for each social class is more or less proportionally related to the total employment rate EMPR; say, $\pi_k = \alpha_k \cdot$ EMPR. Differentiating δ with regard to EMPR then gives:

(5.5) $\dfrac{\partial \delta}{\partial \text{EMPR}} = - \dfrac{\varepsilon_{31}\lambda_3}{(\delta_1+\delta_2)^2} \cdot \alpha_3 \varepsilon_{43}$,

which would lead us to expect a negative impact of EMPR on δ.[21)][22)]

Our own approach to explain the development of the tax rate, through the forces affecting the power coefficient δ, represented by the numerical strength variables and EMPR, can be confronted with other more usual approaches, in which partisan effects and re-election efforts play a role. To that purpose, the variables GVTYP1, GVTYP2 and ELEC have been constructed.

GVTYP1 and GVTYP2 represent the political colour of parliament and cabinet, respectively. The political parties are ordered on a "right"-"left" scale, following the social economic dimension in politics; cf. De Swaan (1973).[23)] GVTYP1, then, equals the sum of the ratings of the political parties weighted by their share of the seats in the Assembly; GVTYP2 equals the sum of the ratings of the parties participating in the cabinet, weighted by the share of each coalition party in the total number of parliamentary seats occupied by the coalition. The more leftist the Assembly or cabinet is, the higher the value of GVTYP1 and GVTYP2, respectively.

ELEC intends to capture possible efforts of the cabinet aimed at stimulating the economy in time before the next general election, in order to enhance the chances of re-election.[24)]

Table 5.2. Estimation results for δ: 1952-1977. [a]

regression number	constant	E_s/E	$(E_c/E)^{-1}$	EMPR	GVTYP1	GVTYP2	ELEC	$\bar{R}^2$	DW
1	1.70 ** (2.99)	-4.02 ** (4.22)	0.084 ** (11.04)	-1.30 ** (2.88)	0.13 (0.41)		-0.002 (0.16)	0.904	2.20
2	2.05 ** (3.93)	-3.82 ** (3.98)	0.081 ** (10.97)	-1.57 ** (3.29)		-0.06 (0.97)	-0.000 (0.04)	0.907	2.03
3	1.21 * (2.60)				-1.41 (1.64)		0.004 (0.14)	0.029	0.24
4	0.46 ** (5.25)					-0.02 (0.12)	0.008 (0.24)	-0.084	0.19
5	1.83 ** (4.02)	-4.03 ** (4.42)	0.083 ** (11.88)	-1.36 ** (3.29)				0.912	2.14
6	2.09 (1.86)			-1.67 (1.46)				0.043	0.21
7	0.35 ** (4.29)	-2.52 * (2.68)	0.076 ** (9.56)					0.874	1.65

a) OLS-estimates; yearly data; $\delta = T/\Pi_{-1}$; E_s/E, $(E_c/E)^{-1}$ and EMPR are lagged one year. Figures within parentheses denote t-ratios; $\bar{R}^2$ denotes the coefficient of determination, adjusted for degrees of freedom; DW is the Durbin-Watson statistic. Two asterisks denote a significance level of 1%, one asterisk a level of 5%.

From the discussion above we can make up regression equations for δ - defined as T/Π_{-1}, in conformity with table 5.1 -, relating it to the relative numerical strength variables E_s/E, E_p/E and E_c/E, and to EMPR, in addition to the alternative explanatory variables GVTYP1, GVTYP2 and ELEC. Because the numerical strength variables sum to one, one of them has to be left out; E_p/E is chosen because its effect is expected to be indeterminate, while furthermore it appears to be highly correlated with the inverse of E_c/E. In the regression equations the numerical strength variables and EMPR will be lagged one year, because of the consideration that pressure has to be built up before it can lead to acknowledged power and vested interests. The results from the regression equations, obtained by OLS, are summarized in table 5.2 (period 1952-1977) and table 5.3 (period 1970-1984; revised data).[25]

Starting with the <u>period 1952-1977</u>, we can first of all point at the insignificant influence of the variables GVTYP1, GVTYP2 and ELEC, both by themselves and in addition to the other variables. This apparent absence of partisan effects and re-election efforts is well in line with our discussion of the multi-party structure of the Dutch democracy in section 5.1. Still, some additional remarks can be made. First, it may be noted that GVTYP1 (indicating the political colour of the Assembly) does not show much variation, which renders it difficult to establish its effect. The fact remains that the dependent variable δ varies between .33 and .55 over the period. In itself, the relative stability of GVTYP1 is of interest, given the dynamic political environment in which the state operated. The type of cabinet variable GVTYP2 shows much more variation. Second, it may be questioned whether any of the GVTYP-variables gives a good indication of the political colour of the government. The ordering of parties along a "right"-"left" scale in fact treats a party as a homogeneous entity; "wings" are neglected. Consequently, larger, or other, differences may be suggested than in fact exist. One should look through the ideological varnish at the social class composition of parties and the associated interest structures. Related to this, the reader is reminded that the Dutch parliamentary seats have predominantly been occupied by people coming from one class, the class of state sector workers.[26]

Next, we turn to the regressions where the alternative explanatory variables GVTYP and ELEC are left out. Regression 5 is very satisfactory as regards the test statistics; the variation in δ explained is substantial, the hypothesis of zero autocorrelation can be maintained. The employment rate has a negative sign, which would be in conformity with eq. (5.5). However, comparing regressions 5, 6 and 7 shows that EMPR does not add much to the variation in δ explained. Thus, the development of δ (and, accordingly, the tax rate) appears to be mainly influenced by the relative numerical strengths of the social classes.

The sign of the highly significant and robust coefficient of E/E_c is in accordance with what we a priori expected.

The negative sign of E_s/E would in terms of our theoretical model demand that $\varepsilon_{12} + \varepsilon_{13} < \varepsilon_{23}$.[27)] Now, although this result may not seem very probable, it is not impossible. After all, the Parkinsonian bureaucrat (who presumably would reveal a high value of ε_{12}) is probably working on a lower echelon, and thereby a less powerful and less representative state sector worker, than the politicians and top bureaucrats who are in a position to determine the amount and the incidence of the tax burden. See on the issue of contrasting interests and objectives between the top officials and the bottom ranks of a bureau also Dunleavy (1985). In this context it is of further interest to note that Aberbach and Rockmann's (1976) positive agency effect on political attitudes of public sector workers (cf. section 2.5.2) need not extend beyond the employees' own agency. The survey results of Courant c.s. (1980) show that the social group most concerned about public expenditure in the state of Michigan is that of the state and local government employees; but least concerned of all social groups are the federal government employees. For the category of public sector workers as a whole it need no longer be obvious then how their relative preference for public provisions compares to that of, e.g., private sector workers. Preliminary Dutch survey findings reported in Pommer c.s. (1987), indeed, suggest that public sector workers might have a (slightly) lower relative preference for public provisions than private sector workers. Returning to the regression results, finally notice that the value of the coefficient of E_s/E is less robust than the coefficient of E/E_c.

Concluding, the empirical results reported in table 5.2 are in conformity with the model presented above. The results suggest that the development of the numerical strength of the class of capitalists (more precisely, the self-employed) has had a major impact on δ.

Table 5.3. Estimation results for δ: 1970-1984.[a]

regression number	constant	E_s/E	$(E_c/E)^{-1}$	EMPR	GVTYP1	GVTYP2	ELEC	$\bar{R}^2$	DW
8	-0.63 (0.53)	-0.79 (0.14)	0.023 (0.29)	0.30 (0.29)	1.43 * (2.84)		0.013 (0.95)	0.774	1.49
9	-0.36 (0.24)	-0.65 (0.09)	0.018 (0.18)	0.77 (0.60)		0.009 (1.28)	0.011 (0.67)	0.637	1.41
10	-0.58 ** (3.87)				1.96 ** (6.87)		0.016 (1.25)	0.780	1.29
11	0.36 ** (7.45)					0.18 (1.85)	0.026 (1.07)	0.157	0.71
12	-0.45 (0.30)	-0.21 (0.03)	0.009 (0.09)	0.92 (0.72)				0.638	1.22
13	-0.40 * (2.68)			0.90 ** (5.69)				0.691	1.20
14	0.64 ** (6.39)	-5.20 ** (3.72)	0.076 (2.11)					0.652	1.01

a) Cf. footnote table 5.2.

Table 5.3 presents the same regression runs as table 5.2, based on the (revised) data for the period 1970-1984. A marked difference with the previous results leaps to the eye; the best job of explaining δ is not done by regression 12. It must immediately be added that there is a serious amount of multicollinearity between E_s/E, E/E_c and EMPR (the simple correlation coefficients between E_s/E and E/E_c and between E_s/E and EMPR both are equal to 0.93), which renders it difficult to establish the precise impact of these variables separately. While regression 14 shows (again) that the numerical strength variables can explain a considerable part of the variation in δ, this apparently is not the whole story, given the relatively low $\bar{R}^2$-value and the DW-statistic in the inconclusive region. EMPR by itself seems to do a better job, but the large positive coefficient cannot easily be fitted in with the theory; here, too, the $\bar{R}^2$- and DW-values are rather low. Interestingly enough, the most important contribution to the explanation of δ is given by GVTYP1 (cf. regressions 8 and 10), while at the same time GVTYP2 and ELEC obtain (once again) insignificant coefficients. Thus, while the political colour or re-election efforts of the cabinet do not seem to have affected economic policy making, the colour of parliament does; the more leftist the composition of the Assembly, the higher δ. Remember that GVTYP1 has been calculated using an ordering of the political parties according to their preference for government intervention, weighted by their relative numerical strength (share of votes in the Assembly); further it has been noted that the Dutch electoral system is marked by proportional representation, and that a clear association exists between the voting behaviour of the electorate and socio-economic background. One could well argue then that the findings do not contradict the theoretical model, as the value of GVTYP1 - contrary, for instance, to GVTYP2 - can be interpreted to be another operational summary measure of the power structure λ of society. But, even if the results might not contradict the theory, they do not as yet provide it with great empirical support either, given the fact that the performance of the relative numerical strength variables E_s/E and E/E_c and GVTYP1 and EMPR differs between the two data sets and periods considered.

Table 5.4. Estimation results for δ: 1952-1984.[a]

regression number	constant	E_s/E	$(E_c/E)^{-1}$	EMPR	GVTYP1	GVTYP2	ELEC	dummy	$\bar{R}^2$	DW
15	0.40 (1.02)	-4.71 ** (4.57)	0.076 ** (6.72)	-0.03 (0.10)	0.41 (1.18)		0.001 (0.06)	-0.02 (1.09)	0.761	1.85
16	0.56 (1.51)	-4.76 ** (4.55)	0.072 ** (6.75)	0.04 (0.15)		0.04 (0.72)	-0.000 (0.01)	-0.01 (0.77)	0.753	1.86
17	0.21 (0.86)				0.37 (0.81)		0.008 (0.41)	0.04 * (2.42)	0.093	0.55
18	0.41 ** (8.55)					0.01 (0.13)	0.009 (0.44)	0.04 * (2.27)	0.073	0.52
19	0.58 (1.62)	-4.78 ** (4.71)	0.070 ** (6.98)	0.05 (0.19)				-0.01 (0.58)	0.766	1.75
20	-0.50 * (2.14)			0.93 ** (3.91)				0.07 ** (4.66)	0.401	0.96
21	0.65 ** (13.55)	-4.94 ** (9.03)	0.071 ** (8.26)					-0.01 (0.62)	0.774	1.74

a) Cf. footnote table 5.2. Dummy = 0, 1952-1969; = 1, 1970-1984.

It then remains of interest to see how our model holds if it is applied to the prolonged 1952-1984 period. To that purpose the 1952-1969 data of the first data set are coupled to the 1970-1984 data of the second. A dummy variable is added to control for the various discontinuities in the data.[28] Table 5.4 presents the estimation results.

Regressions 15 - 18 point out that the (alternative) variables GVTYP1, GVTYP2 and ELEC do not obtain significant coefficients, either by themselves or in combination with the other variables; they can be dispensed with. Further, it appears from regressions 19 - 21 that the employment rate for the period as a whole does not really contribute to the explanation of the variation in δ. The performance of EMPR on its own must be judged to be unsatisfactory, both for statistical (DW, $\bar{R}^2$) and theoretical (the large, positive coefficient) reasons; in addition to the relative numerical strength variables, EMPR is insignificant. The best result, then, is yielded by regression 21. The DW-statistic shows that the hypothesis of zero autocorrelation can be maintained. All coefficients are highly significant, and have the same signs as found in table 5.2. The dummy variable indicates that the discontinuities in the various data series are without consequence; they presumably cancel out.

Summarizing the results of tables 5.2 - 5.4: the relative numerical strength variables E_s/E and E/E_c were the only variables generally found to be successful in the explanation of δ. EMPR made a small additional contribution in the 1952-1977 period. In the 1970-1984 period GVTYP1 had considerable explanatory power; the multicollinearity between E_s/E, E/E_c and EMPR, however, obscured the picture in this case. For the period as a whole the relative numerical strength variables may be deemed to have performed their task as proxy for the power weights λ rather satisfactorily.[29]

At this point it may be observed that the empirical results, while being a useful start for further research in this direction, still remain somewhat meagre. This is especially true of the second subperiod considered, judged by the variance being explained and the signs of some of the relevant explanatory variables (E_s/E, EMPR). Several reasons can be advanced for that finding. Firstly, the coverage and outlays of the social security system have grown drastically since WW II, in particular also during the second of the two periods under consideration (cf. table 0.1). The rapid growth of transfer payments may well have had negative consequences for other components of public sector spending, which effect, however, has not been taken along in the present model specification. Secondly, the economic downturn in the second half of the seventies and the early eighties may have led to a changing attitude towards budget deficits. Stated otherwise, θ may not have been a constant parameter (see also the estimates of θ in section 5.2.2); we will return to this issue in chapter 8. Thirdly, the degree of tax shifting may have changed over the period considered, in response to, e.g., the alternation of excess supply and demand in the labour market. From the mid seventies, and especially since 1980, the Dutch economy has been confronted with high unemployment figures; the degree of tax shifting on to profits may well have diminished by that. Notice that this latter development might help explain the positive coefficient of EMPR in the second subperiod, for it has been observed in chapter 4 that the tax rate will be lower in case of an income tax system without shifting than in case of a profit tax, ceteris paribus. Fourthly, the preference weights ε may have changed over the thirty year period considered here; to mention just one aspect, the preference for privately vs. publicly provided goods and services may have been sensitive to the average income growth since WW II. Finally, the variables which were inserted in the regression runs did only serve as proxies for the power distribution λ; it can not be claimed that they are perfect substitutes. These considerations taken together indicate that the empirical results of this chapter, interesting as they may be, can only have a preliminary and exploratory character, as emphasized in the introduction.

5.2.4. The power coefficient δ; a transformation

The linear tax rate equation of the previous subsection was most useful when it came to the insertion of alternative explanatory variables. However, it must be noted that such a linear equation is not quite conform the equation for δ that was deduced from the model; cf. eq. (5.1). Given the conclusions above that the relative numerical strength variables perform rather satisfactorily as proxies for λ, while the other explanatory variables were not found to play a consistent, significant role, and bearing in mind the exploratory nature of our empirical application, we now wish to employ the model equation for δ in its original form. This may, moreover, permit us to disentangle information on the preference weights ε from the coefficient estimates.

First, notice that eq. (5.1) for δ can readily be transscribed into:

$$(5.6) \qquad \frac{\delta}{1-\delta} = \frac{\varepsilon_{33}}{\varepsilon_{31}} + \frac{\varepsilon_{12}+\varepsilon_{13}}{\varepsilon_{31}} \cdot \frac{\lambda_1}{\lambda_3} + \frac{\varepsilon_{23}}{\varepsilon_{31}} \cdot \frac{\lambda_2}{\lambda_3} .$$

Next, substitute for λ_1, λ_2, λ_3 the relative numerical strengths of the relevant social classes. Assuming further that the preference weights ε can be treated as parameters, the estimation of equation (5.6) does not pose any specific problems. Clearly, from the coefficient estimates of eq. (5.6) we can - at least in principle - derive direct information on the preference weights of the social classes.

Table 5.5 presents the estimation results, for the periods 1952-1977, 1970-1984 and 1952-1984.[30] For each case six regression runs have been undertaken. First, eq. (5.6) is estimated in its regular form; the lagged dependent variable is added to allow for partial adjustment processes with respect to δ and the tax rate.[31] Next, we want to investigate the hypothesis that the preference weights are more or less equal among the social classes. Assuming that the relative preference for publicly provided goods and services is equal for all social classes, i.e. $\varepsilon_{13} = \varepsilon_{23} = \varepsilon_{33} = \varepsilon_{.3}$, eq. (5.6) boils down to

$$(5.7) \qquad \frac{\delta}{1-\delta} = \frac{\varepsilon_{12}}{\varepsilon_{31}} \cdot \frac{\lambda_1}{\lambda_3} + \frac{\varepsilon_{.3}}{\varepsilon_{31}} \cdot \frac{1}{\lambda_3} .$$

The corresponding estimation results are given in the third and fourth row for each period. Rows five and six report the results if it may be assumed in addition that $\varepsilon_{12} = 0$, or, alternatively, if it is assumed that $\varepsilon_{23} = \varepsilon_{33} = \varepsilon_{12} + \varepsilon_{13} = \varepsilon_{.3}$, such that

$$(5.8) \qquad \frac{\delta}{1-\delta} = \frac{\varepsilon_{.3}}{\varepsilon_{31}} \cdot \frac{1}{\lambda_3} .$$

Table 5.5. Estimation results for $\delta/(1-\delta)$.[a]

number	constant	E_s/E_c	E_p/E_c	$E/E_{\bar{c}}$	dummy	$[\delta/(1-\delta)]_{-1}$	$\bar{R}^2$ (RMSE)	DW (Durbin's h)
1952-1977								
22	-0.07 (1.02)	-0.07 (0.16)	0.26** (3.07)				0.874 (0.076)	1.31
23	-0.06 (0.91)	-0.23 (0.51)	0.22* (2.57)			0.29 (1.56)	0.882 (0.073)	2.21 (-2.04)
24		0.70 (1.76)		0.07 (1.53)			0.991 (0.084)	1.14
25		0.34 (0.81)		0.06 (1.24)		0.39 (1.98)	0.992 (0.079)	1.96 (-0.65)
26				0.16** (49.04)			0.990 (0.089)	1.06
27				0.09** (3.22)		0.46* (2.62)	0.992 (0.079)	2.00 (-0.26)
1970-1984								
28	0.21 (0.41)	-1.63** (4.58)	0.44* (2.67)				0.765 (0.066)	1.11
29	0.28 (0.53)	-1.22* (2.38)	0.30 (1.47)			0.27 (1.11)	0.770 (0.065)	1.89 (0.35)
30		-1.91** (9.56)	0.39** (13.56)				0.995 (0.064)	1.06
31		-1.50** (3.82)	0.30** (3.71)			0.27 (1.22)	0.995 (0.062)	1.89 (0.27)
32				0.12** (18.28)			0.960 (0.174)	0.25
33				-0.00 (0.22)		1.02** (6.21)	0.989 (0.91)	1.78 (0.01)

number	constant	E_s/E_c	E_p/E_c	$E/E_{\tilde{c}}$	dummy	$[\delta/(1-\delta)]_{-1}$	$\bar{R}^2$ (RMSE)	DW (Durbin's h)
1952-1984								
34	0.18 * (2.34)	-1.65 ** (9.68)	0.45 ** (11.14)		0.00 (0.01)		0.820 (0.063)	1.71
35	0.13 (1.55)	-1.33 ** (5.12)	0.36 ** (5.08)		-0.00 (0.03)	0.25 (1.58)	0.829 (0.061)	2.14 (-0.97)
36		-1.83 ** (9.70)		0.37 ** (16.26)	0.07 (1.69)		0.993 (0.068)	1.51
37		-1.34 ** (4.47)		0.26 ** (4.61)	0.06 (1.35)	0.32 (2.01)	0.994 (0.065)	1.93 (0.45)
38				0.15 ** (23.13)	-0.25 ** (4.14)		0.970 (0.138)	0.39
39				0.02 (0.90)	-0.05 (1.23)	0.91 ** (7.29)	0.989 (0.083)	2.01 (-0.10)

a) For general comments, see footnote table 5.2. E_s/E_c, E_p/E_c and $E/E_{\tilde{c}}$ are lagged one year. Part of the regressions does not contain a constant term; for those cases $\bar{R}^2$ has been recalculated as $1-\Sigma e_t^2/\Sigma y_t^2$. To enable a comparison of the goodness of fit between the equations with and without constant term, the value of the root mean square error (RMSE) has been added between brackets.
Part of the regressions contains the lagged endogenous variable. To test for autocorrelation in these cases the value of Durbin's h-statistic has been added between brackets.

Statistically, the findings with regard to eq. (5.6) are quite satisfactory (cf. regressions 22, 28, 34). The fit is reasonably good; the hypothesis of zero autocorrelation is not rejected (although, the DW-value lies within the inconclusive region in case of regressions 22 and 28); most coefficients are significantly different from zero. The regressions 23, 29 and 35 show that the addition of the lagged dependent variable hardly means an improvement. The coefficient of the lagged dependent variable is reported to be insignificant; even if we take it at its face value, the implied lag in the adjustment process with regard to δ is very short.

Now, let us turn to the interpretation of the coefficient estimates in terms of the preference weights ε. For the period <u>1952-1977</u>, the intercept term and the coefficient of E_s/E_c - which according to eq. (5.6) correspond to $\varepsilon_{33}/\varepsilon_{31}$ and $(\varepsilon_{12}+\varepsilon_{13})/\varepsilon_{31}$, and thus should be non-negative - are reported to be negative, albeit insignificantly. It should immediately be added that due to multicollinearity - the correlation between E_s/E_c and E_p/E_c is very high (0.977) - it is not well possible to obtain accurate coefficient estimates; omitting the variables E_s/E_c and E_p/E_c one at a time results in a (highly) significant positive coefficient for the remaining variable, while the goodness of fit remains more or less the same. The equality restriction on the preference weights, hypothesized in eq. (5.7), appears to perform quite well. As in regression 24 autocorrelation is on the verge of being accepted, we shall restrict our attention to regression 25. From the comparison of regressions 23 and 25 it appears that the hypothesized equality of the preference weights ($\varepsilon_{13} = \varepsilon_{23} = \varepsilon_{33}$) cannot be rejected. Notice further that the identification of the coefficients in regression 25 is once again hampered by multicollinearity. Notwithstanding, we are tempted to conclude that ε_{12} is not significantly different from zero.[32] Omitting E_s/E_c produces the very nice regression 27. Here, the lagged dependent variable has a coefficient which is significantly different from zero, but still implies a reasonably short adjustment lag. Now, if we are prepared to take one further step and assume that the distribution of the preference weights is fully identical over all social classes, i.e. $\varepsilon_{kg} = \varepsilon_{.g}$ ∀k, g = 1,2,3, then the latter findings would imply: $\varepsilon_{.1} = 0.86$, $\varepsilon_{.2} = 0$, $\varepsilon_{.3} = 0.14$.[33] Thus, it is suggested that the relative preference weight for real disposable income far exceeds the preference for publicly supplied goods and services; the preference weight attached to the numerical strength of the own social group might even be equal to zero (cf. the discussion at eq. (3.1) in chapter 3). Of course, the preference weights that are derived in this manner, should be interpreted with great caution; the result only holds true if the theory can be taken for granted and if the relative numerical strength variables would exactly correspond with the power weights λ.[34]

Turning to the results for <u>1970-1984</u> and for the <u>1952-1984</u> period as a whole, it appears that here too the hypothesis of equal preference weights ε_{13}, ε_{23}, ε_{33} cannot be rejected. On the other hand, it is clear that ε_{12} - more precisely, the coefficient of E_s/E_c in regressions 31 and 37 - is significantly different from zero. More fundamental is the problem that for both observation periods 1970-1984 and 1952-1984 the coefficient of the E_s/E_c-variable is consistently reported to be negative, contrary to what should be expected according to eqs. (5.6) and (5.7). Omitting the E_s/E_c-variable on this theoretical ground, however, does not help, as can be seen from regressions 32/33 and 38/39 which must be deemed quite unsatisfactory. It will be clear that in this situation no useful information on the preference weights ε can be extracted from the coefficient estimates.

Summarizing: eq. (5.6) with the relative numerical strengths of the social classes substituted for the power weights λ, performs quite well statistically. The hypothesis that the relative preference for publicly supplied goods and services is equal for all social classes, could not be rejected by the data. For the first subperiod 1952-1977 the suggestion could be deduced that the relative preference weight for real disposable income far exceeds that attached to public expenditure; the preference weight attached to the numerical strength of the own social class might even be zero. However, the estimation on 1970-1984 data and on data for the prolonged period 1952-1984 does not yield further support for the latter suggestions. Stated more sharply, one could even wonder whether the results - interesting and useful as they are, in view of the performance of the relative numerical strength variables - may be considered to be in line with the theoretical model, given the generally negative sign of E_s.[35] There is no need to reiterate here the reasons that were advanced in the previous subsection as an explanation for defective results in general, and for the second subperiod in particular. Suffice it to stress once again that the empirical application in this chapter necessarily has a preliminary character.

5.3. Conclusions

In this chapter we applied the model of state behaviour that was developed in chapter 4, to Dutch data for the period 1952-1984. Starting with the estimation of behavioural equations for tax receipts and state expenditure, it appeared that the parameters δ, θ and γ cannot be considered to have been constant over time. This result did not really come as a surprise, as according to the model changes in the social power structure λ will lead to changes in the power coefficient δ. Therefore, we turned to the estimation of separate regression equations for this power coefficient δ (and, accordingly, the tax rate τ). The development of the relative numerical strengths of the social classes, and especially that of the capitalist/self-employed, appeared to contribute significantly and substantially to the explanation of the development of δ through time. Furthermore, no indication could be found that the party composition of the cabinet as such influences economic policy making, nor that cabinets try to engineer re-election efforts. Similar findings for the US interbellum period are reported in Van Velthoven and Van Winden (1984).

At several instances we have stressed the exploratory nature of the empirical application in the present chapter; we need not go into that here any further. The reader is referred to chapters 7 and 8, which will be devoted to the study of public sector decision making with respect to social security and the budget discipline.

First, however, we shall investigate in chapter 6 what are the consequences for the dynamic (in)stability of the model, if the power weights λ could indeed be approximated by the relative numerical strengths of the social classes.

CHAPTER 5, APPENDIX   MORE ON THE DATA

Definitions

G_m: material (non-wage) expenditure of the public sector, both for consumption and investment; billions of guilders.

W_s: public sector wage sum; billions of guilders.

Π: private sector profit income; billions of guilders.

T: net tax receipts; billions of guilders.

E_s: public sector labour input; thousands of manyears.

E_p: private sector labour input; thousands of manyears.

E_c: number of self-employed; thousands of manyears.

U: number of unemployed; thousands of persons.

GVTYP1: political colour of the Assembly on a [0,1]-scale; the more leftist, the higher the rating.

GVTYP2: political colour of the cabinet on a [0,1]-scale; the more leftist, the higher the rating.

ELEC: dummy-variable; = 1, in years before (expected) general elections are held, and only if the cabinet has been long enough in power to have had the opportunity to engineer re-election efforts; = 0, otherwise.

Sources and procedures

- G_m, E_s, E_p, and E_c can be drawn directly from the National Accounts.
- Unemployment figures were taken from the Central Economic Plans, issued by the Central Planning Bureau.
- GVTYP1, GVTYP2 were calculated as indicated in the text. If the composition of parliament (or of the cabinet) changed in the course of a year, GVTYP1 (GVTYP2) for that year was calculated by weighing with the number of months parliament (the cabinet) had a particular composition and the concomitant political colour. ELEC was calculated in accordance with the definition given above. The required political data (election dates, election outcomes, the composition of coalition cabinets) were obtained from Parlement en Kiezer (1986).
- Given the structure of the model, the wage sum W_s should be net of contributions for the public production of goods and services, but inclusive of social security premiums and benefits, as the social security system is in our yet simple model considered to be part of the private sector (but see chapter 7). For that reason, we established the sum of direct taxes and social security premiums, net of social security benefits and income transfers from the government, in so far as pertaining to wage income. This (small) amount can be considered to be the contribution of wage income to the public production of goods and services. Given the model assumption that the whole tax burden is borne by profits, the said amount was deducted, proportionally, from the published public and private sector wage sums to obtain our (net) wage sums W_s and W_p, and was imputed to profits and profit taxes, in so far as relevant. Thus, Π was set equal to (gross) private sector production minus W_p.
- T, as indicated in the text, was defined as public sector revenues net of transfers. It was calculated as the sum of: indirect taxes minus subsidies; direct taxes paid by firms; direct taxes, net of transfers, pertaining to non-wage income of households; the (imputed) contribution of private sector wage income to public production, discussed above; and net profit and interest payments from the private to the public sector, vice versa. The data for the compilation of W_s, Π and T were taken from the National Accounts and the Central Economic Plans.

Data sets

Table A.1 (1951) 1952-1977.

Year	G_m	W_s	Π	T	E_s
1951	1.68	1.75	12.26	4.60	376
52	1.89	1.81	12.77	5.07	404
53	2.41	1.94	13.58	4.99	433
54	2.47	2.26	14.93	5.13	461
55	2.76	2.47	16.46	5.56	469
56	3.19	2.74	17.50	6.11	476
57	3.45	3.02	18.77	6.80	481
58	3.06	3.24	18.20	6.20	482
59	3.14	3.33	19.91	7.10	484
60	3.55	3.65	22.42	8.11	490
61	3.91	3.97	23.04	9.04	497
62	4.33	4.55	24.11	9.26	505
63	5.09	5.12	25.32	9.72	509
64	5.82	6.24	29.89	11.81	512
65	6.17	7.17	32.85	13.92	516
66	6.67	8.17	34.48	14.76	528
67	7.53	9.16	38.03	15.87	537
68	8.51	9.96	42.59	18.59	544
69	9.19	11.36	47.34	20.56	558
70	10.69	12.71	52.44	23.23	567
71	12.26	14.84	58.63	27.75	584
72	12.54	17.30	66.73	31.34	601
73	13.02	19.32	77.25	35.06	607
74	15.06	22.60	85.18	39.17	617
75	18.09	27.23	87.56	43.12	630
76	20.37	30.88	104.22	48.32	650
1977	21.12	34.27	112.08	53.98	668

Table A.1 (continued)

E_p	E_c	U	GVTYP1	GVTYP2	ELEC
2395	1016	93	0.563	0.528	1
2364	1003	140	0.560	0.537	0
2416	991	108	0.556	0.563	0
2503	980	77	0.556	0.563	0
2581	966	54	0.556	0.563	1
2649	953	41	0.556	0.564	0
2686	933	53	0.556	0.569	0
2663	917	100	0.556	0.569	0
2715	905	78	0.528	0.449	0
2806	886	50	0.519	0.427	0
2872	874	37	0.519	0.427	0
2960	863	35	0.519	0.427	1
3027	851	35	0.533	0.430	0
3111	841	32	0.543	0.434	0
3160	826	36	0.543	0.532	0
3194	815	46	0.543	0.581	1
3181	805	87	0.525	0.451	0
3231	790	80	0.521	0.427	0
3307	776	62	0.521	0.427	0
3366	763	55	0.521	0.427	1
3388	752	69	0.529	0.420	0
3341	741	115	0.534	0.415	0
3351	727	117	0.545	0.535	0
3355	715	143	0.545	0.616	0
3326	700	206	0.545	0.616	0
3315	684	224	0.545	0.616	1
3328	663	218	0.529	0.616	0

Table A.2 (1969) 1970-1984, revised series.

Year	G_m	W_s	Π	T	E_s
1969	9.28	11.39	52.07	20.44	565
70	10.82	12.73	57.50	23.12	572
71	12.67	14.88	63.67	27.67	589
72	12.74	17.33	72.32	31.22	606
73	13.15	19.40	82.91	34.96	612
74	15.00	22.74	91.88	39.00	624
75	18.01	27.48	94.78	42.67	637
76	20.27	31.28	111.97	47.83	658
77	21.16	34.73	120.98	53.39	676
78	23.11	38.03	129.50	54.93	690
79	24.99	40.72	135.82	57.60	703
80	27.15	42.74	145.32	63.43	714
81	28.83	44.62	154.32	64.17	728
82	29.02	46.76	163.21	59.63	734
83	30.27	46.47	172.67	60.82	733
1984	31.19	46.02	188.71	64.41	727

E_p	E_c	U	GVTYP1	GVTYP2	ELEC
3342	750	73	0.521	0.427	0
3400	737	69	0.521	0.427	1
3417	726	91	0.529	0.420	0
3368	716	145	0.534	0.415	0
3379	702	151	0.545	0.535	0
3386	691	181	0.545	0.616	0
3357	676	260	0.545	0.616	0
3350	661	278	0.545	0.616	1
3364	640	271	0.529	0.616	0
3392	631	273	0.517	0.382	0
3443	627	281	0.517	0.382	0
3468	625	325	0.517	0.382	1
3389	619	480	0.516	0.434	0
3274	611	655	0.509	0.533	0
3186	606	800	0.489	0.359	0
3169	605	822	0.489	0.359	0

CHAPTER 6. A DYNAMIC VERSION OF THE MODEL WITH AN ENDOGENOUS SOCIAL POWER STRUCTURE

6.1. Introduction[1)]

In chapter 4 we presented a politico-economic model, which was built up from an elementary Keynesian income - expenditure model. Analyzing the public sector decision making process with the help of the interest function approach, we obtained behavioural equations for state expenditure, state employment, and the tax rate. These behavioural equations had an important role reserved for the so-called power coefficient δ, which represents the effective interest structure of society, i.e. the preferences of the various social classes for publicly vs privately supplied goods and services (ε_{kg}), weighted by the relative influence of these social classes on state behaviour (λ_k). While in chapter 4 the preferences of the social classes and the power structure of society were taken to be given and fixed, it seems particularly unwarranted to assume that the power distribution will indeed remain unchanged over time. The empirical application in chapter 5 was suggestive in this respect. Several factors were enumerated which may be expected to co-determine the relative influence of the social classes, such as their degree of organization, their financial means, their control over and the relative scarcity of the different factors of production. In chapter 2 - especially section 2.6 - we saw that it is quite a problem to arrive at an appropriate measurement and modelling of such factors. To circumvent this problem, we introduced a first, tentative approach in the previous chapter by considering the relative numerical strengths of the (economically active) social classes as an indicator for the power weights λ_k. The empirical application on Dutch data (1952-1984), indeed, provided some support for this approach. Additional support can be found in Renaud and Van Winden (1987a), studying the Netherlands for the prolonged period 1921-1985, and in Van Velthoven and Van Winden (1984), for the US interbellum period; see also Renaud, Van Velthoven and Van Winden (1986).

Once it is accepted that the power weights λ_k are determined by - or vary in proportion with - the relative numerical strength of the social classes, this process can be included in our politico-economic model as it was developed and analyzed in chapter 4. This addition will turn the model into a fully dynamic, and closed, politico-economic model. The dynamics of this enlarged model will be the subject matter of the present chapter. Section 6.2 contains a general analysis of the model dynamics, centered around the power coefficient δ. Section 6.3 will address a special case, which enables us to present a somewhat more detailed account of the dynamical processes with regard to state sector employment. Section 6.4 concludes.

6.2. <u>General dynamics</u>

Point of departure for our analysis will be the model presented in section 4.3, given by eqs. (4.21) - (4.29), which describes the decision making process in the private and public sectors of the economy with respect to production, distribution and spending, <u>given</u> the power structure λ_k, k = 1,2,3. The dynamic characteristics of this politico-economic model were studied in section 4.4; for stability it proved to be necessary - and in many cases sufficient - that the multiplier m of the model is positive (cf. eq. (4.30)). Let us assume that this model indeed is stable, and that the adjustment to its equilibrium position is fast, relative to the speed of adjustment in the political domain with regard to the distribution of power across the social classes. It takes time for pressure groups to develop, for pressure to be built up, for interests to become vested. Think also of the relatively large intervals between general elections. In line with chapter 5 it will be assumed that the power structure of society is related to the relative numerical strengths of the social classes.

Figure 6.1 portrays the dynamic structure for the enlarged politico-economic model with endogenous power weights λ_k. The index t refers to the length of time it takes the politico-economic system to attain equilibrium, <u>given</u> a certain effective interest structure, summarized by the power coefficient δ. The operating of the system may lead to changes in the level and composition of employment, and, consequently, in the relative numerical strengths of the social classes. This, in its turn, would lead to changes in the power weights λ_k, and in the power coefficient δ. And so on. Note that the number of capital owners E_c is supposed to be constant; our simple Keynesian income-expenditure model does not give us any hold for modelling the development of E_c over time.

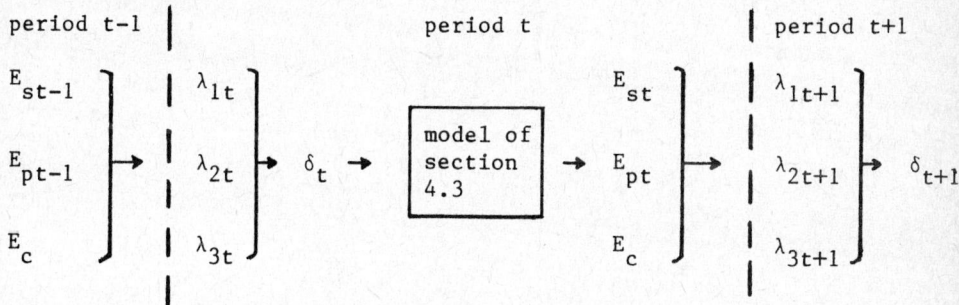

Figure 6.1. The dynamic structure of the model with endogenous power weights λ_k.

The dynamic model of figure 6.1 can be formalized in the following equations (cf. eq. (4.29) for δ, eq. (4.27) for E_s, eqs. (4.25) and (4.30) for E_p):

$$(6.1) \quad \delta_t = \frac{(1-\varepsilon_{11})\lambda_{1t} + \varepsilon_{23}\lambda_{2t} + \varepsilon_{33}\lambda_{3t}}{(1-\varepsilon_{11})\lambda_{1t} + \varepsilon_{23}\lambda_{2t} + (\varepsilon_{31}+\varepsilon_{33})\lambda_{3t}} ,$$

$$(6.2) \quad E_{st} = \delta_t \cdot \frac{\alpha_p^{-w_p}}{\theta(1+\gamma)w_s} \cdot E_{pt} ,$$

$$(6.3) \quad E_{pt} = \frac{1}{\alpha_p} \cdot m_t \cdot (C_o+I_o), \text{ with}$$

$$m_t = [1 - \frac{c_1+\gamma}{\theta(1+\gamma)} \cdot \delta_t(1-\frac{w_p}{\alpha_p}) - c_1\frac{w_p}{\alpha_p} - c_2(1-\delta_t)(1-\frac{w_p}{\alpha_p})]^{-1} ,$$

$$(6.4) \quad \lambda_{kt+1} = \frac{E_{kt}}{\Sigma E_{kt}} , \quad k = 1,2,3 .$$

The model, of course, easily lends itself to the employment of computer simulation techniques.[2] In order to describe the dynamic characteristics of the model in general terms, however, we set out to study its functioning by analytical methods.

Due to the recursive structure, the model can be solved into a first-order non-linear difference equation in δ. Introducing for convenience some additional notation, we obtain:

$$(6.5) \quad \delta_t = \frac{\delta_{t-1}[(1-\varepsilon_{11})a_1 - \varepsilon_{33}E_c(a_3-a_2)] + \varepsilon_{33}E_c a_3 + \varepsilon_{23}a_4}{\delta_{t-1}[(1-\varepsilon_{11})a_1 - (\varepsilon_{31}+\varepsilon_{33})E_c(a_3-a_2)] + (\varepsilon_{31}+\varepsilon_{33})E_c a_3 + \varepsilon_{23}a_4},$$

where:
$$a_1 = \frac{(\alpha_p - w_p)}{\theta(1+\gamma)w_s}(C_o + I_o),$$

$$a_2 = \alpha_p - c_1 w_p - \frac{c_1 + \gamma}{\theta(1+\gamma)}(\alpha_p - w_p),$$

$$a_3 = \alpha_p - c_1 w_p - c_2(\alpha_p - w_p),$$

$$a_4 = C_o + I_o.$$

Assuming, as in chapter 4, that $\alpha_p > w_p > 0$, $0 < c_2 \leq c_1 < 1$, $C_o + I_o > 0$, $w_s > 0$, $\gamma > 0$, and $\theta > 0$, it immediately follows:

$$(6.6) \quad \begin{array}{l} a_1 > 0,\ a_3 > 0,\ a_4 > 0, \\[4pt] a_2 \gtreqless 0 \text{ if } \theta \gtreqless \dfrac{(c_1+\gamma)(\alpha_p-w_p)}{(1+\gamma)(\alpha_p - c_1 w_p)}, \end{array}$$

with the latter expression being < 1.

Computing from eq. (6.5) the <u>long-run equilibrium solution</u>, defined by $\delta_t = \delta_{t-1} = \delta^*$, yields a quadratic equation in δ^*. Apart from some special cases ($\varepsilon_{31} = 0$, in which case $\delta^* = 1$; or $\varepsilon_{23} = \varepsilon_{33} = 0$, cf. section 6.3), no nice looking and easily tractable equilibrium solution is obtained, due to the many parameters involved. More specifically, the two roots of the quadratic equation in δ^* are given by:

$$(6.7) \quad \frac{(a_5 - a_6) \pm \sqrt{(a_5+a_6)^2 + 4\varepsilon_{31}E_c a_2 a_6}}{2[a_5 + \varepsilon_{31}E_c a_2]},$$

where: $a_5 = (1-\varepsilon_{11})a_1 + \varepsilon_{33}E_c a_2 - (\varepsilon_{31}+\varepsilon_{33})E_c a_3$,

$a_6 = \varepsilon_{23}a_4 + \varepsilon_{33}E_c a_3$, > 0 .

If the discriminant $D = (a_5+a_6)^2 + 4\varepsilon_{31}E_c a_2 a_6$ is negative, no long-run equilibrium solution appears to exist; for this case to occur it is necessary (but not sufficient) that $a_2 < 0$. Let us for the sequel assume that the discriminant D is positive, such that expression (6.7) does give us two distinct real roots; δ_-^* will denote the root corresponding with the minus-sign between the terms in the numerator of (6.7), δ_+^* the other one. For either of these roots to be a potential long-run equilibrium solution it should lie within the [0,1]-interval. Analysis of the corresponding phase-diagrams[3] then can bring clarity on the dynamic stability of these (potential) equilibrium points. We do not want to bore the reader with the ensuing, very tedious, but quite straightforward derivations; we content ourselves with the presentation of the results in the form of two (sets of) figures.

From the phase-diagrams in figure 6.3 it can be seen whether a long-run equilibrium solution exists, and whether it is stable. Figure 6.2 demarcates which of the phase-diagrams of figure 6.3 corresponds with any (sub)set of parameter values. Note from eq. (6.6) that a_2 varies with θ, and that $a_3 > 0$.

In the cases I, II and III one (long-run) equilibrium exists, which is moreover globally stable. Starting from an initial (disequilibrium) value of the power coefficient δ, new levels of state and private sector activity and employment are generated, which result in a change in the power weights λ_k. This, in its turn, induces a change of the power coefficient, bringing it closer to its equilibrium value; and so on. Following a step-wise pattern, the politico-economic processes thus lead δ to its long-run equilibrium value δ_+^*, which can be read from eq. (6.7). The corresponding equilibrium levels of private and state sector employment then can be derived from eqs. (6.2) and (6.3).[4]

It may be added that from eq. (6.3) it follows that $\frac{\partial m}{\partial \delta} > 0$ if $a_3 > a_2$. If so, an increase in δ goes along with a growth of both state and private sector employment, E_s and E_p, inducing a further increase in

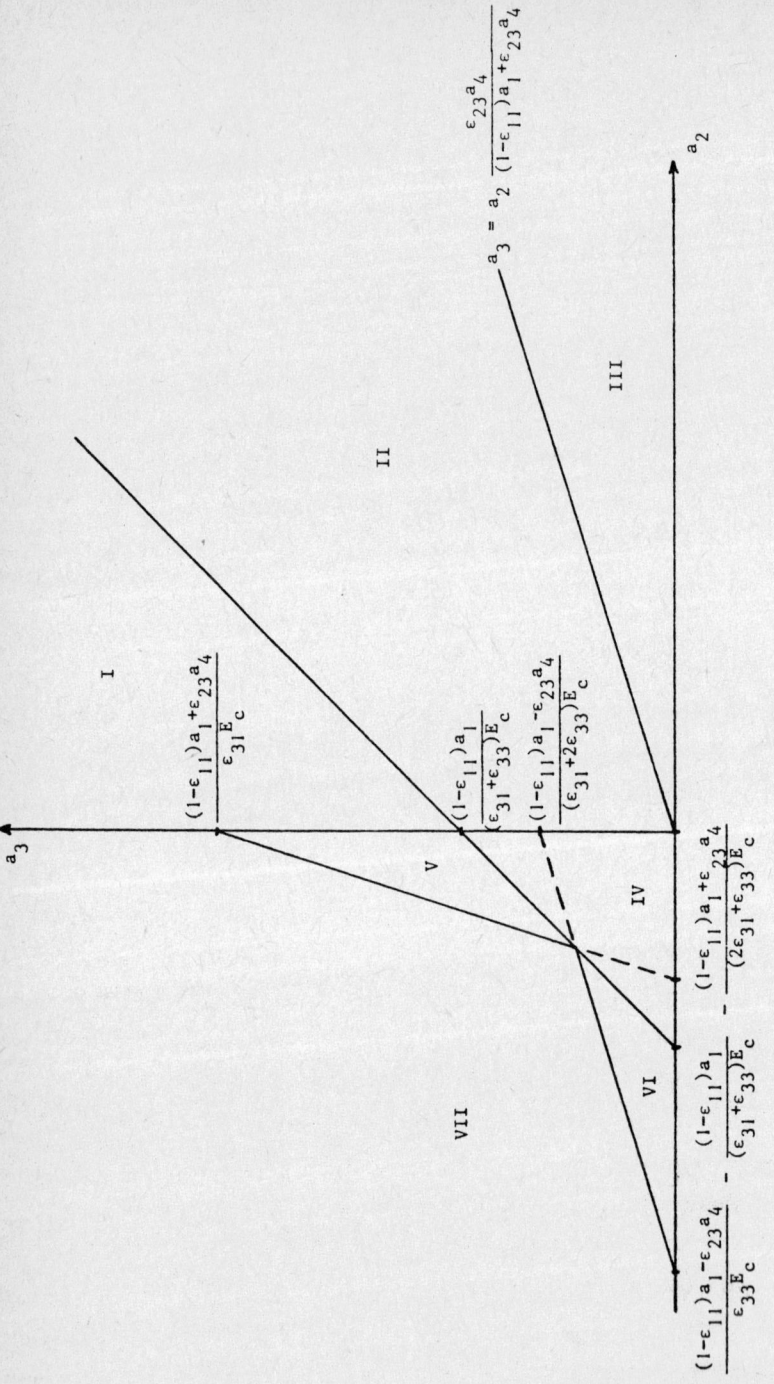

Figure 6.2 Subdivision of the set of parameter values. The numbers I till VII refer to the phase-diagrams of figure 6.3.

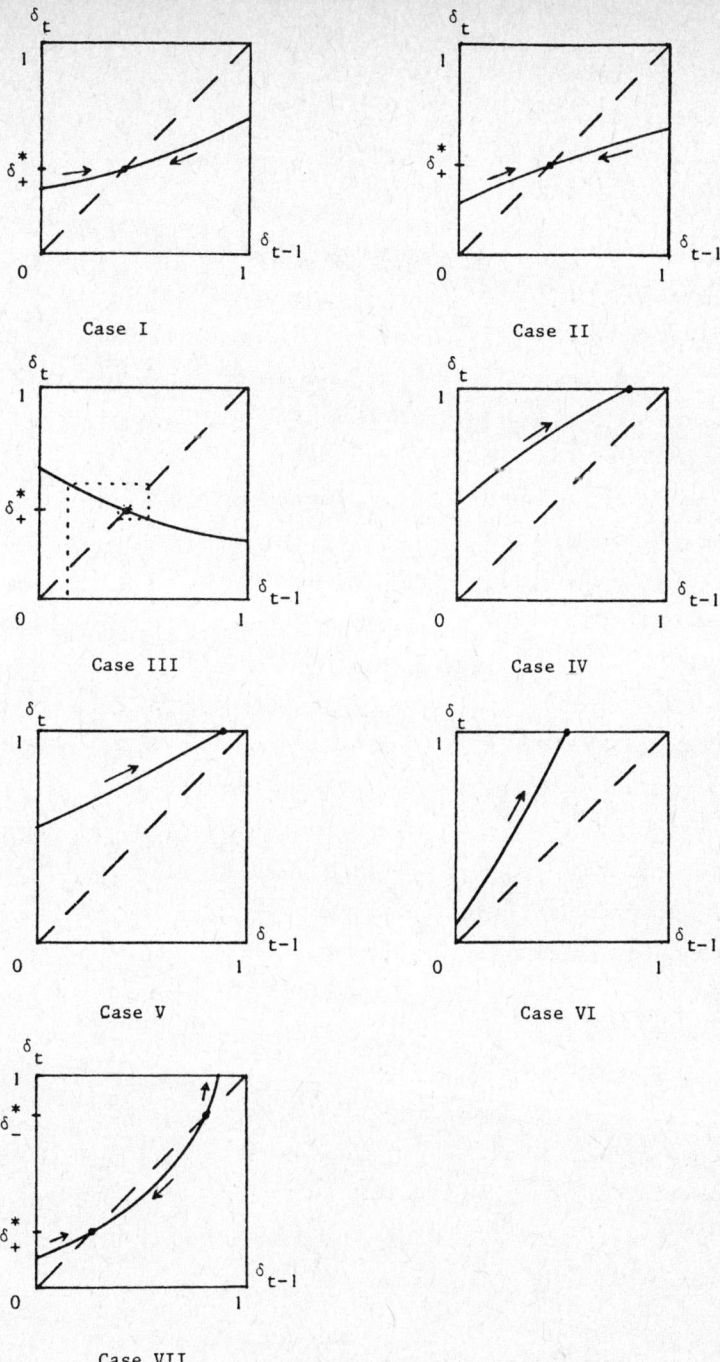

Figure 6.3   The set of phase-diagrams, corresponding to the subsets of parameter values in figure 6.2.

δ, until equilibrium is reached. If on the other hand $a_3 < a_2$ or, stated otherwise, if

$$\theta > \frac{c_1+\gamma}{c_2(1+\gamma)} \quad (> 1) ,$$

then an increase in δ is followed by an increase in E_s and a decrease in E_p (see also table 4.1). In case II the total effect of this opposite developments of E_s and E_p is still some further increase in δ. Equilibrium will be approached monotonically. In case III, however, a cyclic movement results. Starting from a relatively low (i.e. below equilibrium) value of δ, with a corresponding, relatively high multiplier value, levels of E_s and E_p are generated which induce a growth of δ. This enlarged value of δ generates an increase in E_s, but results in a decrease of the multiplier m and of E_p. In all, the power coefficient decreases. Then, E_s diminishes, m and E_p increase; the power coefficient increases again. The alternation continues until the equilibrium δ_+^* has been reached.

Let us next turn to the cases IV, V, and VI. It can be seen from the phase-diagrams of figure 6.3 that no long-run equilibrium exists. An initial (disequilibrium) value of δ leads to a growth in state sector employment E_s, with a concomitant growth in X_p and E_p. A growth of the power coefficient results, and so on, until the stability boundaries for the politico-economic submodel taken from section 4.3 are reached.[5] The politico-economic system as a whole is explosive.

In case VII, finally, two long-run equilibrium positions seem to exist. Seem to, because for a subset of parameter values within this region the multiplier m is negative, implying that the values of E_s and E_p underlying the (equilibrium) values of δ are negative, too. But then no meaning can be attached to the results. For the other subset of parameter values in the region,[6] the multiplier is positive. Of the two equilibrium positions figuring in the phase-diagram, one is unstable (δ_-^*), while the other (δ_+^*) is only locally stable.

We can now draw some general <u>conclusions</u>.
<u>a</u>. A necessary and sufficient condition for global stability of the politico-economic processes turns out to be $a_2 > 0$, or stated otherwise:

$$\theta > \frac{(c_1+\gamma)(\alpha_p-w_p)}{(1+\gamma)(\alpha_p-c_1 w_p)} .$$

Observe that the ratio on the right hand side of the latter inequality is smaller than one, as $c_1 < 1$. This implies that the stability condition at any rate is satisfied if a balanced budget is strived for ($\theta = 1$), or more broadly, if a budget deficit is being avoided ($\theta \geq 1$).

<u>b</u>. If

$$\theta < \frac{(c_1+\gamma)(\alpha_p-w_p)}{(1+\gamma)(\alpha_p-c_1 w_p)} ,$$

such that $a_2 < 0$, then either no long-run politico-economic equilibrium exists at all[7], or the equilibrium that may exist is at the most locally stable.

<u>c</u>. Given the time-path and long-run equilibrium value of δ, the time-path and equilibrium levels of, for example, E_s, E_p, and X_p can be derived. It will be clear that there is no chance of the state crowding out the private sector. On the one hand, because the private sector forms the tax base; on the other hand, because the state (for its non-wage expenditure) and the state sector workers (for their consumption expenditures) depend on the private sector for the provision in their expenditures.

More precisely: a rising δ induces a rising level of activity in the private sector, as long as

$$\theta < \frac{c_1+\gamma}{c_2(1+\gamma)} .$$

Then, X_p and E_p reach their minimum level if $\delta = 0$, and the state sector vanishes. The result simply is:

$$Y = X_p = \frac{1}{1 - c_1 \cdot \frac{w_p}{\alpha_p} - c_2(1-\frac{w_p}{\alpha_p})} \cdot (C_o+I_o) .$$

On the other hand, if $\theta > \frac{c_1+\gamma}{c_2(1+\gamma)}$ (> 1)

a growing state sector would lead to a shrinking private sector. The lower bound for the size of the private sector would be reached for $\delta = 1$, and would be equal to:

$$X_p = \frac{1}{1 - c_1 \cdot \frac{w_p}{\alpha_p} - \frac{c_1 + \gamma}{\theta(1+\gamma)} \cdot (1 - \frac{w_p}{\alpha_p})} \cdot (C_o + I_o),$$

which remains definitely positive.

6.3. A special case

It is no easy job to handle the dynamic politico-economic model presented above in its general form, if one is interested in the contribution of the various parameters to the level and the stability of the equilibrium position. To that purpose, we shall follow Van Velthoven and Van Winden (1986), who discussed a special case which yields a more easily manageable solution. It will be assumed that private sector workers and capitalists do not <u>reveal</u> any interest in the amount of public goods made available by the state; thus, $\varepsilon_{23} = \varepsilon_{33} = 0$. Certainly for the capital owners, it may be quite rational to conceal their interest in publicly provided goods and services. As we saw in chapter 4, the other classes will already press for – from the point of view of the capitalist class – more than enough public provisions, given that taxes ultimately fall on profits.

Under the assumption $\varepsilon_{23} = \varepsilon_{33} = 0$, the power coefficient δ simply boils down to

$$(6.1') \quad \delta_t = \frac{(1-\varepsilon_{11})\lambda_{1t}}{(1-\varepsilon_{11})\lambda_{1t} + \varepsilon_{31}\lambda_{3t}}.$$

The model, now consisting of eqs. (6.1') and (6.2) – (6.4), can be reduced to the following first-order non-linear difference equation in δ:

$$(6.5') \quad \delta_t = \frac{\delta_{t-1}(1-\varepsilon_{11})a_1}{\delta_{t-1}[(1-\varepsilon_{11})a_1 - \varepsilon_{31}E_c(a_3 - a_2)] + \varepsilon_{31}E_c a_3}.$$

It follows that the long-run equilibrium value(s) for δ are given by the (trivial) solution $\delta^* = 0$, and by

(6.8) $$\delta^* = \frac{(1-\varepsilon_{11})a_1 - \varepsilon_{31}E_c a_3}{(1-\varepsilon_{11})a_1 - \varepsilon_{31}E_c(a_3-a_2)} ,$$

provided the latter solution is within the [0,1]-interval.

Next, we have to reconsider figures 6.2 and 6.3. As the parameters ε_{23} and ε_{33} move towards zero, the demarcation lines between the subsets of parameter values in figure 6.2 will shift (more specifically, the regions III and V will vanish), while, at the same time, in figure 6.3 the equilibrium positions may shift (more specifically, δ^*_+ moves towards zero, if $(1-\varepsilon_{11})a_1 - \varepsilon_{31}E_c a_3 < 0$). Figures 6.4. and 6.5 depict the results.

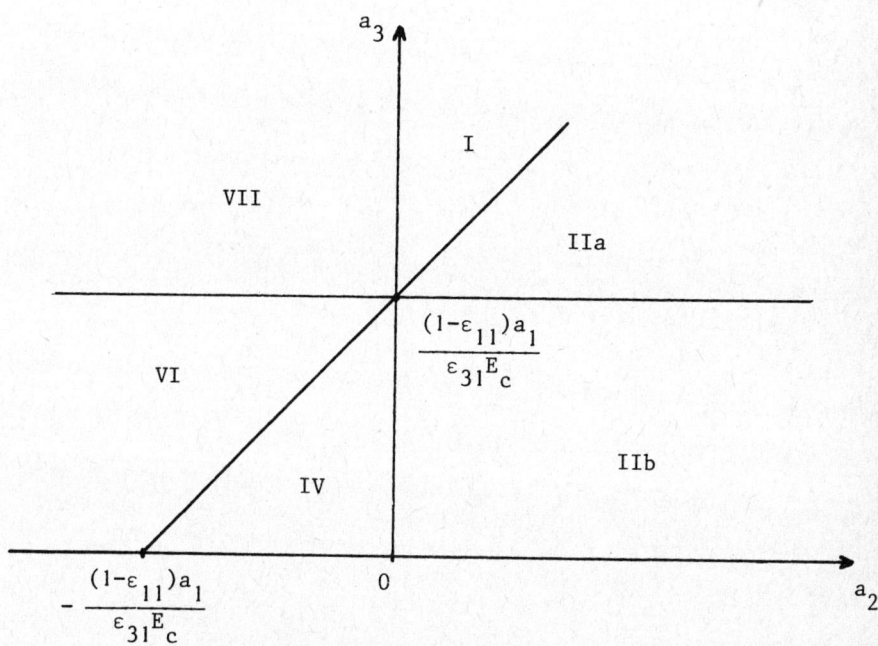

Figure 6.4   Subdivision of the set of parameter values; the numbers I till VII refer to the phase-diagrams of figure 6.5.

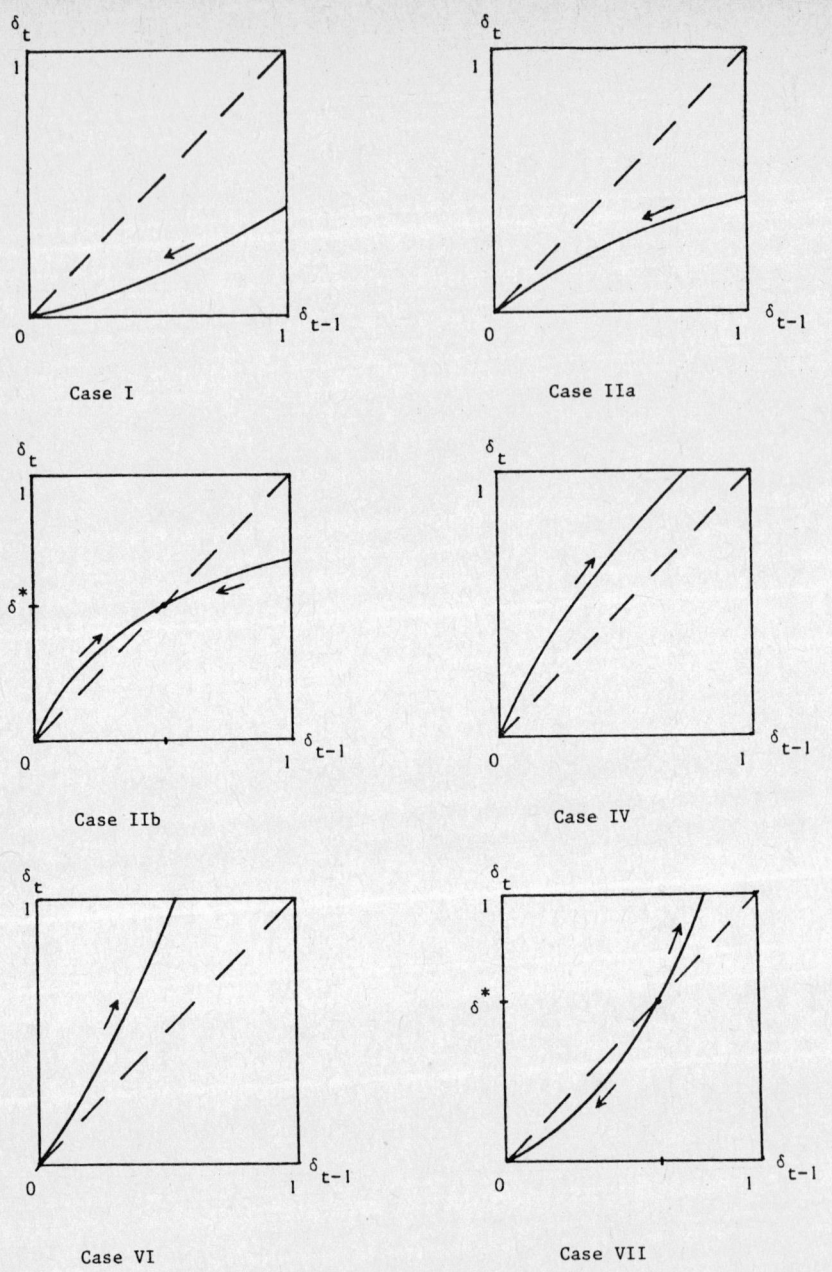

Figure 6.5 The set of phase-diagrams for δ, corresponding to the subsets of parameter values in figure 6.4.

The important difference between the general analysis in section 6.2 and the special case under consideration is that the analysis need not stop here. The model can also be solved into a first-order non-linear difference equation in E_s:

$$(6.9) \quad E_{st} = \frac{(1-\varepsilon_{11})a_1 E_{st-1}}{(1-\varepsilon_{11})a_2 E_{st-1} + \varepsilon_{31} a_3 E_c} .$$

The long-run equilibrium values of E_s are given by the trivial solution $E_s^* = 0$, and by

$$(6.10) \quad E_s^* = \frac{(1-\varepsilon_{11})a_1 - \varepsilon_{31} a_3 E_c}{(1-\varepsilon_{11})a_2} ,$$

provided the latter expression is non-negative. It further follows from eq. (6.9) that the horizontal asymptote, denoted by $\bar{E}_s$, is equal to a_1/a_2; the vertical asymptote, denoted by $\underline{E}_s$, is given by

$$\underline{E}_s = - \frac{\varepsilon_{31} a_3 E_c}{(1-\varepsilon_{11})a_2} .$$

As a_1, $a_3 > 0$, it is obtained that $\bar{E}_s \lessgtr 0$ and $\underline{E}_s \gtrless 0$, if $a_2 \lessgtr 0$. All in all, four patterns can be distinguished for the time-path of state sector employment; these are represented in figure 6.6.[8]

Let us now <u>discuss</u> the results.

<u>a</u>. If $a_2 < 0$, either no long-run equilibrium exists at all, or the non-zero equilibrium is unstable, such that either the size of the state sector will grow explosively, or it is subject to a persistent contraction.[9] Because of the absence of a stable long-run equilibrium with a non-zero size of the public sector, the cases IV, VI and VII will not interest us any further.

If $a_2 > 0$, global stability of the politico-economic processes is assured. However, the stable long-run equilibrium position not necessarily entails positive values for the power coefficient δ and for E_s. In the cases I and IIa, the politico-economic system appears to be too

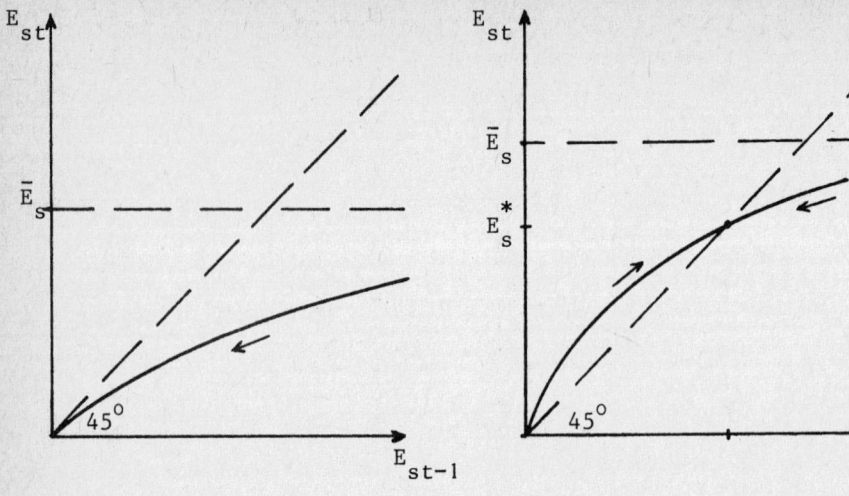

Cases I+IIa: Persistent contraction

Case IIb: Stable (non-zero) equilibrium E_s^*

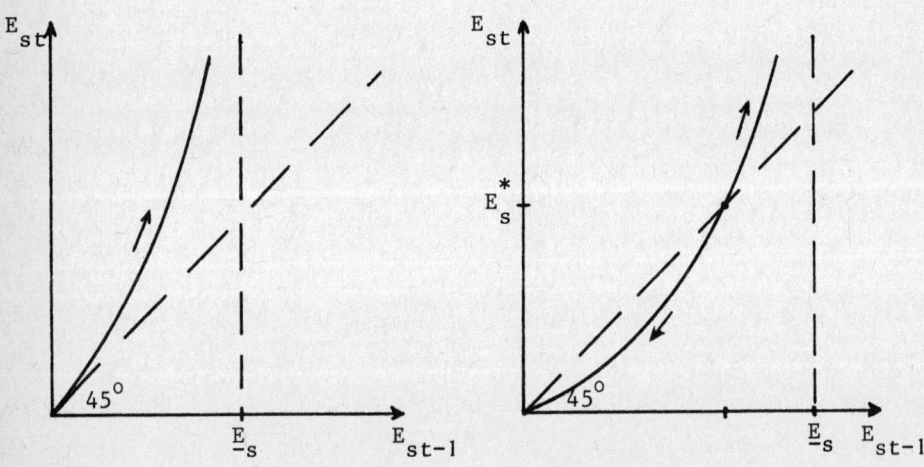

Cases IV+VI: Accelerating expansion

Case VII: Unstable (non-zero) equilibrium E_s^*

Figure 6.6.   The time-path of state sector employment. The numbers I till VII correspond with those in figures 6.4. and 6.5.

restrictive to sustain a non-zero public sector. The only interesting case, then, that remains for further discussion, is case IIb. Here, a public sector manifests itself which will attain a well-defined, positive size in the long run.

The condition for global stability, $a_2 > 0$, can also be written as:

$$(6.11) \qquad \theta > \frac{(c_1+\gamma)(\alpha_p-w_p)}{(1+\gamma)(\alpha_p-c_1 w_p)} .$$

For the existence of a non-zero equilibrium, it should be added that $(1-\varepsilon_{11})a_1 - \varepsilon_{31} E_c a_3 > 0$, or stated in terms of the model parameters:

$$(6.12) \qquad \theta < \frac{(1-\varepsilon_{11})(\alpha_p-w_p)(C_o+I_o)}{\varepsilon_{31}[\alpha_p-c_1 w_p-c_2(\alpha_p-w_p)](1+\gamma)w_s E_c} .$$

This inequality brings out which elements are determinant for the restrictiveness of the politico-economic system. Both political and economic factors play a role. For a positive state size to persist, the members of the social classes should not be too much interested in market goods and real disposable income (i.e., ε_{11} and ε_{31} should not be too high), while the "natural opponents" of a large public sector (in the context of our model, the capital owners, E_c) should not be too numerous. At the same time, the economic basis should be large enough to bear a sizeable public sector; more specifically, $C_o + I_o$, c_1 and c_2 should not be too small. Furthermore, the budget parameter θ should not be too large, nor γ and w_s. Observe in this context that the ratio on the right-hand side of eq. (6.11) is smaller than one. That is, (6.11) will be satisfied, and the global stability of the system assured, if the state balances its budget ($\theta = 1$). But note that the possibility remains that $\theta = 1$ violates eq. (6.12), such that the state would be forced to vanish.

<u>b</u>. Analogous to the time-path and stationary state of E_s, the time-path and equilibrium levels of private sector activity can be derived. Cf. section 6.2 for a general discussion. For the special case under consideration it can be deduced that the level of E_p corresponding with a long-run politico-economic equilibrium is given by:

$$(6.13) \quad E_p^* = \frac{(C_o+I_o) - \frac{\varepsilon_{31}}{1-\varepsilon_{11}} [\frac{c_1+\gamma}{\theta(1+\gamma)} - c_2] \theta(1+\gamma) w_s E_c}{\alpha_p - c_1 w_p - \frac{c_1+\gamma}{\theta(1+\gamma)} (\alpha_p - w_p)}.$$

<u>c</u>. Under the present specification of the model, the number of capitalists has no effect on total profits; the latter is related to the production level in the private sector only, given labour productivity and the wage rate. A change in E_c should, therefore, be considered as resulting from concentration and deconcentration in ownership. Its only effect is to alter λ_3, and consequently, δ; cf. eqs. (6.1), (6.4) and (6.1'). As a result, the equilibrium value of the power coefficient is, restricting attention to the "regular" case IIb, negatively related to the number of capitalists, as is the equilibrium level of state sector employment. The long-run effect of an increase in E_c on private sector employment may vary, but it certainly is negative as long as $\theta \leq 1$.

<u>d</u>. Apart from the number of capital owners, there are many other factors determining the long-run equilibrium position, as can be seen from eqs. (6.8) for δ^*, (6.10) for E_s^*, and (6.13) for E_p^*.

It can be ascertained for case IIb, that a rise in autonomous expenditure, e.g., has a positive impact on both E_p^*, E_s^* and δ^*. The equilibrium state size is also positively affected by increases in the marginal propensities to consume, c_1 and c_2.

A growth in the private sector labour productivity α_p tends to an increase of the state sector employment level; the effect on E_p^* is ambiguous.

Turning to the parameters of state sector behaviour, it can firstly be derived that the larger θ, i.e. the more stringent budget discipline is, the lower will be the equilibrium levels of δ and E_s. The effect on E_p^* varies. With respect to changes in the state sector wage rate w_s, it was noted in chapter 4 that the only effect in the short run was on E_s; due to unitelasticity, the total state wage sum would not change, leaving X_p and E_p unaffected. In the present chapter, however, we saw that on a longer term the change in E_s will alter the value of the power coefficient δ, and hence the level of taxation, state expenditure, and so on. A decrease in the wage rate for state sector workers, then, not only enhances state sector employment in the short term, but also in the long term because of an improved social power position; δ^* and E_s^* increase as a result of a fall in w_s.

Finally, about the influence of the parameter γ no explicit, unambiguous statements can be made.

6.4. Conclusion

In this chapter we transformed the initial macroeconomic model with endogenous state behaviour that was developed and analyzed in chapter 4, into a fully dynamic and closed politico-economic model. To that purpose we made use of the assumption - for which empirical support was obtained in chapter 5 - that the relative strength with which the different social classes get their interests promoted by the state, depends on their relative numerical strength.

The analysis should be considered as a first attempt to take account, within the confines of our model, of the changes in the social power structure that are due to politico-economic processes. As such, only the Frey-Schneider popularity surplus/deficit model seems to come up to it (see figure 2.1 and section 2.4.4). However, the critical review of the latter model in chapter 2 pointed out a series of deficiencies. Most important in the present context: the Frey-Schneider model is not well applicable to multi-party systems; it only accounts for political influence through elections; the ideology of the political parties is ill-defined and without any further theoretical underpinning. Our model, then, does not seem to stand out bad at all, as it solves or circumvents these deficiencies by the employment of the interest function approach (cf. chapter 3).[10]

It further has to be emphasized that the model in this chapter is a truly politico-economic model. Political developments - the promotion of interests and the exertion of pressure, finding expression in the determination of the power weights λ_k and the power coefficient δ - and economic developments - the determination of the levels of production and employment - continually interact with one another; cf. figure 6.1. Note, also, that there is no question of a simple one-sided economic determinism.

Finally, we summarize some specific results from this chapter.
- If the state balances its budget, the politico-economic system turns out to be globally stable. Whether in a long-run equilibrium a sizeable public sector subsists, depends on a large number of parameters, which together - one might say - determine the restrictiveness of the system.
- In so far as numerical strength is a determinant of the relative influence with which the social classes get their interests promoted by the state, it is clear that changes in the composition of the (dependent and independent) labour force may have important consequences for politico-economic processes. The model suggested for instance, that the equilibrium state size may be negatively related to the number of capital owners. Along similar lines, it followed that a fall in the wage rate for state sector workers may not only enhance state sector employment directly; because of a resulting improved social power position the effect may become reinforced in the longer run.

CHAPTER 7. TOWARDS A POLITICO-ECONOMIC THEORY OF SOCIAL SECURITY

7.1. Introduction[1]

Social security - which will be taken here in its wide, European sense, not only encompassing public pension schemes, but also other income transfers, such as to unemployed, sick and disabled persons and to widows and orphans - nowadays figures large among government outlays, after its continuous and fast expansion over especially the past two decades; see, e.g., Saunders and Klau (1985), and table 0.1. Accordingly, social security is receiving increasing attention in the economic profession. Recent discussions have focused on the effects of social security on capital accumulation and on its ability to achieve a more desirable distribution of income. In these studies social security programs are typically treated as exogenously determined. Little attention has hitherto been paid to the explanation of social security policies.

Roughly speaking, three approaches for the study of social security policies can be discerned in the public choice literature. Firstly, a series of interesting exploratory studies apply the median voter concept to develop a more formal quantitative analysis of the determinants of social security programs. Meltzer and Richard (1981, 1983) analyze the collective decision making process with regard to - intratemporal - income transfers. Their model implies that the size of social security programs will increase, the more mean income surpasses the income of the decisive, median voter. Browning (1975) and Hu (1982) model public decision making on the intertemporal redistribution of income which is related to old age (pay-as-you-go) pension schemes. In their analysis the preferences of the voter with median age are decisive. Browning shows that, given a once-and-for-all decision at the start of the public pension scheme, the pension benefit level will be too large relative to that which maximizes lifetime utility of a person at the start of his working life. The bill is disproportionately paid by the younger members of society. This creates incentives for the younger voters to misrepresent their preferences in case revoting opportunities exist. Hu argues that a static analysis of the demand for social security in a majority-voting process will tend to overstate its tendency towards overexpansion. For an application of a median voter type of analysis suggesting a gradually declining public support of the Dutch pay-as-you-go public pension scheme, see Verbon and Van Winden (1985). As the median voter approach has already been discussed and critically evaluated in general terms earlier in this book (cf. section 2.2), we need not go any further into it here.[2]

A <u>second</u> entry for the explanation of the development of social security policies can be found in the studies employing policy reaction functions. Here, income transfers are typically treated as just another instrument of economic policy on a par with government expenditure and taxation, without explicit consideration of their special characteristics. See, especially, Frey and Schneider (1978a, b; 1979). A critique of this type of studies was given in section 2.4.

A <u>third</u> approach is based on the functioning of pressure groups, as income transfer programs are typically concerned with redistribution. Interestingly enough, the beneficiaries of social security programs tend to be badly organized. Several factors can be enumerated which hamper and retard the organization of and collective action by these beneficiaries (cf. section 2.6): social security arrangements have a public good character; the beneficiaries in general have quite limited financial means at their disposal; as they, moreover, do not partake in the production process their threat potential is typically low; for various categories of social security arrangements (think of sickness or unemployment) receiving a benefit generally will only have a temporary character; between beneficiaries quite large income and status differentials exist. For the Netherlands, for instance, Wiebrens (1982) and Van Wijngaarden (1985) observe that the beneficiaries of the social security programs have hardly organized themselves at the public level, such that for the present they are as an interest group of no real importance for public sector decision making. The growth of the social security system over the past decades thus cannot well be attributed to pressure group activities of the beneficiaries themselves.

While the three approaches mentioned thus far may yield interesting pieces of insight into the determination of social security policies, they do not present a satisfactory, coherent explanation. In chapter 4 we developed an alternative model for the analysis of public sector behaviour, by employing the interest function approach discussed in chapter 3. Hitherto, social security transfer payments were treated in the model as an internal affair of the private sector. The theme of the present chapter is to study social security explicitly as an element of public sector policy making. By employing the interest function approach we do not just concentrate on voting as the only way to influence state behaviour; also other kinds of internal and external pressure on public sector decision makers are allowed for. Another characteristic of our model will be that social security outlays are considered simultaneously with state expenditure; as will be shown below, the two are intimately related. We shall analyze the impact of preferences, the social power configuration, and the carrying capacity of the economy, with respect to the size of these two components of state outlays.

To illustrate some implications for macroeconomic modelling of the social security programs thus brought about, we shall trace their effects on the levels of production and employment and on the stability of the economy, within the simple textbook Keynesian income-expenditure model used before. Even in that context, it turns out that it is not at all evident that social security tends to stabilize the economy, nor that it has a positive effect on the levels of production and employment. Moreover, it appears that the kind of social security program considered is important in these respects.

The chapter is organized as follows. Section 7.2 analyzes the behaviour of the state, and is in particular concerned with the social security policies that the state will choose. In section 7.3 we introduce the behaviour of the private sector in the form of the simple Keynesian demand model, and analyze the equilibrium properties of the full model. An empirical application of the model to the Netherlands is presented in section 7.4. Section 7.5 concludes.

7.2. The behaviour of the state; social security policies

7.2.1. Social classes and interests

In chapter 3 it has been observed that the particular form in which the basic interests of people will manifest themselves, as well as their action space and control over marketed and non-marketed goods, are shaped by the position they have with respect to the production process in the economy. Four elementary types of economic positions have been distinguished:
1. state sector worker (politician or bureaucrat),
2. private sector worker,
3. capital owner (capitalist),
4. dependant ("unemployed" in a wide sense).

The set of agents in each elementary economic position has been referred to as a social class. Of course, the four elementary economic positions mentioned above are no more than "archetypes". Actually, as a person may occupy more than one position at the same time, or because of ideological considerations or (anticipated) mobility in time from one economic position to another, an individual may well take account of the interests connected with more than just one elementary economic position. Stated otherwise, more than one elementary interest function may play a part in the determination of the behaviour of an individual.[3] In this chapter we shall explicitly deal with the last aspect, by taking a closer view of social mobility as far as it is related to the social security system.

The class of dependants is made up by all people with an income out of social security transfers. For reasons of exposition, we shall divide these transfer payments in two groups:
- unemployment benefits in the usual sense, for those people who are available to the labour market (we shall call this labour market related social security); and
- the remainder, such as old age pensions (to be called labour market unrelated social security).

Corresponding to this partitioning of the social security system, two kinds of mobility will be considered in this chapter:
- mobility which is due to the fact that people get unemployed (in the

usual, strict, sense), which means a transition from the class of private or state sector workers to the (sub)class of dependants that still partake in the labour market, or the converse;
- mobility which is related to the transition from one of the classes that partake in the labour market to the (sub)class of dependants, that stand outside of it, such as pensioners (the reverse will not be considered, for simplicity).

In the sequel the two subclasses of dependants will be indexed by k = 4d (dependent on the labour market), and k = 4i (independent of the labour market). The social security benefits that are transferred by the state to the (representative) members of these subclasses, will be denoted by w_{4d} and w_{4i}, respectively.

People generally will reckon with a (subjective) probability that in the future they will be subject to one or the other of the two kinds of mobility mentioned above. If people take account of this (anticipated) mobility, more than one elementary interest function becomes pertinent to an individual. The interest function for a representative member of social class k is transformed into a so-called complex interest function, indicated by P_k, which is a function of the relevant elementary interest functions. In what follows the following specifications will be used:

(7.1) $\quad P_1 = w_1^{\varepsilon_{11}} \cdot x_s^{\varepsilon_{12}} \cdot w_{4i}^{\varepsilon_{13}} \cdot w_{4d}^{\varepsilon_{14}}$,

(7.2) $\quad P_2 = w_2^{\varepsilon_{21}} \cdot x_s^{\varepsilon_{22}} \cdot w_{4i}^{\varepsilon_{23}} \cdot w_{4d}^{\varepsilon_{24}}$,

(7.3) $\quad P_3 = w_3^{\varepsilon_{31}} \cdot x_s^{\varepsilon_{32}} \cdot w_{4i}^{\varepsilon_{33}}$,

(7.4) $\quad P_{4d} = w_{4d}^{\varepsilon_{4d1}} \cdot x_s^{\varepsilon_{4d2}} \cdot w_{4i}^{\varepsilon_{4d3}} \cdot w_1^{\varepsilon_{4d4}} \cdot w_2^{\varepsilon_{4d5}}$,

(7.5) $\quad P_{4i} = w_{4i}^{\varepsilon_{4i1}} \cdot x_s^{\varepsilon_{4i2}}$,

with $\varepsilon_{kg} \geq 0 \ \forall k, g, \ \Sigma_g \varepsilon_{kg} = 1 \ \forall k$,

where the subscript g denotes the relevant argument in the interest function.

We make some comments:
- We distinguish two elementary interests, to wit the real disposable income of the representative member of each social class, w_k, and the bundle of (purely collective) goods and services provided by the state, x_s. The relative numerical strengths of the social classes, e_k, have been left out for theoretical and empirical reasons (cf. chapters 3 and 5), in addition to notational efficiency, without real loss of substance.[4)]
- A state or private sector worker is first of all interested in his own basic class interests (represented by w_1 and w_2, respectively, and by x_s), but because one day he can become unemployed or a pensioner, for example, he will also take some interest in the level of the respective social security benefits w_{4d} and w_{4i}.[5)] Capital owners are generally not entitled to unemployment benefits, but may receive one day some other social security benefits; hence eq. (7.3).
- In eq. (7.4) it is being expressed that those who are currently unemployed may anticipate getting a new job again, either in the public or the private sector, or to abandon the labour force some day.
- As was already announced above, a return of the dependants outside the labour market to the labour force is left out of account; hence eq. (7.5).

7.2.2. The behaviour of the state

In conformity with the discussion in chapter 3 (see, especially, eq. (3.8)), it will be assumed that the behaviour of the state is in accordance with the (constrained) maximization (as a tendency, and not necessarily on purpose) of the interest function P_s, specified as:

$$(7.6) \quad P_s = P_1^{\lambda_1} \cdot P_2^{\lambda_2} \cdot P_3^{\lambda_3} \cdot P_{4d}^{\lambda_{4d}} \cdot P_{4i}^{\lambda_{4i}}, \quad \lambda_k \geq 0 \ \forall k, \ \Sigma_k \lambda_k = 1.$$

Let us next turn to the constraints. E_s and E_p, again, indicate the numbers of state and private sector workers. N comprises the fixed total dependent and independent labour force, L and E_c respectively, as well as the dependants who do not partake in the labour market (E_{4i}, which is also given). It follows that:

(7.7) $E_{4d} = L - E_s - E_p$.

As noted, state goods are supposed to be purely collective in nature. Their full cost of production consists of the state wage sum $W_s = w_s E_s$ and non-wage (material) expenditure G_m; G_m is assumed to be proportionally related to W_s. Thus:

(7.8) $G_m = \gamma W_s$, $\gamma > 0$,

(7.9) $X_s = G_m + W_s = (1+\gamma) w_s E_s$.

Taxes will be supposed to fall on profits (because of a single profit tax or because of full shifting).[6] The tax rate will be labelled τ. Real disposable profit income (all income and expenditure is in real terms) equals:

(7.10) $w_3 = (1-\tau)\Pi/E_c$,

where total before-tax profits Π are equal to private sector output X_p minus the private wage sum $W_p = w_p E_p$. As labour productivity α_p is supposed to be given, Π can be written as:

(7.11) $\Pi = (\alpha_p - w_p) E_p$, $\alpha_p > w_p > 0$.

We assume that the state because of lack of information, naiveté, or a short time horizon, takes the expected level of private sector employment as well as the private sector wage rate as given.

With respect to the determination of the state sector wage rate w_s and the unemployment benefit rate w_{4d} all kinds of labour market considerations play a role. In actual practice, for instance in the Netherlands, both have been coupled in a more or less steady fashion to the wage rate of the private sector. As the functioning of the labour market is not the primary subject of this study, we consider w_s and w_{4d} as exogenously given.

Then, using eqs. (7.1) through (7.11), $w_1 = w_s$ and $w_2 = w_p$, P_s can be written in terms of the instruments E_s, τ and w_{4i} as:

(7.12) $P_s = A \cdot E_s^{\delta_1} \cdot (1-\tau)^{\delta_2} \cdot w_{4i}^{\delta_3}$, where

$$\delta_1 = \lambda_1 \varepsilon_{12} + \lambda_2 \varepsilon_{22} + \lambda_3 \varepsilon_{32} + \lambda_{4d} \varepsilon_{4d2} + \lambda_{4i} \varepsilon_{4i2},$$

$$\delta_2 = \lambda_3 \varepsilon_{31},$$

$$\delta_3 = \lambda_1 \varepsilon_{13} + \lambda_2 \varepsilon_{23} + \lambda_3 \varepsilon_{33} + \lambda_{4d} \varepsilon_{4d3} + \lambda_{4i} \varepsilon_{4i1}.$$

A comprises all the (with respect to the state) exogenously determined variables.

Maximization of P_s is subject to the budget constraint:

(7.13) $\theta(W_s + G_m + W_4) = \tau \Pi,$

where θ indicates the fraction of total state outlays to be covered by taxation, and W_4 stands for total social security outlays, that is $W_4 = w_{4d}E_{4d} + w_{4i}E_{4i}$.

Maximization of the state interest function (7.12) with respect to the instruments E_s, τ and w_{4i}, subject to the budget constraint (7.13), recalling from eq. (7.7) that $E_{4d} = L - E_s - E_p$, and given the level of the unemployment benefit w_{4d}, yields the following <u>behavioural equations</u> for the state:

(7.14) $E_s = \Delta_1 \cdot \dfrac{\Pi - \theta w_{4d}(L-E_p)}{\theta[(1+\gamma)w_s - w_{4d}]},$

(7.15) $\tau = 1 - \Delta_2 \cdot \dfrac{\Pi - \theta w_{4d}(L-E_p)}{\Pi},$

(7.16) $w_{4i} = \Delta_3 \cdot \dfrac{\Pi - \theta w_{4d}(L-E_p)}{\theta E_{4i}},$

with: $\Delta_i = \dfrac{\delta_i}{\delta_1 + \delta_2 + \delta_3}$, $i = 1,2,3$.

Note that from $\varepsilon_{kg} \geq 0$ ∀k,g and $\lambda_k \geq 0$ ∀k, it follows that $\delta_i \geq 0$ ∀i, $0 \leq \Delta_i \leq 1$ ∀i, and $\Sigma_i \Delta_i = 1$.

For the instrument values to be economically meaningful, the conditions $\Pi - \theta w_{4d}(L-E_p) \geq 0$ and $(1+\gamma)w_s - w_{4d} > 0$ should hold. We shall assume henceforth that these conditions are satisfied, so that $E_s \geq 0$, $0 \leq \tau \leq 1$, $w_{4i} \geq 0$.

Discussion

<u>a</u>. The budget constraint (7.13) can easily be rewritten into:

$$(7.17) \qquad \theta[(1+\gamma)w_s - w_{4d}]E_s + (1-\tau)\Pi + \theta w_{4i}E_{4i} = \Pi - \theta w_{4d}(L-E_p) .$$

Now it can be noted that maximization of (7.12) under this budget constraint, with w_{4d} as a constant, is formally equivalent to the well-known linear expenditure system from consumer theory. The expression $\Pi - \theta w_{4d}(L-E_p)$ may be called the <u>supernumerary tax capacity</u> of the economy. It denotes the tax capacity which remains having taken account of the "basic income" w_{4d} that is guaranteed by the state to the - potentially - unemployed dependent labour force through its labour market related social security program.

Because of w_{4d} the (supernumerary) "price" for the state of a state sector worker equals $\theta[(1+\gamma)w_s - w_{4d}]$; it is the demand that the employment of one additional state sector worker is making on the (supernumerary) tax capacity of the economy. It is reminded that γ refers to the material state expenditure accompanying state sector employment.

<u>b</u>. Our model can be said to distinguish between three departments: a spending department, producing collective goods; a transfer department, taking care of social security benefits; and a finance department, concerned with taxation. Note that the (supernumerary) tax covered expenditures of these departments - where the "expenditure" of the finance department is considered to be given by disposable profit income $(1-\tau)\Pi$ - are proportionally related to the (supernumerary) tax capacity. The

proportions Δ_i can be said to summarize the <u>effective interest structure</u> of society. They are determined by the preference weights ε_{kg} that the classes attach to their respective interests, weighted by the relative strengths λ_k with which the classes get their interests vested with and promoted by the state (see eq. (7.12)). Following the terminology of chapter 4, the Δ_i's could also be named power coefficients.

The model sheds some new light on the observed <u>incremental behaviour</u> of the budgetary process and the <u>sudden changes</u> ("displacement effects" or "shift points") by which it is marked from time to time. Cf. Peacock and Wiseman (1961), Davis, Dempster and Wildavsky (1966). Denoting the budget of department i at time t by B_{it}, and the (supernumerary) tax capacity of the economy by $\bar{T}$ our model suggests that $B_{it} = B_{it-1} + \Delta_i(\bar{T}_t - \bar{T}_{t-1})$, where Δ_i indicates the effective interest of society in the output of department i. It follows that given a gradually changing tax capacity, incrementally changing budgets will show up. Shift points will occur if either the tax capacity would show a sharp discontinuity or the effective interest structure Δ would suddenly change.

<u>c</u>. From eq. (7.15) and the condition $\Pi - \theta w_{4d}(L-E_p) \geq 0$ it immediately follows:

(7.18) $\quad \theta w_{4d}(L-E_p)/\Pi \leq \tau \leq 1$.

Within these boundaries, the tax burden is (co)determined by the relative power of the social classes (given their interests). The right hand side of (7.18) obtains if $\Delta_2 = 0$, the left hand side if $\Delta_2 = 1$.

Observe that $\Delta_2 = \lambda_3 \varepsilon_{31}/(\delta_1+\delta_2+\delta_3)$, which implies that the tax burden is especially dependent on the interest that capitalists take in real disposable income (indicated by ε_{31}) and the relative strength with which they get this interest promoted by the state (λ_3). The latter depends on the internal (because of multiple positions) and external (via political parties and other pressure groups) pressure that they can bring to bear upon the behaviour of the state. Notice that $\Delta_2 = 1$ if $\lambda_3 = 1$ and $\varepsilon_{31} = 1$. If $\lambda_3 = 0$, then $\Delta_2 = 0$, and hence $\tau = 1$.

d. The labour market unrelated social security benefit w_{4i} is (co)determined by the effective interest weight $\Delta_3 = \delta_3/(\delta_1+\delta_2+\delta_3)$. According to eq. (7.12):

$$\delta_3 = \lambda_1 \varepsilon_{13} + \lambda_2 \varepsilon_{23} + \lambda_3 \varepsilon_{33} + \lambda_{4d} \varepsilon_{4d3} + \lambda_{4i} \varepsilon_{4i1}.$$

Thus, the level of w_{4i} depends not only (not even in the first place) on the direct interest that the dependants E_{4i} themselves take in their real disposable income and on their influence on state behaviour. Even if $\lambda_{4i} = 0$ (cf. section 7.1 on the degree of organization of the social security beneficiaries), the benefit w_{4i} quite likely will be positive, due to the indirect interest that the other social classes attach to this kind of social security (because they take the consequences of anticipated future social mobility into account).

e. We now turn to the effects of the unemployment benefit level w_{4d}. First, note that $\partial\tau/\partial w_{4d} \geq 0$. Further, the partial derivative of w_{4i} with respect to w_{4d} is negative. The two social security arrangements are, to a certain extent, competing with one another.

The effect of w_{4d} on the level of state sector employment E_s cannot be determined unambiguously. For, an increase in w_{4d}, besides lowering the supernumerary tax capacity, also lowers the (supernumerary) "price" for employing state sector workers. The relationship between E_s and w_{4d} appears to depend on the fact whether the tax capacity Π is sufficient to employ in the state sector all those not employed in the private sector. Cf. figure 7.1. The relations in figure 7.1 will play an important role when we trace out the effects of the endogenization of w_{4d} in the next subsection.

f. As regards <u>demographic developments</u>, it should be noted that an increase in E_{4i} and/or L, i.e. in the (actual or potential) number of social security beneficiaries, has a negative impact on the benefit level w_{4i}.[7]

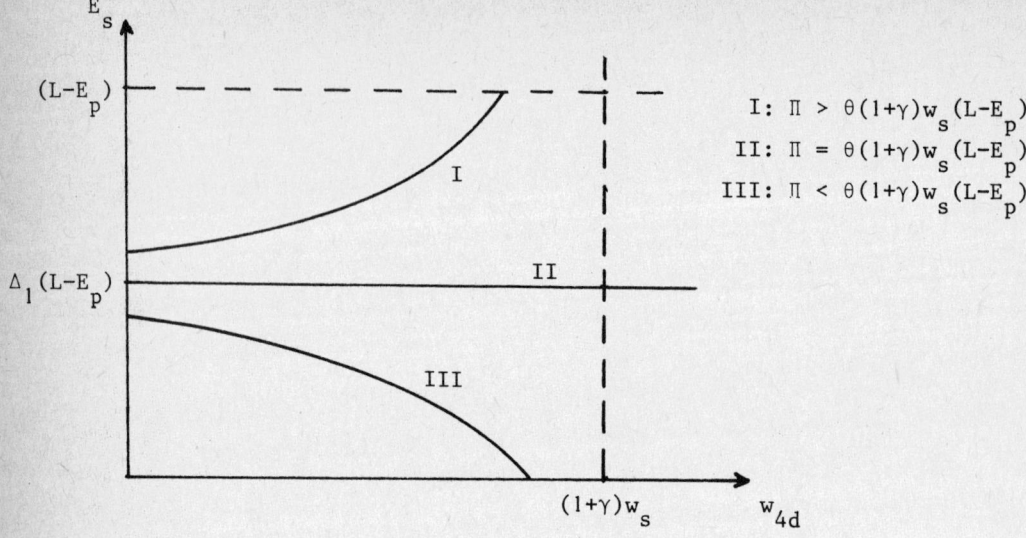

Figure 7.1   The relationship between E_s and w_{4d} for different regimes with regard to Π.

7.2.3. Endogenization of the unemployment benefit level

In the previous subsection, the unemployment benefit rate w_{4d} was taken to be exogenously determined. Such an assumption may perhaps, to a certain extent, be justified by pointing at the necessary upkeep of the human capital of the labour force, demanding that w_{4d} becomes not too far removed from w_p (and w_s). Nevertheless, it would be interesting to know more about the consequences of the endogenization of w_{4d}. In the subsection it will become apparent that the introduction of w_{4d} as an instrument in the model considerably complicates the analysis, taking for granted that the state takes account of the direct effect of state sector employment on the level of unemployment ($E_{4d} = L - E_p - E_s$).

Eqs. (7.14) - (7.16) recorded the optimal values of E_s, τ and w_{4i}, for given levels of w_{4d}. Now, once w_{4d} is considered to be an instrument in public sector decision making, eq. (7.12) for P_s should be rewritten as:

(7.19) $P_s = A' \cdot E_s^{\delta_1} \cdot (1-\tau)^{\delta_2} \cdot w_{4i}^{\delta_3} \cdot w_{4d}^{\delta_4}$,   where

$$\delta_4 = \lambda_1 \varepsilon_{14} + \lambda_2 \varepsilon_{24} + \lambda_{4d} \varepsilon_{4d1} ,$$

while δ_1, δ_2, δ_3 remain as defined above, and with A' containing all the exogenous variables. After the insertion of the optimal values of E_s, τ and w_{4i} as functions of w_{4d}, (7.19) can be maximized with respect to the unemployment benefit level. The first-order condition appears to involve a quadratic function in w_{4d}. The roots of this function are given by:

$$(7.20) \quad w_{4d} = \frac{-\Pi(\delta_1 - \delta_4) + \theta(1+\gamma)w_s(L-E_p)(\delta_1 + \delta_2 + \delta_3 + \delta_4) \pm \sqrt{D}}{2\,\theta(L-E_p)(\delta_2 + \delta_3 + \delta_4)} \quad, \text{ with}$$

$$D = \Pi^2(\delta_1 - \delta_4)^2 + [\theta(1+\gamma)w_s(L-E_p)(\delta_1 + \delta_2 + \delta_3 + \delta_4)]^2$$
$$- 2\Pi\theta(1+\gamma)w_s(L-E_p)[\delta_1(\delta_1 + \delta_2 + \delta_3) + \delta_4(\delta_2 + \delta_3 + \delta_4)] .$$

Although eq. (7.20) is not quite easy to handle, it still appears to be possible to say something more about the solution of w_{4d}.

First, not surprisingly, $w_{4d} = 0$ if $\delta_4 = 0$.[8)] That is, if the effective interest of society in the labour market related social security program is nil, it will not come into existence. Notice from eq. (7.19) that for δ_4 to become positive, it is not necessary that the beneficiaries themselves have any political influence; even if $\lambda_{4d} = 0$, the effective interest attached to an unemployment benefit scheme may well become positive due to the fact that the current state and private sector workers have an (indirect) interest in such a scheme.

Assuming from now on that $\delta_4 > 0$, a crucial condition in the analysis of eq. (7.20) appears to be whether $\Pi \lessgtr \theta(1+\gamma)w_s(L-E_p)$, i.e. whether the tax capacity is large enough to finance the employment of all non-private sector workers in the state sector (including the material inputs accompanying state sector employment, and taking account of the tax-coverage parameter θ). Recall from figure 7.1 that this condition was determinant for the sign of $\partial E_1/\partial w_{4d}$.

a. If $\Pi < \theta(1+\gamma)w_s(L-E_p)$, then P_s attains a global maximum for $w_{4d} = \bar{w}_{4d}$; the value of $\bar{w}_{4d}$ is given by eq. (7.20) where the minus sign before $\sqrt{D}$ holds, and it lies in the interval $(0, \Pi/[\theta(L-E_p)])$. Hence, $w_{4d} < (1+\gamma)w_s$.

It can be shown that changes in the size of the labour force have a negative effect on w_{4d} in this case; i.e. $\partial w_{4d}/\partial L < 0$.

<u>b</u>. If $\Pi = \theta(1+\gamma)w_s(L-E_p)$, then P_s attains a global maximum for $w_{4d} = [\delta_4/(\delta_2+\delta_3+\delta_4)](1+\gamma)w_s$.

<u>c</u>. If $\Pi > \theta(1+\gamma)w_s(L-E_p)$, then P_s goes to infinity as w_{4d} approaches $(1+\gamma)w_s$. Thus, in this case no interior (global) solution exists. If however, $\Pi < \bar{\Pi}$ with $\bar{\Pi}$ denoting the smallest root of Π for the discriminant D in eq. (7.20), then P_s attains a local maximum for a value of w_{4d} in the interval $(0, (1+\gamma)w_s)$.

Of course, in the situation dealt with here, one should take certain boundaries into account. For instance, the labour force constraint will become active, as E_s will tend to surpass $L - E_p$; but then $E_{4d} = 0$, and the benefit level w_{4d} is no longer relevant. There may also be (further) restrictions on the domain of w_{4d} (e.g., the condition that $w_{4d} \leq w_1$), in which case w_{4d} may become a "corner solution" (such as $w_{4d} = w_1$), or the local maximum may even become the global maximum.

Finally, let us take a look at the wage-benefit structure. Because of the intractability of the general expression for w_{4d}, attention will be restricted to the case $\delta_1 = 0$ (which implies $E_s = 0$, such that $E_{4d} = L - E_p$). If $\delta_1 = 0$, it follows that $w_{4i} = \Delta_3\Pi/[\theta E_{4i}]$, $w_{4d} = \Delta_4\Pi/[\theta(L-E_p)]$, with $\Delta_i = \delta_i/(\delta_2+\delta_3+\delta_4)$. Thus:

$$(7.21) \quad \begin{aligned} \frac{w_{4i}}{w_p} &= \frac{\Delta_3}{\theta} \cdot \frac{\alpha_p - w_p}{w_p} \cdot \frac{E_p}{E_{4i}}, \\ \frac{w_{4d}}{w_p} &= \frac{\Delta_4}{\theta} \cdot \frac{\alpha_p - w_p}{w_p} \cdot \frac{E_p}{(L-E_p)}, \\ \frac{w_{4d}}{w_{4i}} &= \frac{\Delta_4}{\Delta_3} \cdot \frac{E_{4i}}{(L-E_p)}. \end{aligned}$$

Both ratio's w_{4d}/w_p and w_{4i}/w_p are positively affected by an increase in the ratio between profits and the private wage sum; e.g., they are positively influenced by an increase in the labour productivity in the private sector, ceteris paribus. An increase in labour productivity which is attended by a proportional increase in wage rates will lead the social security benefit rates to rise with that same percentage.[9] Equation (7.21) further predicts that in a period of economic recession, when private sector employment E_p slows down and unemployment grows, the social security benefit rates will be reduced relative to w_p, and w_{4d} more so than w_{4i}.[10] The ratio between w_{4d} and w_{4i} is strictly determined by the relevant effective interest weights and (the inverse of) the size of the two subclasses of dependants.

Summarizing: in this subsection it has been demonstrated that the endogenization of the unemployment benefit rate is possible and can produce valuable insights. However, the general expression for w_{4d} which was derived above, is too intractable to incorporate it in the more complete politico-economic model which will be presented and analyzed in the next section. Moreover, as was observed before and confirmed by our analysis of eq. (7.20), the determination of w_{4d} will be subject to all kinds of labour market considerations and constraints, the modelling of which is outside the scope of this book; presumably, the value of w_{4d} will be fixed somewhere below and not too far removed from w_p. For those reasons, we will consider w_{4d} to be exogenously determined in the following, and take our starting point from the equations (7.14) - (7.16).

7.2.4. Some additional remarks

The analysis in this section has shown that it is possible to relate the development of social security policies to preferences, the social power structure, and the tax capacity of the economy.

If the tax capacity, the labour force and the population keep pace, the benefit level will be stable, in accordance with the (power weighted) preferences. If the wage rates are rising in proportion to the growth of labour productivity, so may the social security benefits. In a period of growth, even an extension of the social security system is likely, as it may be expected that the preferences for social security are income-elastic.

Problems arise if the number of beneficiaries starts rising fast(er), and/or if the tax capacity starts shrinking. As has been suggested in the literature, these problems may even have been created by the (growth of the) social security system itself.[11] To study the interaction between social security policies and the economy, we whall present and analyze in the next section a more complete politico-economic model.

7.3. Social security in a complete politico-economic model

7.3.1. The model

The endogenization of state behaviour in general and social security policies here in particular may have important consequences for the functioning of macroeconomic models. To explore the issues involved we shall take our starting point at a simple Keynesian income-expenditure model (cf. chapter 4). This will suit our purpose of showing that the conclusions of macroeconomic analysis may be fully reversed by endogenizing state behaviour.

For the <u>private sector</u> it is assumed that production X_p is adapted to the demand for output consisting of private consumption C, private investment I, non-wage state expenditure G_m, and net exports Ex - M. The marginal propensities to consume out of non-profit and profit income are denoted by c_1 and c_2, respectively. For investment two possible determinants are considered: total private output and after-tax profits, with coefficients i_1 and i_2. Exports (Ex) are assumed to be autonomous. Imports (M) are related to private output, the marginal propensity to import being given by β.

The economic behaviour of the private sector, then, can be represented by the following set of equations, where the subscript o denotes the autonomous components of expenditure, and α_p indicates the private sector labour productivity:

(7.22) $C = c_1(w_s E_s + w_p E_p + W_4) + c_2(1-\tau)\Pi + C_o, \quad 0 < c_2 \leq c_1 < 1$,

(7.23) $I = i_1 X_p + i_2(1-\tau)\Pi + I_o$, $i_1, i_2 \geq 0$,

(7.24) $Ex = Ex_o$,

(7.25) $M = \beta X_p + M_o$, $\beta \geq 0$,

(7.26) $X_p = C + I + G_m + Ex - M$,

(7.27) $\Pi = X_p - w_p E_p$,

(7.28) $X_p = \alpha_p E_p$.

It wil be assumed throughout that $\alpha_p > w_p > 0$.

Notice that eq. (7.26) can also be written in terms of national income, labelled Y:

(7.26') $Y = C + I + G + Ex - M$,

where: $Y = X_p + w_s E_s$, $G = G_m + w_s E_s$.

To obtain a complete politico-economic model the <u>behavioural equations for the state</u> derived above must be added to the eqs. (7.22) - (7.28) describing the behaviour of the private sector. For convenience we duplicate here the relevant equations:

(7.29) $G_m = \gamma w_s E_s$,

(7.30) $E_s = \Delta_1 \cdot \dfrac{\Pi - \theta w_{4d}(L - E_p)}{\theta[(1+\gamma)w_s - w_{4d}]}$,

(7.31) $\tau = 1 - \Delta_2 \cdot \dfrac{\Pi - \theta w_{4d}(L - E_p)}{\Pi}$,

(7.32) $w_{4i} = \Delta_3 \cdot \dfrac{\Pi - \theta w_{4d}(L - E_p)}{\theta E_{4i}}$,

(7.33) $W_4 = w_{4d} E_{4d} + w_{4i} E_{4i}$,

(7.34) $E_{4d} = L - E_s - E_p$.

The equations (7.22) - (7.34) represent the politico-economic model, which will be scrutinized in the sequel. To start the analysis, we solve the model and derive its <u>equilibrium solution</u>. In terms of private output X_p the equilibrium solution of the model is given by:

(7.35) $\quad X_p = m.A$, with

$$m = \alpha_p\Big(\alpha_p^* - c_1(w_p - w_{4d}) - (\alpha_p - w_p + \theta w_{4d})[\Delta_1 \frac{c_1(w_s - w_{4d}) + \gamma w_s}{\theta[(1-\gamma)w_s - w_{4d}]} + \Delta_2 c_2^* + \Delta_3 c_1/\theta$$

$$A = C_o + I_o + Ex_o - M_o + w_{4d}L\Big(c_1 - \Delta_1[\frac{c_1(w_s - w_{4d}) + \gamma w_s}{(1+\gamma)w_s - w_{4d}}] - \Delta_2 \theta c_2^* - \Delta_3 c_1\Big) ,$$

$$\alpha_p^* = (1 - i_1 + \beta)\alpha_p ,$$

$$c_2^* = c_2 + i_2 .$$

<u>Discussion</u>

<u>a</u>. X_p is determined in the familiar way by a multiplier m and autonomous expenditure A.

<u>Autonomous expenditure</u> now comprises the expenditure generated by the existence of a "basic income" w_{4d} for the dependent labour force. This basic income $w_{4d}L$ leads to consumption, the direct marginal expenditure rate being c_1. On the other hand, aggregate expenditure is negatively affected by the financing of this basic income. For, its financing implies partly (Δ_1) a reduction in state sector employment, partly (Δ_2) an increase of taxation and a decrease of disposable profit income, and partly (Δ_3) a lower level of the social security benefits for the dependants outside the labour force (w_{4i}), with the concomitant reductions in consumption, investment, and material state expenditure.

The <u>multiplier</u> m indicates how (an increase in) autonomous expenditure, giving rise to (additional) private sector employment and production, induces further private product demand. First, of course, private sector workers consume part of their (additional) wage income. The budget of the state is affected in two ways: the tax capacity Π of the economy grows, while the transfer payments to the unemployed diminish. The space that is thus created in and for the budget, is partly (Δ_1) used for (additional) state employment, inducing additional non-wage expenditure by the state and consumption by the state sector workers, partly (Δ_3) for improving on the labour market unrelated social security benefit level w_{4i}, while the rest (Δ_2) leads to additional disposable profit income with a marginal propensity to spend c_2^*.

<u>b</u>. For an economically meaningful equilibrium to exist, the multiplier m should be positive. The latter is, for instance, assured if $\theta = 1$, $w_{4d} = 0$, $i_1 = 0$. Contrary to chapter 4 (cf. figure 4.1), no well-interpretable general conditions for the existence of an equilibrium can be formulated, due to the multiplicity of parameters involved. Thus, it will be assumed henceforth that m is positive. It is noticed that the impact of several of the parameters on the multiplier value will be the subject of subsequent subsections.

<u>c</u>. Observe from eq. (7.35) that the role played by output induced investment (i_1) and production induced imports (β) is straightforward. The parameters i_1 and β only make their appearance in the multiplier, independent from politically relevant parameters such as Δ_i. This in contrast with, e.g., i_2.

Starting from the equilibrium solution (7.35) the following subsections will be addressed to a study of the impact of the social security system on the economy. In section 7.3.2 we look into the effect of social security on the levels of production and employment: X_p, E_p (= X_p/α_p), and E_s. In section 7.3.3 we investigate the influence on the value of the multiplier, as a measure of stability of the economy. Section 7.3.4 then will summarize some first conclusions. The effects of demographic changes and of changes in the effective interest structure Δ wil shortly be explored in sections 7.3.5 and 7.3.6.

It is noted at the outset that the results in the following subsections are derived from rather straightforward algebraic manipulations, which are space absorbing and tiring and are therefore omitted.

7.3.2. The effects of social security on production and employment

The effect of a social security program on the levels of production and employment can be measured in two ways, i.e.:
- through the effect of variations in the benefit rate given the existence of the social security program, and
- through the effect of the introduction of the program as such given a specific benefit rate.

For the labour market related social security, where w_{4d} is treated as an exogenous variable, both approaches are open. Under certain conditions it is then possible to obtain all information required from the first approach. For the labour market unrelated social security in our model the first approach will not work, because the benefit rate w_{4i} is endogenously determined once the program is installed; thus, only the second approach will yield results.

Note in this connection that previous to or on the occasion of the introduction of a social security program a shift in the effective interest structure Δ may occur. Not so much because the preferences or the relative power of the social classes themselves will change, as well because the installation of a social security program involves a certain institutionalization (e.g. a new department or a new office comes into being), such that a new entry is created within the state organization for (the promotion of) some specific preferences/ interests. In order not to overload the exposition we shall assume that the effective interest structure Δ may change at the introduction of a new program, but that the underlying parameters δ_i (cf. eq. (7.12)) are not subject to changes.

The introduction of labour market unrelated social security (w_{4i})

Let X_p^o, E_p^o and E_s^o denote the equilibrium levels of private output, private sector employment, and state sector employment in case of the absence of labour market unrelated social security, and X_p, E_p and E_s the respective equilibrium values in case of its existence. Let, furthermore, $\Delta_i^o = \delta_i/(\delta_1+\delta_2)$, $i = 1,2$, stand for the effective interest structure in the former case, whereas $\Delta_i = \delta_i/(\delta_1+\delta_2+\delta_3)$, $i = 1,2,3$, holds after the introduction of w_{4i}. That is, after the introduction of the labour market unrelated social security program effective interest is attached to (because internal and external pressure is brought to bear on state decision making for) the maintenance and improvement of the benefit level w_{4i}, vis-à-vis the maintenance and enlargement of the provision of public goods and services and real disposable (profit) income.

It can be derived that:

(7.36)[12] $X_p \gtreqless X_p^o$ iff $\delta_3 \{\delta_2(c_1-\theta c_2^*) - \delta_1 \dfrac{(1-c_1)\gamma w_s}{(1+\gamma)w_s - w_{4d}}\} \gtreqless 0$,

(7.37) $E_s \gtreqless E_s^o$ iff $\delta_1 \delta_3 \{\alpha_p^* - c_1 w_p - c_1(\alpha_p - w_p)/\theta\} \lesseqgtr 0$.

Of course $E_p \gtreqless E_p^o$ iff $X_p \gtreqless X_p^o$, given the assumedly constant private sector labour productivity α_p.

Discussion

<u>a</u>. As to X_p, inequality (7.36) indicates under which condition the increase in consumption of the beneficiaries is large enough to compensate for the decrease of state sector employment induced expenditure, and for the decline of consumption and investment out of profits due to the financing of the benefits.

With respect to E_s two effects are to be discerned: a direct negative effect due to the shift in the effective interest structure Δ, and an indirect effect via E_p on the tax capacity of the economy.

<u>b</u>. Note the importance of the effective interest structure, assuming $\delta_3 > 0$ (if $\delta_3 = 0$, w_{4i} will remain zero even after the installation of the program).

If $\delta_1 = 0$ and $\delta_2, \delta_3 > 0$, E_s equals zero (or, formulated more broadly, is exogenously determined); the effect on X_p depends entirely on the sign of $c_1 - \theta c_2^*$. $X_p \gtreqless X_p^o$ iff $c_1 - \theta(c_2 + i_2) \gtreqless 0$. In case the "<u>classic</u>" assumptions hold that the state budget balances ($\theta = 1$) and all after-tax profits are reserved for investment, so that $i_2 = 1$ and $c_2 = 0$ (while $i_1 = 0$, only profits induce investments), then the effect of the introduction of w_{4i} will be non-positive, and negative if $c_1 < 1$. In a "<u>Keynesian</u>" perspective, where the state budget shows a deficit ($\theta < 1$), investments are only output-determined ($i_1 > 0$, $i_2 = 0$), and the marginal propensity to consume of wage earners exceeds that of capital-owners

($c_2 < c_1 < 1$), the effect on X_p will be positive.

Now, let us consider the more general case, with $\delta_1 > 0$, where state production and employment are endogenous. With the "<u>classic</u>" assumptions the effect on X_p remains negative; the effect on E_s is, accordingly, negative too. In a "<u>Keynesian</u>" perspective, however, it is no longer obvious now that X_p will be affected positively. As to the impact of the introduction of w_{4i} on E_s, it will only be positive if $\delta_1, \delta_3 > 0$ and $\theta < \dfrac{c_1(\alpha_p - w_p)}{\alpha_p^* - c_1 w_p}$. Thus, even if $c_2 < c_1 < 1$, social security may have a negative impact on economic activity, because via the state budget constraint it "crowds out" state sector employment. The corresponding loss of state employment induced expenditure (c_1 and γ), plus the expenditure loss from reduced disposable profit income, may not be compensated for by the extra consumption from the social security beneficiaries.

Variations in the unemployment benefit rate w_{4d}

To obtain information on the impact of the labour market related social security program we calculated the partial derivates of the equilibrium with respect to w_{4d}.[13] For E_p (and, analogously, for $X_p = \alpha_p E_p$) and for E_s it follows:

$$(7.38) \quad \frac{\partial E_p}{\partial w_{4d}} = \frac{m}{\alpha_p} \cdot \{ \Delta_1 \cdot \frac{(1-c_1)\gamma w_s}{\theta[(1+\gamma)w_s - w_{4d}]^2} \cdot [\Pi - \theta(1+\gamma)w_s(L-E_p)]$$

$$+ \Delta_2(c_1 - \theta c_2^*)(L-E_p) \}$$

$$(7.39)^{14)} \quad \frac{\partial E_s}{\partial w_{4d}} \gtreqless 0 \text{ if } \frac{\partial E_p}{\partial w_{4d}} \gtreqless \frac{\theta(1+\gamma)w_s(L-E_p) - \Pi}{(\alpha_p - w_p + \theta w_{4d})[(1+\gamma)w_s - w_{4d}]}$$

The effect on E_p, X_p and E_s depends on the relative magnitude of δ_1 and δ_2, and on the signs of $c_1 - \theta c_2^*$ and $\Pi - \theta(1+\gamma)w_s(L-E_p)$. For the latter expression we call to mind subsection 7.2.2; it indicates whether the tax capacity of the economy is large enough to have all non-private sector workers employed in the state sector. More specific results have been tabulated in table 7.1, where we set out the "Keynesian" and "classic" views sketched above against $\Pi \gtreqless \theta(1+\gamma)w_s(L-E_p)$. Table 7.1

points out that it is not sure that the impact of the unemployment benefit is always positive from a "Keynesian" perspective. Nor, contrary to the partial result of figure 7.1, is the effect always positive if $\Pi > \theta(1+\gamma)w_s(L-E_p)$.

Table 7.1 The equilibrium effects of a change in the unemployment benefit rate w_{4d}

$\delta_1, \delta_2 > 0$	Keynesian assumptions: $\theta < 1, i_1 > 0, i_2 = 0,$ $0 < c_2' < c_1' < 1$		Classic assumptions: $\theta = 1, i_1 = 0, i_2 = 1,$ $c_2' = 0$	
	$\dfrac{\partial E_p}{\partial w_{4d}}$	$\dfrac{\partial E_s}{\partial w_{4d}}$	$\dfrac{\partial E_p}{\partial w_{4d}}$	$\dfrac{\partial E_s}{\partial w_{4d}}$
$\Pi < \theta(1+\gamma)w_s(L-E_p)$	±	±	−	−
$\Pi = \theta(1+\gamma)w_s(L-E_p)$	+	+	−	−
$\Pi > \theta(1+\gamma)w_s(L-E_p)$	+	+	±	±

7.3.3. The effect of social security on the stability of the economy

In the context of our comparative-static analysis of the equilibrium solution of the politico-economic model of section 7.3.1, the economy is defined to be more stable if its reaction to changes in autonomous expenditure is less volatile, that is if the multiplier value is smaller.

First, we take a look at the introduction of the labour market unrelated social security program (w_{4i}). Let m^o and m respectively stand for the multiplier value in the absence and presence of the social security program. The introduction of w_{4i} will have a positive effect on the stability of the economy, i.e.

(7.40) $m < m^o$, iff $\delta_3\{\delta_2(c_1 - \theta c_2^*) - \delta_1 \dfrac{(1-c_1)\gamma w_s}{(1+\gamma)w_s - w_{4d}}\} < 0$.

A comparison of this result with eq. (7.36) points out that if the introduction of the labour market unrelated social security scheme is favourable for X_p, it will negatively affect the stability of the economy, and vice versa. For a further discussion of the elements of (7.40), see at (7.36).

Turning to the impact of the <u>labour market related social security program</u> w_{4d}, the following results can be deduced:

$$(7.41) \quad \frac{\partial m}{\partial w_{4d}} = \frac{m^2}{\alpha_p} \{\Delta_1 \cdot \frac{(1-c_1)\gamma w_s}{\theta[(1+\gamma)w_s - w_{4d}]^2} \cdot [\alpha_p - w_p + \theta(1+\gamma)w_s] - \Delta_2(c_1 - \theta c_2^*)\} .$$

The unemployment benefit enhances the stability of the economy, if $\partial m / \partial w_{4d} < 0$.[15] If so, then $\partial E_p / \partial w_{4d} > 0$, as can be seen from eq. (7.38); the reverse need not be true.

What processes are behind the (de)stabilizing influence of the unemployment benefit scheme? Observe that with a fall in autonomous expenditure private sector output and employment will go down; the tax capacity for the state shrinks, and hence state sector employment will be reduced. Consequently, the transfer payments to the unemployed will increase, which, given their marginal propensity to consume c_1, will dampen the fall in expenditure and thus tends to be stabilizing. However, notice that the means for financing this growth of unemployment benefits must be found, given θ, from a reshuffling of the budget. The state will opt for - a mixture of - a reduction in the provision of public goods and services, curtailing the labour market unrelated social security program, and raising tax rates; but, these measures will tend to affect aggregate expenditure negatively. By how much is a matter of the relative importance of, and of the marginal contributions to expenditure corresponding with, these three kinds of measures. Whether, ultimately, the unemployment benefit scheme is stabilizing or destabilizing can be deduced from a comparison of this latter negative (and hence destabiling) and the initial positive (stabilizing) influence on expenditure.

With the "<u>classic</u>" assumptions we have, unambiguously, $\partial m / \partial w_{4d} \gtreqless 0$. In the "<u>Keynesian</u>" perspective it is not certain that $\partial m / \partial w_{4d} < 0$. A positive effect of w_{4d} on the economy's stability becomes more likely the smaller the value of θ, c_2^*, w_{4d} and Δ_1, and the higher the value of Δ_2 (that is, the greater the influence of the capitalists).

From the confrontation of the equations (7.40) and (7.41) an important conclusion emerges. It turns out that no parameter configurations exist for which both social security programs are stabilizing. If a situation arises in which one of the two social security programs has a positive effect on the stability of the economy, then the other one has a negative effect on stability. Also, parameter configurations exist, notably if:

$$\delta_1 \frac{(1-c_1)\gamma w_s}{(1+\gamma)w_s - w_{4d}} < \delta_2(c_1 - \theta c_2^*) < \delta_1 \frac{(1-c_1)\gamma w_s}{\theta[(1+\gamma)w_s - w_{4d}]^2} \cdot [\alpha_p - w_p + \theta(1+\gamma)w_s]$$

for which both social security programs are destabilizing.

7.3.4. Some first conclusions

The results derived above show that the effects of the introduction of and changes in social security policies (apart from supply-side effects, which are not taken into consideration here) not only depend on the various propensities to spend, but also on the effective interest structure Δ. It appears that, from a theoretical point of view, no distinct positive or negative signs can be attributed to most of the effects. With endogenous state behaviour the world becomes more complicated.

To explore the change in perspective, let us start from the Keynesian assumptions on spending - i.e. $0 < c_2 < c_1 < 1$, $i_2 = 0$, $\theta < 1$ - and consider state behaviour, and especially E_s and w_{4i}, to be determined exogenously. Then it can be shown that the unemployment benefit unambiguously contributes to stabilization of the economy, while the labour market unrelated social security program has no effect at all on stability;[16] both programs tend to increase production and employment in the private sector.

As soon as state behaviour is recognized to be endogenous, these results do not go unchanged. Even while the model can be characterized as a pure demand model, it is not at all evident that a social security program has a positive effect on the levels of production and employment. The same result holds for the stabilizing impact of the presence of social security programs. It appears that the introduction of the labour market unrelated social security, the benefit rate of which is treated as an endogenous variable, has a stabilizing effect when it affects the level of production itself negatively, and vice versa. Furthermore, it appears that if one of the social security programs affects the stability of the economy positively, the other one has a negative impact on stability. While it is thus precluded that both labour market related and unrelated social security stabilize the economy at the same time, the possibility remains that they have simultaneously a negative impact on stability.[17]

At this point it is of interest to take notice of the findings of Snyder (1970, p. 271): ".. the social security system had virtually no stabilizing effects in the UK, and in France the effects were an important <u>destabilizing</u> factor (probably more due to discretionary changes than to any procyclical features inherent in the automatic functioning of the system)", and of Brittain (1972): ".. it (the payroll tax for social security) is not very effective as an automatic stabilizer, as the payroll tax has often been increased in times of substantial slack".

7.3.5. <u>Demographic developments</u>

Demographic developments are co-determining the use of social security arrangements. It is interesting therefore to look in the present context at the effects of changes in the dependent labour force, L, and in the number of dependants outside the labour force, E_{4i}.

First, notice from the equilibrium solution for X_p, eq. (7.35), that E_{4i} does not occur. The specification of the interest functions is such that the impact of a change in E_{4i} is completely absorbed by a change in w_{4i} (unit-elasticity). Accordingly, changes in E_{4i} have no effect on E_s and E_p.

With respect to the impact of a change in the size of the dependent labour force the following results can be established:

$$(7.42) \quad \frac{\partial E_p}{\partial L} = w_{4d} \cdot \frac{m}{\alpha_p} \cdot \{\Delta_2(c_1 - \theta c_2^*) - \Delta_1 \frac{(1-c_1)\gamma w_s}{(1+\gamma)w_s - w_{4d}}\},$$

$$(7.43) \quad \frac{\partial E_s}{\partial L} = -\frac{w_{4d}}{(1+\gamma)w_s - w_{4d}} \cdot \frac{m}{\alpha_p} \cdot \Delta_1 \cdot \{\alpha_p^* - c_1 w_p - c_1(\alpha_p - w_p)/\theta\}.$$

We want to make the following remarks:
- If $w_{4d} = 0$, a change in L, of course, will have no effect on either E_s or E_p in the present model.
- Notice the conformity of the eqs. (7.42) and (7.43) with (7.36) and (7.37). That is, an increase in L affects E_s and E_p in the same direction as did the introduction of w_{4i}. In both cases the state budget is confronted with an additional, but (essentially) fixed burden.
- Combining eqs. (7.42) and (7.43), we conclude that under the "classic" assumptions total employment is affected negatively by a growth of the labour force. Under the "Keynesian" assumptions the total effect on employment may both be positive or negative.
- The (equilibrium) effect of a growth in the labour force L on the benefit rate w_{4i}, $\partial w_{4i}/\partial L$, has the same sign as $\partial E_s/\partial L$. It is not necessarily negative, contrary to what was concluded from the partial analysis in section 7.2.2. On the other hand, the effect will be positive only if the private sector employment and accordingly the tax capacity of the economy grow sufficiently (cf. eq. (7.42)).

7.3.6. Changes in the effective interest structure Δ

The effective interest structure is, according to eqs. (7.14) - (7.16), given by $\Delta_i = \delta_i/(\delta_1 + \delta_2 + \delta_3)$, $i = 1,2,3$. The coefficients δ_i are composed of the preference weights ε_{kg} and the power weights λ_k, as specified in eq. (7.12). It will be clear that a change in one Δ, due to a changing configuration of ε's and/or λ's, may involve changes in the other Δ's too.

In the context of this chapter we are especially interested in (changes in) Δ_3. A change in Δ_3, indicating the effective, i.e. power weighted, (direct and indirect) interest that the members of the different social classes take in the social security benefit w_{4i}, and/or a change in Δ_1, indicating the effective, power weighted interest that they take in state provided collective goods and services, has the following effects on E_s and E_p (remember that $\Sigma_i \Delta_i = 1$, and thus $\Sigma_i d\Delta_i = 0$):

$$(7.44) \quad dE_p = \frac{1}{\theta} \cdot \frac{m}{\alpha_p} [\Pi - \theta w_{4d}(L-E_p)] \cdot \{ \frac{(1-c_1)\gamma w_s}{(1+\gamma)w_s - w_{4d}} \cdot d\Delta_1 + (c_1 - \theta c_2^*)(d\Delta_1 + d\Delta_3) \} ,$$

$$(7.45) \quad dE_s = \frac{\Pi - \theta w_{4d}(L-E_p)}{\theta[(1+\gamma)w_s - w_{4d}]} \cdot d\Delta_1 + \Delta_1 \frac{\alpha_p - w_p + \theta w_{4d}}{\theta[(1+\gamma)w_s - w_{4d}]} \cdot dE_p .$$

An increase in the effective interest weight given to labour market unrelated social security, Δ_3, at the expense of Δ_2, the effective interest that is taken in real disposable profit income, will have a positive effect on E_p and E_s if $c_1 - \theta c_2^* > 0$. On the other hand, an increase in Δ_3 at the expense of Δ_1 will have a negative effect on E_p and E_s, assuming $c_1 < 1$. Notice that in this latter case the ultimate impact on the benefit rate w_{4i} itself is not necessarily positive; the initial positive impuls, due to the greater weight being given to social security in the effective interest structure, is counteracted by a decrease of the (supernumerary) tax capacity.

Concluding, it is not sufficient to know that social security has been given a greater weight in the state's decision making process; it is also important to know from which direction this increase has been fostered.

7.4. Empirical application

7.4.1. Introduction

In chapter 5 we made a first attempt to apply our model of state behaviour to data for the Netherlands. Attention was restricted to state expenditure, employment, and taxation; social security was considered to be a private sector affair. It was found that the relative numerical strengths of the social classes, substituted for the power weights λ_k, performed quite well statistically in explaining state behaviour. However, on closer inspection it appeared that, while the coefficient estimates for the period 1952-1977 had the expected signs, this was not the case - at least not uniformly - for the second subperiod 1970-1984. Several reasons were advanced as possible explanations for this result, such as the imperfect nature of the relative numerical strength variables as proxies for the λ's, changes in the attitudes towards budget deficits over the period considered, changes in the degree of tax shifting, changes in the preference weights ε_{kj}, but also the growth of the social security system. As the model of state behaviour has been extended in the present chapter to explicitly account for (the size of) the social security system as part of public sector activity, it would be of interest to see how this extended model behaves in a confrontation with the data.

In this section, therefore, we shall apply the model for state behaviour that has been developed in section 7.2 to Dutch data for the period 1953-1984. For details on these data and the data sets themselves the reader may be referred to the Appendix.[18] Suffice it here to remind the reader from section 5.2.1 that, due to a major revision of the national accounts, two separate, partly overlapping time series can be constructed, one for the period (1951)1953-1977, the other for the period (1969)1971-1984.[19]

7.4.2. Regression results

In section 7.2.2 we derived behavioural equations for the state: eq. (7.14) for the level of public sector employment E_s, eq. (7.15) for the rate of taxation τ, and eq. (7.16) for the social security benefit rate w_{4i}. Estimating these equations as such would not be wise given that the coefficients Δ_i, summarizing the effective interest structure of society, can hardly be deemed constant over time; they are determined by the preference weights ε_{kg} and the power weights λ_k, and thus are themselves the outcomes of politico-economic processes. Cf. the discussion of earlier results in section 5.2.2.

We, therefore, proceed by calculating from the data sets the values of the Δ_i's on a yearly basis, using eqs. (7.14) - (7.16), and then try to explain the development of these coefficients over time.[20] By definition, $\Delta_i = \delta_i/(\delta_1+\delta_2+\delta_3)$, $i = 1,2,3$, with the δ_i's given by eq. (7.12). If additional information would be available on the ε's and/or λ's, regression equations could be composed. As no independent information on the preference weights ε_{kg} is available, we adopt the procedure already employed in chapter 5, and use the relative numerical strengths of the social classes as proxies for the power weights λ_k. To obtain linear regression equations - while, moreover, $\Sigma_i \Delta_i = 1$ - we pass on to the ratio's Δ_1/Δ_2 (= δ_1/δ_2) and Δ_3/Δ_2 (= δ_3/δ_2). With the help of eq. (7.12) the following equations are obtained.

$$(7.46) \quad \frac{\Delta_1}{\Delta_2} = (\frac{\varepsilon_{32}}{\varepsilon_{31}}) + (\frac{\varepsilon_{12}}{\varepsilon_{31}}) \cdot \frac{\lambda_1}{\lambda_3} + (\frac{\varepsilon_{22}}{\varepsilon_{31}}) \cdot \frac{\lambda_2}{\lambda_3} + (\frac{\varepsilon_{4d2}}{\varepsilon_{31}}) \cdot \frac{\lambda_{4d}}{\lambda_3} + (\frac{\varepsilon_{4i2}}{\varepsilon_{31}}) \cdot \frac{\lambda_{4i}}{\lambda_3} ,$$

$$(7.47) \quad \frac{\Delta_3}{\Delta_2} = (\frac{\varepsilon_{33}}{\varepsilon_{31}}) + (\frac{\varepsilon_{13}}{\varepsilon_{31}}) \cdot \frac{\lambda_1}{\lambda_3} + (\frac{\varepsilon_{23}}{\varepsilon_{31}}) \cdot \frac{\lambda_2}{\lambda_3} + (\frac{\varepsilon_{4d3}}{\varepsilon_{31}}) \cdot \frac{\lambda_{4d}}{\lambda_3} + (\frac{\varepsilon_{4i1}}{\varepsilon_{31}}) \cdot \frac{\lambda_{4i}}{\lambda_3} .$$

Because of the consideration that pressure has to be built up before it can lead to acknowledged power and vested interests, a partial adjustment model will be used, with the numerical strength variables lagged one year.

Table 7.2 presents the estimation results for the first (sub)period 1953-1977. Regressions 1 and 5, based on (7.46) and (7.47), yield satisfactory results, statistically. The fit is good, autocorrelation seems to be absent. Most of the coefficients significantly differ from zero; only the lagged dependent variable does not seem to play an important role. However, it should be acknowledged that several of the coefficient estimates do not obey the non-negativity restriction on the ε's; some of them are even significantly negative.

Our earlier work suggested the hypothesis that the economically active members of society attach the same preference weight to public goods and services; i.e., $\varepsilon_{12} = \varepsilon_{22} = \varepsilon_{32} = \varepsilon_{.2}$. Similarly, they might attach the same weight to social security; i.e., $\varepsilon_{13} = \varepsilon_{23} = \varepsilon_{33} = \varepsilon_{.3}$. The estimation results under these assumptions are reported in regressions 2 and 6, respectively. Statistically, the hypotheses are in this case rejected, however.

With regard to the hypothesis that the dependants are without political power or influence, the evidence is somewhat mixed. Regressions

Table 7.2 The model of state behaviour applied to the Netherlands, period 1953-1977; estimation results for Δ_1/Δ_2 and Δ_3/Δ_2.[a]

regression number	dependent variable	Constant	E_s/E_c	E_p/E_c	E_{4d}/E_c	E_{4i}/E_c	lagged dependent variable	$\bar{R}^2$	(RMSE)	Durbin's h (LM)
1	Δ_1/Δ_2	-0.25 (1.47)	-1.83* (2.74)	0.64** (4.81)	1.29** (3.26)	-0.21* (2.16)	-0.10 (0.52)	0.910	(0.044)	1.86
2			0.07** (3.05)		-0.08 (0.36)	0.03 (1.04)	0.31 (1.46)	0.991	(0.059)	— (12.37)
3			0.07** (3.38)			—	0.38 (2.00)	0.992	(0.058)	-0.04
4				0.05** (3.07)	—		0.40 (1.97)	0.991	(0.060)	— (0.80)
5	Δ_3/Δ_2	-0.60** (3.48)	-0.36 (0.66)	0.37** (3.57)	1.03* (2.80)	-0.09 (1.10)	0.01 (0.04)	0.973	(0.039)	— (1.33)
6			0.001 (0.13)		0.10 (0.41)	0.14* (2.11)	0.52* (2.14)	0.991	(0.050)	— (7.37)
7				0.000 (0.04)		0.13* (2.14)	0.58** (3.10)	0.991	(0.050)	-2.91
8				0.01 (1.54)			0.91** (10.18)	0.990	(0.053)	-1.01

a) OLS-estimates; yearly data. All explanatory variables are lagged one year. The figures within parentheses underneath the coefficient estimates denote t-ratio's; two asterisks denote a significance level of 1%, one asterisk a level of 5%. $\bar{R}^2$ denotes the coefficient of determination, adjusted for degrees of freedom. Part of the regressions does not contain a constant term; for these cases R^2 has been recalculated as $1 - \Sigma e_t^2/\Sigma y_t^2$. To enable a comparison of the goodness of fit between the equations with and without constant term, the value of the root mean square error (RMSE) has been added between brackets. As the regressions contain the lagged dependent variable, the value of Durbin's h-statistic has been reported to test on autocorrelation. In those instances in which Durbin's h could not be computed, we have carried out a Lagrange multiplier test on first-order autocorrelation; the LM-statistic reported has a F-distribution with 1, n-k-1 degrees of freedom, n being the number of observations and k the number of parameters.

1 and 5 indicate that the hypothesis should be rejected. As to Δ_1/Δ_2, regressions 2 and 3 would support the hypothesis, but see regression 4, which is statistically as good as regression 2. As to Δ_3/Δ_2, in regression 6 $\varepsilon_{.3}$ and ε_{4d3} are not significantly different from zero, nor from each other. Hence, it is assumed in regression 7 that $\varepsilon_{12} = \varepsilon_{23} = \varepsilon_{33} = \varepsilon_{4d3}$, i.e. all people currently not receiving a benefit w_{4i} attach the same weight to this kind of social security, which may differ from the weight given to it by the beneficiaries themselves for whom w_{4i} is their current source of income. Contrary to regression 5, the results of regressions 6 and 7 point out that the dependants outside the labour force might play a role in the decision making process on social security. On the whole, and especially from regressions 1 and 5 which statistically yielded the best results, it is suggested that the dependants may have (had) political influence.

Next, let us take a look at the second (sub)period 1971-1984. Regressions 9 and 13 in table 7.3 report the estimation results according to the standard form of eqs. (7.46) and (7.47). None of the explanatory variables obtains a coefficient which is significantly different from zero. However, although the goodness of fit is inferior to that for the first subperiod, the hypothesis that the regressions are useless is rejected. Multicollinearity is a very serious problem here, indeed. It appears to be impossible to identify the separate impact of (each of) the explanatory variables. Regressions 10 - 12 and 14 - 16 - with approximately equal goodness of fit measures, yet quite different values and significance levels for the coefficient estimates - just present some fine examples of the latter statement. The only conclusion to be drawn from table 7.3 is that the relative numerical strength variables can help to explain the ratio's Δ_1/Δ_2 and Δ_3/Δ_2.

Finally, we apply the model to the prolonged period 1953-1984. To that purpose we couple the 1953-1970 data of the first data set to the 1971-1984 data of the second. A dummy variable is added to control for the various discontinuities in the data between the two sets.[21]

Regressions 17 and 21 in table 7.4 report the estimation results according to the standard form of eqs. (7.46) and (7.47). Statistically,

Table 7.3 Estimation results for Δ_1/Δ_2 and Δ_3/Δ_2, period 1971-1984.[a]

regression number	dependent variable	Constant	E_s/E_c	E_p/E_c	E_{4d}/E_c	E_{41}/E_c	lagged dependent variable	$\bar{R}^2$ (RMSE)	Durbin's h (LM)
9	Δ_1/Δ_2	-1.38 (0.68)	-2.22 (0.90)	0.83 (1.21)	0.49 (0.88)	-0.14 (0.23)	0.38 (1.23)	0.770 (0.049)	- (0.59)
10		0.09 (0.26)	-0.98* (2.60)	0.26 (1.76)	-	-	0.25 (0.99)	0.797 (0.046)	1.96
11			0.15* (3.10)			-0.17* (2.64)	0.25 (0.89)	0.994 (0.047)	- (0.58)
12				0.11* (2.40)		-0.18* (2.56)	0.61* (3.07)	0.993 (0.052)	0.86
13	Δ_3/Δ_2	-2.61 (1.24)	-1.08 (0.39)	1.05 (1.42)	0.69 (1.15)	-0.53 (0.81)	0.75* (2.80)	0.620 (0.052)	- (0.28)
14		-0.13 (0.29)	-0.61 (1.87)	0.19 (1.18)	-	-	0.64* (2.95)	0.640 (0.050)	-0.03
15			0.07* (2.53)			-0.07 (0.52)	0.64* (2.74)	0.994 (0.051)	0.06
16				0.07* (2.62)		-0.13* (3.04)	0.82** (4.99)	0.994 (0.051)	0.06

a) For comments, see the footnote at table 7.2.

Table 7.4 Estimation results for Δ_1/Δ_2 and Δ_3/Δ_2, period 1953-1984.[a]

regression number	dependent variable	Constant	E_s/E_c	E_p/E_c	E_{4d}/E_c	E_{41}/E_c	dummy	lagged dependent variable	$\bar{R}^2$ (RMSE)	Durbin's h
17	Δ_1/Δ_2	-0.15 (0.79)	-0.84 (2.02)	0.37** (4.39)	0.12 (1.07)	-0.13 (1.33)	-0.05 (1.28)	0.22 (1.34)	0.830 (0.044)	1.15
18		0.08 (1.36)	-1.01** (4.94)	0.27** (4.88)	—	—	-0.03 (0.82)	0.25 (1.55)	0.828 (0.044)	-0.10
19			0.06* (2.51)		-0.21* (2.16)	-0.02 (0.59)	-0.03 (0.65)	0.57** (3.26)	0.991 (0.055)	1.74
20				0.03 (1.25)		-0.04 (1.20)	-0.01 (0.15)	0.88** (7.01)	0.989 (0.059)	0.27
21	Δ_3/Δ_2	-0.24 (1.47)	-0.40 (1.17)	0.21** (3.42)	0.02 (0.20)	-0.06 (0.75)	0.01 (0.28)	0.60** (4.28)	0.959 (0.038)	0.13
22		-0.13* (2.07)	-0.59** (4.97)	0.19** (4.24)	—	—	0.02 (0.82)	0.60** (4.53)	0.961 (0.037)	-0.24
23			0.01 (1.86)		-0.19* (2.15)	0.02 (0.59)	0.03 (0.89)	0.80** (5.40)	0.993 (0.044)	0.29
24				0.01 (1.54)		-0.05* (2.13)	0.02 (0.64)	1.05** (10.19)	0.992 (0.047)	0.56

a) For comments, see the footnote at table 7.2

the two regressions perform very well. The fit is good, autocorrelation absent.

With regard to the three economically active social classes, it should be mentioned that the hypotheses of equal preference weights ($\varepsilon_{12} = \varepsilon_{22} = \varepsilon_{32} = \varepsilon_{.2}$, and $\varepsilon_{13} = \varepsilon_{23} = \varepsilon_{33} = \varepsilon_{.3}$) are both rejected; see also regressions 19 and 23. It is furthermore suggested by regressions 17 and 21 that the two subclasses of dependants do not play a role of significance in public sector decision making; the relevant coefficients are not significantly different from zero. Of course, the latter conclusion should be handled with some care, as the actual state of affairs may be obscured by collinearity between the explanatory variables (the correlation between E_s/E_c and E_{4i}/E_c is 0.994).

Omitting the numerical strength variables for the two subclasses of dependants, E_{4d}/E_c and E_{4i}/E_c, yields regressions 18 and 22, which produce the best results statistically, with a good fit and no autocorrelation. The relative numerical strength variables contribute significantly to the explanation of the effective interest structure Δ. Although, it should be acknowledged that, once again, E_s/E_c obtains a negative coefficient, as does the constant term in regression 22. The lagged dependent variable is only significant in regression 22, pertaining to public sector decision making on social security outlays, the average lag implied being still rather short (1½ year).

Summarizing:
- The relative numerical strength variables as proxies for the power weights λ_k can produce a quite statisfactory explanation of the effective interest structure Δ, and, with that, of state behaviour.[22]
- The evidence on the political influence of the subclasses of dependants is still somewhat mixed. We reported some significant coefficients for the first subperiod, while multicollinearity precluded that inferences could be made for the second. However, in table 7.4 no significant impact of the (number of) dependants was found over the period as a whole.
- With respect to the preference weights ε it does not seem warranted to draw firm conclusions. As in chapter 5, the coefficient of the E_s/E_c-variable was quite consistently reported to have a negative sign.

The hypotheses of equality of preference weights across social classes were rejected, both for the first subperiod and for the period as a whole; the finding that the hypotheses could not be rejected for the second subperiod must be deemed of little importance, given the high degree of multicollinearity.

7.4.3. An exercise in revealed preference

While the empirical application of the extended model points out that it is possible to explain the development of state sector activities encompassing the social security system, one could at the same time question whether the findings lend sufficient support to the theoretical model employed, in view of the generally negative sign of E_s (see also chapter 5). Given the preliminary, exploratory character of the empirical application, firm conclusions cannot be drawn here. Several important factors and developments, enumerated earlier, have not yet been taken into account, either in the theoretical model and/or in the empirical work. As a reminder: the relative numerical strength variables may be imperfect proxies for the λ's; the attitudes towards budget deficits may have altered (cf. chapter 8); the degree of tax shifting may have changed over the period considered, in response, for instance, to the alternation of excess demand and supply in the labour market; for the same reason, the subjective probabilities with regard to anticipated social mobility, implicitly contained in the interest functions P_k, may not have remained unaltered over time; even the preference weights proper need not have been constant given the economic growth since WW II.

With respect to the last mentioned issue some suggestive results of an exercise in revealed preference can be presented. We are well aware of the problems involved in this kind of exercise (cf. section 1.5.1; see also Basu (1980)), while furthermore the summary of findings in the previous subsection hardly can be read to imply a stimulus in that direction. The results are only reported to show that the issue of preference changes may be of interest; and it illustrates that our approach may open up interesting opportunities for further research here.

Table 7.5. The development of the interest weights, 1952-1984.

Year	Δ_1	Δ_2	Δ_3	$\varepsilon_{.1}$	$\varepsilon_{.2}$	$\varepsilon_{.3}$
1952	0.292	0.584	0.124	0.84	0.11	0.05
53	0.285	0.604	0.111	0.85	0.11	0.04
54	0.269	0.616	0.115	0.86	0.10	0.04
55	0.269	0.615	0.116	0.87	0.09	0.04
56	0.272	0.617	0.111	0.87	0.09	0.04
57	0.280	0.584	0.136	0.86	0.10	0.05
58	0.228	0.637	0.134	0.89	0.07	0.04
59	0.258	0.585	0.157	0.86	0.09	0.05
1960	0.271	0.561	0.168	0.85	0.09	0.06
61	0.269	0.569	0.162	0.86	0.09	0.05
62	0.276	0.557	0.167	0.86	0.09	0.05
63	0.281	0.535	0.184	0.85	0.09	0.06
64	0.320	0.477	0.203	0.82	0.11	0.07
65	0.307	0.476	0.217	0.83	0.10	0.07
66	0.295	0.487	0.219	0.84	0.09	0.07
67	0.300	0.478	0.222	0.84	0.09	0.07
68	0.315	0.448	0.237	0.82	0.10	0.08
69	0.307	0.448	0.245	0.82	0.10	0.08
1970	0.310	0.437	0.253	0.82	0.10	0.08
71	0.327	0.398	0.275	0.80	0.11	0.09
72	0.315	0.394	0.291	0.80	0.10	0.09
73	0.298	0.402	0.300	0.81	0.09	0.10
74	0.291	0.410	0.299	0.82	0.09	0.09
75	0.296	0.392	0.311	0.81	0.09	0.10
76	0.312	0.352	0.336	0.78	0.10	0.11
77	0.286	0.389	0.324	0.81	0.09	0.10
1970	0.284	0.484	0.231	0.85	0.08	0.07
71	0.304	0.446	0.251	0.84	0.09	0.07
72	0.293	0.438	0.269	0.84	0.09	0.08
73	0.278	0.444	0.278	0.84	0.08	0.08
74	0.272	0.447	0.281	0.84	0.08	0.08
75	0.275	0.435	0.290	0.84	0.08	0.08
76	0.289	0.397	0.313	0.82	0.09	0.09
77	0.268	0.429	0.303	0.84	0.07	0.08
78	0.258	0.443	0.299	0.85	0.07	0.08
79	0.254	0.450	0.297	0.86	0.06	0.08
1980	0.261	0.431	0.308	0.85	0.07	0.08
81	0.246	0.454	0.300	0.86	0.06	0.07
82	0.222	0.499	0.280	0.88	0.05	0.06
83	0.211	0.526	0.263	0.89	0.05	0.06
1984	0.211	0.533	0.257	0.89	0.05	0.06

To derive the results, we start from the Δ_i's (cf. table 7.5), and make a few assumptions that find support in the regressions reported above: (1) λ_1, λ_2, λ_3 are assumed to correspond with the relative numerical strengths of the social classes involved, with a one-year lag; (2) dependants do not possess politico-economic power, i.e. $\lambda_{4d} = \lambda_{4i} = 0$. Further, it is assumed that the preference weights are identically distributed for the different social classes, i.e. $\varepsilon_{kg} = \varepsilon_{.g}$, ∀k, g. Then, yearly values for $\varepsilon_{.g}$, $g = 1,2,3$, can be calculated.[23)] For the results, see table 7.5. The value ranges suggest that there has been a substantial shift in preferences during the period of economic growth since WW II until the mid seventies, from $\varepsilon_{.1}$, the (relative) preference weight given to real disposable income, to $\varepsilon_{.3}$, the preference weight given to social security; $\varepsilon_{.2}$, the (relative) preference for publicly provided goods and services, remainêd more or less constant. Since the mid seventies, in a period of economic slow-down and recession, the pendulum seems to have gone in the opposite direction, of accentuating private sector activities and private spending and driving back the public sector. Observe that if the theoretical model (including the additional assumptions) is correct and the implied shift in preference weights has actually taken place, this might help explain why the regressions in tables 7.2 - 7.4 did not perform better.

If one is prepared to accept the values of the preference weights from table 7.5, then it becomes possible to split up the changes in the effective interest structure Δ in one part due to changes in preferences and the other part due to changes in the power structure of society. For 1952-1977 (based on the first data set) and 1977-1984 (based on the second data set) we get:

	1952	due to changes in ε's		due to changes in λ's	1977
Δ_1	0.292				0.286
Δ_2	0.584	0.538	→		0.389
Δ_3	0.124				0.324
		0.217			
		0.246			

	1977	due to changes in ε's		due to changes in λ's	1984
Δ_1	0.268		0.203		0.211
Δ_2	0.429	→	0.547	→	0.533
Δ_3	0.303		0.250		0.257

For the period 1952-1977 it appears that the substantial increase in Δ_3 should be attributed both to the preference shift and to a favourable shift in the power structure. On the whole, Δ_1 remained at a roughly constant level as the effects of preference and power shifts cancelled one another. As a consequence, Δ_2 fell sharply. The change in the effective interest structure since 1977, an increase of Δ_2 at the expense of Δ_1 and Δ_3, appears to be mainly attributable to the change in the preference weights described earlier.

As it has already been noted before that the exercise in revealed preference in this subsection is suggestive, but most of all tentative or even speculative, this warning to the reader need not be repeated.

7.5. Conclusion

This chapter has shown how it is possible to formulate a model of state behaviour including the social security system, where due attention is given to the interest structure and the power relations in the economy. From the model, the precise impact of changes in preferences and in the power structure of society on matters such as the benefit rate of social security or the level of state employment and the number of social security beneficiaries can be derived. The model also gives an explanation for the observed incremental behaviour of the budgetary process; the displacement effects by which this process can be marked from time to time can, among other things, be attributed to changes in the power-interest-configuration. In response to changes in the unemployment benefit rate, it appears that state sector employment may grow as well as diminish, and that unemployment may decrease as well as increase, dependent on the tax capacity of the economy.

To study the possible consequences of endogenizing social security policies for the functioning of macroeconomic models, the behavioural equations for the state were inserted in a simple Keynesian income-expenditure model. Even in that context, some widely held views on the effect of social security on the level and stability of national income and employment need correction or, at least, amplification.[24] For instance, it is not all evident that a social security program has a positive effect on the levels of production and employment. The same result holds for the stabilizing impact of the presence of social security programs. Furthermore, it appears to be precluded that both the labour market related and labour market unrelated social security programs stabilize the economy at the same time; the possibility remains that they have simultaneously a negative impact on stability. As to demographic developments, our model points out that a growth of the labour force, ceteris paribus, most probably leads to a decrease in state sector employment due to pressure from rising social security outlays; private sector employment may grow, however.

A first attempt was made to apply the extended model of this chapter to Dutch data. It turned out that the relative numerical strength variables as proxies for the power weights λ_k are capable of producing an – although certainly not perfect – explanation of the effective interest structure Δ, and, with that, of state behaviour. For the (number of) dependants no significant influence on public sector decision making was found, over the period as a whole. With respect to the preference weights some suggestive – but, admittedly, tentative – figures were produced to illustrate that preferences may well have been subject to change, in response to economic developments since WW II. The latter phenomenon, in combination with some other factors discussed above, might help explain why the empirical results were not totally satisfactory from a theoretical point of view.

CHAPTER 7, APPENDIX DATA FOR APPLICATION OF THE MODEL INCLUDING THE SOCIAL SECURITY SYSTEM

Definitions

G_m : material (non-wage) expenditure of the public sector, both for consumption and investment; billions of guilders

W_s : public sector wage sum; billions of guilders

Π : private sector profit income; billions of guilders

T : public sector receipts of taxes and social security premiums; billions of guilders

W_4 : income transfers from the public sector to households; billions of guilders

W_{4d} : unemployment benefits; billions of guilders

W_{4i} : $= W_4 - W_{4d}$

E_s : public sector labour input; thousands of manyears

E_p : private sector labour input; thousands of manyears

E_c : number of self-employed; thousands of manyears

E_{4d} : number of persons receiving unemployment benefits; thousands of persons

E_{4i} : number of dependants receiving income transfers other than unemployment benefits (sickness payments, disabled persons' benefits, old age pensions, widows' pensions); thousands of persons.

Sources and procedures

Like in chapter 5, most data could be obtained from the National Accounts, issued by the Dutch Central Bureau of Statistics. Additional data sources were the Central Economic Plans issued by the Central Planning Bureau, the Pocket Yearbooks issued by the Central Bureau of Statistics, and the yearly accounts of the General Unemployment Fund. Some manipulations with the data had to be carried out in order to fit them to the model structure, because of the fact that taxes are supposed to be ultimately borne by profits. In more detail:

- G_m, E_s, E_p and E_c can be drawn directly from the National Accounts.
- Given the structure of the model, the wage sum W_s should be net of contributions for the public provision of goods and services, and exclusive of social security premiums and benefits as the social security system is considered separately, as bearing upon the class of dependants. For that reason, we established the sum of direct taxes and social security premiums as far as pertaining to wage and transfer income. Given the model assumption that the whole tax burden is borne by profits, the said amount was deducted, proportionally, from the published public and private sector wage sums and transfer income to obtain our (net) wage sums W_s and W_p and (net) transfer income W_4; it was subsequently imputed to profits and profit taxes, as far as relevant. Thus, Π was set equal to (gross) private sector production minus W_p.
- T has been defined as public sector revenues. It was calculated as the sum of: indirect taxes minus subsidies; direct taxes paid by firms; direct taxes and premiums pertaining to non-wage income of households; the (imputed) contribution of private sector wage income to public revenues, discussed above, which in the present model is taken to be borne by profits; and net profit and interest payments from the private to the public sector, vice versa. The data for the compilation of W_s, W_4, Π and T were taken from the National Accounts and the Central Economic Plans.
- The amount of (net) unemployment benefits W_{4d} and the number of beneficiaries E_{4d} have been constructed by considering for each year the then existing social insurance and social provision arrangements for

unemployed persons. The amounts of benefit payments (netted as well as possible) and the number of persons receiving an unemployment benefit have been summed over the various arrangements. The data were obtained from the Pocket Yearbooks (Statistisch Zakboek) issued by the Central Bureau of Statistics, and the yearly accounts (Jaarverslag) of the General Unemployment Fund (Algemeen Werkloosheids Fonds).

- E_{4i} has been calculated by summing the numbers of persons receiving sickness payments, disabled workers' pensions, old age pensions and widows' pensions. Data sources were:
  - Centraal Bureau voor de Statistiek, Tachtig jaren statistiek in tijdreeksen, 's-Gravenhage, 1979;
  - Financiële nota Sociale Zekerheid 1987, Tweede Kamer, Vergaderjaar 1986-1987, 19708, nrs 1-2.

Data sets

Table A.1. (1951) 1952-1977.

Year	G_m	W_s	W_4	Π	T
1951	1.68	1.52	1.14	13.22	5.51
52	1.89	1.55	1.30	13.89	6.11
53	2.41	1.66	1.40	14.77	6.11
54	2.47	1.94	1.58	16.26	6.39
55	2.76	2.12	1.76	17.95	6.97
56	3.19	2.36	1.89	19.10	7.62
57	3.45	2.54	2.39	20.80	8.71
58	3.06	2.68	2.79	20.54	8.43
59	3.14	2.75	2.89	22.34	9.41
1960	3.55	3.01	3.25	25.16	10.72
61	3.91	3.29	3.47	25.96	11.83
62	4.33	3.75	3.99	27.43	12.45
63	5.09	4.12	4.95	29.44	13.67
64	5.82	5.03	5.72	34.61	16.32
65	6.17	5.69	6.86	38.51	19.30
66	6.67	6.41	8.02	41.09	21.02
67	7.53	7.11	9.12	45.50	22.94
68	8.51	7.66	10.33	51.07	26.62
69	9.19	8.72	11.96	57.18	29.88
1970	10.69	9.72	13.83	63.89	34.07
71	12.26	11.21	16.38	72.16	40.50
72	12.54	12.85	19.43	82.60	46.32
73	13.02	14.26	22.41	95.57	52.41
74	15.06	16.54	26.80	106.78	59.91
75	18.09	19.45	33.55	114.21	68.89
76	20.37	21.76	38.78	134.83	77.98
1977	21.12	23.97	43.39	146.30	87.07

Table A.1. (continued)

Year	W_{4d}	E_s	E_p	E_c	E_{4d}	E_{4i}
1951	0.060	376	2395	1016	36	504
52	0.137	404	2364	1003	77	520
53	0.120	433	2416	991	64	522
54	0.108	461	2503	980	51	553
55	0.090	469	2581	966	40	573
56	0.078	476	2649	953	32	580
57	0.070	481	2686	933	26	964
58	0.163	482	2663	917	58	991
59	0.118	484	2715	905	41	1134
1960	0.075	490	2806	886	24	1181
61	0.057	497	2872	874	17	1202
62	0.057	505	2960	863	17	1254
63	0.065	509	3027	851	17	1296
64	0.063	512	3111	841	15	1351
65	0.106	516	3160	826	21	1406
66	0.163	528	3194	815	30	1461
67	0.432	537	3181	805	70	1488
68	0.462	544	3231	790	74	1570
69	0.398	558	3307	776	58	1650
1970	0.421	567	3366	763	54	1712
71	0.586	584	3388	752	65	1760
72	1.130	601	3341	741	107	1820
73	1.275	607	3351	727	109	1881
74	1.771	617	3355	715	132	1946
75	2.986	630	3326	700	198	2011
76	3.464	650	3315	684	215	2154
77	3.505	668	3328	663	211	2240

Table A.2. (1969) 1970-1984, revised series.

Year	G_m	W_s	W_4	Π	T
1969	9.28	8.80	12.04	62.05	29.90
70	10.82	9.79	13.90	69.08	34.08
71	12.67	11.30	16.48	77.36	40.57
72	12.74	12.95	19.54	88.37	46.38
73	13.15	14.42	22.54	101.44	52.52
74	15.00	16.76	26.98	113.74	60.00
75	18.01	19.78	33.81	121.77	68.78
76	20.27	22.23	39.17	143.03	77.94
77	21.16	24.52	43.77	155.67	86.95
78	23.11	26.59	48.78	168.12	92.26
79	24.99	28.30	53.06	177.94	98.25
80	27.15	29.49	57.21	191.01	107.38
81	28.83	30.14	62.53	204.16	112.22
82	29.02	30.86	68.05	217.25	111.78
83	30.27	30.21	69.84	228.23	114.39
1984	31.19	29.84	70.19	244.91	118.43

Year	W_{4d}	E_s	E_p	E_c	E_{4d}	E_{4i}
1969	0.355	565	3342	750	58	1650
70	0.375	572	3400	737	54	1712
71	0.510	589	3417	726	65	1760
72	0.967	606	3368	716	107	1820
73	1.103	612	3379	702	109	1881
74	1.502	624	3386	691	132	1946
75	2.548	637	3357	676	198	2011
76	2.958	658	3350	661	215	2154
77	2.992	676	3364	640	211	2240
78	3.115	690	3392	631	210	2325
79	3.188	703	3443	627	211	2392
80	3.881	714	3468	625	244	2452
81	6.249	728	3389	619	357	2485
82	8.710	734	3274	611	496	2512
83	11.304	733	3186	606	614	2540
1984	11.588	727	3169	605	650	2594

CHAPTER 8.   TOWARDS A BEHAVIOURAL-THEORETIC ANALYSIS OF
            BUDGET DEFICITS[1)]

8.1. Introduction

   For quite some time now public sectors in Western countries have been running budget deficits (cf. Saunders and Klau (1985)). The economic literature on these budget deficits and their financing is extensive. It is discussed whether government debt represents a burden or net wealth, and whether the so-called Ricardian equivalence theorem between debt and tax financing holds; the macroeconomic analysis of the consequences of budget deficits has been given a new impulse through the explicit modelling of the government budget restraint since Christ (1967); all kinds of budget norms have been presented and defended. Rather rare, however, are the studies in which a positive analysis of the economic and political causes of the occurrence of budget deficits is given.[2)] We will briefly survey the latter approaches.
   First, it could be hypothesized that policy makers maximize some social welfare function in terms of, say, unemployment, inflation and the balance-of-payments position, within the constraints imposed by the functioning of the economy. Then, assuming non-neutrality of debt financing[3)], policy reaction functions might be derived with respect to budget deficits (see, further, chapter 1). Secondly, as suggested by Walters (1967), interest rates may differ between citizens (especially the poor) and the state due to capital market imperfections (e.g., collateral requirements). Debt instead of tax financing by the state then would enable the (poor) citizens to borrow at the low interest rates enjoyed by the state (and the rich). Thirdly, Barro (1979), taking the Ricardian equivalence for granted, has presented a model for the determination of the public debt in which it is the assumed objective of the state to minimize the costs associated with tax collection. His central proposition is that deficits are varied countercyclically in response to temporary income movements in order to keep the tax/income ratio constant. It is interesting to note that Kremers (1983) has applied the Barro-model to the Netherlands, period 1953-1980. While the model does not fit the fifties

and sixties, it follows public debt growth surprisingly well during the seventies. However, Kremers is not very confident in the relevancy of the Barro-model, as the Ricardian equivalence has not been tested but was assumed to be valid; the order of causation between income and public debt growth might well be the reverse.

The approaches hitherto do not take explicit account of political factors, and hence it remains obscure how the proposed budget policies would come into operation. Let us now take a look at some studies which do take account of political processes.

Fassbender (1981) transformed the well-known Blinder-Solow model into a politico-economic model by introducing policy reaction functions for government expenditure and taxation, in line with the Frey-Schneider approach (see also chapter 2). According to these reaction functions the government changes the instrument variables depending on its popularity level, which in its turn depends on the state of the economy. Due to the budget constraint, then, the budget deficit is endogenously determined and, albeit implicitly, a function of the popularity of the government. Apart from the fact that no really satisfactory behavioural-theoretic underpinning of government behaviour is given, two serious problems stand out. First, apparently no (future) costs of deficit financing are taken into consideration; only popularity related to the (present) state of the economy counts. Secondly, no difference is made in this respect between bond and money financing.[4]

Explicit studies of the causes of the frequent occurrence of budget deficits can be found in Buchanan and Wagner (1977)[5] and Crain and Ekelund (1978). The main assertion of Buchanan and Wagner is that the fiscal perceptions of individuals are systematically biased. The costs related to debt financing are underestimated, because people are not fully informed and have no perfect foresight. Furthermore, it is argued that the encumbrances represented by public debt may not have to be fully borne by the present (generation of) taxpayers, due to a finite lifetime. Crain and Ekelund develop the argument that the burden of debt financing for the current generation will be different depending upon whether the taxes to service the debt fall upon human or non-human capital.[6] While it is likely that taxes on non-human capital will be fully capitalized, this needs not be the case for taxes on human income, since liabilities for the repayment of the debt cannot be carried beyond the tax-paying lifetime. One way or another, debt financing reduces the (average) perceived price of publicly provided goods and services, compared to tax financing. In response, voters are likely to increase their demand for such provisions. In a democratic environment politicians, competing for re-election, will translate this demand in higher spending levels, financed through debt creation.

Some aspects of the two studies just discussed deserve further attention. First, they start from the typical assumption of a homogeneous electorate; no social groups are distinguished. This is very remarkable in view of the importance attached to the distinction between human and non-human wealth, which is implicit in the study of Buchanan and Wagner, and explicit in that of Crain and Ekelund. Aranson (1983) points out that it is important to consider the impact on public sector deficits of organized interest groups, but fails to come up with a clearly elaborated account of it. Secondly, the debt illusion thesis in the sense of a biased perception of the future obligations stemming from the issuance of public debt, should be handled with care. Imperfect information and foresight need not only pertain to these encumbrances, but may also be associated with the future benefits of public investment and other expenditures which entail future benefits. Further, debt illusion due to ignorance and myopia will last only one period; after this initial period the newly issued debt must be serviced, and the issue turns into one of tax perception. One step further, in case of regularly returning deficits voters might exhibit learning behaviour; they might not only come to take account of the future consequences of present deficits but even of the future consequences of future borrowing.[7] Thirdly, although both studies present a behavioural-theoretic analysis of the occurrence of budget deficits in the present era, they cannot explain from this theory why deficits did not emerge for may decades in the past. Rather curious for public choice adepts (at least in our view), a decisive influence is attributed to "philosophical change", in the form of the development and spread of the Keynesian view on the economic process. It is argued that the moral constraints that inhibited massive resort to debt financing for ordinary outlays were effectively undermined by the policy advocacy of Keynes and the

Keynesians. That the modern regime of continuous and increasing deficits is dating from the sixties and not from the thirties, is attributed to the fact that it took quite some time for the Keynesian revolution to affect the thinking of political decision makers and the general public. In addition to this philosophical change, Crain and Ekelund point at two other factors to explain the emergence of budget deficits in recent times. The shift in the structure of sources of tax revenue in the twentieth century has resulted in a dramatic increase in the relative importance of human capital as a taxable base; further, it is noted, has the tie between gold and the money supply been disconnected, facilitating the use of inflation as a tax. However, why these developments should have taken place remains obscure. Finally, we want to stress that the Buchanan-Wagner and Crain-Ekelund studies lack a more rigorous formal analysis.

In preceding chapters we have presented and analyzed a formal model of state behaviour, based on the interest function approach to the study of political-economic phenomena. This approach started from individual behaviour, but at the same time it was recognized that individuals share basic political-economic interests if they have the same position with respect to the production process in the economy. Accordingly, some social classes were distinguished, among other things related to the distinction between human and non-human capital. Hitherto, decision making on the size of and the way of financing the public sector budget deficit/surplus was not taken along in our modelling of state behaviour; more precisely, the ratio between state revenues and outlays was governed by the - exogenously determined - parameter θ. In the present chapter we shall try to fill this gap in the analysis, and incorporate in our model the decision making on budget deficits and bond financing, along with state expenditure and taxation. To that purpose the model will be extended to encompass multi-period decision making, in order to be able to specify both present and future costs and benefits for the different social classes of the various courses of action open to the state.

The chapter is organized as follows. Section 8.2 presents the model and reviews the assumptions. Section 8.3 is devoted to a discussion of the results that can be derived from the model with regard to public sector decision making in a given period t. The impact of the various parameters of the model (within- and between-period preferences, the social power structure, economic growth, the rate of interest, time horizons, and so on) on the occurrence and the size of budget deficits is carefully examined. Section 8.4 contains some preliminary results with respect to the development of the state's budget balance over time. As it is beyond the scope of this book to try to incorporate the rather complicated equations for state behaviour derived in section 8.2 in a full-scale dynamic model of the economy encompassing goods as well as money and bond markets, attention will be restricted to an analysis of the development of the budget deficit in the context of a steady growth path and of a regular cyclic pattern of the economy. Section 8.5 concludes.

8.2. The model

8.2.1. Introduction

According to the interest function approach presented and discussed in chapter 3, public sector behaviour originates from (is in accordance with) the constrained maximization of the state interest function P_s, which is a weighted representation of the elementary interest functions P_k of the social classes. An elementary interest function represents the interest (utility) function of the (politically) representative member of a social class; it is a function of the amounts of goods and services that can be obtained both in and outside the market. As regards the latter, attention will be restricted here to the goods and services supplied by the public sector; the bundle of goods and services that can be obtained in the market is reflected by real disposable income.

In the preceding chapters the analysis referred to one-period decision making, both for the members of the social classes and for the state. The current costs and benefits of public sector provisions and taxation were weighted against one another, given the state budget constraint; saving, or dissaving, was neglected. We now want to address the issues related to the public sector decision making process on budget deficits (surpluses) in connection with bond financing. It should be noted at the outset that money finance will not be taken into consideration, as it would necessitate the explicit introduction of a (another) monetary authority – the central bank – with its peculiar legal status and its specific position in the decision making process on economic policy; this would lead us outside the scope of this book.[8] When it comes to bond finance of current public sector activities, one should include in the model the future costs associated with interest payments and redemptions, estimate how these will affect the (anticipated) future tax burdens of the various social classes, and assess how the members of the social classes will weigh the benefits of public sector provisions against the costs of present and/or future taxation. In the ensuing multi-period framework for the analysis of public sector decision making, it further is not at all evident that processes of saving and dissaving by the members of the social classes can be ignored without consequence.

Our first concern then is to specify how an individual member of class k is affected by and evaluates a given time-path of public expenditure and taxation. Let x_{kt} denote the amount of goods and services obtained in the market, G_{kt} the amount of goods and services provided by the public sector, τ_{kt} the tax rate, and w_{kt} the level of income of the representative member of social class k in period t. In line with the functional formulation adopted since chapter 3, it is assumed that the intertemporal utility function of the representative member of class k is given by

$$(8.1) \quad P_{kt} = \prod_{j=0}^{H_k} [x_{kt+j}^{\varepsilon_{k1}} \cdot G_{kt+j}^{\varepsilon_{k2}}]^{\mu_{kj}}, \quad \varepsilon_{kg} \geq 0 \; \forall g, \; \Sigma_g \varepsilon_{kg} = 1,$$
$$\mu_{kj} \geq 0 \; \forall j, \; \Sigma_j \mu_{kj} = 1,$$

with H_k indicating the time horizon, $H_k > 0$; the parameters μ_{kj} represent the time preference schedule. The intertemporal budget constraint is represented by:

$$(8.2) \quad \sum_{j=0}^{H_k} P_{t+j} \cdot x_{kt+j}/(1+r)^j = \sum_{j=0}^{H_k} (1-\tau_{kt+j}) w_{kt+j}/(1+r)^j,$$

where P_t denotes the price of marketed goods and services and r the interest rate, which will be taken to be given and fixed. The life-cycle model of maximizing (8.1) under the constraint (8.2)[9] yields the following optimal time-path for private consumption x_k, given expected values for public sector provisions G_k and taxation τ_k:

(8.3) $\quad x_{kt+j} = \dfrac{(1+r)^j}{P_{t+j}} \cdot \mu_{kj} \cdot Z_{kt}$, $j = 0,1,\ldots,H_k$,

$$\text{with: } Z_{kt} = \sum_{j=0}^{H_k} (1-\tau_{kt+j})w_{kt+j}/(1+r)^j .$$

Substituting (8.3) back into (8.1), and collecting all the variables which are assumed to be exogenous to the state decision making process in a term A_{kt}, would produce the elementary interest function for social class k in terms of G_k and τ_k relevant for public sector decision making in period t:

(8.4) $\quad P_{kt} = A_{kt} \cdot Z_{kt}^{\varepsilon_{k1}} \cdot \prod_{j=0}^{H_k} G_{kt+j}^{\varepsilon_{k2}\mu_{kj}}$.

As a consequence of this formulation it can immediately be deduced that in case of a life-cycle model the exact timing of taxation is of no importance to the representative member of class k, as long as the discounted value of his tax payments remains unaltered. When this holds true for all k, and when the time horizon is equal for all social classes while moreover r is also the rate of interest bearing upon the state, the political struggle in the public sector decision making process will be about the distribution over the various social classes of the total discounted value of the tax revenue to be levied; once that has been settled, timing is irrelevant for each class. As - apart from a sum restriction over the time horizon under consideration - tax rates would be indeterminate, so would be the budget deficit. The budget deficit/surplus of the state would just be the antipole of the budget surpluses/deficits of the social classes. Of course, this is the Ricardian equivalence case referred to in section 8.1.

Several objections can be raised to the formulation of the programming problems for the social classes and the state contained in the preceding equations and the concomitant discussion.
a. Capital markets generally are not without imperfections. Ordinary citizens, certainly the less wealthy ones who are only in possession of

their human capital, are not treated on equal terms with the state with regard to collateral requirements and/or interest rates when it comes to borrowing money. In such a situation it could make sense for the citizens to delegate the process of borrowing and lending to the state. Through a proper timing of taxation, and budget deficits/ surpluses, the state could arrange for a time-path of real disposable income for each social class that would correspond with the optimal consumption pattern (8.3). In each period the members of the social classes could directly attune their consumption expenditure to the disposable income of the period involved; i.e. x_{kt+j} would be directly related to $(1-\tau_{kt+j})w_{kt+j}$.[10] If so, the elementary interest functions (8.1) would come to read:

$$(8.5) \qquad P_{kt} = A_{kt} \cdot \prod_{j=0}^{H_k} [(1-\tau_{kt+j})^{\varepsilon_{k1}} \cdot G_{kt+j}^{\varepsilon_{k2}}]^{\mu_{kj}},$$

with A_{kt} again containing all those variables which are assumed to be exogenous to the public sector decision making process at time t.

b. All kinds of informational discrepancies and distortions may arise in the process of transmitting the preferences of the citizens into the elementary interest functions taken account of in public sector decision making. First, because of computational and informational restrictions citizens may not take account of life-cycle considerations, but may just use simple rules of thumb. Consumption, for instance, might be directly related to disposable income, given some a priori fixed savings rate. Secondly, even if the citizens employ a life-cycle model, the state sector workers need not be fully informed of all ins and outs of private sector planning; as a reasonable first-order approximation they might hypothesize a fixed relationship between consumption and current disposable income. Thirdly, there could be a Stackelberg-type relation between citizens and state, where at each moment of time citizens - for lack of better information - hold the current tax rate as indicative for the future value of this variable, while the state is aware and taking account of this.

In all these instances, the elementary interest function of social class k, relevant for the analysis of public sector decision making, would read like eq. (8.5).

c. Some other problems arise in connection with the time horizon H_k and the time preference schedule μ_{kj}.

First, one could point at the circumstance that each social class is composed of persons of different generations, with different ages and time horizons, and with different time preference schedules for the remainder of their lives. However, in the context of the interest function approach this is not a real problem. Taking for granted that the various generations within each social class - apart from their time horizon and time preferences - have very much in common (especially tax rates and the amounts of publicly supplied goods and services), eq. (8.5) can be interpreted to be a weighted average of the preferences of all generations of class k, hence to be representative for class k.[11] That is, μ_{kj} can be interpreted to be a weighted average of the time preferences of the different generations, where the weights presumably will be related to the age frequencies in the group; the horizon index H_k can be considered to be determined by the horizon of the youngest member, and thus may be quite large.

Secondly, it is not self-evident that the time horizon H_k - or, for that matter, the time preference schedule μ_{kj} - will be equal among the social classes, or between the social classes and the state. A first reason why this might not be the case, readily comes to mind: the age structure of the social groups may differ. It may, furthermore, be presumed that the time horizon of capital owners will be relatively large and their rate of time preference relatively small. The possession and management of capital will urge them to pay extra attention to the future and to de-emphasize the present. The "strategic bequest motive" of Bernheim c.s. (1985) may also play a role here. We shall return to these issues later on.

The time horizon of the state deserves yet some special attention. As in addition to the present also all relevant future interests of the various social classes are brought to bear upon the state decision making process - through pressure, multiple positions, anticipated social mobility and/or altruism -, it stands to reason that the time horizon of the state, denoted by H, will be at least as large as the largest time horizon of the social classes (i.e., of those social classes for which $\lambda_k > 0$). H might even be substantially larger, in view of the fact that the state is in principle an infinitely-lived organization. That is, while the interests of the members of the social classes are only taken account of and promoted up to period $t + H_k$, one might well be aware of and take into consideration that taxes can be levied, interest paid and debt redeemed beyond that date.

<u>d</u>. The formulation above did not account for an already existing level of state debt at time t, nor allow for the possibility of a non-zero level of state indebtedness at the end of the time horizon. If the time horizon is taken to be finite, it does not seem to be obvious that the state debt will be fully redeemed at the end of that interval; generations that will live afterwards could in principle be burdened with that task. On the other hand, once the state debt is allowed to be positive at the end of the time horizon, its admissible level should be specified, in order to prevent that the tax burden is shifted indefinitely into the future. Capital market considerations with regard to the maximum amount of loanable funds come into play here.

Bearing in mind the foregoing discussion we will now unfold in more detail our multi-period model of state behaviour that will be used for the analysis of state decision making on budget deficits.

8.2.2. The model

With regard to the state activities to be considered in this chapter, attention will be restricted to the supply of non-marketed goods and services and to taxation, in relation to bond financing. As the emphasis is on the latter issue, income transfers under the social security system will not be explicitly modelled here in order not to overload the notation; the preceding chapter makes sufficiently clear how such transfers could be integrated in the analysis. For the same reason, attention will be restricted to the classes of state and private sector workers and capital owners; dependants will be assumed to have no political power ($\lambda_4 = 0$; cf. chapter 7). The goods and services supplied by the state will be assumed to be purely collective in nature (G).

Bonds are taken to be perpetuities paying one currency unit of interest per period; cf. Blinder and Solow (1973). With B measuring the number of bonds outstanding, and r being the interest rate (which is taken to be fixed), interest payments by the state for the period concerned will be equal to B, while the market value of the stock of bonds is given by B/r.

State behaviour in period t is assumed to be in accordance with the (constrained) maximization of the <u>state interest function</u> P_{st}:

$$(8.6) \quad P_{st} = \prod_{k=1}^{3} P_{kt}^{\lambda_{kt}}, \quad \lambda_{kt} \geq 0 \; \forall k, \; \Sigma_k \lambda_{kt} = 1 .$$

The interests of social class k as taken into account in the decision making process within the state organization are represented by the elementary interest functions P_{kt} for which, for the reasons discussed above, the following specification will be used:

$$(8.7) \quad P_{kt} = A_{kt} \cdot \prod_{j=0}^{H_k} [(1-\tau_{kt+j})^{\varepsilon_{k1}} \cdot G_{t+j}^{\varepsilon_{k2}}]^{\mu_{kj}} ,$$

$$\varepsilon_{kg} \geq 0 \; \forall g, \; \Sigma_g \varepsilon_{kg} = 1 ,$$

$$\mu_{kj} \geq 0 \; \forall j, \; \Sigma_j \mu_{kj} = 1 .$$

Here, ε_{k1} and ε_{k2} denote the relative importance attached by the average member of social class k to real disposable income and the consumption of non-marketed (collective) state goods; μ_{kj} indicates his time preference schedule. As point of departure, the time horizon H_k is assumed to be finite; it is allowed to differ among social classes. The time horizon of the state will be denoted by H; as P_s encompasses all elementary interest functions P_k, it is presumed that H is at least as large as the largest H_k.

As we shall mostly be examining the state's decision making process in period t, there seems to be no need to introduce a double time-index to mark activities that are planned or expected at one time to take place at another. Thus, for example, unless stated otherwise, G_{t+j} will denote the level of public provisions planned or expected in period t to be supplied in period t + j.

Let us now turn to the specification of the <u>constraints</u> subject to which P_s is being maximized. Above, it has already - implicitly - been assumed that the income levels of the individual members of the social classes are taken as exogenous - that is, as determined in labour and product markets - by the state. The same assumption will be employed for the total level of income of each class - the tax base - denoted by Y_k; Y_1 is equal to the state wage sum W_s, Y_2 to the private sector wage sum W_p, and Y_3 to gross business profits Π. Consequently, national income Y - $Y = \Sigma_k Y_k$ - is also considered as an exogenous variable by the state. Our state is rather naive in the sense that no account will be taken, for example, of possible multiplier effects of state expenditure. Notice that we are concerned here with the way the state actually operates, and in that perspective such assumptions may be quite realistic after all (for one thing, which economic model would the state have to employ to take account of such effects?).

The most important restriction on the behaviour of the state that we have to deal with in the context of this chapter is, of course, the budget constraint. This constraint is made up on the spending side by the outlays on collective goods and services (G) and the interest paid on outstanding bonds (B); on the revenue side we meet the collected amount of taxes ($\Sigma_k \tau_k Y_k$), and the proceeds from the issuance of new bonds at their market value ($\Delta B/r$). The budget equation for each period from t onwards reads as follows:

(8.8) $\qquad G_{t+j} + B_{t+j-1} = \Sigma_k \tau_{kt+j} Y_{kt+j} + \Delta B_{t+j}/r , \qquad j = 0,1,\ldots,H ,$

with B_{t+H} denoting the level of state debt - measured in terms of interest payments due - at the end of the time horizon.

Let us first examine, in line with previous chapters (cf. the argumentation in section 4.2), the case of a <u>single profit tax</u> with rate τ. Then, inserting the P_k's and rearranging terms, the state interest function P_s can be written as:

(8.9) $\qquad P_{st} = A_t \cdot \prod_{j=0}^{H} (1-\tau_{t+j})^{\alpha_{3j}} \cdot G_{t+j}^{\beta_j} ,$

with: $\quad \alpha_{3j} = \lambda_{3t}\mu_{3j}\varepsilon_{31}$, $\forall j$,

$\quad\quad\quad\quad \beta_j = \Sigma_k \lambda_{kt}\mu_{kj}\varepsilon_{k2}$, $\forall j$,

where: $\quad H \geq \max_k H_k$, and

$\quad\quad\quad\quad \mu_{kj} = 0$, $H_k < j \leq H$,

and where A_t comprises all the variables assumed to be exogenous to the state decision making process at time t. The parameters α_{3j} and β_j can be said to denote the <u>influence weighted</u> or <u>effective interest weight</u> attached at time t to the various interests within the time horizon.

The budget equations (8.8) can be summarized into one budget constraint over the entire horizon:

(8.10) $\quad \sum_{j=0}^{H} G_{t+j}/(1+r)^j + \sum_{j=0}^{H} (1-\tau_{t+j})\Pi_{t+j}/(1+r)^j = Z_t$,

with: $\quad Z_t = \sum_{j=0}^{H} \Pi_{t+j}/(1+r)^j - (1+r)B_{t-1}/r + B_{t+H}/(r(1+r)^H)$.

Z_t may be called the <u>intertemporal discretionary tax capacity</u>; it is determined by the discounted present and future levels of the tax base, corrected for the service of the presently outstanding debt (negative) and for the (discounted) admissible final level of the state debt (positive).

The behaviour of the state can be derived, according to our earlier observations, from the maximization of (8.9) subject to the constraint (8.10). This programming problem yields the following solution:

(8.11) $\quad \tau_{t+j} = 1 - \dfrac{\alpha_{3j}}{\Sigma_h \alpha_{3h}+\beta_h} \cdot \dfrac{(1+r)^j Z_t}{\Pi_{t+j}}$, $j = 0,1,\ldots,H$,

(8.12) $\quad G_{t+j} = \dfrac{\beta_j}{\Sigma_h \alpha_{3h}+\beta_h} \cdot (1+r)^j Z_t$, $j = 0,1,\ldots,H$.

The equations pertaining to the rate of taxation τ and the level of state expenditure G in period t (j = 0) should be considered to be the <u>behavioural equations</u> for the state for the period under consideration; the solution for the periods beyond t has the character of a plan.

Given these behavioural equations for τ_t and G_t, the size of the budget deficit in period t, to be denoted by D_t ($D_t = \Delta B_t/r$), can be straightforwardly derived from the budget equation:

(8.13) $\quad D_t = \mu_{s0} Z_t + B_{t-1} - \Pi_t$, with:

$$\mu_{sj} = \frac{\alpha_{3j} + \beta_j}{\Sigma_h \alpha_{3h} + \beta_h} = \frac{\lambda_{1t}\mu_{1j}\epsilon_{12} + \lambda_{2t}\mu_{2j}\epsilon_{22} + \lambda_{3t}\mu_{3j}}{\lambda_{1t}\epsilon_{12} + \lambda_{2t}\epsilon_{22} + \lambda_{3t}} , \quad j = 0,1,\ldots,H.$$

Here, μ_{sj} denotes what might be termed the effective time preference schedule; μ_{sj} is the relative weight attached in the state decision making process to the goods and services in period j in comparison with the goods and services over the entire time horizon under consideration. It is a weighted average of the time preferences μ_{kj} of the social classes.[12]

8.2.3. Alternative formulations

For the sake of comparison we shall present here some variations of the model of state behaviour developed above, in which we consider some alternative assumptions with regard to the nature of public provisions and the tax system.

Firstly, public provisions may not be of a purely collective nature. Class specific instead of (or next to) collective public provisions can be straightforwardly taken account of in the model. For instance, if the one public expenditure category G_{t+j} would have to be replaced by three class specific expenditure instruments G_{kt+j}, $k = 1,2,3$, then eq. (8.12) should be substituted by:

$$G_{kt+j} = \frac{\beta_{kj}}{\Sigma_h(\alpha_{3h}+\Sigma_k \beta_{kh})} \cdot (1+r)^j Z_t, \quad k = 1,2,3, \quad j = 0,1,\ldots,H,$$

with: $\quad \beta_{kj} = \lambda_{kt}\mu_{kj}\epsilon_{k2}$.

However, total state expenditure ($\Sigma_k G_{kt+j}$) would remain unchanged for each period, as would the tax rate. Hence, the budget deficit in period t would, again, be given by eq. (8.13).

One might also be interested in the case of a <u>differentiated income tax system</u> with tax rates τ_k, $k = 1,2,3$, as opposed to the single profit tax above. To analyze an income tax system, the model of state behaviour contained in eqs. (8.9) and (8.10) has to be modified somewhat; whenever the definitions and values of parameters and variables deviate from those introduced above at the profit tax model, primes will be added to the notation. The programming problem becomes:

$$(8.9') \quad \max_{\tau'_{kt+j},\, G'_{t+j}} P'_{st} = A'_t \cdot \prod_{j=0}^{H} \left[\prod_{k=1}^{3} (1-\tau'_{kt+j})^{\alpha_{kj}} \right] \cdot G'^{\beta_j}_{t+j}$$

with: $\alpha_{kj} = \lambda_{kt} \mu_{kj} \varepsilon_{k1}$, $\forall k,j$,

$\beta_j = \Sigma_k \lambda_{kt} \mu_{kj} \varepsilon_{k2}$, $\forall j$,

subject to the budget constraint

$$(8.10') \quad \sum_{j=0}^{H} G'_{t+j}/(1+r)^j + \sum_{j=0}^{H} \sum_{k=1}^{3} (1-\tau'_{kt+j}) Y_{kt+j}/(1+r)^j = Z'_t,$$

with: $Z'_t = \sum_{j=0}^{H} Y_{t+j}/(1+r)^j - (1+r)B_{t-1}/r + B_{t+H}/(r(1+r)^H)$.

Remember that $Y (= \Sigma_k Y_k)$ denotes national income.

The solution to this programming problem reads:[13]

$$(8.11') \quad \tau'_{kt+j} = 1 - \alpha_{kj}(1+r)^j Z'_t/Y_{kt+j}, \quad k = 1,2,3; \; j = 0,1,\ldots,H,$$

$$(8.12') \quad G'_{t+j} = \beta_j (1+r)^j Z'_t, \quad j = 0,1,\ldots,H.$$

For the <u>budget deficit</u> in period t it then follows:

$$(8.13') \quad D'_t = \mu'_{s0} Z'_t + B_{t-1} - Y_t,$$

with: $\mu'_{sj} = \beta_j + \Sigma_k \alpha_{kj} = \Sigma_k \lambda_{kt} \mu_{kj}$, $j = 0,1,\ldots,H$.

Notice from eq. (8.11') that the average tax rate in case of a differentiated income tax system is given by:

$$\tau'_{t+j} = 1 - (\Sigma_k \alpha_{kj})(1+r)^j Z'_t / Y_{t+j} \ , \quad j = 0,1,\ldots,H \ .$$

This same tax rate would result in case of a <u>uniform income tax system</u> ($\tau_{kt+j} = \tau_{t+j}$, $k = 1,2,3$, $\forall j$). For the case of a uniform income tax it further follows from the above equations (8.9') and (8.10') that total tax revenue and total state outlays remain unchanged, as compared with the solution of the differentiated income tax system. The budget deficit in period t in case of a uniform income would then, again, be given by eq. (8.13').

8.3. Discussion

8.3.1. Introduction

It seems useful to start our discussion of the behavioural equations of the profit tax model - eqs. (8.11) through (8.13) - by making reference to the assumption of previous chapters of this book, that the ratio of tax revenue to state expenses can be treated as a priori given, in the form of the budget deficit parameter θ. Now, for the said ratio, it is obtained from eqs. (8.11) and (8.12), neglecting B_{t-1} and B_{t-H}:

$$(8.14) \quad \theta_t = \frac{\tau_t \Pi_t}{G_t} = \frac{1 - \dfrac{\alpha_{30}}{\Sigma_h \alpha_{3h} + \beta_h} \cdot \dfrac{Z_t}{\Pi_t}}{\dfrac{\beta_0}{\Sigma_h \alpha_{3h} + \beta_h} \cdot \dfrac{Z_t}{\Pi_t}} ,$$

with: $\alpha_{30} = \lambda_{3t} \mu_{30} \varepsilon_{31}$,

$\beta_0 = \Sigma_k \lambda_{kt} \mu_{k0} \varepsilon_{k2}$,

$\Sigma_h \alpha_{3h} + \beta_h = \lambda_{1t} \varepsilon_{12} + \lambda_{2t} \varepsilon_{22} + \lambda_{3t}$.

From (8.14) it follows that θ_t depends on the preference schedules in society (ε_{kg}, μ_{kj}), on the distribution of political influence (λ_{kt}), and on the expected (discounted) growth path of the economy (Z_t/Π_t). In a simple, static one-period model for the analysis of state decision making on taxation and public spending θ may be considered constant. However, as soon as more than one period makes its appearance in either the theoretical analysis or the empirical application, θ no longer can be treated as a parameter; for instance, the expected growth path of the economy may be subject to change, or the power structure of society. Notice that this point can help us to understand - along with the other reasons mentioned earlier - why the empirical application in chapters 5 and 7 was not a full success. It should be observed, on the other hand, that it is also not immediately clear how to apply the eqs. (8.11) and (8.12) to a relatively simple empirical test.[14] For that reason we shall not engage in such an effort here.

Let us now look in more detail at the (theoretical) impact of the various elements of the model on state behaviour in general and the budget deficit in particular.

8.3.2. Impact of the preferences for private and public goods

From eqs. (8.11) and (8.12) it appears that disposable profit income $(1-\tau_{t+j})\Pi_{t+j}$ and the availability of state provided goods G_{t+j} as effectuated or planned by the state are proportionally related to the intertemporal discretionary tax capacity Z_t. These proportions $(\alpha_{3j}/\Sigma_h(\alpha_{3h}+\beta_h)$, and $\beta_j/\Sigma_h(\alpha_{3h}+\beta_h))$, reflecting the effective interest weights attached by society to privately and publicly provided goods and services, are determined by the ε's, μ's and λ's.

First, notice that the ratio of $(1-\tau)\Pi$ and G for period t is equal to $\alpha_{30}/\beta_0 = \lambda_{3t}\mu_{30}\varepsilon_{31}/\Sigma_k\lambda_{kt}\mu_{k0}\varepsilon_{k2}$, which quite generally (taking for granted that $\varepsilon_{31} > 0$, $\lambda_{3t} < 1$) will be less than what the capitalist class would like it to be (namely, $\varepsilon_{31}/\varepsilon_{32}$). State and private sector workers, in their turn, are profiting from a free-rider position, as the result of taxes being fully borne by business profits. In the special case of equal preferences among the social classes, that is $\varepsilon_{kg} = \varepsilon_{.g}$ for all k, we would have $\alpha_{30}/\beta_0 = (\lambda_{3t}\mu_{30}/\Sigma_k\lambda_{kt}\mu_{k0}) \cdot \varepsilon_{.1}/\varepsilon_{.2}$, which is smaller than $\varepsilon_{.1}/\varepsilon_{.2}$ as long as $\lambda_{3t} < 1$. It is obvious then that (i) political influence does matter, and (ii) the effective interest structure relevant for the state's decision making deviates from the underlying individual preferences. Furthermore, as this result depends on the presence of a pure profit tax, it must be added that the amount of state expenditure and the way it is financed may not only depend on political power but also on the opportunity of social classes to shift the tax burden using their market power. For, the profit tax may have come about by political decisions, but it may also be thought of as the result of a full shifting of taxes on profits which has taken place in the product and labour markets, outside the political sphere.

Secondly, turning from the within-period relation between disposable income and public provisions to their distribution over time, we have:

$$(8.15) \quad \frac{(1-\tau_{t+j})\Pi_{t+j}/(1+r)^j}{(1-\tau_{t+h})\Pi_{t+h}/(1+r)^h} = \frac{\alpha_{3j}}{\alpha_{3h}} = \frac{\mu_{3j}}{\mu_{3h}},$$

$$(8.16) \quad \frac{G_{t+j}/(1+r)^j}{G_{t+h}/(1+r)^h} = \frac{\beta_j}{\beta_h} = \frac{\Sigma_k \lambda_{kt} \mu_{kj} \varepsilon_{k2}}{\Sigma_k \lambda_{kt} \mu_{kh} \varepsilon_{k2}}.$$

Hence, if for all social classes the time preference schedule μ_{kj} would be equal, say $\mu_{.j}$, then the planned distribution over time of the availability of private and public goods (in terms of their present value) would be in correspondence with this time preference schedule $\mu_{.j}$. Moreover, if the time discount rate implicitly defined by the time preference schedule $\mu_{.j}$ would equal the rate of interest r, disposable profit income and state expenditure would be planned to be evenly spread over the time horizon under consideration.

Once the time preference schedules μ_{kj} of the social classes differ, it depends on the distribution of the λ's and ε's by how much the time path of G is deviating from these time preferences. Notice that the distribution over time of $(1-\tau)\Pi$ still is in conformity with the time preference schedule of the social class that is at stake, the class of capital owners.

Thirdly, as we have seen that the preferences ε_{kg}, weighted with λ's and μ's, may affect the within- and between-period distribution of taxation and public expenditure, we should record their effect on state behaviour in period t more fully. With regard to ε_{k2}, the relative preference weight attached within social class k to publicly supplied goods and services, it is obtained:

(8.17)
$$\frac{\partial \tau_t}{\partial \varepsilon_{12}} = \frac{\lambda_{1t}}{\Sigma_h \alpha_{3h} + \beta_h} \cdot (1-\tau_t), \geq 0$$

$$\frac{\partial \tau_t}{\partial \varepsilon_{22}} = \frac{\lambda_{2t}}{\Sigma_h \alpha_{3h} + \beta_h} \cdot (1-\tau_t), \geq 0$$

$$\frac{\partial \tau_t}{\partial \varepsilon_{32}} = \frac{1}{\varepsilon_{31}} \cdot (1-\tau_t), \geq 0$$

(8.18)
$$\frac{\partial G_t}{\partial \varepsilon_{12}} = \frac{\lambda_{1t} Z_t}{(\Sigma_h \alpha_{3h} + \beta_h)^2} \cdot \{(\mu_{10}-\mu_{20})\lambda_{2t}\varepsilon_{22} + (\mu_{10}-\mu_{30}\varepsilon_{32})\lambda_{3t}\},$$

$$\frac{\partial G_t}{\partial \varepsilon_{22}} = \frac{\lambda_{2t} Z_t}{(\Sigma_h \alpha_{3h} + \beta_h)^2} \cdot \{(\mu_{20}-\mu_{10})\lambda_{1t}\varepsilon_{12} + (\mu_{20}-\mu_{30}\varepsilon_{32})\lambda_{3t}\},$$

$$\frac{\partial G_t}{\partial \varepsilon_{32}} = \frac{\lambda_{3t}\mu_{30}}{\Sigma_h \alpha_{3h} + \beta_h} \cdot Z_t, \geq 0$$

The sign of $\partial G_t/\partial \varepsilon_{12}$, $\partial G_t/\partial \varepsilon_{22}$ will tend to be positive if it can be assumed - as we will come to argue shortly - that μ_{10} and μ_{20} are more or less equal and larger than μ_{30}. Thus, eqs. (8.17) and (8.18) indicate that current state expenditure and taxation will tend to rise with an increased preference for public goods of any social class.

As both tax revenue and state outlays are increased, but to a different degree, the impact of an increase in ε_{k2} on the budget deficit of period t, D_t, is not immediately obvious. It appears that:

$$\frac{\partial D_t}{\partial \varepsilon_{12}} = \frac{\lambda_{1t} Z_t}{(\Sigma_h \alpha_{3h} + \beta_h)^2} \cdot \{(\mu_{10} - \mu_{20}) \lambda_{2t} \varepsilon_{22} + (\mu_{10} - \mu_{30}) \lambda_{3t}\} ,$$

(8.19) $$\frac{\partial D_t}{\partial \varepsilon_{22}} = \frac{\lambda_{2t} Z_t}{(\Sigma_h \alpha_{3h} + \beta_h)^2} \cdot \{(\mu_{20} - \mu_{10}) \lambda_{1t} \varepsilon_{12} + (\mu_{20} - \mu_{30}) \lambda_{3t}\} ,$$

$$\frac{\partial D_t}{\partial \varepsilon_{32}} = 0 .$$

Assuming again that μ_{10} and μ_{20} are more or less equal and larger than μ_{30}, it is suggested by eq. (8.19) that $\partial D_t / \partial \varepsilon_{12} > 0$, $\partial D_t / \partial \varepsilon_{22} > 0$. Hence, the size of the budget deficit is not independent of the (within-period) preference weights ε_{kg} of the social classes, not even if these weights are equal among the social classes.[15]

8.3.3. Impact of the time preferences and time horizons

In the present context it should be recognized that the time preference schedules of the state and the various social classes in general need not be identical. First, because the length of the time horizon may differ among the social classes and between the social classes and the state. Secondly, because the rate of time preference implicitly contained in the time preference schedules μ_{kj}, $k = 1,2,3$ and μ_{sj} may vary. As to the occurrence and the size of budget deficits, these possible differences can be of great importance.

Let us start our discussion of the time preference schedules by focussing first on the time horizons. In case the time horizon H of the state surpasses any of the time horizons H_k of (the presently living generations of) the social classes, the analysis of Buchanan and Wagner becomes relevant.[16] In the public sector decision making process as formalized in eqs. (8.9) and (8.10) the interests of future generations of social class k living beyond H_k are not taken into account ($\mu_{kj} = 0$, $H_k < j \leq H$), while the potential tax base formed by their (discounted) future income between H_k and H is. As a result, state planning over the time horizon H will give less weight to state expenditure G and to disposable income of the social class(es) concerned beyond H_k. Referring to eqs. (8.9) and (8.12): β_j will be lower, ceteris paribus, for $H_k < j \leq H$. Accordingly, G_{t+j} will tend to be lower for $H_k < j \leq H$, and higher for $0 \leq j \leq H_k$. Furthermore, according to eqs. (8.9) and (8.11): $\tau_{t+j} = 1$, $H_3 < j \leq H$. Of course, the shift in the supply of public goods and services to the present, and the shift in tax levying to the future, will tend to create budget deficits in the current period t; cf. eq. (8.13).[17]

One might presume that the budget deficit D_t will become very large if H would be considerably larger than (the largest) H_k. A simple example may suffice to show that D_t need not at all be explosive if H tends to infinity, although its value may become substantial.[18] Of course, it is questionable whether H is actually infinite; if not, the value of D_t is adjusted downwards accordingly. Furthermore, it should be noticed that over time some factors may be at work that are not taken along in our model, which will tend to dampen an excessive growth of budget deficits and public debt. Administrative and legislative restrictions, for instance, may become active if the state budget is expanded by substantial amounts. Also capital market considerations may come into play here, as heavy borrowing will sooner or later affect the creditworthiness of the state, and the interest rate. As will be shown in section 8.3.5, the budget deficit will tend to become lower, ceteris paribus, the higher is the rate of interest; the outstanding level of public debt may also have a decreasing impact on the size of the deficit.

Leaving the issue of differential time horizons, we now turn to the course of the time preference schedules μ_{kj} and μ_{sj} and the rate of time preference contained within them.

Taxation and state expenditure in period t (only) depend on the μ_{k0}'s, the relative time preference attached within the social classes to the present. The effect of an increase in μ_{k0} is given by:

(8.20) $\quad \dfrac{\partial \tau_t}{\partial \mu_{10}} = \dfrac{\partial \tau_t}{\partial \mu_{20}} = 0 \; ; \; \dfrac{\partial \tau_t}{\partial \mu_{30}} = - \dfrac{1}{\mu_{30}} \cdot (1-\tau_t), \; \leq 0 \; ,$

(8.21) $\quad \dfrac{\partial G_t}{\partial \mu_{k0}} = \dfrac{\lambda_{kt} \varepsilon_{k2}}{\Sigma_h \alpha_{3h} + \beta_h} \cdot Z_t \; , \; \geq 0 \; .$

With regard to the budget deficit it follows from eq. (8.13):

(8.22) $\quad \partial D_t / \partial \mu_{s0} = Z_t$, > 0 ,

as the intertemporal discretionary tax capacity may safely be assumed to be positive. As the effective time preference μ_{s0} is a weighted average of the time preference weights μ_{k0}, it further follows that $\partial D_t / \partial \mu_{k0} > 0$, $\forall k$; more precisely:

(8.23) $\quad \dfrac{\partial D_t}{\partial \mu_{k0}} = \dfrac{\lambda_{kt} \varepsilon_{k2}}{\Sigma_h \alpha_{3h} + \beta_h} \cdot Z_t$, $k = 1,2$; $\dfrac{\partial D_t}{\partial \mu_{30}} = \dfrac{\lambda_{3t}}{\Sigma_h \alpha_{3h} + \beta_h} \cdot Z_t$.

A shift in the time preference schedule μ_{kj} such that relatively more weight is given to the present, induces, as would be expected, more public provisions and/or less taxation in period t, and a larger budget deficit.

To illustrate this effect of the time preferences, suppose there is no outstanding debt. Then, if $\mu_{k0} = 1$ for all social classes, the budget deficit of period t will be at its largest, being equal to the discounted value of the total expected future tax base; for $j > 0$ $G_{t+j} = 0$ and $\tau_{t+j} = 1$. If, on the other hand, $\mu_{k0} = 0$ for all k, then present profit income will be fully taxed away and in the form of a budget surplus be saved for the future; thus, $\tau_t = 1$, $G_t = 0$.

As the possibility has been left open in the model that the time preference schedules μ_{kj} may differ among the social classes, it remains to be seen whether such differences indeed can be expected to exist, and in which direction they operate.

A factor that has already been alluded to is a possible different age structure per social group (which co-determines the interests that are by the state perceived as representative for the group). The higher the average age, the higher μ_{k0} is likely to be. In this respect the group of dependants especially distinguishes itself, because of the dominating proportion of old aged people. For this reason (taken in isolation) it is to be expected that μ_{40} is relatively high. However, this result is not of much significance here, as the class of dependants does not seem to have much political influence by itself ($\lambda_4 = 0$ in our model specification). As regards the age structure of the classes of state sector workers, private sector workers and capital owners, no unidirectional differences seem to exist between them.

There are several reasons that can be mentioned as to why the time preference μ_{30} of capital owners is presumably relatively small, compared to μ_{10} and μ_{20}. These reasons are related to differences connected with the possession of human and non-human wealth. The first has to do with the fact that the possession and management of capital will urge people to pay (extra) attention to the future and to de-emphasize the present. Secondly, while it is likely that future tax liabilities on capital will be fully capitalized into its present value, this need not be the case for taxes on income out of human wealth, due to the lack of transferability of the latter. This difference will show up in the intertemporal budget constraints of (the representative individuals of) the social classes, underlying the elementary interest functions P_k (cf. the derivation of (8.5)). Consequently, future tax obligations will be more strongly taken account of by capital owners than by state and private sector workers. In terms of P_k, this would amount to a relatively low value of μ_{30} vis-à-vis μ_{10} and μ_{20}. A third reason is related to the "strategic bequest motive" of Bernheim, Shleifer and Summers (1985). According to Bernheim c.s. the welfare of testators and their beneficiaries not only depends on income but also on particular actions taken by a potential beneficiary, such as attention or care from children or grandchildren. To evoke such behaviour wealth would be held in bequethable form. In the context of our model this theory suggests that capital owners may take account of the (monetary income related) interest functions of the younger generations in exchange for the actions earlier referred to, which are not explicitly considered in our model. The result would seem to be, then, that also for this reason μ_{30} may be lower than the time preference for the present of the non-capital owning social classes.

The foregoing analysis would lead us to expect that $\mu_{30} < \mu_{10}$, $\mu_{20} < \mu_{40}$, where μ_{10} and μ_{20} might be more or less equal. Granted that the present time preference of capital owners (μ_{30}) is smaller than that of state and private sector workers (μ_{10}, μ_{20}), if the former have to give in to the latter with respect to political influence, the effective time preference μ_{s0} will be increased;[19] this will show up in a larger budget deficit D_t.

If this kind of relationship holds true, there are two demographic developments that are interesting to point at here. The first is the structural decline of the relative numerical strength of capitalists (more specifically, selfemployed) to the numerical benefit of, in particular, state sector workers. The empirical applications in earlier chapters of this book suggested that the relative numerical strengths of the social classes that are actively involved in the production process may be good proxies for the parameters λ_{kt}. In so far as this is a reliable result, and if in addition the μ_{k0}'s are distributed as discussed above, the aforementioned change in the numerical strengths of the social classes would entail a gradual increase in the budget deficit, ceteris paribus. A second development that may become important is the expected substantial and structural increase in the number of old-aged; in the Netherlands, for example, from a present 11% of the population to around 20% in 2030.[20] Although the direct political influence of those dependent on transfers presumably is not great, it cannot be neglected, of course, that this social group is becoming a potentially important electoral group. To the extent that the old-aged do not belong to the class of capitalists, this development may again stimulate an enlargement of the budget deficit according to our model, given the relatively high time preference of dependants for the present (μ_{40}).

As final comment it is noted that in the special event of equal time preferences among the social classes, i.e. $\mu_{k0} = \mu_{.0}$ ∀k, it follows from eq. (8.13) that the effective time preference of the state μ_{s0} also equals this value $\mu_{.0}$, irrespective of the power distribution λ_{kt}.

The effective time preference schedule for the state is given by the μ_{sj}'s, $j = 0,1,...,H$, as defined in eq. (8.13). To be more precise, μ_{sj} indicates the relative weight attached within public sector decision making to goods and services in period j, in comparison with goods and services over the entire time horizon; μ_{sj}/μ_{sj+1} gives the relative weight attached to the availability of goods and services in two consecutive periods. We may call $\mu_{sj}/\mu_{sj+1} - 1$ the **rate** of pure **time preference**. Henceforth, this rate of time preference will be assumed to be equal between any two consecutive periods, and be denoted by ρ. As ρ thus equals $\mu_{sj}/\mu_{sj+1} - 1$ ∀j, while furthermore $\Sigma_j \mu_{sj} = 1$, it follows:

$$(8.24) \quad \mu_{s0} = \left[\sum_{j=0}^{H} \left(\frac{1}{1+\rho}\right)^j \right]^{-1} = \frac{\rho(1+\rho)^H}{(1+\rho)^{H+1} - 1}.$$

Notice that through μ_{sj} ρ is made up by the time preference schedules μ_{kj} holding for the different social classes and their political influence λ_{kt}. Ultimately its value is, therefore, determined by private discount rates; it should not be expected to reflect a "social discount rate" as plays a role in normative cost-benefit analysis. As the rate of time preference of state and private sector workers is probably higher than that of capital owners (see above), while the time preference rate of the latter is presumably closely related to the interest rate, it may be hypothesized that the rate of time preference of the state, μ, exceeds the rate of interest, r.

In this connection it is interesting to mention some results obtained by Zuidema (1982). He derived time preference rates for the three largest political parties in the Netherlands from a question put to the members of parliament of those parties involving a choice between immediate expenditure benefits to citizens and alternative streams of future benefits. The time preference rate for the social-democrats (PvdA) appeared to be 10%, for the christian-democrats (CDA) 4%, and for the liberal-conservatives (VVD) 2%, as compared with a real interest rate of 3.5% for the same year. As CDA and VVD formed the ruling coalition in that year, Zuidema tentatively concludes that politicians do not appear to be more future orientated than individual citizens (cf. Crain and Ekelund (1978), p. 817). Although it is clear that one should be very careful with results like these, it is remarkable that compared with the interest rate no low values, suggesting anything like a "social discount rate", are reported and that the value distribution over the parties is in accordance with what would be expected because of the human versus non-human wealth issue given the constituencies of the parties.

8.3.4. Income versus profit taxes

Above we have seen how the size of the budget deficit D_t is affected by the time preferences μ_{k0} of the social classes (cf. eq. (8.23)). In addition, it appeared that the extent of debt finance is also affected by the political power structure of society (λ_{kt}) and by the preference weights attached within the different social classes to the consumption of private versus state goods (ε_{kg}), provided that the time preferences μ_{k0} differ among the social classes (cf. eq. (8.19) and the discussion in section 8.3.3). These results were derived in the context of a profit tax system.

In section 8.2.3 we considered some alternative model formulations, with an income tax system, either uniform or differentiated. The general form of the solution does not deviate from that of the profit tax model; only the gross profits variable Π indicating the tax base has to be replaced by national income Y, while, furthermore the definition of the effective interest weights has been modified somewhat. Thus, most results carry over, with the exception of those related to the absolute size of the tax base and the impact of the ε's, μ's and λ's. The difference between the uniform and differentiated income tax systems only pertains to the distribution of the tax burden within each period (see also section 4.2).

As to the level of state expenditure and taxation, it can be shown that the effective interest taken in current state expenditure is lower in the income tax model than in the profit tax model, ceteris paribus (free riding is eliminated); the effective interest in current disposable income is higher, at least if the plausible distribution of the time preferences μ_{k0} discussed earlier is accepted. In addition, the intertemporal discretionary tax capacity will be higher in the income tax model, as the tax base is larger. Because of the counteracting forces, however, no general comparative statement can be made on the levels of tax revenue and state expenditure.

This brings us to the budget deficit. Contrary to what could be concluded from the profit tax model, the preference weights ε_{kg} do not appear to have any influence on debt finance in case of an income tax system. According to eq. (8.13') the effective time preference of the state in the income tax model is given by: $\mu'_{s0} = \Sigma_k \lambda_{kt} \mu_{k0}$. That is, μ'_{s0} is determined by the present time preferences of the social classes, weighted with their relative political influence. Only if the time preferences of the social classes are equal, say $\mu_{k0} = \mu_{.0}$ $\forall k$, is the effective time preference of the state independent of the political power structure of society; in that case $\mu'_{s0} = \mu_{.0}$.

To compare the effective time preference of the income tax model (μ'_{s0}) with that of the profit tax model (μ_{s0}), we adhere to the plausible assumption that the time preference for the present of state and private sector workers is higher than that of the capital owners ($\mu_{10} = \mu_{20} > \mu_{30}$). Under that assumption, it appears that $\mu'_{s0} \geq \mu_{s0}$. Combining this finding with the size of the respective tax bases, it can be concluded that the reliance on debt finance (if positive, and neglecting the outstanding state debt) will tend to be larger in case of an income tax system than in case of a single profit tax (or full shifting of the tax burden to profits in the market sector).

8.3.5. Impact of the level of state debt and the rate of interest

In 1985 public debt redemptions and interest payments in the Netherlands amounted to, respectively, 2.3% and 5.2% of net national income.[21] In state finance these burdens do not play a similar role. The reason, of course, is that in case of debt redemptions additional financial means become available in the capital market such that in general the debt can be reissued without problem. These bonds in fact function as perpetual bonds. For that reason the target variable in Dutch public finance generally has been the balance of the budget exclusive of debt redemptions; only the interest payments are focussed upon.

In our model the interest payments on the existing debt in period t are measured by B_{t-1}. The extent to which the state plans its outstanding debt to be redeemed at the end of the time horizon can be read from B_{t+H}. To be more specific on the relationships between the intertemporal discretionary tax capacity Z_t and the budget deficit D_t, on the one hand, and the levels of B_{t-1}, B_{t+H} and the interest rate r, on the other hand, we rewrite Z_t into:

$$(8.25) \quad Z_t = \sum_{j=0}^{H} (\Pi_{t+j} - B_{t-1})/(1+r)^j + (B_{t+H} - B_{t-1})/(r(1+r)^H) .$$

It is easily seen that the lower B_{t-1} and/or the higher B_{t+H}, the higher is Z_t. With respect to the interest rate we conclude that in general (that is, if the existing state debt is not exceptionally high) $\partial Z_t/\partial r < 0$.[22] Consequently:

(8.26)
$$\frac{\partial \tau_t}{\partial B_{t-1}} > 0 , \quad \frac{\partial \tau_t}{\partial B_{t+H}} < 0 , \quad \frac{\partial \tau_t}{\partial r} > 0 ,$$

$$\frac{\partial G_t}{\partial B_{t-1}} < 0 , \quad \frac{\partial G_t}{\partial B_{t+H}} > 0 , \quad \frac{\partial G_t}{\partial r} < 0 .$$

Next we turn to the budget deficit D_t (= $\mu_{s0} Z_t + B_{t-1} - \Pi_t$). Clearly, if the time horizon is short and if, indeed, redemption of currently issued debt is left out of account - that is, by pari passu increasing B_{t+H} - this would entail a strong bias in favour of debt finance; the cost of borrowing one dollar now would only be reckoned to amount to r dollars interest in the next few years. On the other hand, it could well be argued that the time horizon of the state may after all be quite long. The state interest function encompasses all the elementary interest functions P_k, while these P_k's (cf. section 8.2.1) can be considered to be some weighted average of the preferences of the various generations within social class k, the horizon H_k being determined by the time horizon of the youngest generation in class k. If so, the time horizon of the state could well exceed 50 years, such that for practical purposes H might be set equal to infinity. Then also B_{t+H}, provided its value remains finite, could be omitted from the analysis as the second term in (8.25) goes to zero.

The partial impact of B_{t-1} on the budget deficit is given by:

(8.27) $\quad \dfrac{\partial D_t}{\partial B_{t-1}} = 1 - \mu_{s0} \dfrac{1+r}{r}$, which is $\gtreqless 0$ if $r \gtreqless \rho + \dfrac{\rho}{(1+\rho)^H - 1}$,

using the assumption of a uniform rate of time preference ρ of eq. (8.24). When $H \to \infty$, the inequality of (8.27) simplifies into: $\partial D_t/\partial B_{t-1} \gtreqless 0$ if $r \gtreqless \rho$.[23] If indeed a higher ρ can be related to a more "leftist" state (see section 8.3.3), then this result suggests that the more "leftist" the state, the more it will be concerned about and take corrective action at a high level of (interest obligations on) outstanding state debt, ceteris paribus.

For the impact of B_{t+H} (provided that H is finite) and of the interest rate (as long as B_{t-1} is not too high) it is obtained:

$$(8.28) \quad \frac{\partial D_t}{\partial B_{t+H}} > 0 \, , \, \frac{\partial D_t}{\partial r} < 0 \, .$$

8.3.6. Impact of the size and the growth rate of the tax base

In the behavioural equations for the state both present and (expected) future values of the tax base, i.e. gross profit income Π, play a part. To analyze the impact of the tax base, we shall distinguish between its current level Π_t, and the expected future growth in the form of the (uniform) growth rate γ. Thus, $\Pi_{t+j} = (1+\gamma)^j \cdot \Pi_t$, $j = 0,1,\ldots,H$. We shall consider three different kinds of development with regard to Π:
1. an incidental increase in Π_t, without any effect on the expected future time path of the economy;
2. an increase in Π_t of a structural nature, in the sense that the whole future time path of Π is raised with it;
3. an increase in the expected growth rate γ of the economy.

First, for the <u>incidental change</u> in Π_t it follows from eqs. (8.11) – (8.13):

$$(8.29) \quad \begin{aligned}
\frac{\partial \tau_t}{\partial \Pi_t} &= \frac{\alpha_{30}}{\Sigma_h \alpha_{3h} + \beta_h} \cdot \frac{Z_t - \Pi_t}{\Pi_t^2} \, , \, > 0 \, , \\[4pt]
\frac{\partial G_t}{\partial \Pi_t} &= \frac{\beta_0}{\Sigma_h \alpha_{3h} + \beta_h} \, , \, > 0 \, , \\[4pt]
\frac{\partial D_t}{\partial \Pi_t} &= \mu_{s0} - 1 \, , \, < 0 \, ,
\end{aligned}$$

where it is taken for granted that $Z_t > \Pi_t$. An incidental increase in the tax base of period t is only for a small part used for making available additional public and private goods in the present; it is largely transferred to the future, in order to spread the benefits evenly over the entire time horizon. As a consequence, taxation in period t is progressive, and the budget deficit will be reduced.

Secondly, for a <u>shift in the growth path</u> of Π in period t - that is, an increase in Π_t, maintaining $\Pi_{t+j} = (1+\gamma)^j \Pi_t$ for $j > 0$ - it is obtained:

$$\frac{\partial \tau_t}{\partial \Pi_t} = \frac{\alpha_{30}}{\Sigma_h \alpha_{3h} + \beta_h} \cdot \frac{1}{\Pi_t^2} \cdot \frac{1}{(1+r)^H} \cdot \{\frac{B_{t+H}}{r} - (1+r)^{H+1} \cdot \frac{B_{t-1}}{r}\},$$

(8.30) $$\frac{\partial G_t}{\partial \Pi_t} = \frac{\beta_0}{\Sigma_h \alpha_{3h} + \beta_h} \cdot \sum_{h=0}^{H} (\frac{1+\gamma}{1+r})^h, > 0,$$

$$\frac{\partial D_t}{\partial \Pi_t} = \mu_{s0} \sum_{h=0}^{H} (\frac{1+\gamma}{1+r})^h - 1 = \mu_{s0} \sum_{h=0}^{H} [(\frac{1+\gamma}{1+r})^h - (\frac{1}{1+\rho})^h],$$

which is $\gtreqless 0$ if $(1+\gamma)(1+\rho) \gtreqless (1+r)$.

It now follows that $\partial \tau_t / \partial \Pi_t \geq 0$ only if $B_{t+H} \geq (1+r)^{H+1} B_{t-1}$, that is only if the already existing interest payment obligations are allowed to be accumulated and integrated in the outstanding level of state debt. Assuming that current state behaviour is neutral with respect to the outstanding level of state debt ($B_{t+H} = (1+r)^{H+1} B_{t-1}$), we would have $\partial \tau_t / \partial \Pi_t = 0$; tax rates would be flat, and G_t and $(1-\tau_t)\Pi_t$ would grow proportionally with Π_t (unit elasticity).

Turning to the budget deficit, the effect of Π_t is not immediately clear; state expenditure G_t grows, but so does the tax base Π_t, while the direction the tax rate τ_t will take remains somewhat questionable. However, eq. (8.30) points out that $\partial D_t / \partial \Pi_t > 0$ if $(1+\gamma)(1+\rho) > (1+r)$, which would hold as long as $\gamma \geq 0$, given that we may plausibly assume $\rho > r$. Thus, an incidental increase in Π_t would induce a "countercyclical" state reaction in the form of a decreasing budget deficit; an increase of Π_t which is expected to work through in the future tax base, would, on the contrary, seem to lead to a "pro-cyclical" behaviour of the state, entailing an expansion of state expenditure and an increase of the deficit.

We now proceed to our third case, and consider an increase in the expected <u>rate of growth</u> γ. In that case it is obtained:

(8.31) $$\frac{\partial \tau_t}{\partial \gamma} < 0, \frac{\partial G_t}{\partial \gamma} > 0, \frac{\partial D_t}{\partial \gamma} > 0.$$

These results quite unambiguously point at a "pro-cyclical" behaviour of the state.

The results reported in (8.31) also suggest that periods of economic growth will witness - ceteris paribus - larger budget deficits than times of stagnation. Observe that, with the help of γ and ρ as the uniform rates of growth and time preference, eq. (8.13) can be rewritten as:

$$(8.32) \quad D_t = \mu_{s0} \{ \Pi_t \cdot \sum_{h=0}^{H} [(\frac{1+\gamma}{1+r})^h - (\frac{1}{1+\rho})^h] - B_{t-1} \cdot \sum_{h=0}^{H} [(\frac{1}{1+r})^h - (\frac{1}{1+\rho})^h] + (B_{t+H} - B_{t-1})/[r(1+r)^H] \} .$$

Whether the state plans its budget to show a deficit depends on a whole range of parameters (γ, ρ, r, Π_t, B_{t-1}, B_{t+H}). The third term on the right-hand side of (8.32) will be positive, if, as was suggested above, redemption of presently outstanding debt is not taken into consideration ($B_{t+H} \geq B_{t-1}$), and it will at any rate be small if the time horizon (H) is not too short; for those reasons we will further ignore it. As to the first and second term on the right-hand side of (8.32), it is very plausible that $\Pi_t > B_{t-1}$. Then, if $\gamma > 0$ - while further assuming that $(1+\gamma)(1+\rho) > (1+r)$, which will not be too problematic once $\gamma > 0$ - it follows that $D_t > 0$. And the higher γ, the greater this budget deficit will tend to be. On the other hand, if γ becomes (sufficiently) negative, then the budget deficit turns into a surplus; that is, $D_t < 0$.

From this analysis it can be concluded that the deficits after World War II, ascribed to the influence of the Keynesian theory by writers such as Buchanan and Wagner (cf. section 8.1), may in fact have been caused by the behavioural reaction of the state to - a prolonged period of - economic growth. Of course, the same phenomenon may also have been caused (or have been corroborated) by changes in the social power configuration (cf. section 8.3.3).

Until now, we analyzed the influence of the interest rate and the growth rate of the tax base, ignoring inflation. It is time to make up for this omission. The problem of inflation can be addressed quite easily, if it is agreed that inflation raises the growth rate of the (nominal) tax base and the (nominal) interest rate to the same degree. The (real)

discounted value of the future tax base in Z_t will not be affected, then. However, the (real) discounted values of B_{t-1} and B_{t+H}, assuming these are fixed in nominal terms (non-indexed), will be affected by the rate of inflation. It can be concluded from eqs. (8.9) - (8.13) that inflation tends to raise Z_t and, as a result, D_t;
at least, if B_{t+H} is not too high ($B_{t+H} < B_{t-1} \frac{(1+r)^{H+1}}{1+(H+1)r}$).

8.3.7. Impact of the time horizon

Our model assumes that the state looks H periods ahead, with H finite. Now, what happens, if this time horizon would be lengthened, say, with one period from H to H+1? The solution of the model would be affected in two ways, ceteris paribus. First, the intertemporal discretionary tax capacity Z_t most probably is increased, as one period is added with its tax base Π_{t+H+1} (but also with interest payments obligations). On the other hand, the effective time preference μ_{s0} attached to the consumption of public and private goods in the present will diminish somewhat; see eq. (8.24).[24]

For the impact on the state budget deficit the following differential can be calculated (cf. eq. 8.32):

$$(8.33) \quad D_t(H+1) - D_t(H) = \Pi_t \cdot \left\{ \frac{\sum_{h=0}^{H+1} (\frac{1+\gamma}{1+r})^h}{\sum_{h=0}^{H+1} (\frac{1}{1+\rho})^h} - \frac{\sum_{h=0}^{H} (\frac{1+\gamma}{1+r})^h}{\sum_{h=0}^{H} (\frac{1}{1+\rho})^h} \right\}$$

$$- B_{t-1} \left\{ \frac{\sum_{h=0}^{H+1} (\frac{1}{1+r})^h}{\sum_{h=0}^{H+1} (\frac{1}{1+\rho})^h} - \frac{\sum_{h=0}^{H} (\frac{1}{1+r})^h}{\sum_{h=0}^{H} (\frac{1}{1+\rho})^h} \right\}$$

$$+ (B_{t+H-1} - B_{t-1}) \cdot \frac{\rho(1+\rho)^{H+1}}{r(1+r)^{H+1}} \cdot \frac{1}{(1+\rho)^{H+2}-1}$$

$$- (B_{t+H} - B_{t-1}) \cdot \frac{\rho(1+\rho)^{H}}{r(1+r)^{H}} \cdot \frac{1}{(1+\rho)^{H+1}-1} \cdot$$

The impact thus depends on the whole range of parameter values. As in the preceding section, suppose that the third and fourth term can be neglected, as they will tend to be small and to cancel one another. The first term on the right-hand side of (8.33) is positive if $(1+\gamma)(1+\rho) > (1+r)$. As Π_t may well be assumed to exceed B_{t-1}, it is then suggested by eq. (8.33) that, in case $\gamma > 0$ and $(1+\gamma)(1+\rho) > (1+r)$, a lengthening of the time horizon will induce a rising budget deficit.

An interesting further question is what value the budget deficit will attain, if the length of the time horizon H grows infinitely large.[25] First, eq. (8.24) yields for $H \to \infty$: $\mu_{s0} \to \rho/(1+\rho)$. From eq. (8.32) it is immediately apparent that no (upper) bound exists for D_t if $\gamma > r$. Stated otherwise, the state decision making process in case of an infinite H only can yield a well-defined, finite value for the budget balance if $\gamma < r$.

Let us consider the infinite horizon case more closely yet. If it may be assumed that $\gamma < r$, eq. (8.32) reduces to:

$$(8.34) \quad D_t = \Pi_t [\frac{\rho(1+r)}{(1+\rho)(r-\gamma)} - 1] - B_{t-1}[\frac{\rho(1+r)}{(1+\rho)r} - 1].$$

Once again, the first term is positive of $(1+\gamma)(1+\rho) > (1+r)$; the second term is positive if $(1+r) > (1+\rho)$. Observe that eq. (8.34) is highly simplified if the effective rate of time preference ρ more or less equals the (real) interest rate r, ignoring problems of inflation, it then reads:

$$(8.35) \quad D_t = \frac{\gamma}{r-\gamma} \cdot \Pi_t,$$

where γ is the (long-run, real) rate of growth of the tax base. Thus, it appears that the budget deficit in proportion to the tax base might become excessively large if $H \to \infty$ and $\gamma > 0$. Since this result is not very likely to occur in reality, two conclusions can be drawn: either H is actually finite, or — in spite of the infinite time horizon — real growth is not expected to endure for ever. Letting the principle of insufficient reason dominate expectations with respect to the more distant future, expected real growth may be taken to die out gradually, or to last only for some given finite number of periods. For instance, if within an infinite time horizon economic growth would be expected to last for T periods only, T being a finite number, eq. (8.35) should be replaced by:

$$(8.36) \qquad D_t = \frac{\gamma}{1+r} \cdot \left[\sum_{h=0}^{T-1} \left(\frac{1+\gamma}{1+r}\right)^h \right] \cdot \Pi_t .$$

By a proper choice of T eq. (8.36) could easily yield values for the budget deficit D_t, that would be in conformity with the figures of reality. Notice, finally, that for the limit of eq. (8.36) to exist it is no longer required that $\gamma < r$.

8.3.8. Conclusions

In the preceding subsections we discussed how the various parameters of the model affect the occurrence and the size of the state budget deficit. We summarize the main results.

First, in correspondence with the analysis of Buchanan and Wagner, budget deficits are furthered if the time horizon of the state surpasses that of the social classes, i.e. of the current generations of tax payers/beneficiaries. (The effect of a general lenghtening of the time horizon, for social classes and state alike, was seen to depend on the other parameter values). Relatedly, the budget deficit will be higher, the higher the rate(s) of time preference of the social classes. As the effective time preference schedule of the state is a weighted average of the time preference schedules of the social classes, the weights being given by their political influence, (changes in) the social power structure may also affect the size of the budget deficit, as long as the rates of time preference of the social classes differ. For instance, a decrease in the political influence of the capital owners, or an increase in the political influence of the dependants, presumably will lead to a rise of the budget deficit. In connection with the possibility of tax shifting in the market sector it has also been found that the budget deficit need not be independent of the within-period preferences with regard to the consumption of public vis-à-vis private goods. The above findings point out that it is relevant for the problem at hand to distinguish between the social classes, and to take account of both political and market power. Thus, by treating society as a homogeneous entity one eliminates from the analysis important intertemporal redistributive aspects of the public sector decision making process.

The rate of interest was found to have in general a negative impact on the size of the deficit. As to the growth of the tax base, it makes a difference whether the increase is of an incidental or a structural nature. An incidental increase produces a "countercyclical" reaction, a structural increase induces a growth of the budget deficit. In the next section we shall take a closer look at the development of the budget over time.

8.4. The budget deficit over time; some preliminary results

8.4.1. Introduction

In the present chapter we have analyzed public sector decision making on state expenditure, taxation and the budget balance within a multi-period framework. Until now the analysis of actual state behaviour has been confined to period t, also referred to as the "present"; state behaviour pertaining to future periods only consisted of plans and intentions. Of course, it is also of interest to study the (actual) development of state behaviour, and of the budget balance in particular, over time. To that purpose we could endeavour to insert the equations for state behaviour in period t, derived above, in a suitable macroeconomic model; with that extended model we could then analyze the dynamic interaction between the course of the economy and state behaviour, including the payment of interest on state debt and the issuing of new bonds as a consequence of budget deficits. Given the present state of the art of macroeconomic analysis as to the consequences of the government budget restraint on the one hand (cf. Christ (1979) and the literature cited there, Rau (1985)), and the rather intractable form of the solution of our model with regard to the budget deficit D_t on the other hand, it does not seem wise to engage on such an operation here. Thus, we shall undertake no effort here to model the dynamic functioning of the money and bond markets of the economy, nor shall we be concerned with a full-scale stability analysis of the economy under bond financing of the - endogenously determined - budget deficit. This does not imply that we cannot say anything at all about the development of the budget balance over time. Carefully holding our own ground - eq. (8.13) - we can superimpose certain assumptions with regard to the structural and cyclical development of the economy - i.c. the tax base - over time, and see which time path of the budget balance would be implied by it. In section 8.4.2 we shall discuss the properties of the budget deficit along a steady growth path, and in section 8.4.3 its behaviour in reaction to the business cycle.

8.4.2. The budget deficit along a steady growth path

In this subsection it is assumed that the economy is developing over time along a steady growth path; the growth rate of the tax base is equal to γ, the interest rate equals r. The central question we want to consider now is whether and under which conditions period-by-period state decision making in this set-up will result in budget deficits, public debt levels and interest obligations that maintain constant ratio's to the tax base through time, as to be compatible with steady state growth.

For the analysis it is assumed that the state, being aware of the steady growth of the economy, is anticipating it in its process of planning at time t in so far that it allows the state debt and interest obligations at the end of the time horizon considered to have grown at the rate γ, such that $B_{t+H} = (1+\gamma)^{H+1} B_{t-1}$.

Let η denote the ratio of the interest payments to the tax base, and, similarly, ϕ the ratio of the budget deficit to the tax base. Thus:

(8.37)
$$\eta_t = \frac{B_{t-1}}{\Pi_t}, \forall t,$$

$$\phi_t = \frac{D_t}{\Pi_t} = \frac{\Delta B_t / r}{\Pi_t} = \frac{B_t - B_{t-1}}{r \Pi_t}, \forall t.$$

If the state at time t is indeed reckoning with $\Pi_{t+h} = (1+\gamma)^h \Pi_t$, $h = 0, 1, \ldots H$ and $B_{t+H} = (1+\gamma)^{H+1} B_{t-1}$, eq. (8.13) for the budget deficit, using eq. (8.37) and the definition of Z_t in eq. (8.10), can be rewritten into:

$$(8.38)^{26)} \quad \eta_t = \eta_{t-1} + \left(1 - \frac{\sum_{h=0}^{H}\left(\frac{1+\gamma}{1+r}\right)^h}{\sum_{h=0}^{H}\left(\frac{1}{1+\rho}\right)^h}\right) \left(\frac{r-\gamma}{1+\gamma}\right) \left(\eta_{t-1} - \frac{r}{r-\gamma}\right),$$

$$\phi_t = \left(1 - \frac{r-\gamma}{r}\eta_t\right) \frac{\sum_{h=0}^{H}\left(\frac{1+\gamma}{1+r}\right)^h}{\sum_{h=0}^{H}\left(\frac{1}{1+\rho}\right)^h} + (\eta_t - 1).$$

This equation gives us hold for tracing the development of the state interest obligations, and with that of the public debt level and the budget balance, over time.

First, we shall address the case $(1+\gamma)(1+\rho) \neq (1+r)$. It directly follows from eq. (8.38) that η will be subject to change over time as long as it has not reached the "steady state solution"

$$(8.39) \quad \eta = \frac{r}{r-\gamma}.$$

The concomitant steady state value of ϕ (see also Domar (1944)) is given by

$$(8.40) \quad \phi = \frac{\gamma}{r-\gamma}.$$

It can be observed from eqs. (8.10) - (8.13) that the "steady state solution" (8.39) and (8.40) implies that $Z_t = 0$, $G_t = 0$, $\tau_t = 1$, $D_t = B_{t-1} - \Pi_t$ $\forall t$; i.e., the entire tax base is taxed away and used for the payment of interest on public debt. Of course, that can only be considered to be a perverse solution. Hence, it must be concluded that as to public sector behaviour no real steady state solution exists if $(1+\gamma)(1+\rho) \neq (1+r)$.

The reason behind that result is that even if the state (B_{t-1}) is on the steady state growth path at time t and may take it for granted to be on that path at the end of the time horizon (B_{t+H}), its planning need not keep it on that path in between. As long as $(1+\gamma)(1+\rho) \neq (1+r)$ it is in its interest, that is in the interests of those it actually represents, to reallocate disposable income and public provisions over time. The consequence is a budget balance at time t that changes the public debt level and hence the burden of interest payments relative to the tax base from period t to period t+1. In period t+1 the programming problem for the state repeats itself, the time horizon being shifted one period ahead; and so on. Proceeding in this way the state will manoeuvre itself over time into problems, as indicated by eq. (8.38).[27] However, that would not be the end of the story, in view of the partial nature of our model which only deals with (the explanation of) state behaviour. Suffice it here to point at some factors that will be at work in the economy, at least some of them in opposite direction: the rate of interest need not remain constant, certainly not if the state is borrowing substantial amounts, nor is it to be expected that the rate of growth γ or the rate of inflation will remain unaltered, while also the power structure of society and with that the rate of time preference ρ may be subject to change. It requires a complete macroeconomic model to study the interactions and feedback effects involved more fully.

Whatever may be the outcome of such modelling exercises, for our purposes it is sufficient to point out that our model of state behaviour is compatible with a (any) real steady state growth path of the economy if the condition $\underline{(1+\gamma)(1+\rho) = (1+r)}$ is satisfied. It is easily seen from eq. (8.38) that η and ϕ will remain constant over time then, given any initial situation $\eta_t = B_{t-1}/\Pi_t$. From eq. (8.38) it further follows:

$$\phi = \frac{Y}{r} \eta, \quad \text{i.e.} \quad D_t = \frac{Y}{r} B_{t-1} . \quad [28]$$

8.4.3. The budget deficit along the business cycle

After having considered the properties of the budget deficit in a steady growth environment, we shall now address the behaviour of the budget deficit along the business cycle. To that purpose it is assumed that the tax base - in deviation of its steady growth path - exhibits a regular cyclic pattern over time. The subsequent analysis of the development of the budget deficit over time, in deviation of the (any) steady state growth path, will provide more insight in the pro- or counter-cyclical pattern inherent in state behaviour.

The analysis can best take its start from the budget deficit equation (8.13) using the definition of Z_t in eq. (8.10):

$$D_t = \mu_{s0} [\sum_{h=0}^{H} \frac{\Pi_{t+h}}{(1+r)^h} - \frac{(1+r)B_{t-1}}{r} + \frac{B_{t+H}}{r(1+r)^H}] - \Pi_t + B_{t-1} .$$

Let the (any) steady state growth path be given by Π_t^*, B_t^*, D_t^* such that $\Pi_{t+h}^* = (1+\gamma)^h \Pi_t^*$, $B_{t-1}^* = \eta \Pi_t^*$, $D_t^* = \phi \Pi_t^*$, $B_{t+H}^* = (1+\gamma)^{H+1} B_{t-1}^*$, as discussed in the previous subsection. The relevant variables in deviation from this steady state growth path will be denoted by undercast symbols: $d_t = D_t - D_t^*$, $p_t = \Pi_t - \Pi_t^*$, $b_t = B_t - B_t^*$. Now it will be assumed that the development of p_t over time is characterized by a regular cycle. More specifically:[29)]

(8.41) $\quad p_t = a \cdot \sin \omega t, \quad a > 0, \quad 0 < \omega < \frac{\pi}{2}.$

The state is presumed to be aware of this cyclical pattern in the tax base and to effectively employ this knowledge in its multi-period planning process. It is further assumed that $B_{t+H} = B_{t+H}^*$; i.e. the state debt planned to stand out at the end of the time horizon is not affected by the incidental position in the business cycle but is governed by structural considerations.

Substituting and rearranging terms yields the following equation for the outstanding level of state debt at the end of period t:

(8.42) $\quad \frac{b_t}{r} = \alpha_1 \sin \omega t + \alpha_2 \cos \omega t + \alpha_3 \frac{b_{t-1}}{r} ,$

with: $\alpha_1 = a \cdot [\mu_{s0} \cdot \sum_{h=0}^{H} \frac{\cos \omega h}{(1+r)^h} - 1] ,$

$\alpha_2 = a \cdot \mu_{s0} \cdot \sum_{h=0}^{H} \frac{\sin \omega h}{(1+r)^h} ,$

$\alpha_3 = (1-\mu_{s0})(1+r) .$

This first-order difference equation can be solved for the level of state debt b_t/r along familiar lines. Next, we can calculate the budget deficit d_t ($= b_t/r - b_{t-1}/r$). The result reads:

(8.43) $\quad d_t = \beta_1 \sin \omega t + \beta_2 \cos \omega t + \beta_3 \cdot \alpha_3^t$,

$$\text{with: } \beta_1 = \frac{(1+\alpha_3)\alpha_1(1-\cos \omega) - (1-\alpha_3)\alpha_2 \sin \omega}{1 - 2\alpha_3 \cos \omega + \alpha_3^2},$$

$$\beta_2 = \frac{(1-\alpha_3)\alpha_1 \sin \omega + (1+\alpha_3)\alpha_2(1-\cos \omega)}{1 - 2\alpha_3 \cos \omega + \alpha_3^2},$$

while β_3 is a constant which is of no further interest to us. First, observe, using eq. (8.24) for μ_{s0}, that $0 < \alpha_3 < 1$ if $r < \rho + \rho/[(1+\rho)^H - 1]$, which seems quite plausible, and is taken to hold in the sequel. Thus, the third term on the right-hand side of (8.43) will die out over time and can be neglected. Notice, further, that $\Sigma_h \cos \omega h/(1+r)^h$ will be (much) smaller than $\Sigma_h 1/(1+r)^h$. Generally then, unless perhaps ρ would exceed r greatly, $\alpha_1 < 0$. Moreover, in general, $\alpha_2 > 0$. Hence, it follows that $\beta_1 < 0$. As to the sign of β_2 we remain uncertain. Bearing in mind the sign condition on β_1, (8.43) can be rewritten into:

(8.44) $\quad d_t = \beta_4 \sin(\omega t + z), \frac{\pi}{2} < z = \arctan(\beta_2/\beta_1) < \frac{3\pi}{2}$,

$$\beta_4 = \beta_1/\cos z > 0 .$$

From this equation we can draw our conclusions. First, in reaction to the tax base, the budget deficit also appears to follow a sinusoidal, cyclic pattern over time. Secondly, the oscillation period for the budget balance is the same as for the tax base. Thirdly, the time pattern of the budget balance has a phase difference in comparison to the tax base of at least a quarter and at the most three quarters of a cycle. See, for instance, figure 8.1 for the case of a regular cycle of six time periods ($\omega = \pi/3$). It is apparent that the budget deficit in general will have a - although not necessarily perfect - countercyclical relationship to the tax base. That is, if the tax base is above (below) its steady growth path, the budget balance d_t tends to be in surplus (deficit).

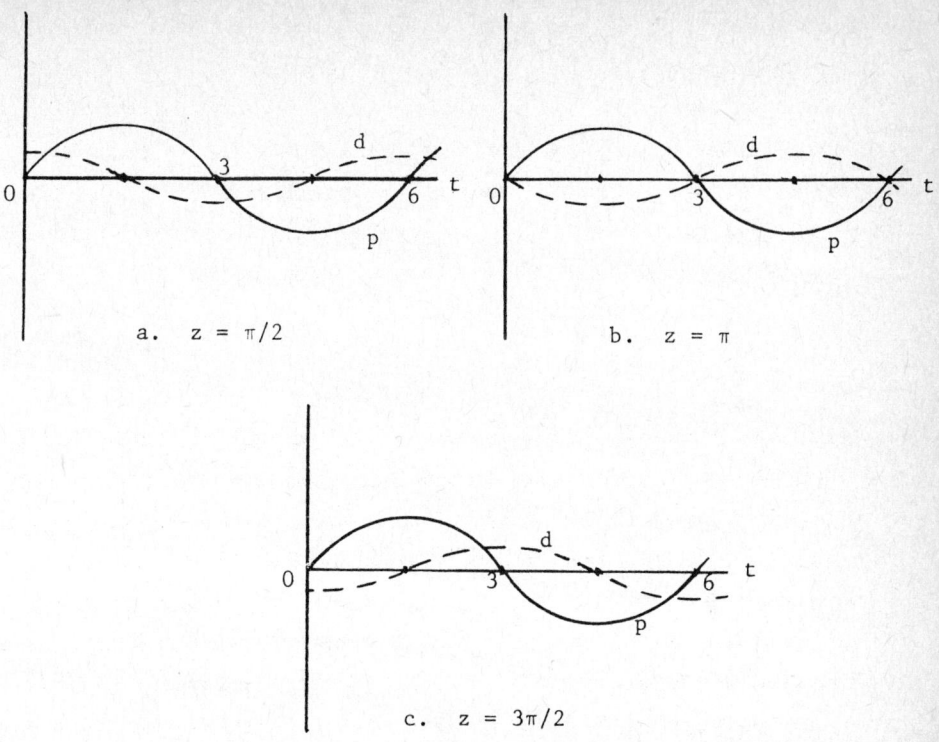

Figure 8.1　　The time paths of p_t and d_t (cf. eqs. (8.41) and (8.44)), for various values of z; $\pi/2 < z < 3\pi/2$.

The latter finding differs from our preliminary conclusions in section 8.3.6, but does not contradict them. All depends on (the assumption made with respect to) the future development of the tax base as it is anticipated by the state. In the upward (above trend) phase of the business cycle one could on the one hand become highly optimistic, extrapolating the current growth (or above average level) of the tax base into the future; this anticipation of an economically favourable future would lead to an increasing budget deficit now, i.e. to a pro-cyclically orientated reaction of the state (cf. section 8.3.6). On the other hand one could also turn pessimistic, thinking of and anticipating the downturn in economic life and the subsequent decline (below average level) of the tax base. This gloomy perspective would be translated in a reduction of the present budget deficit, i.e. in countercyclically orientated state behaviour (cf. figure 8.1).

It thus is becoming a relevant empirical question - to which we have no answer here - how the public sector is actually forming expectations. Is the state inclined to be optimistic or pessimistic, or could it be that optimistic and pessimistic governments are alternating?

8.5. Conclusion

In this chapter we extended the formal model of state behaviour developed earlier in this book to encompass multi-period planning, in order to study public sector decision making on the size of the budget deficit/surplus, in addition to state expenditure and taxation. In this modified model the state takes account of both the present and the future costs and benefits of its course of action for the various social classes in so far their interests play a role (are effective) in the state decision making process. Possible budget deficits are assumed to be fully covered by the issuing of bonds; financing through money creation has not yet been taken into consideration because of the institutional peculiarities and the nature of the future costs that are involved.

From the model behavioural equations could be derived for the rate of taxation, the level of public expenditure, and the size of the state's budget deficit. Subsequently, we discussed in section 8.3 how the various parameters of the model affect the occurrence and the size of a public budget deficit in a given period t. The deficit will tend to be larger, the further the time horizon of the state surpasses the time horizons of the social classes; the higher the rates of time preference of the social classes and therefore of the state; the higher the expected growth rate of the economy; the lower the rate of interest; and the longer the time horizon of the state and the social classes in general (provided, most notably, that the growth rate of the economy is positive). Moreover, as the time preferences of the social classes quite likely will diverge because of differences in their holdings of human and non-human wealth, changes in the social power structure will also affect the budget balance. It thus appears to be important to distinguish between different social groups in the present context.

It further turned out that the budget deficit may react both pro- and countercyclically to changes in the tax base, dependent on whether the change is expected to be of a structural or an incidental nature. This issue was explored somewhat more deeply in section 8.4, which explicitly addressed the development of the budget balance over time. In case the economy is characterized by a regular cyclic pattern, the budget deficit reacts in a, although not necessarily perfect, countercyclical manner. It thus follows from our analyses that a pro- or countercyclical pattern of the budget balance is dependent on how the public sector is actually forming expectations on the future development of the economy.[30] Of course, a related question - which we have assumed can be answered in the negative - is whether (and to which degree) the state actually takes account of the feedback effects of its own actions on the course of the economy and the development of the tax base. Although casual observation suggests that the state is rather naïve in this respect, it seems that important empirical work remains to be done here.

Given the results of this chapter we want to return, finally, to an issue that was raised in the introductory section 8.1, which was how to account for the historical transition from classical fiscal discipline to post-war "democracy in deficit". Several important developments can now be pointed at. Given the distribution of time preferences over the social classes, connected to the distribution of human versus non-human wealth, the structural decline of the relative numerical strength of the capitalist class (more specifically, the self-employed) may have entailed an increase in the rate of time preference of the state. Secondly, the post-war period witnessed a structurally and historically high rate of economic growth. According to our model, these developments would suffice to explain the acceptance of structural budget deficits during this period. That is, we would no longer have to rely on "philosophical change" as a decisive influence.

During the last decade severe economic problems showed up, in the shape of oil crises and a world-wide economic recession. (Expected) economic growth diminished, and even became negative. Besides, the (real) rate of interest has risen considerably. According to our model, both developments would lead the deficit of the budget to become subject to downward pressure. The deep concern shown by politicians, representing a wide political spectrum, with the present size of the deficit is in agreement with this result. The model suggests that it depends on a series of factors to which degree a reduction of the deficit is actually brought about. To mention some of them: Has the decline of the relative numerical strength of the capitalist class continued, or has the shift in the social power structure been reversed? Are the estimates with regard to future economic growth rates generally correct, or do they tend to be overoptimistic time and again? How serious are the administrative and legislative restrictions when it comes to budget cuts? The relative importance and the effect of these kinds of developments, and hence the actual reduction of the deficit, may vary between countries. In the Netherlands, for instance, the state has been lagging behind the facts for quite some time since the mid seventies; the result has been a continual increase of the deficit, instead of the planned reduction.

CHAPTER 9. EPILOGUE

The purpose of this book has been to critically discuss the issues involved in and to make a contribution to the endogenization of public sector behaviour in macroeconomic models.

Firstly, it turned out to be highly desirable, if not outright necessary, to analyze the behaviour of the public sector in the context of macroeconomic model-building. Apart from the intrinsic value of such an analysis given the huge share of the public sector in, and its large influence on, the economy, it would also help to avoid certain errors in the specification and estimation of macroeconomic models, and in the future possibly add to the production of better forecasts (cf. chapter 1).

As soon as one embarks on a positive study of economic policy decision making, however, it has to be acknowledged that political processes and institutions play an important role when it comes to the choice and weighing of the policy targets. An inspection of the relevant - public choice and Marxist - literature on public sector decision making processes yielded a multitude of theories, approaches and suggestions as to the objectives and behaviour of voters, politicians, political parties, the government, bureaucrats and interest groups, without much coherence and with only limited empirical support up to now. No general theory appeared to exist which combines and confronts the influence of the various participants in public sector decision making processes in a multi-party system, and which can be used for tracing out the economic and political factors underlying economic policy making (cf. chapter 2).

For the endogenization of public sector behaviour in macroeconomic modelling it thus seemed a wise research strategy not to enter at once into the details of the intricate relationships and interactions between all the agents that partake in public sector decision making. Borrowing the terminology of industrial organization theory: as a first approach we better skip the question of just how conduct forms the bridge between structure and performance. Here the interest function approach to the study of public sector decision making proved to be of great value (cf. chapter 3). Based on the distinction of only a limited number of elementary economic positions in society, and the concomitant distinction of only a limited number of social classes, it directly links public sector behaviour to the interests of the representative members of these social classes, and to the power structure of society which summarizes the (relative) political influence of these social classes through all available channels and by all available means combined. Adopting the interest function approach we indeed were able to build an explanatory model of public sector decision making, yielding behavioural equations for public expenditure, public employment and taxation which were suited for insertion in a macroeconomic model (chapter 4). We also found that the model could be generalized to explicitly account for a social security system and its income transfers (chapter 7). Furthermore, the model could be extended to allow for multi-period decision making on bond financed budget deficits/surpluses (chapter 8). A first application of the model to data for the Netherlands suggested that the model can be provided with empirical support and that the social power structure can be proxied by the relative numerical strengths of the economically active social classes (chapters 5, 7). Taking the latter finding for granted, a fully closed model of politico-economic interaction could be obtained (chapter 6). With that the task we set ourselves to endogenize public sector behaviour in macroeconomic modelling has been accomplished.

Having arrived at this stage, we want to add some observations to place our results in a proper perspective.

_a_. The empirical support obtained so far for the employment of the interest function approach, useful as it may be, may not be deemed convincing yet. That the results reported above are still ambiguous, may be imputed to such factors as the impact of anticipated social mobility, the changing degree of tax shifting over time which was not allowed for in the model, the proxy nature of the relative numerical strength variables, and so on. The fact remains that our empirical application is to be considered as no more than a first attempt; the results strongly need further corroboration. Moreover, further inquiry is needed into how the multi-period model with regard to public sector decision making on budget deficits/surpluses can be cast in a suitable mould for empirical testing.

_b_. The above analysis of public sector decision making has not been complete, in the sense that not all - kinds of - economic policy instruments have been examined. Firstly, in modelling public expenditure we did not properly distinguish between consumption and investment. Within the multi-period version of our model it should now be possible, although perhaps not easy, to introduce that distinction. Next, while we included income transfers into the analysis, we did not do so with capital transfers. Finally, and perhaps most importantly, we did not consider monetary policy in our model of economic policy making. The latter omission has been justified by pointing to the fact that the inclusion of monetary policy would have necessitated the explicit introduction of the central bank, with its peculiar legal status and its specific, allegedly more or less independent, position; moreover, it would not be a straightforward matter to model the future costs and benefits for the different social classes due to money creation and destruction. On the other hand, it might also be argued that in the context of the interest function approach to the study of public sector decision making the insertion of monetary policy would just amount to reformulating and generalizing the public sector interest function, taking account of the inflation tax aspect of (excessive) money creation, within a multi-period decision making framework. It will be clear that here too further work remains to be done.

<u>c</u>. With respect to the interest function approach itself it can be remarked that its elegance and applicability do highly recommend it for the task in this book. However, one has to pay a price for that, in accepting that the interest function approach reduces public sector decision making to a black box. This black box nature can give rise to problems of multi-interpretability with regard to the underlying decision making processes, as we saw in chapter 3. It should be welcomed if future research could more firmly ground the approach in a concrete analysis of the processes of voting, interest representation, pressure, coalition formation, bargaining a.s.o., which together make up public sector decision making.

This book put forward the hypothesis that economic policy has a logic of its own. Public sector behaviour is considered to be the outcome of conflicts of interests, the outcome of compromises that are produced in a more or less systematic manner in society. Hence, economic policy would be predictable. Arguing further along these lines, one can even end up with a fully closed politico-economic model, and become tempted to conclude that the interaction between political and economic processes over time is, in principle, fully predictable.

In connection with the latter - tentative - conclusion we feel that we may not end this book without having drawn the reader's attention to two topics that have recently been under discussion in the public choice literature. It concerns the role of the economic policy adviser and the possibility of changing the institutional arrangements and rules in the process of public sector decision making.

As to the first, and most familiar, of these topics: What potential is there for economic policy advice, if economic policy is predictable? In a certain sense, enough. It is not likely that the decision maker at the emergence of each new policy problem will be fully acquainted with the various consequences of the courses of action that are open to him. Thus, it could be useful to him, if his advisers set out to obtain and provide such information. Quite another matter is whether the policy advice by an individual economist or agency really makes a difference for the economic policy actions that are actually carried into effect. For one thing, many advices turn out to be mutually contradictory, leaving the decision maker with the task to decide which one might be appropriate. Further, given the competition that is going on between government agencies, universities, interest groups, it is not very likely that any advice will be completely new. Also, the decision maker presumably has already, perhaps unconsciously, been aware of the direction and order of magnitude of the effects involved. Finally, and most importantly, even if the information is really new and unique, much depends on the interests and power relations of the moment. It is to be expected that policy advices will only have effect if the decision maker who is being advised, perceives them as beneficial to the furtherance of the interests that he represents.

The second topic that deserves our attention here, bears upon the distinction that has recently been accentuated by Brennan and Buchanan (1980, 1985), Frey (1983), Buchanan (1986), between the choice of action within a well-defined set of rules (institutions, laws) and the choice of the rules themselves; see also Buchanan and Tullock (1962). This classification of two different types of activities would give rise to two categorically different types of analysis, to wit the theory of economic policy[1]) on the one hand and constitutional political economy on the other.

The views of public sector decision making and the influence of policy advice and advisers that have been expounded in this book up to now, can in the first instance be thought to apply to the field of economic policy, where alternative policy actions are studied under given institutional arrangements. However, one might seek to apply those ideas in an analogous manner to the domain of constitutional political economy. In that field attention is directed to the incidence and effects of, and the process of decision making on, alternative rules, regimes and institutions within which policy choices are made by designated agents. As well as it has been presumed that the behaviour of agents empowered to make choices under given institutional arrangements can be explained and predicted, it can be hypothesized that the behaviour of agents involved in making changes in the basic rules and institutions is predictable. Such behaviour might be explained too from the prevailing interest and the social power structure, which can change over time due to the politico-economic interactions referred to earlier. Given the fact that the area of constitutional political economy is rather novel and uncultivated yet with especially the contractarian approach of Brennan and Buchanan standing out, while apparently it may constitute a logical extension of the analysis in this book, we want to seize the opportunity to discuss some aspects that are of interest in this context.

First, it should be observed that the distinction between acting within the rules and acting to change the rules may have some use from the point of view of the private sector, as the former can refer to activities in the market place and the latter to political activities. However, within the public sector the distinction is necessarily a blurred one. For instance, acting within the rules in the sense of conducting economic policy frequently amounts to changing rules; adjusting tax rates in the Netherlands, e.g., generally requires passing tax laws by Parliament. Further, changing the institutional arrangements is most frequently done within (other) rules; changing the constitution in the Netherlands, e.g., must follow rules and procedures laid down in the existing constitution. Moreover, in a democratic country both conducting economic policy within the existing rules and changing the rules of public sector decision making require sufficient political support in society. Viewed at in this way there appears to be no fundamental difference between the two types of activity. The main motive for making the distinction after all seems to be that in the real world some rules and arrangements are changed quite frequently, while other rules and institutions last for decades. But given that observation the distinction should not be introduced as a premise; rather it should follow from the analysis which rules, arrangements and institutions are altered more frequently than others, and why.

Further accepting the distinction as it stands, the next topic is how rule changes can be thought to come about. In that context Brennan and Buchanan (1985) oppose their own contractarian analysis to the non-contractarian, more specifically the evolutionary approach. The evolutionary position embodies the notion that the rules of social order are not artificial creations subject to constructive reform; they may change in the course of time, but only through an organic evolutionary process. This position is rejected by Brennan and Buchanan, because "if the rules of the socio-economic-political game are not themselves subject to contructive change, there is little left to do but to endure the forces of history."; "... surely we must be given hope that the institutions of social order are subject to reform and change" (p. 21). Here, they argue, enters the contractarian approach, which basically amounts to applying the Pareto-criterion to the field of institutional arrangements. The contractarian explanation (or justification) of social order is obtained if the individuals in society, led by their own evaluation of alternative prospects, can be shown to accept it (not to reject it) by unanimous agreement. They further maintain that "if ... the state can be legitimized "as if" it emerged contractually, the way is left open for constructive constitutional reform. Existing rules can be changed contractually even if they did not so emerge" (p. 22). This position of Brennan and Buchanan should be criticized on two related grounds, familiar to public choice theorists.

First, as to the field of economic policy it is argued by Brennan and Buchanan that it is misleading to examine the set of all conceivable social outcomes and select an ideal according to some normative criteria, whithout investigating how that best outcome might emerge from the political process, in order to ascertain that it is feasible. The same argument would seem to hold on the constitutional level, as here too changes have to come about through the political process. Here too, it is not sufficient to outline an ideal and give society the advice to change its institutional arrangement accordingly; one should also make clear that attainment is feasible.[2]

That brings us to the second point: What potential is there for changes in the rules and institutions of social order? Brennan and Buchanan (1985) try to formulate an answer. It is observed that changes in the rules will modify personal expectations about future distributional patterns. To the extent that proposed changes embody time lags between approval and implementation, and to the extent that the rules can be expected to remain in effect over an extended sequence of periods and tend to have a more general character bearing upon numbers of instances, people who are potentially affected will be less able to predict how the rule changes will affect their relative positions. Thus, people will evaluate the propositions behind some "veil of uncertainty". Brennan and Buchanan hopefully remark that the effect of this uncertainty is "to mitigate substantially any purely distributional aspects of genuine constitutional choice" (p. 140), such that one will tend to agree more easily.

A first aspect deserving attention in that context is the collective action problem that will become more serious, the more the benefits of the changes in the rules indeed would accrue publicly to all members of society, without individually identifiable, differential claims. "To the extent that "investment" in institutional analysis, design, argument, dialogue, discussion, and persuasion is costly in a personal sense, the individual of the orthodox [public choice] model will forgo such investment in favor of more immediate gratification of privately directed desires".[3] Secondly, it should be acknowledged that distributional implications of proposed changes in rules in actual practice cannot a priori be excluded. People know that they are in different positions now, and they can make predictions about their future economic positions which will be correlated with the current ones; besides, they will only consider a limited period of time given their finite time horizon. Hence, they may well foresee a differential impact on identifiable individuals and groups. Finally, institutional change in practice need not at all be restricted to contractarian solutions that satisfy the Pareto-criterion of unanimous consent, as long as changing the institutional arrangements is subject to the rules of social order presently in existence. The latter assumedly only requires a majority decision in the legislature.

Concluding, the contractarian approach to constitutional political economy is <u>incomplete</u>, as it lacks as yet a positive theory to analyze and predict the behaviour of persons and groups involved in making changes in the basic rules and institutions of society, and <u>too restrictive</u>, as it is only interested in these changes in the rules that satisfy the Pareto-criterion.

What has the above discussion of constitutional political economy in the context of this book been good for? First, it has been shown that the distinction between acting within the rules and changes of the rules, and hence the distinction between the theory of economic policy and constitutional political economy, is not a fundamental one. Relatedly, it has been argued that before engaging in proffering advice with regard to changing the rules and institutional arrangements of society one should inquire into its feasibility. For that, one needs a "positive theory of constitutional choice", i.e. a positive analysis of the behaviour of persons and groups involved in making changes in the basic rules or institutions; cf. Buchanan (1986). It is suggested that the approach to the field of constitutional polical economy could basically be the same as the approach to the field of economic policy that has been set out in this book. Here too, behaviour should be explained from the prevailing interests and the power structure of society, while taking account of the own character of the issues involved.[4)]

If we would succeed in developing such an explanatory positive theory of constitutional choice, the entire course of history might seem to become predictable. However, the possibility of formulating "laws of historical development" has been negated by Popper (1957). The chance of really new information turning up as a result of the growth of human knowledge becomes larger the longer is the time horizon taken into consideration. Precisely this development of knowledge over time must by the nature of things be deemed unpredictable. Within a public choice perspective it should be added that people will only tend to react to new insights, and to proposals for change in policy actions and in the rules of the game, if there are incentives to do so and the power relations permit it. Thus, while the emergence of new insights and the growth of human knowledge may be unpredictable, their success or failure in affecting decision making processes in society can again be subjected to (economic) inquiry. Nevertheless, grasping for "laws of historical development" after all seems to be reaching too high. Yet, we need not mourn for long as the field for future research opening up here is large enough for the present, quite apart still from the topics for further inquiry enumerated earlier in this epilogue.

NOTES

Chapter 1

1. For a survey of empirical reaction function studies for the US and several other countries, see Fase and Den Butter (1977). As almost all these studies estimate reaction functions in the form of (1.7), without accounting for (1.1), they may be subject to a similar specification error as will be discussed later in section 1.4 with regard to the estimation of the model (1.1). Friedlaender (1973) notes "that there is some chance of simultaneous bias here", but contents herself with remarking that "this however, is equally true of other studies of this nature". For an approach to circumvent the problem, using consistent expectations estimates of the macroeconomic target variables, see Abrams, Froyen and Waud (1980).

2. In this context the reader can also be referred to table IX.2 in Kirschen et al. (1964), vol I. That table gives a synthesis for eight western countries of the preferences of political parties - grouped into three families: socialists, centre, conservatives - with regard to the objectives of economic policy. The rankings show marked differences. To give just one example: for the socialists the dominant objectives are reported to be full employment and improvement in the income distribution, for the conservatives the dominant objective is price stability.

3. Cf. Centraal Planbureau (1955), Centraal Economisch Plan 1955, 's-Gravenhage; Bijlage C.

4. Cf.- Centraal Planbureau (1961), Centraal Economisch Plan 1961, 's-Gravenhage; Bijlage I.
   - P.J. Verdoorn (1967), "The short-term model of the Central Planning Bureau and its forecasting performance", in: United Nations, Macroeconomic models for planning and policy making, Geneva.
   - Centraal Planbureau (1971), Centraal Economisch Plan 1971, 's-Gravenhage; Bijlage A.

5. Cf. W. Driehuis (1972), Fluctuations and growth in a near full employment economy, Universitaire Pers Rotterdam.

6. Cf.- C.A. van den Beld (1967), Dynamiek der ontwikkeling op de middellange termijn, Rotterdam.
   - Centraal Planbureau (1977), Een macro model voor de Nederlandse economie op middellange termijn (Vintaf-II), Occasional Paper 12, 's-Gravenhage.

7. Cf.- P.J.C.M. van den Berg, F.J.M. Don en J. Sandee (1983), KOMPAS, Kwartaalmodel voor prognose, analyse en simulatie, Centraal Planbureau Monografie 26, 's-Gravenhage.
   - B.H. Hasselman, V.R. Okker en R.J.A. de Haan (1983), FREIA, Een macroeconomisch model voor de middellange termijn, Centraal Planbureau Monografie 25, 's-Gravenhage.

- Centraal Planbureau (1985), FREIA-KOMPAS '85; een kwartaalmodel voor Nederland voor de korte en middellange termijn, Monografie 28, 's-Gravenhage.

8. A more extensive discussion of the role and performance of the CPB is contained in Griffiths (1980). Den Butter (1984) gives a survey of the history of macroeconometric model building in the Netherlands, the US and several other countries.

9. It may be added that in a Dutch context a somewhat similar procedure has been employed by Knegt (1978). Starting from the premisse that government behaviour - at least to a certain degree - is following a systematic pattern, he sets out to endogenize public sector behaviour to incorporate it in the CPB-model VINTAF-I. The endogenization of the public sector, however, is brought about mainly through the employment of empirical methods, without (much) theoretical underpinning. As interesting conclusion it emerges that at least part of government activity (notably, exhaustive government expenditure, and the number of government employees) has a pro-cyclic character.

10. Reasoning further along this line, combining the natural rate hypothesis with the assumption that expectations are rational, the so-called policy-ineffectiveness or neutrality proposition has been derived, positing that there is no sense in which the monetary authorities can conduct countercyclical policy by using a policy rule. See, e.g., Sargent and Wallace (1976). However, note that the rational expectations school of thought does not maintain that economic policy per se is pointless; only that the instrument variables should be searched for in the realm of relative prices, both at the same moment and over time.
    Another neutrality result with respect to the use of certain instruments, the Ricardian equivalence of tax and debt financing of government outlays, will call for our attention in Chapter 8.

11. This point has also led to a discussion of the applicability in general of optimal control theory to economic stabilization and planning. See Kydland and Prescott (1977) and the volume edited by Brunner and Meltzer (1977).

12. Cf. footnote 2.

13. In this context it should be observed that in actual practice the policymaker might not be prepared, or able, to give complete information on his preferences even to his policy adviser who carries out the calculation of the "optimal" solution. For these cases interactive optimization procedures have been developed in the literature to be used in the deliberations between decision makers and policy analysts. See, e.g., Hafkamp (1983).
    Clearly, such an interactive decision making procedure, from iteration to iteration, not only gives information to the decision maker on the actual trade-offs between the objectives, but also allows the policy adviser to deduce, from the choices being made by the policy maker, his actual preferences. However, in order to

arrive at an accurate assessment of these preferences, it might be necessary that the procedure is carried out over a rather large number of observations.

14. For a quadratic version of this specific welfare function, see Sandee (1977). For some other attempts to specify welfare functions along this line, cf. the references cited in Theil (2nd ed. 1961, Ch. 8.6).

15. In this connection it is noted that a quadratic formulation of the preference function as in eq. (1.3) may be too restrictive. The quadratic terms imply that deviations of actual and desired target values of the same size in upward and in downward direction have equivalent consequences for the policy makers' welfare level. This actually need not hold for all target variables. A balance of payments deficit of certain size, e.g., in general will give the policy maker much more trouble than a similar balance of payments surplus. Such an asymmetry in the preference function is reflected in an asymmetric reaction function.

16. In 1977 the three separate christian-democratic parties KVP (catholic), ARP and CHU (both protestant) merged into one party, the CDA.

17. The instability of the findings is once more demonstrated by the (preliminary) results of Merkies and Hofkes (1986). They have taken direct interviews from a series of Dutch political parties in 1983, along the same lines as followed by Merkies and Vermaat (1981) in 1977. The relative weights attached to the unemployment rate are found to be drastically lower in 1983 than they were in 1977, apparently due to the very high actual unemployment rate in the more recent years.

18. Cf. Friedlaender (1973), who assumes that the welfare function W is quadratic and matrix A diagonal, and then can obtain revealed preference weights only after having dropped the linear terms a, b.

19. For a full discussion of the politico-economic model of Frey and Schneider, see chapter 2.

20. For the period 1954-1973 the DW-statistics reported by Mosley (1984) in tables 4.6 and 4.7 are too low to attach any meaning to the significance levels of the coefficients. Even apart from that, in six out of ten cases the coefficients for crisis and non-crisis periods do not seem to be significantly different, and in one of the four other cases the differential is in the wrong direction (i.e. the coefficient for the non-crisis period being significantly different from zero). Estimation of single reaction functions to the period as a whole gives 7 out of 10 (seemingly) significant coefficients between targets and instruments.
For the period 1974-1982, the results reported in table 5.5 are in general contrary to the predictions of the satisficing theory: with one exception, the response is stronger and more significant in non-crisis than in crisis periods. Here too, single reaction functions applied to the period as a whole produce significant coefficients.

21. Cf. Mosley (1984), chapter 3. In his footnote 21 he cites the UK Committee on Policy Optimisation: "It has been put to us that, in the recent past, no options seriously recommended by respected outside observers have gone unanalysed in the Treasury. .... all "known" policy instruments have been in the minds of the simulators composing their analyses".

22. Cf. footnote 11. See also Lucas (1987).

Chapter 2

1. An ordering is a binary relation, say R, between a (any) pair of elements of a set, say S, such that this relation is reflexive, transitive and complete. A relation is said to be
   - reflexive, if $\forall x \in S : xRx$;
   - transitive, if $\forall x,y,z \in S$ xRy and yRz implies xRz;
   - complete,   if $\forall x,y \in S$ (x≠y) : xRy and/or yRx.

   See on this, and on social welfare functions in general, Sen (1970)

2. See further on the median voter model Enelow and Hinich (1984), Riker (1980), Romer and Rosenthal (1979).

3. Kristensen (1982), p. 41. His allegation that to confirm the median voter proposition the difference between the percentage of respondents favouring less spending on an item and the percentage of respondents favouring more should be zero seems mistaken. We give a simple example. If the distribution of the respondents' attitudes with regard to education for instance would have been: 37% favouring less spending. 52% satisfied with the current level, and 11% favouring more, which would have resulted in the reported percentage difference between those favouring less and more spending of 26%, then according to the median voter the current level of spending would have been adequate.
   Nevertheless, at any rate 4 out of the 9 items considered can rather safely be assumed not to fit the median voter proposition (i.e., old age pensions with a percentage difference of 60, defence with a percentage difference of -49, environmental protection with a percentage difference of 46, and police with a percentage difference of 41).

4. Applying this latter result to Wagner's Law, Meltzer and Richard suggest that it is not absolute (average) income growth as such which is important for the growth of government, but that it is conditional on relative income, notably the ratio of mean and median income.
   Much of the discussion in this book has connections with the literature on the size and growth of the public sector, emanating from Wagner's Law. Our angle of incidence, however, is different, in that we are interested in a theoretical underpinning of government behaviour such as to be able to integrate it in (macro)economic modelling. Only sideways shall we pay attention to the literature on Wagner's Law and the growth of government. For some recent

surveys of the literature, see Cameron (1978), Larkey, Stolp and Winer (1981), Lowery and Berry (1983), Peltzman (1980).

5. For an extension of the model to an economy with two products, opening the possibility of analyzing a rational choice between transfers in cash and in kind, cf. Meltzer and Richard (1985).

6. Although the specification of the series of median income y_d used in the empirical application is somewhat obscure, cf. Meltzer and Richard (1983, pp. 409 and 416), it might be deduced that y_d is computed as the median labour income of all <u>workers</u>. Apart from the problem that capital income apparently is hypothesized to be irrelevant in practice for the level of the tax rate, this specification of y_d would not be in conformity with the theoretical model. According to the theory y_d should be taken to be the earned income of the decisive voter, which is the voter with median (potential) productivity. The median is thus derived from the distribution of productivity, which encompasses all voters <u>including</u> those who choose <u>not</u> to work.
It can be added that Fratianni and Spinelli (1982) for the case of Italy also had to contend with data problems, and were not able to find empirical support for the Meltzer-Richard-model.

7. Going from the evaluation and choice of the individual voter to overall popularity of parties or candidates or to election outcomes requires aggregation. Some solutions to the aggregation question are presented in Fair (1978b) and Borooah and Van der Ploeg (1983).

8. Plausible alternative formulations would be:
   - that political support for the government responds to deviations of current performance from the customary level;
   - that the government's accumulated discounted performance is evaluated relative to the customary situation prior to the beginning of the government's current term.

   See Hibbs and Vasilatos (1981). They apply the different formulations to popularity data for the US president and the UK government during the period 1961:I-1976:IV. The differences in fit are so small that it is "virtually impossible to choose" between the formulations using goodness of fit criteria. However, it should be noticed that the political messages embedded in the coefficient estimates differ in important respects.

9. If the voters indeed react to the general economic situation, say the rate of unemployment or the rate of inflation, a further question could be whether they react to the <u>actual</u> levels of these variables as published by the official statistical office, or to the <u>perceived</u> levels. Mosley (1984) suggests that these perceived levels could be the values as they are being published in the popular press. And as he points out: "Only at times of economic crisis, it is clear, do the popular media pull back the curtains from the windows through which the mass electorate perceives trends in the economy". His empirical results for the UK government popularity function suggest that replacing the official figures for unemployment and inflation by the most recent figures published in the Daily Mirror greatly

increases the explanatory power of the model.

10. See, however, Kramer (1983), who argues that "individual-level survey data, at least when analyzed with the usual methods, are not really very useful for studying the effects of short-term economic fluctuations on individual voting decisions" (p. 94).

11. This statement is not entirely correct as the policy-ineffectiveness proposition refers to macroeconomic policies of demand management, not to microeconomic policies which might lower the natural rate of unemployment.

12. For US voting functions the reader can be referred to Kramer (1971), Fair (1978b), Kirchgässner (1984); on US presidential popularity see, e.g., Mueller (1970), Frey and Schneider (1978a, 1981a), Golden and Poterba (1980). As to the popularity of the UK government, cf. Goodhart and Bhansali (1970), Frey and Schneider (1978b, 1981b), Hibbs and Vasilatos (1981), Borooah and Van der Ploeg (1983), Mosley (1984). For references to studies on other countries, see Schneider (1984). See also the surveys by Paldam (1981), Kiewiet and Rivers (1984).

13. It is (implicitly) assumed here that only current values of inflation and unemployment are taken into account by the electorate. This assumption is in no way essential for the argument. Nordhaus (1975) assumes that voters take account of the development of inflation and unemployment during the whole incumbency period, with a rate of decay of voters' memories equal to µ; in MacRae (1977) the value of µ is even equal to zero. Essential for the argument is only that voters do not look forward, i.e. beyond election day.

14. Tufte, e.g., reports that in 19 of the 27 democracies taken into consideration short-run accelerations in real disposable income are more likely to occur in election years than in years without elections. On closer scrutiny, however, his evidence appears to be not at all conclusive for 8 out of these 19 countries, while for the remaining countries it is only indicative, based as it is on a short time period with on average only 3 election years. Cf. Tufte (1978), table 1.1, p. 12. For a critical evaluation of Tufte's procedures and results, see Thompson and Zuk (1983).

Similarly, we would call Soh's inferences into doubt. He states that 8 out of 20 countries considered have a political-business-cycle-like pattern of unemployment; 5 countries have a corresponding pattern in real disposable income growth. Only Sweden scores on both accounts. However, it is not at all evident – on the contrary, we would say – that the cases in which the average rate of unemployment in election years is equal or almost equal to the average in non-election-years, should be counted as supportive of the political business cycle hypothesis. For Austria and Sweden, Soh reports the ratio of these two averages to be equal to 1, and yet concludes that these countries show signs of a political business cycle. The same conclusion is drawn for:

	ratio	election year mean	non-election year mean	number of election years	standard deviation
Canada	0.97	5.85	6.05	8	1.41
West-Germany	0.95	1.97	2.08	5	1.60
Ireland	0.90	7.34	8.15	4	2.31
Switzerland	0.90	0.30	0.42	1	0.17
Norway	0.88	1.28	1.45	4	0.42

In view of the number of observations and the standard deviations involved, the differences can not be considered as serious evidence for the existence of a political business cycle. Even for the UK the evidence (0.79, 2.84, 3.61, 5, 1.83, respectively) may be questioned. Problematic is also the way Soh proceeds with regard to inflation. While it may be taken for granted that according to the political business cycle hypothesis inflation is comparatively low in election years (which, however, Soh reports to be the case in only 8 out of the 20 countries considered), it need not at all be true that inflation should be decelerating in election years. Inflation might well be accelerating, instead. Cf. Nordhaus (1975, p. 185), Kirchgässner (1984, p. 180).

15. As we announced in the introductory section 2.4.1, the Frey-Schneider and related results will be considered in section 2.4.4. Although re-election efforts are also accounted for in the Frey-Schneider model, they differ from the Nordhaus-like re-election activities in an important respect. According to Frey and Schneider re-election efforts are undertaken only if popularity is below some critical level, while their employment depends on the size of the popularity deficit.

16. Cf. MacRae (1977), Kirchgässner (1984), Van der Ploeg (1984); but see Lächler (1984).

17. Cf. Coleman (1971) on the strategy of a politician in a two-step election procedure, who has to trade off the party median (relevant for winning the party's nomination) and the population median (relevant for winning the election).

18. The effect on the (equilibrium) unemployment level, revealed by the model, is given by the following table.

	effect	change in government,	at date
1.	-.19	Labour in	1965.4
2.	.20	Labour out	1966.12
3.	-.13	Labour in	1973.5
4.	-.18	Labour out	1977.5
5.	-1.47	Labour in	1981.9
6.	2.16	Labour out	1982.5

The first five of these effects were statistically significant, but note that the fourth case does show the wrong sign (cf. Alt (1985b), pp. 1025, 1033).
It may be added that De Grauwe (1985), using only one dummy to distinguish between centre-right and centre-left governments, does not find a significant partisan difference in unemployment or inflation figures for the Netherlands for the period 1961-1985.

19. These goals could stem from the purely personal interests of the politicians, but more likely they will correspond to the interests of the core supporters of the political parties and politicians.

20. In addition to econometric estimation the model has also been subject to computer simulation in order to study its dynamic characteristics (cf. Frey and Schneider (1975)). It appears that the model generates a political business cycle, but due to the higher complexity of the model this cycle is of an irregular shape between any two elections. See our discussion in section 2.4.2. See also Kirchgässner (1984).

21. Apparently, the columns in Frey and Schneider (1978b) table 1 and (1981b) table 2, presenting the results for the adjustment speeds with respect to re-election efforts and ideological goals, have been interchanged. Probably, the same two coefficients have also been interchanged in the reaction function estimate in Frey and Schneider (1982), p. 245. If not, the latter would imply that the adjustment speed with respect to re-election efforts is slower than with respect to ideological goals.

22. It is of further interest to note that Frey and Schneider (1981c) have extended their model to encompass the central bank as a separate policy-making unit. The officials of a central bank are considered as deriving utility from keeping the price level as stable as possible. This corresponds to the organization's most important official goal, which its officers internalize as an ideology, and reflects the feeling prevalent in the financial community, their most important reference group. A vigorous policy to achieve a low rate of inflation gives them prestige (and, potentially, attractive job offers from private business). The central bank operates largely independent of the voters' wishes and public opinion, but it faces certain constraints, imposed by the structure of the economy, the exchange rate regime and the government. With respect to the latter, it is argued that the central bank can maximize its utility only if the direction (contractionary or expansionary) of its policy coincides with that pursued by the government. Frey and Schneider assume that in case of a conflict, the central bank will be forced by the government to change its policy and to follow the direction taken by the government. But then the central bank always acts, with possibly a small lag, in accordance with government policy; there seems to be no need for separate modelling. Monetary instruments could just be treated as other - fiscal - instruments, possibly with a slightly different lag structure.

23. Alt and Chrystal (1983), p. 117.

24. With respect to Germany, the formulation of the ideological variable in Frey and Schneider (1979), p. 33 reads:

    $[b_R R + b_L L + (1-R)(1-L)] (POP-POP^*)^2 (1-D)$ where:

    R = 1, at the time of a right-wing (CDU) dominated government (1951-1966); otherwise R = 0;
    L = 1, at the time of a left-wing (SPD) dominated government (1970-1974); otherwise L = 0;
    such that R = L = 0, at the time of the 'grand coalition' between CDU and SPD (1967-1969).
    It is expected that $b_R < 0$, $b_L > 0$. Indeed it is found that b_R ranges between -0.03 and 0.001 while b_L ranges from 0.005 for government wages and employment via 0.46 for expenditure to 0.73 for transfers. Apparently, $b_L < 1$.
    In our view, the logic of the formulation above and the empirical results should be called into question. For, why is the parameter of the ideology of the 'grand coalition' a priori set equal to one? And secondly, why would the 'grand coalition' be ideologically more inclined towards increasing government activity than a left-wing dominated government?
    In connection with the previous it is to be observed that Frey and Schneider in their (1981c) article (cf. pp. 298, 305) apparently have set the coefficient of (1-R)(1-L) equal to zero - but without any comment or reference to their earlier work.

25. For the discussion between Frey-Schneider and Alt-Chrystal the reader is referred to Chrystal and Alt (1981), Alt and Chrystal (1981, 1983), Frey and Schneider (1981b, 1982, 1983). A great deal of their discussion handles about the comparison of model forecasts. Frey and Schneider claim support for their model through superior forecasting results compared with, among others, the permanent income model of Alt and Chrystal. According to the latter, however the alleged forecasting superiority of the Frey-Schneider model rests at best on comparisons between the full Frey-Schneider model and a subset of the Alt-Chrystal model in which factors which had been described as extremely important, were omitted. It does not seem very useful to go further into the details of this (part of the) discussion.

26. Notice that Mosley's formalization for the case $y \leq y^*$ does not seem to be in accordance with the last feature of his model, mentioned earlier.

27. Further, it is unclear why for the same policy instrument and for overlapping periods, looking at different target variables, separate equations of the form (2.3) have been estimated. For the UK, e.g., one equation suggests that in the crisis years 1967 and 1972 taxes were lowered, in reaction to high unemployment, while according to another equation taxes were raised, in reaction to the balance of payments deficit. Cf. Mosley (1984), p. 104, table 4.4 (a) and (b).

28. Somewhat related is the incremental budgeting approach, analyzed by Wildavsky c.s. See Davis, Dempster and Wildavsky (1966). As the latter paper explicitly deals with the interaction between the bureaucracy (agency requests for funds) and the politicians (Congressional appropriations) we shall return to it in section 2.5.

29. Alt and Chrystal (1983), p. 116.

30. With regard to the last channel of influence mentioned – organizing in interest groups –, the reader may be referred to the recent review of research on US public sector labour relations by Freeman (1986).
His general conclusion is that researchers for the most part have applied the same models and tools as have been used to analyze the economic impact of private sector unionism, concentrating on wage and other compensation effects of collective bargaining. Most studies have failed to address the differences in constraints (legal, budgetary, political) between public and private sector bargaining. For this reason this line of research cannot help us any further, here.
Some specific conclusions may yet be mentioned:
   - "Much of the literature concludes that public sector unions have had relatively modest effects on wages compared to the effects of private sector unions on wages" (p. 42).
   - "The evidence available on the effects of public sector unions on productivity shows that unionism is not inimical to productivity" (p. 43).
   - "With respect to public budgets, studies suggest that unionization does, indeed, increase the share of a municipality's budget going to the organized workers" (p.43).

31. Think of the probability, in the context of the median voter model, that the median will change noticeably. One possibility is that the persons becoming publicly employed change their preferences for public spending from low or average to high. Another possibility is that the persons becoming publicly employed are mostly recruited from high-preference groups, but start to participate more in voting than before they became publicly employed.

32. For a first attempt at an alternative approach, presenting a dynamic model of three-way interaction among bureaucracy, politicians and interest groups, where the ill-informed participants make their choices adaptively rather than in a maximizing way, see Bendor and Moe (1985).

33. This motivational assumption leads to a rather strange two-regime solution with respect to the technical efficiency of the bureaucracy: a "cost-constrained" solution (B = C) which is technically efficient, and a "demand-constrained" solution (B > C) which is not.
Also from various other sides question marks have been placed at the motivational assumption. Breton and Wintrobe (1975) note that a positive monotonic relationship between (budget) size and the salary and other amenities of office may well exist <u>within</u> a given bureau, but need not exist <u>between</u> bureaus. Officials in the top echelons,

searching a suitable career path among the bureaus, may improve their salaries etc. by moving from one position, at the head of a relatively large bureau, to another, at the head of a smaller one. In such a context of mobility among agencies, it also becomes understandable that bureaucrats sometimes cut budgets, as a means to further advancement.
Dunleavy (1985) further notes that there may be a collective action problem confronting budget maximizing bureaucrats, as the realization of collective benefits for the bureau members is likely to require concerted action by a number of officials. However, at the top the scope for exploiting individual strategies will be much greater than in the bottom ranks (see above); hence, the inclination to resort to collective strategies is correspondigly reduced.

34. One case in which the public sector is smaller than the social optimum, is offered by Miller and Moe. In that case it is assumed that the government (or legislature) ultimately decides on the production level Q and on the budget B being allocated. The information on costs is provided for by the bureaucracy, in the form of a flat amount p per unit of output, after the demand function for Q has been revealed by the politicians. From eq. (2.4) this demand function reads $p = a - 2bQ$. If the bureaucracy then maximizes (2.7) - substituting (2.8) -, given $B = p \cdot Q = aQ - 2bQ^2$, while $C = cQ + dQ^2$, the solution becomes:

(2.9') $\quad Q^* = \frac{\beta+\gamma}{\beta+2\gamma} \cdot \frac{a-c}{2b+d}$.

The information on unit costs transferred to the politicians is set equal to $p_* = a - 2bQ^*$ by the bureaucracy, such that the politicians maximizing net social welfare $aQ - bQ^2 - p_* Q$, end up with a final decision on the level of output equal to Q^*.
It is easily shown that the production of Q^* is technically inefficient if $\gamma > 0$, and that Q^* is lower than the social optimum if γ is sufficiently high ($\gamma > \beta d/2b$).

Another case is discussed by Moene. There it is assumed that the government (or legislature) decides on the budget B being allocated, while the bureaucracy establishes the production level Q given the budget B. When allocating the budget, however, the politicians know the true cost function and the reaction function of the bureaucracy $Q = F(B)$. This reaction function can be deduced from the maximization problem of the bureaucracy: maximize (2.7) - substituting (2.8) - with respect to Q, given B and given $C = cQ + dQ^2$. The programming problem of the politicians is to maximize net social welfare $aQ - bQ^2 - B$, subject to $Q = F(B)$. The final solution reads:

(2.9'') $\quad Q = \frac{\beta a-(\beta+\gamma)c}{2[\beta b+(\beta+2\gamma)d]}$.

The level of output is equal to the social optimum if $\gamma = 0$, and falls below it if $\gamma > 0$.
Production is also technically inefficient if $\gamma > 0$.

35. Larger populations can be expected to be more heterogeneous, thus to require more interest groups to represent the diverse interests. Moreover, if there are some fixed costs or scale economies to interest group formation then, holding heterogeneity constant, the larger the population the more interest groups of an optimal size a society can accommodate.
With respect to the decentralization of government, it can be argued that the more decentralized political power is, the more potential for interest group influence there is and the greater the number of interest groups will be.

36. The reason why voters are uninformed is not of interest here. It may well be that it is a rational decision of voters to remain relatively uninformed, using only the information that is readily available through the media. Cf. Section 2.3. Crucial is that voting behaviour <u>can</u> be affected.

37. See on the latter aspect Denzau and Munger (1986). They argue that, if voters are fully informed, spending resources on advertizing will have no effect. The politicians are induced to serve the preferences of their constituency; they do not have any incentive to serve interest groups, unless there is a coincidence of an interest group's and his voters' wishes. On the other hand, if voters are fully ignorant, only advertizing expenditures can mobilize voters. A politician will employ those activities that maximize the resources he receives from interest groups. The result is extreme interest group influence. But even then, "departures by legislators from their voters' preferences are constrained by the strong preferences voters have on some issues, and by the threat of informing and mobilizing public opinion that the news media and potential competitors always represent" (o.c., p. 103).

38. These activities are measured by "the number of motions and applications to the government, parliament, and parliamentary commissions concerning the preferred use of a specific spending category. Also statements in the same line outside the parliament are counted" (o.c., p. 302).
The theoretically expected signs of the coefficients for the activities of the four interest groups over the preferred use of the instruments were derived from observed behaviour.

39. But note that section 2.5.3 provides an alternative explanation for this push.

40. Mosley (1984) gives it a sort of a try. He tests "the proposition that some indicator of the state of business welfare can influence the direction of macro-policy <u>independently</u> of conventional targets of economic policy such as inflation or the balance of payments" (p. 191). He concludes: "It does seem, then, that the government does sometimes spontaneously deflate the economy in a manner not required by the state of the prevailing target variables nor, therefore, explained by the 'satisficing' response pattern .... But to the extent that this happens, it seems to happen for reasons quite separate from the desire of Kalecki's capitalists to undermine the

'self-assurance and class-consciousness of the working class'. It seems rather, to be a short-term attempt by the government to retain the 'confidence' of the financial community at times when this has been called into question" (p. 197).

41. Cf. Salamon and Siegfried (1977, p. 1035).

42. Bain (1959, p. 421). His reasons for this approach can be summarized in three points:
First, the inclusion of conduct variables is not essential to the development of an operational theory of industrial organization.
Secondly, a priori theory based upon structure-conduct and conduct-performance links yields ambiguous predictions.
Thirdly, much published information on business conduct is incomplete and unreliable, while business firms in general are not very willing to allow researchers access to internal information.
See also Scherer (1970).

Chapter 3

1. This section mainly draws upon Van Winden (1983), especially chapter 1, chapter 4 pp. 88-100, chapter 7 pp. 216-222. In some instances we also consulted Van Winden (1987), Van Velthoven and Van Winden (1986).

2. Van Winden (1983) prefers to use the term "state" to denote the "institution that has the monopoly of legitimate violence and taxation within a certain territory" (p. 1). We will use the terms "public sector" and "state" interchangeably.

3. To mention some of the aspects: state sector workers have direct access to the most important means of violence (the police and the military); they have potential control over more or less collective goods; they are part of one organization, which makes it relatively easy for them to promote their interests in a unified way; the "survival" problem is less urgent for the state bureaucracy than for a firm, because state departments are often monopolistic suppliers, and because political upheavals are typically directed against the government (the bureaucracy with its possession of expert knowledge generally will not be superseded).
See also section 2.5.

4. Cf. Van Winden (1983, p. 91, 93, 99, 170).

5. Van Winden prefers to use the term "interest function" instead of "utility function", as the functions are not defined on a purely individual level. Cf. Van Winden (1983), p. 255.

6. For the sake of clarity: it is not assumed here that the members of a social class will automatically organize themselves and engage in collective action to further their common interests. Eqs. (3.1) and (3.2) only bring out that the interests of each individual class

member are structurally related to, and for the analysis of political processes can be represented by the interests of the <u>representative member</u> of the social class. P_k remains an individual interest function.

7. As Van Winden (1987) points out, many ideological, behavioural norms — i.e., opinions about how one should behave — are the result of intensive influencing accompanied by rewards and punishments (positive and negative sanctions), which may eventually lead people to show the desired behaviour <u>as if</u> voluntarily. A clear example is the education of children by parents and teachers. See also Mueller (1986). For the moment it suffices to observe that due to continuous pressure, individuals may (behave as if they voluntarily) pay heed to other people's interests. We shall return to this issue shortly.

8. Van Winden (1983, p. 95), citing R. Radner.

9. As these interest functions will typically represent processes of power and conflict between interests, Van Winden prefers not to speak of "objective functions", or "social welfare functions". Cf. Van Winden (1983, p. 255; 1984, p. 495).

10. If one is talking about level-specific interest bloc i on decision-making level h, Van Winden (1983, p. 99) suggests, it may be useful or necessary to particularize the elementary interest functions P_k into functions $P_{k,hi}$. It should be expected that people in interest bloc hi are not only interested in the real disposable income level that holds on average for the social class to which they belong, when this is at stake (meso- (class-) level political processes), but in addition in the income level that holds for their particular bloc, when this is perceived or expected to be affected (micro-level political processes).
We will not go further into this.

11. Note that the impact of external pressure, e.g. from pressure groups, will explicitly be dealt with below.

12. A similar reasoning also holds for P_{11}. P_{11} may be a complex interest function, in case of anticipated mobility (the next election might work out badly) or multiple positions of politicians in the economy. P_{11} might also be formulated as a nested complex interest function, Van Winden (1983, p. 170) suggests, if the level-specific (complex) interest functions of the politicians in government and parliament would differ.

13. As in all underlying interest functions — cf. (3.3) and (3.4) — the relevant weights λ were assumed to be non-negative and sum to one, this also holds for P_s, due to the multiplicative structure.

14. Van Winden (1983, p. 217) uses the term pressure groups in a more general sense, i.e. for collectivities that try to influence the behaviour of another collectivity.

15. Van Winden (1983), p. 220, mutatis mutandis. That is, throughout our exposition (see also note 14) we have interpreted c_h to be the public sector, and c_i the pressure group(s).

16. An additional problem may arise if the information regarding the nature of the interest functions P_k gets distorted before it can be brought to bear upon public sector decision making. We need not go into this problem here. What counts for our analysis is that P_k can be interpreted to be the perception by public sector decision makers of the interest function of (the representative member of) social class k.

17. Van Winden (1983), p. 95, pp. 102/103.

18. Van Winden (1983), pp. 169/170.

19. Van Winden (1983), p. 216.

20. It may be added that Borooah and Van der Ploeg (1983) only apply the interest function approach to the analysis of the "day-to-day running of an economy with different interest groups". In passing on to the analysis of "medium term economic policy", the interest function approach is replaced by - more accurately, but in our opinion it amounts to the same thing, is subordinated to - an approach based on vote functions and government ideology, without an indication of the reason why and of the relation between the two approaches.
With respect to the specific outcomes for the day-to-day decision making of the state, it should be observed that they hinge on the assumption that the state reckons with full crowding out of private sector activities, in the sense that an increase in income generated in the public sector decreases private sector (gross) income by the same amount. It is further assumed that state expenditure and employment can be varied in the short term while tax rates are considered to be fixed, implying that the costs of state expenditure in terms of present or future taxation - and the concomitant conflicts of interest - are neglected.
Overlooking the various elements touched on above, the approach adopted by Borooah and Van der Ploeg to implement the interest function approach does not seem very appealing to us.

21. Cf. Van Winden (1983, p. 237; 1987, p. 22).

22. For a more extensive treatment of this model, see Van Winden (1983), chapter 5. To see how such a model might work out, he presents some simulation results.
It may be added that Van Winden (1983) also outlines some ideas - inspired by the interest function approach and the treatment of voting behaviour - to cope with the analysis of coalition formation.

23. The first proxy variable to come across one's mind would seem to be relative numerical strength. Cf. Van Winden (1983), for instance pp. 157, 171, 175, 192.

24. The Nash bargaining solution originates from cooperative game theory. Within a static, axiomatic representation of a bargaining problem it can be shown to be the solution satisfying certain plausible conditions. See Nash (1950, 1953) for two-person games, and Harsanyi (1963) for the generalization to n-person games; see also Roth (1979).

    It might be added here that the static, axiomatic approach of cooperative game theory tells us virtually nothing about the details of the bargaining process and procedures. For that reason game theorists involved in what has come to be called the "Nash program", are currently working on the construction of non-cooperative games to explicitly describe the process of bargaining. Cf. Rubinstein (1982), Binmore, Rubinstein and Wolinsky (1986). The perfect equilibrium outcomes of such games have been shown to coincide in the limit with the Nash bargaining solution.

25. See, e.g., Roth (1979).

26. The discussion hitherto pertained to the so-called symmetric Nash solution. It may be noticed, however, that the bargaining theory also considers asymmetric solutions, characterized by the maximization of a weighted Nash-product

$$\Pi_k (P_k - P_k^T)^{\alpha_k}, \quad 0 \leq \alpha_k \leq 1 \; \forall k, \quad \Sigma_k \alpha_k = 1,$$

where a large exponent α_k is interpreted as representing a relatively high "bargaining power" of participant k. Cf. Roth (1979), Svejnar (1986), Binmore, Rubinstein and Wolinsky (1986). This asymmetric Nash solution attempts to capture some - imprecisely defined - differences in bargaining power between the participants, due to institutional, economic and other factors, other than those arising from asymmetries in preferences and threat points (the latter are already taken account of in the symmetric Nash solution). One could think of asymmetries in the bargaining procedure, or of differences in the participants' beliefs about the determinants of the environment.

If the asymmetric Nash solution would obtain eq. (3.12) should be replaced by:

$$(3.12') \quad f' = -\frac{\alpha_2}{\alpha_1} \cdot \frac{(P_1 - P_1^T)}{(P_2 - P_2^T)}.$$

Hence, eq. (3.14) should be rewritten as:

$$(3.14') \quad \frac{\lambda_1}{\lambda_2} = \frac{\alpha_1}{\alpha_2} \cdot \frac{P_1^*}{P_2^*} \cdot \frac{P_2^* - P_2^T}{P_1^* - P_1^T}.$$

The (distribution of the) power weights λ would not only be related to the bargaining power of the participants connected with the position of the threat point in the bargaining game, but also to their bargaining power arising from other sources; as should be expected.

27. Going back from - say, an estimate of - P_s to the underlying decision structure would confront us with the problem which of the three models mentioned - or maybe even an other model - is the proper one. We shall not venture on such an operation.

Chapter 4

1. The first three sections of this chapter heavily draw on Van Velthoven and Van Winden (1986).

2. Cf. Samuelson (1980), chapters 11-13; Lipsey, Steiner and Purvis (1987), chapter 26. See also section 1.5.2.

3. This statement is a little bit too strong. Both Samuelson (1980, p. 244) and Lipsey, Steiner and Purvis (1987, p. 561) make mention of Nordhaus' political business cycle hypothesis; however, without incorporating it in the analysis of the functioning of the economy, or drawing conclusions from it for the practice of economic policy advising.

4. The national income multiplier with respect to autonomous expenditure, $[1-c(1-t)-g]^{-1}$, is increasing in g.

5. This specification allows us to derive analytically well-defined behavioural equations which can be used straightforwardly in the empirical application in chapter 5. Alternative specifications of the elementary interest functions P_k, such as a CES or a quadratic formulation, are of course theoretically admitted but readily lead to analytical intractabilities.

6. In chapter 7 we shall be explicitly concerned with public sector decision making on income transfers, and integrate the social security system in our politico-economic model. The empirical application in that chapter, using data for the Netherlands, will show that with respect to state expenditure the hypothesis that the dependants are without direct political influence, can not be rejected.
Note, however, that even if the dependants themselves are without direct political influence, it is not necessarily so that their interests are completely disregarded. For reasons discussed in section 3.2 - altruism, multiple positions, and, presumably most important here, anticipated mobility - the interests of this social class may still be taken account of by the other, politically more powerful, social groups. We shall return to this issue in chapter 5.

7. All variables should be read as being expressed in real terms.

8. In a more sophisticated set-up, one should recognize that the mixture of public and private production of the goods and services to be supplied by the state, may be subject to political dispute too. The

amount of "load shedding" and "contracting out" may vary. See also section 5.2.2.

9. There are many studies on the Netherlands which find a considerable degree of shifting. Empirical evidence for full or nearly full shifting is presented by Knegt (1978), Knoester (1983), Brandsma and Van der Windt (1983). See also the discussion between Koefoed (1985) and Knoester (1985).
Knoester (1983), who finds full shifting for the Netherlands, also considered the cases of Germany, the UK, and the US, for which countries he finds a considerable degree of forward shifting too; respectively 0.71, 0.50, 0.41.

10. Cf. section 3.3, point d.

11. The implication is that the state, partly because of lack of knowledge, partly because of a short time horizon, does not take account of second-order and feedback-effects of its activities on the tax base.

12. With $w_s E_s$ and G_m exogenously determined and fixed, either the budget surplus/deficit (parameter θ) or the tax rate (τ) have to accommodate in view of the public sector budget constraint; cf. eq. (4.7). If $\tau = \delta$ and θ accommodates, then the statement in the text is always true. If θ is fixed and τ accommodates, the statement is true if
$$\theta < \frac{c_1+\gamma}{c_2(1+\gamma)}, \text{ where } \frac{c_1+\gamma}{c_2(1+\gamma)} > 1.$$

13. That is, if $\theta < \frac{c_1+\gamma}{c_2(1+\gamma)}$.

14. Gandenberger (1985) also points out that in a Keynesian perspective the emphasis would be on the positive effects of deficits-and-borrowing on real output and employment.
In economic theory no general agreement has yet been reached on the effects of a budget deficit and the way it is financed, nor is it clear what information on this issue is available to and used by the state.
For a more extensive analysis of state decision making on budget deficits and borrowing, taking account of future interest and redemption obligations, see chapter 8.

15. Other lag structures might also be proposed for the model; for instance, only a lag in the consumption function, or just lags in the expenditure equations for C and G_m. However, note that in these cases the dynamic stability condition would be the same: m > 0.

16. That is, if $1 \leq v < 1 + \frac{c_1 \delta(1-w_p/\alpha_p)}{\theta(1+\gamma)}$, and m > 0.

Chapter 5

1. This chapter draws on Van Velthoven and Van Winden (1986) and Van Velthoven, Van Winden and Renaud (1984). However, while in these references the empirical application was limited to the period 1952-1977 because of problems of data availability, the present chapter will be concerned with the extended period 1952-1984.

2. More precisely, for the Assembly (the Second Chamber).
Dutch parliament consists of two chambers: an Assembly and a Senate (the First Chamber). Contrary to the Assembly, the Senate is elected indirectly. Moreover, it lacks some of the legislative prerogatives of the Assembly, to wit the right of amendment and of initiative. The Senate has a legislative right of veto over the bills that have been passed by the Assembly, which, however, it is expected to exercise with considerable restraint. At the time of cabinet formations only (the chairmen of the fractions in) the Assembly plays a role. The government program is debated in the Assembly alone. No cabinet has ever been ousted by a Senate majority.
For all these reasons, prevalent opinion has it that the cabinet ought to conform to the political relations within the Assembly, the branch of parliament that directly represents the electorate. Cf. De Swaan (1973, p. 206). Accordingly, we shall ignore the Senate in the sequel and restrict attention to the Assembly and the cabinet.

3. De Swaan (1973), p. 221.

4. Another factor which further aggravates the problem of assigning responsibility for economic developments, is the highly open character of the Dutch economy.

5. Recently, the Netherlands has seen some fine examples of the latter phenomenon.
The last coalition discussed in De Swaan (1973) was started in 1973, and lasted until 1977. It resigned because of an internal conflict, and was replaced by a new coalition in December 1977, after the election of May (!) 1977. Remarkably, the new coalition did not contain the previous prime minister's party (PvdA) that "won" the election with an increase in its seat share from 43 to 53 (on a total of 150).
Just the reverse could be observed in 1986, after the CDA-VVD-coalition cabinet "Lubbers-I" had completed its regular four-year parliamentary period. In the general elections, the VVD lost 9 of its original 36 seats, while the main opposition party won 5. The christian-democratic party CDA, itself winning 9 seats, and still in the key position in parliament, chose for continuation of the CDA-VVD-coalition (cabinet "Lubbers-II").

6. For a nice illustration, the reader is referred to the 1977 cabinet formation, touched upon in footnote 5.

7. Cf. De Swaan (1973).

8. With a few exceptions, that is. Some economic data, such as unemployment figures, and the division of taxes, social security premiums and income transfers between wage and non-wage incomes, were taken from the Central Economic Plans, issued by the Central Planning Bureau. Political data, such as election dates, election outcomes, and the composition of coalition cabinets, were obtained from Parlement en Kiezer (1986).

9. Cf. Centraal Bureau voor de Statistiek, Nationale Rekeningen 1969-1981, met herziene reeksen over de jaren 1969-1976, 's-Gravenhage, 1985.

10. It should be noticed that the estimation equations will contain some one-year lags; hence 1970. Similarly because of the lag, some figures for 1951 have been added to the data set.

11. The reader is reminded that the empirical application in this chapter has the character of a first approach. While the hypothesis of tax shifting is quite generally accepted for the first subperiod under consideration (1952-1977) - cf. the literature cited in chapter 4, footnote 9 -, this is less so for more recent times. Due to high and rising unemployment figures, especially since 1980, wage increases have been tempered; the degree of tax shifting on to profits may well have diminished at that. A shift in market power between labour and capital might necessitate, as we argued in chapter 4, an adaptation of the model of state behaviour.
There are also some other reasons that might lead us to expect at the outset that our yet simple model will perform better for the first subperiod than, in particular, for the years after 1980. The fact that public sector decision making on income transfers and the level of the budget deficit is not explicitly modelled, is likely to be important here. The set-up of the Dutch social security system - in the latter half of the sixties and the first half of the seventies mainly - took place rather smoothly due to the prospering state of the economy which kept demand for transfers low. This situation drastically changed in the beginning of the eighties, when unemployment sharply increased and the budget deficit soared. Our model as yet neglects the possible substitution effects between transfers and expenditure, nor does it go into the choice between taxation and debt finance.
We shall return to these issues later on.

12. Simultaneity bias need not be present here, given the recursive nature of the three equations, and the one-year lag in Π.

13. The two sets of parameter estimates also point in that direction, but for that the data revision might be responsible too.

14. Van Winden (1983, pp. 221) brings these factors together in three categories: objective threat potential, group cohesiveness, and an information factor.
The reader is reminded that for the class of dependants, who are not directly involved in the production process and for that reason have the weakest position in politico-economic affairs, it has been

assumed in chapter 4 that $\lambda_4 = 0$. Hence eq. (5.1). For the potentiality of $\lambda_4 \neq 0$, see chapter 7.

15. See also the discussion in section 3.3, under point e.

16. In the Netherlands, in 1975, 89.6% of the income of the self-employed was obtained from profits, while the figure was 0.6% for directors. The latter obtained 88.5% of their income from wages. Source: Centraal Bureau voor de Statistiek (1980), De personele inkomensverdeling 1975, deel 2, 's-Gravenhage.
Similar figures for 1954, 1959 and 1967 can be found in: Centraal Planbureau (1975), De personele inkomensverdeling 1952-1967, Monografie 19, 's-Gravenhage.

17. It is implicitly assumed here that $\varepsilon_{12} + \varepsilon_{13}$, ε_{23}, ε_{31} and λ_3 are unequal to zero. The reader is reminded that ε_{12} denotes the weight attached by state sector workers to their employment level (as revealed), whereas ε_{13} and ε_{23} stand for the weight that state and private sector workers, respectively, attach to the consumption of state provided goods.

18. In the Netherlands, the distribution of the chances of being involuntarily dismissed has been (and still is, albeit to a gradually less extent) quite uneven between the private and the public sector; in the latter case the chance was close to nil.

19. This alternative formulation was suggested in Renaud, Van Velthoven and Van Winden (1986).

20. Observe that the analysis of state behaviour in chapter 4 assumed $\lambda_4 = 0$. For that reason, the social mobility of those who are presently unemployed, which may be anticipated for good reasons, can be left out of consideration here.
Notice, further, that according to eq. (5.3) the interests of the unemployed may well be taken account of in society, despite the fact that $\lambda_4 = 0$.

21. It may be observed that the variable EMPR might also represent a motivation for state behaviour which quite differs from our present model, to wit stabilization policy. Cf. chapter 1. In the latter case, however, the sign of the effect of EMPR on δ (and, hence, the tax rate) will be expected to be positive.

22. Given the interpretation of state behaviour in terms of eqs. (5.3) and (5.4), the analysis of the impact of changes in the power distribution λ on δ has to be reconsidered. It turns out that, again, E_c/E is expected to be inversely related to δ; further, δ is positively related to E_s/E, if

$$[(\varepsilon_{12}+\varepsilon_{13}) - \varepsilon_{43}]\pi_1 - [\varepsilon_{23} - \varepsilon_{43}]\pi_2 > 0,$$

which would hold if it can be expected that $\varepsilon_{12} + \varepsilon_{13} > \varepsilon_{43} > \varepsilon_{23}$.

23. Use is made of the ordering of the Dutch parties presented by De Swaan (1973), which is based on the crucial criterion of the degree

of government intervention in the national economy that a party advocates. Parties with less than 2.5% of the vote are neglected. The ratings of the political parties are determined on a [0,1]-interval, and kept fixed over the whole period whether the party existed at all times or not. The ratings are: BP (peasants), 0.1; VVD (liberal-conservatives), 0.2; DS70, 0.3; CHU, 0.4; KVP (catholics) and ARP, 0.5; D66, 0.6; PvdA (social-democrats), 0.7; PPR, 0.8; PSP, 0.9; CPN (communists), 1.0. Thus, the more leftist a party, the higher its rating. As noted earlier, in 1977 KVP, ARP and CHU merged into one party, the CDA. The rating of this single christian-democratic party since 1977 is set equal to the weighted average rating of the three separate parties at the last general election before 1977 (i.e., 0.485).

24. Of course, our discussion in section 5.1 of the characteristics of the Dutch democracy and the empirical results found thus far, does not leave much hope for finding any effect of this variable.
Among the many possibilities that can be chosen for the formulation of ELEC (cf. Allen, Sulock and Sabo (1986)), we opt for a straightforward approach. ELEC is defined to be a 0,1-variable; ELEC = 1 in the years before (anticipated) general elections are held, and only if the cabinet has been long enough in power to have had the opportunity to engineer re-election efforts; otherwise, ELEC = 0.

25. For the error terms in the equations the usual assumption is made that they are independently, normally distributed.
Notice that no simultaneity bias need be present here, as the relative numerical strength variables are all lagged.
The regressions of table 5.2 can also be found, in broad outline, in Van Velthoven and Van Winden (1986). Because of the addition of ELEC and a somewhat different procedure for the calculation of the GVTYP-variables (a change in the type of cabinet in the course of a year is now taken account of, by weighing with the number of months each type of cabinet has been in power during that year), while the underlying data series have been rounded off somewhat less, the coefficient estimates presented here differ to a certain extent. However, the general line of the results (signs, significancy, goodness of fit, absence of autocorrelation) remains unchanged.

26. See Van den Berg (1981).

27. Cf. eq. (5.2). Allowing for social mobility - cf. eq. (5.4) - the negative sign of E_s/E would demand that
$$[(\varepsilon_{12}+\varepsilon_{13}) - \varepsilon_{43}] \pi_1 - [\varepsilon_{23} - \varepsilon_{43}] \pi_2 < 0,$$
for which $\varepsilon_{12} + \varepsilon_{13} < \varepsilon_{43} \leq \varepsilon_{23}$ is a sufficient condition. As it may be taken for granted that π_1 was much larger over the period considered than π_2, it is presumably even sufficient for the inequality to hold if $\varepsilon_{12} + \varepsilon_{13} < \varepsilon_{43}$.

28. Dummy = 0, 1952-1969; = 1, 1970-1984. For the data, see the Appendix. Alternatively, one could try to eliminate the break in each of the underlying data series separately, by linking up the 1952-1969 data

with a multiplicative or additive transformation to the 1970-1984 sequel. Such a procedure would certainly be as arbitrary as the one chosen here. Moreover, for the variables in our regression equations additive transformations seem to be the most proper ones. In that case, introducing a dummy variable will serve the same job, and yield an estimate of the significancy of its role, in addition.

29. It could be argued that the translation of changes in the power structure of society, through the exertion of pressure and the build-up of vested interests, into changes in the power coefficient δ and, hence, the tax rate, takes time. Then, a partial adjustment model would be applicable. However, rerunning the regressions of tables 5.2 - 5.4 with the addition of the lagged dependent variable does not improve the results reported above. In most instances the coefficient of the lagged dependent variable is small and not significantly different from zero; in those cases in which it is significant, the other regression coefficients do not lend themselves for useful interpretation. In order not to overload the exposition, we have decided not to include these regression results in the main text. For the interested reader the following table presents those regressions which were considered above to be the most useful ones for the different periods, with the lagged dependent variable included.

30. The data for the period 1952-1984 were obtained by coupling the 1952-1969 data of the first data set to the 1970-1984 figures of the second, to enable the inclusion of the lagged dependent variable; cf. table 5.5. The dummy variable is redefined accordingly.

31. In view of the earlier results with regard to the inclusion of the lagged dependent variable reported in footnote 29, its contribution may be expected to be rather small.

32. Alternatively, comparison of regressions 23 and 27 points out that the hypothesis $\varepsilon_{23} = \varepsilon_{33} = \varepsilon_{12} + \varepsilon_{13}$ cannot be rejected.

33. From regression 27 it follows that the structural value (i.e. corrected for the lagged adjustment process) of the coefficient $\varepsilon_{.3}/\varepsilon_{31}$ is equal to $0.09/(1 - 0.46) = 0.16$.
Introducing the equality assumption $\varepsilon_{kg} = \varepsilon_{.g}$ $\forall k$, and taking account of the sum restriction $\Sigma_g \varepsilon_{.g} = 1$, then yields the figures reported in the text.
It is interesting to add that Schram and Van Winden (1986b) in an analysis of voting intentions in the Netherlands obtain quite similar values for these preference parameters, indicating a relatively high preference for private consumption relative to government consumption (0.82 as opposed to 0.18).

34. For the problems surrounding revealed preference methods, cf. section 1.5.1. See also Basu (1980).

35. Both in this and in the previous subsection.

Table at note 29. Estimation results for δ.

	constant	E_s/E	$(E_c/E)^{-1}$	EMPR	GVTYP1	ELEC	dummy	lagged endogenous variable	$\bar{R}^2$	Durbin's h
1953-1977										
5a	1.75 * (2.48)	-3.85 * (2.76)	0.082** (4.91)	-1.30 * (2.18)				0.00 (0.02)	0.906	-1.57
7a	0.23 * (2.34)	-1.58 (1.57)	0.059** (4.21)					0.22 (1.24)	0.889	-1.99
1971-1984										
8a	0.17 (0.18)	0.79 (0.20)	-0.050 (0.86)	0.54 (0.65)	-0.46 (0.81)	0.05 ** (4.13)		0.56 (2.20)	0.922	-3.39
10a	-0.40 * (2.29)				1.26 * (2.56)	0.03 (2.04)		0.41 (1.63)	0.820	3.28
13a	-0.42 * (2.75)			0.81 ** (3.24)				0.24 (0.93)	0.786	1.53
14a	0.52 * (3.09)	-3.04 (1.87)	0.026 (0.71)					0.39 (1.63)	0.778	0.88
1953-1984										
21a	0.57 ** (4.84)	-4.48 ** (4.82)	0.059** (4.39)				-0.00 (0.01)	0.20 (1.14)	0.814	-1.72

Chapter 6

1. This chapter relies partly on Van Velthoven and Van Winden (1986). Section 6.3 reproduces material from section 4 of the latter paper, while section 6.2 presents a generalization of the results in that paper.

2. For applications of computer simulation in politico-economic analysis, see Kirchgässner (1984), Van Winden (1983), and several studies of Frey c.s. cited in Frey and Schneider (1981a).

3. Cf. Gandolfo (1980), pp. 455-459.

4. Note from eqs. (6.3) and (6.5) that:
$$m_t = \alpha_p [a_3(1-\delta_t) + a_2 \delta_t]^{-1}.$$

   For the first quadrant of figure 6.2 (cases I, II, III), we have $a_2 > 0$, $a_3 > 0$, $0 \leq \delta_t \leq 1$ $\forall t$, such that m_t is well-defined and guaranteed to be > 0, $\forall t$.

5. A necessary condition for the (sub)model of section 4.3 to have a well-defined and stable solution is: $m > 0$. If
$$\theta < \frac{(c_1+\gamma)(\alpha_p-w_p)}{(1+\gamma)(\alpha_p-c_1 w_p)},$$
   or in the notation of the present chapter (cf. eq. (6.6)), if $a_2 < 0$, then we know from figure 4.1 that a continuously growing δ on the [0,1]-interval will sooner or later break the condition $m > 0$. The model becomes explosive.

6. For the two equilibrium positions, it holds:
$$m \gtrless 0 \text{ if } a_3[(1-\varepsilon_{11})a_1 - \varepsilon_{23}a_4 + \varepsilon_{33}E_c a_2 - (\varepsilon_{31}+2\varepsilon_{33})E_c a_3] +$$
$$a_2[(1-\varepsilon_{11})a_1 + \varepsilon_{23}a_4 + (2\varepsilon_{31}+\varepsilon_{33})E_c a_2 - \varepsilon_{31}E_c a_3] \gtrless 0.$$
   Both the expressions within hooked brackets are negative for case VII, as can be seen from figure 6.2, while $a_3 > 0$, $a_2 < 0$.

7. In this statement we summarize three potentialities that we met in the course of the exposition: the discriminant D may be negative, one of the cases IV, V, VI may obtain, or case VII may obtain with a negative multiplier value m.

8. If $a_2 = 0$, eq. (6.9) degenerates into a linear first-order difference equation in E_s, which leads to a continuing expansion, a constancy or a persistent contraction of E_s, depending on whether
$$\frac{(1-\varepsilon_{11})a_1}{\varepsilon_{31} a_3 E_c} \gtreqless 1.$$

9. The suggested occurrence of a continuing expansion of the size of the public sector brings out that the model is not fully specified to

analyze these cases. For instance, in cases IV, VI and VII in figure 6.6, what happens if E_s surpasses the asymptotic value $\overline{E}_s$? To deal with this kind of issues, upper and lower limits (productive capacity, labour market constraints, non-negativity constraints) should explicitly be added to the model.

10. It may be added that Van Winden (1983, chapter 6) presents and analyzes a politico-economic model with an endogenous type of state, which combines some elements of the Frey-Schneider and the present approach. His model is based upon the interest function approach; the power weights λ_k, however, are set by the political party that, in a two party system, wins the election. With each of the two parties corresponds one set of power weights λ_k.

Chapter 7

1. This chapter heavily draws on Van Velthoven and Van Winden (1985). However, while in this reference the empirical application was limited to the period 1952-1977 because of problems of data availability, the present chapter (cf. section 7.4) will be concerned with the extended period till 1984; also some minor other modifications will be introduced. Section 7.2.3 is newly added.

2. According to Dutch survey data (cf. Sociaal en Cultureel Planbureau (1986), bijlage 11.18) median respondents were in recent years quite content with the existing social security benefit levels, with the exception of the Algemene Bijstandwet for which benefit levels were deemed too low. At the same time, the government has been curtailing social security programs.

3. For a first, preliminary step in that direction, see section 5.2.3, eq. (5.3).

4. In section 3.2 it was argued that the suggestion in Van Winden (1983) to include e_k in the elementary interest functions presumably should be justified by interpreting these interest functions as some sort of indirect utility functions. Moreover, in the empirical application in chapter 5 the preference weight attached to e_k was consistently reported to be non-positive.
Of course, the relative numerical strength variables can be added to eqs. (7.1) till (7.5), in a quite straightforward manner. The consequence of this will be that δ_1 in eq. (7.12) has to be redefined, such that it not only includes the preference weights attached to the supply of public goods and services x_s, but also the preference weights attached to the relative number of state sector workers e_1. (Note that x_s is directly related to e_1, via the production function of state goods). But then the whole difference just amounts to a matter of interpretation of the preference weights ε_{k2} in eq. (7.12). The (formal) derivations in the remainder of the chapter are not affected.

5. Note that the various preference weights are likely to include the subjective probability estimates for the events of remaining

employed, becoming unemployed, or becoming a pensioner, for example. Cf. eq. (5.3).

6. For a discussion of this assumption and an analysis of the consequences related with the introduction of some alternative tax systems, see section 4.2.

7. Due to the specific functional form of the interest functions, implying unitelasticity, the number of dependants E_{4i} does not show up in the equation for E_s, nor does the state wage rate w_s appear in the equation for w_{4i}.

8. The reader might be tempted to conclude from eq. (7.20), substituting $\delta_4 = 0$, that in some cases other, positive values would yield better results in terms of the value of P_s. However, in those cases state sector labour demand surpasses the available supply in the labour market, $L - E_p$, such that $E_{4d} = 0$; the labour market related social security scheme loses its relevance. For those cases, the constraint $E_{4d} \geq 0$ should be made explicit in the model.

9. In a prolonged period of more or less stable growth such a phenomenon may even become institutionalized, e.g. by legally coupling the development of w_{4i} to an index of w_p, as it has occurred in the Netherlands.

10. Ergo, the coupling of the preceding footnote will most probably come to an end in a period of recession.

11. See, e.g., Van Praag and Halberstadt (1980), Van Praag and Emanuel (1981).

12. For the more general case that the δ_i's themselves would have changed (due to a shift the power weights λ_k^i or the preference weights ε_{kg}), such that $\Delta_i^o = \delta_i^o/(\delta_1^o+\delta_2^o)$, $i = 1,2$ before the introduction, and $\Delta_i = \delta_i/(\delta_1+\delta_2+\delta_3)$, $i = 1,2,3$, afterwards, then the condition in (7.36) would have read

$$(\Delta_1-\Delta_1^o) \frac{c_1(w_s-w_{4d})+\gamma w_s}{(1+\gamma)w_s-w_{4d}} + (\Delta_2-\Delta_2^o)\theta c_2^* + \Delta_3 c_1 \gtreqless 0 \ .$$

Analogous conditions can be derived for the inequalities to follow.

13. As noted before, the impact of the unemployment benefit program can also be studied by comparing the values of E_p and E_s before and after the introduction of the program. The results obtained in that manner are very similar to (7.38) and (7.39) and need not be reproduced here.

14. It may be noticed that the inequality (7.39) conforms with the partial result portrayed in figure 7.1. In analyzing state decision making it was assumed that E_p is considered to be fixed; hence, $\partial E_p/\partial w_{4d}$ is taken to be zero. The analysis of state behaviour, then, pointed out (see figure 7.1) that

$$\frac{\partial E_s}{\partial w_{4d}} \gtreqless 0 \quad \text{if} \quad \Pi - \theta(1+\gamma)w_s(L-E_p) \gtreqless 0 \ .$$

In the present context of equilibrium analysis $\partial E_p/\partial w_{4d}$ of course need not be equal to zero.

15. The result which is obtained when comparing m^o and m, before and after the introduction of w_{4d}, as in eq. (7.40), is very similar to eq. (7.41).

16. Bearing in mind the conclusions of chapter 4, this statement should be read with some care. In section 4.4, in a discussion of the automatic stabilizing nature of taxation, it was noticed that one should study the dynamic properties of the politico-economic model. It was found that much depends on the particular specification and lag structure of the model. Of course, the same holds true for the present model, which has a very similar structure.

17. However - cf. the conclusions of section 4.4 already referred to in the preceding footnote -, at a dynamic respecification of the model the above conclusions might well be reversed.

18. These data sets differ substantially from those constructed for the empirical application in chapter 5, due to the treatment of social security: as a private sector affair in chapter 5, and as a public sector activity in this chapter.

19. More specifically: the data sets pertain to the periods 1951-1977 and 1969-1984. Because of a lag which is introduced in the computation of the dependent variable, while furthermore the lagged dependent variable will be inserted in the regressions, the regressions will pertain to the periods 1953-1977 and 1971-1984.

20. To be more precise, the Δ_i's have been calculated as:

$$\Delta_1 = \frac{\theta[(1+\gamma)w_s - w_{4d}]E_s}{\Pi - \theta w_{4d}(L-E_p)} ,$$

$$\Delta_2 = \frac{\Pi - T}{\Pi - \theta w_{4d}(L-E_p)} ,$$

$$\Delta_3 = \frac{\theta(W_4 - W_{4d})}{\Pi - \theta w_{4d}(L-E_p)} ,$$

with: $\theta = T/(G_m + W_s + W_4)$, $\gamma = G_m/W_s$, $w_s = W_s/E_s$, $w_{4d} = W_{4d}/E_{4d}$, $L = E_s + E_p + E_{4d}$, while a one-year-lag has been applied with regard to Π, in conformity with the procedure in chapter 5.
It is noticed that the figures on the Δ_i's - and hence the results - in this chapter differ in some minor respects from those in Van Velthoven and Van Winden (1985), as Π has been lagged one year, and L

has been calculated using the number of persons receiving unemployment benefits instead of the registered unemployment level.

21. Dummy = 0, 1953 - 1970; = 1, 1971 - 1984. See also chapter 5, footnote 28.

22. Due to the sum restriction $\Sigma_i \Delta_i = 1$, the values of Δ_1, Δ_2, Δ_3 can be computed, once the ratio's Δ_1/Δ_2 and Δ_3/Δ_2 are given.

23. From the definition of the Δ_i's in eqs (7.14) - (7.16) and from eq. (7.12) it follows:

    $\varepsilon_{.1} = \Delta_2 / [\Delta_2 + (\Delta_1 + \Delta_3)\lambda_3]$,

    $\varepsilon_{.2} = \Delta_1 \lambda_3 / [\Delta_2 + (\Delta_1 + \Delta_3)\lambda_3]$,

    $\varepsilon_{.3} = \Delta_3 \lambda_3 / [\Delta_2 + (\Delta_1 + \Delta_3)\lambda_3]$,

    where

    $\lambda_3 = [E_c / (E_s + E_p + E_c)]_{-1}$.

24. It is not impossible, of course, that our results in their turn may need amendment when the supply-side of the economy is taken into account. Cf. Van Praag and Halberstadt (1980) and Van Praag and Emanuel (1981), who analyze the impact of the social security system from the supply-side of the economy. Their model predicts that the higher the benefit/wage ratio, the higher unemployment will be.

Chapter 8

1. This chapter is a thoroughly revised version of the paper "Towards a behavioural-theoretic explanation of budget deficits" (co-author Frans van Winden) that was presented at the 5th World Congress of the Econometric Society, Cambridge (Ma), august 1985.

2. Barro (1979) is of the same opinion:
   ".... proponents of the Ricardian view that the choice between debt and taxes does not matter are left with an embarassing absence of a theory of public debt creation". "However, opponents of the Ricardian view seem also to lack an interesting positive theory of the public debt" (pp. 940-941).

3. That is, debt financing may have effects different from tax financing, or the policy maker may think so.

4. Note that these objections are serious indeed, as the size and the way of financing the deficit are of crucial importance in determining the dynamic behaviour of the model. The (in)stability of the model is the central topic of the article.

5. Comments about the major thesis of this book by R.J. Barro, D.F. Gordon, W.A. Niskanen, P.C. Roberts and J. Tobin, presented at a symposium organized by K. Brunner, together with a reply by the authors, can be found in the Journal of Monetary Economics, 1978, vol. 4, pp. 567-636.

6. See on this, extensively, Cavaco Silva (1977).

7. For a discussion of the various aspects of debt and fiscal illusion, the reader is referred to Cavaco Silva (1977), Gandenberger (1985). It might be added that Gandenberger suggests that the degree of debt illusion and perception may vary over the business cycle. In a period of economic recovery and boom, budget deficits will tend to diminish, ceteris paribus, as tax receipts rise and unemployment related outlays fall. Voters will perceive the situation as one of reduced fiscal strain; pressure for additional expenditure and tax reductions will mount, increasing structural deficits. In a period of economic recession the previous increases in the structural deficit will become apparent; deficits and borrowing will rise sharply. Expenditure cuts and tax increases will be on the agenda, but ratchet-type effects then may well prevent a downward correction of the structural deficit.

8. For some tentative approaches to the analysis of central bank behaviour, see Acheson and Chant (1973), Chant and Acheson (1973), Kane (1980), Frey and Schneider (1981c). See also Brennan and Buchanan (1981).

9. Notice that this formulation is in conformity with the standard life-cycle model with d (-d being the elasticity of marginal utility with respect to consumption) tending to 1; the rate of time preference ρ is implicitly contained in the schedule μ_{kj}. See, e.g., White (1978) and Söderström (1982).

10. Cf. Seater (1985). In an evaluation of the evidence for the validity of the equivalence hypothesis he notes, first, that "most (but not all) of the favorable evidence consists of failures to reject the hypothesis and therefore may be of questionable power". Secondly, and in the present context most importantly, he points out that "studies of the consumption function consistently find that consumption expenditure seems "too sensitive" to current income. One possible explanation is that a significant number of households are wealth-constrained. Such households would not obey the predictions of the equivalence theorem" (p. 125).

11. From the point of view of the interest function approach, each generation - index g - may be characterized by its own elementary interest function, say

$$(8.5') \quad P_{kt}^g = A_k^g \cdot \prod_{j=0}^{H_k^g} [(1-\tau_{kt+j})^{\varepsilon_{k1}} \cdot G_{kt+j}^{\varepsilon_{k2}}]^{\mu_{kj}^g}, \quad \sum_{j=0}^{H_k^g} \mu_{kj}^g = 1.$$

Due to altruism, anticipated mobility and pressure the different generations will to a certain extent take account of the interests of the other generations of their group; see with regard to pressure among generations Bernheim, Shleifer, Summers (1985). Through pressure, multiple positions, anticipated mobility and altruism the interests of the different generations of social class k will be taken into account by the state sector workers. Let λ_k^g denote the relative influence of each generation, through all channels combined, in public sector affairs. Then the representative elementary interest function of social class k is given by:

$$(8.5'') \quad P_{kt} = \prod_g P_{kt}^{g \, \lambda_k^g},$$

$$= A_k \cdot \prod_{j=0}^{H_k} [(1-\tau_{kt+j})^{\varepsilon_{k1}} \cdot G_{kt+j}^{\varepsilon_{k2}}]^{\mu_{kj}},$$

where: $H_k = \max_g H_k^g$,

$$\mu_{kj} = \sum_g \lambda_k^g \cdot \mu_{kj}^g, \; 0 \leq j \leq H_k, \text{ with } \mu_{kj}^g = 0 \; H_k^g < j \leq H_k.$$

If $\sum_g \lambda_k^g = 1$, $\sum_{j=0}^{H} \mu_{kj}^g = \sum_{j=0}^{H_g} \mu_{kj}^g = 1$, then $\sum_{j=0}^{H} \mu_{kj} = 1$ too.

12. From their definition in eqs. (8.9) and (8.13) it is apparent that the effective interest weights α_{3j}, β_j and μ_{sj} (j = 0,1,...,H) are functions of the power weights λ_{kt}^{3j} of the social classes, which may vary as time goes by. As we will mostly be concerned here with period t, we have not explicitly given expression to this dependence of α_{3j}, β_j and μ_{sj} on t, in order not to burden the notation.

13. It should be observed that $\sum_j (\beta_j + \sum_k \alpha_{kj}) = 1$, as $\sum_g \varepsilon_{kg} = 1 \; \forall k$, $\sum_j \mu_{kj} = 1 \; \forall k$, $\sum_k \lambda_{kt} = 1$.

14. Apart from the problems associated with the supposed constancy of the preference schedules over time and the approximation of the power weights λ_{kt} by the relative numerical strengths of the social classes, we now have to deal with the time horizon H and the expected future economic growth path, as well as to find a suitable, estimable transformation of the behavioural equations for the state. This is a proper subject for further research.

15. At least, as long as μ_{10}, μ_{20}, μ_{30} differ, and $0 < \lambda_{3t} < 1$. See also section 8.3.4.

16. Notice that H has been presumed to be at least as large as the largest H_k, given that P_s encompasses all the elementary interest functions P_k.

17. This effect on D_t can be illustrated in two ways:
    - an increase in H, given H_k, k = 1,2,3, means an increase in Z_t, and hence in D_t;
    - a decrease in any of the H_k's, given H, means an increase in the relative weight attached to the present within social class k, hence in μ_{s0}, and in D_t.

    It is noted that the impact of a general increase or decrease of the time horizons in society (H_k's as well as H) will be discussed later.

18. Disregard for a moment outstanding public debt, economic growth, and all differences in the preference schedules of the social classes, and assume that H_k = 50 ∀k, while H is infinite. Let the rate of interest be 5%, as well as the time discount rate implicitly contained in the time preference schedules μ_{kj}. It is easily predicted then that at time t it is planned to fully tax away the tax base beyond period t+50. The present value at time t of those future (planned) tax revenues amounts to some 1.8 times the tax base. The benefits of those (potential) tax receipts will be spread over the time horizon (H_k) of 50 periods, in the form of (planned) additional state spending and/or tax reductions to the amount of some 9% of the tax base in each of these periods. The concomitant budget deficit in period t then also amounts to 9% of the tax base.

19. This immediately follows from the definition of μ_{s0} as a weighted average of the μ_{k0}'s in eq. (8.13):

$$\mu_{s0} = \frac{\lambda_{1t}\varepsilon_{12}\mu_{10} + \lambda_{2t}\varepsilon_{22}\mu_{20} + \lambda_{3t}\mu_{30}}{\lambda_{1t}\varepsilon_{12} + \lambda_{2t}\varepsilon_{22} + \lambda_{3t}},$$

granted that $\varepsilon_{12}, \varepsilon_{22} > 0$.

20. Cf. CBS, Prognose van de bevolking van Nederland na 1980, 's-Gravenhage, 1982.

21. Cf. Miljoenennota 1987 (Ministerial report on the Dutch state budget for 1987), Staatsuitgeverij, 's-Gravenhage, 1986, p. 143.

22. A rise in r means a fall in the market value of the outstanding state debt. If this effect, with its positive impact on Z, would be large enough, it could offset the negative effect of an increase in r on the discounted value of future income streams.

23. This same result – $\partial D_t/\partial B_{t-1} \gtreqless 0$ if $r \gtreqless \rho$ – is also obtained for finite H, in case $B_{t+H} = B_{t-1}$.

24. At least, if the time horizons H_k of (at least some of) the social classes grow too. If these H_k's would remain unchanged, so would the time preference schedules μ_{kj}, and hence, according to eq. (8.13), μ_{sj}, j = 0,1,...,H; for j = H+1 we would get $\mu_{kj} = 0$ ∀k, $\mu_{sj} = 0$. Then we are back at the case discussed in section 8.3.3.

If, however, the time horizons of the social classes are lengthened parallel to H, it may be presumed that the rate of time preference ρ will also hold between periods H and H+1. According to eq. (8.24), μ_{s0} for a time horizon of H+1 periods would be given by:

$$\mu_{s0} = [\sum_{j=0}^{H+1} (\frac{1}{1+\rho})^j]^{-1} = \frac{\rho(1+\rho)^{H+1}}{(1+\rho)^{H+2}-1}.$$

25. Taking for granted that $\rho > 0$, and that B_{t+H} remains finite (at least, that $B_{t+H}/(1+r)^H \to 0$ if $H \to \infty$).

26. This equation also applies for the case that the horizon H grows infinitely large, provided $\gamma < r$ (otherwise D_t is not defined; see also eq. (8.34)). It is guaranteed then that $B_{t+H}/(1+r)^H \to 0$.
It may be noticed that eq. (8.34) in section 8.3.7 is equivalent to (8.38) for the case H is infinite. If it could further be assumed that $\rho = r$, eq. (8.35) results; in that special case the "steady state solution" of ϕ - cf. eq. (8.40) - is reached instantaneously.

27. Either because the time path of η is dynamically stable, leading the state to the perverse solution (8.39), or because the time path of η is unstable.

28. In subsection 8.4.2 it has been surmised that the state in case of a steady growth situation will take account of such a development in advance, in the sense that it will plan $B_{t+H} = (1+\gamma)^{H+1} B_{t-1}$. More generally, substituting $\eta = B_{t-1}/\Pi_t$, $\phi = D_t/\Pi_t$, $\eta = r\phi/\gamma$ into the budget deficit equation (8.13), and rearranging terms, yields the following equation for the steady state solution of ϕ (H finite):

$$\phi(\frac{r-\gamma}{\gamma})[\mu_{s0} \cdot \frac{1+r}{r-\gamma} \cdot (1-\frac{1}{(1+r)^{H+1}} \frac{B_{t+H}}{B_{t-1}})-1] = \mu_{s0}(\frac{1+r}{r-\gamma})(1-(\frac{1+\gamma}{1+r})^{H+1}) - 1.$$

Provided that the ratio B_{t+H}/B_{t-1} is independent of t, ϕ in general can be solved from this equation.
Notice that in the specific case that $B_{t+H} = (1+\gamma)^{H+1} B_{t-1}$, indeed, $\phi = \gamma/(r-\gamma)$ if $(1+\gamma)(1+\rho) \neq (1+r)$, while the equality is satisfied for any value of ϕ if $(1+\gamma)(1+\rho) = (1+r)$. For an infinite horizon, $H \to \infty$, the same solution for ϕ is obtained, provided $\gamma < r$. In the infinite horizon case the precise assumption as to the state's view of B_{t+H} is rather irrelevant, as long as $B_{t+H}/(1+r)^H \to 0$ as $H \to \infty$, which condition, for instance, would hold if $B_{t+H} = (1+\gamma)^{H+1} B_{t-1}$ and $\gamma < r$.

29. It must be noted that the specific functional form for the sinusoidal pattern of p_t is chosen for ease of reference, without loss of generality. The only real restriction imposed is $\omega < \pi/2$, which states, quite reasonably for a business cycle, that the economy has a period of oscillation of at least four periods.

30. In this connection it is of interest to quote some studies on public policy and public budget deficits in the Netherlands. Apart from the general statement by the Dutch Council of Economic Experts (1984)

that pro-cyclical measures predominated in the period 1952-1982, we may refer to Meijerink (1974). He concludes from a factor-analytical study of the period 1953-1971 that the boom of a business cycle coincided with relatively large budget deficits. Moreover, confronted with the choice of issuing bonds or liquidity creation, the state turned out to opt for a pro-cyclical manner of financing the deficit. During boom periods, when interest rates tend to be high and the capital market tense, the state did not engage in attempts to lower the supply of money by issuing more bonds than would be necessary to cover the deficit; on the contrary. Kremers (1983) subscribes to these conclusions as far as the pre-1970s period is concerned. Since then, he argues, public debt creation "just follows the course of events"; it is used as a buffer to absorb temporary deviations of spending and/or revenue from trend, in a counter-cyclical manner, as in the Barro-model.

Chapter 9

1. To avoid confusion: the theory of economic policy as it is here understood, comprises both the traditional normative theory of economic policy (cf. chapter 1), as well as the positive analysis of the use of economic policy instruments (as discussed in chapters 2 through 8). See Buchanan (1986).

2. That indeed problems may arise in that context is admitted by Brennan and Buchanan at the end of their book. "If the status quo set of rules is, indeed, nonoptimal, or inefficient, there must exist potential agreement on some change in structure. The working out of such an agreement, even for conceptual evaluative purposes may, however, require a complex network that includes various compromises, side payments, compensations, bribes, exchanges, trade-offs - a network aimed precisely at offsetting the predictable adverse distributional properties of the proposed changes. .... The discovery of such mutually beneficial proposals, best considered as complex exchange propositions, is the proper task of the specialist in political economy. The problem worthy of our attention here concerns the willingness of those who may be direct beneficiaries of structural change to pay the compensations that may be required to secure general agreement. ... All parties in the political community may be unwilling to accept the status quo distribution of entitlements generated under the operation of existing rules. This distribution of entitlements may not be acceptable to many persons as the appropriate starting point from which genuine constitutional reform is to be made" (p. 140/141).

3. Brennan and Buchanan (1985), p. 145/146.
To escape from the free-rider problem in genuine constitutional choice, Brennan and Buchanan suggest that we move beyond the strict individualistic model. "Applied to the problem at hand, which is that of deriving some conceptual explanation of why individuals might be expected to seek out, design, argue for, and support changes in the general rules of the sociopolitical order when, by presumption, such behavior would be contrary to identifiable self-interest, it is

necessary to resort to some version of "general interest" or "public interest" as the embodiment of a shared moral norm. That is to say, persons must be alleged to place positive private value on "public good" for the whole community of persons, over and beyond the value placed on their own individualized or partitioned shares" (p. 147). Notice that in a positive theory of constitutional choice this might be a helpful and interesting hypothesis, to be subjected to empirical testing. However, postulating it in a normative context does not help to demonstrate the feasibility of constitutional choice.

4. In the terminology of Brennan and Buchanan this would amount to an evolutionary position.

REFERENCES

Aberbach, Joel D., and Bert A. Rockman (1976), "Clashing beliefs within the executive branch: the Nixon administration bureaucracy", American Political Science Review, vol. 70, pp. 456-468.

Abrams, Richard K., Richard Froyen and Roger N. Waud (1980), "Monetary policy reaction functions, consistent expectations, and the Burns era", Journal of Money, Credit and Banking, vol. 12, pp. 30-42.

Acheson, K., and J.F. Chant (1973), "Bureaucratic theory and the choice of central bank goals. The case of the Bank of Canada", Journal of Money, Credit and Banking, vol. 5, pp. 637-655.

Ahmad, Kabir U., (1983), "An empirical study of politico-economic interaction in the United States: A comment", Review of Economics and Statistics, vol. 65, pp. 173-178..

Allen, Stuart D., Joseph M. Sulock and William A. Sabo (1986), "The political business cycle: how significant?", Public Finance Quarterly, vol. 14, pp. 107-112.

Alt, James E., (1985a), "Party stategies, world demand, and unemployment in Britain and the United States, 1947-1983", Political Behavior, vol. 7, pp. 7-36.

Alt, James E., (1985b), "Political parties, world demand and unemployment: domestic and international sources of economic activity", American Political Science Review, vol. 79, pp. 1016-1040.

Alt, James, and Alec Chrystal (1981), "Politico-economic models of British fiscal policy", Ch. 11 in: D.A. Hibbs jr. and H. Fassbender (eds.), Contemporary Political Economy, North Holland PC, Amsterdam, pp. 185-208.

Alt, James, and K. Alec Chrystal (1983), "The criteria for choosing a politico-economic model, forecast results for British expenditures 1976-79: A reply to Frey and Schneider, European Journal of Political Research, vol. 11, pp. 115-123.

Amacher, Ryan C., and William J. Boyes (1982), "Unemployment rates and political outcomes: an incentive for manufacturing a political business cycle", Public Choice, vol. 38, pp. 197-203.

Andeweg, Rudy B., (1982), Dutch voters adrift. On explanations of electoral change (1963-1977), Ph.D. dissertation, Leyden University.

Aranson, Peter H., (1983), "Public deficits in normative economics and positive political theory", Ch. 5 in: L.H. Meyer (ed.), The economic consequences of government deficits, Kluwer-Nijhoff, Boston, pp. 157-182.

Aubin, Christian, Jean-Pierre Berdot, Daniel Goyeau, Jean-Dominique Lafay (1985), "A complete politico-economic model of the French economy (1966-1982)", paper presented at the 1985 Congress of the European Public Choice Society, Alcalá de Henares; discussion paper, University of Poitiers.

Aubin, Christian, and Daniel Goyeau (1986), "Political influences on private economic behaviour: An empirical study of the French case", paper presented at the 1986 Congress of the European Public Choice Society, Noordwijkerhout; discussion paper, University of Poitiers.

Bain, Joe S., (1959), Industrial organization, John Wiley and sons, New York.

Barro, Robert J., (1979), "On the determination of the public debt", Journal of Political Economy, vol. 87, pp. 940-971.

Basu, K., (1980), Revealed preference of government, Cambridge University Press.

Beck, Nathaniel, (1982a), "Does there exist a political business cycle: a Box-Tiao analysis", Public Choice, vol. 38, pp. 205-209.

Beck, Nathaniel, (1982b), "Presidential influence on the Federal Reserve in the 1970's", American Journal of Political Science, vol. 26, pp. 415-445.

Beck, Nathaniel, (1982c), "Parties, administrations, and American macro-economic outcomes", American Political Science Review, vol. 76, pp. 83-93.

Becker, Gary S., (1983), "A theory of competition among pressure groups for political influence", Quarterly Journal of Economics, vol. 98, pp. 371-400.

Bendor, Jonathan, and Terry M. Moe (1985), "An adaptive model of bureaucratic politics", American Political Science Review, vol. 79, pp. 755-774.

Bennett, James T., and William P. Orzechowski (1983), "The voting behaviour of bureaucrats: some empirical evidence", Public Choice, vol. 41, pp. 271-283.

Berg, Sven, (1985), "Paradox of voting under an urn-model. The effect of homogeneity", Public Choice, vol. 47, pp. 377-387.

Bernheim, B.D., A. Shleifer and L.A. Summers (1985), "The strategic bequest motive", Journal of Political Economy, vol. 93, pp. 1045-1076.

Binmore, Ken, Ariel Rubinstein and Asher Wolinsky (1986), "The Nash bargaining solution in economic modelling", Rand Journal of Economics, vol. 17, pp. 176-188.

Black, D., (1948), "On the rationale of group decision making", Journal of Political Economy, vol. 56, pp. 23-34.

Blinder, A.S., and R.M. Solow (1973), "Does fiscal policy matter?", Journal of Public Economics, vol. 2, pp. 319-337.

Blinder, Allan S., and Robert M. Solow (1974), "Analytical foundations of fiscal policy", in: A.S. Blinder et al., The economics of public finance, The Brookings Institution, Washington, pp. 3-115.

Boddy, R., and J. Crotty (1975), "Class conflict and macro-policy: the political business cycle", Review of Radical Political Economics, vol. 7, pp. 1-19.

Borooah, Vani K., and Frederick van der Ploeg (1983), Political aspects of the economy, Cambridge University Press.

Brandsma, Andries S., and Nico van der Windt (1983), "Wage bargaining and the Phillips curve: a macroeconomic view", Applied Economics, vol. 15, pp. 61-71.

Brennan, Geoffrey, and James M. Buchanan (1980), The power to tax. Analytical foundations of a fiscal constitution, Cambridge University Press.

Brennan, H.G., and J.M. Buchanan (1981), Monopoly in money and inflation. The case for a constitution to discipline government, Hobart Paper 88, Institute for Economic Affairs, London.

Brennan, Geoffrey, and James M. Buchanan (1985), The reason of rules, Constitutional political economy, Cambridge University Press.

Breton, Albert, and Ronald Wintrobe (1975), "The equilibrium size of a budget-maximizing bureau: A note on Niskanen's theory of bureaucracy", Journal of Political Economy, vol. 83, pp. 195-207.

Brittain, J.A., (1972), The payroll tax for social security, Brookings Institution, Washington D.C..

Brosio, Giorgio, and Antonio Manzini (1986), "Comparing public and private efficiency: market structure vs. property rights", paper presented at the 1986 Congress of the European Public Choice Society, Noordwijkerhout.

Browning, E.K., (1975), "Why the social insurance budget is too large in a democratic society", Economic Inquiry, vol. 13, pp. 375-388.

Brunner, Karl, and Allan H. Meltzer (eds.) (1977), Optimal policies, control theory and technology exports, Carnegie-Rochester conference series on public policy, vol. 7, North-Holland PC, Amsterdam.

Buchanan, J.M., and G. Tullock (1962), The calculus of consent, University of Michigan Press, Ann Arbor.

Buchanan, J.M., and R.E. Wagner (1977), <u>Democracy in deficit</u>, Academic Press, New York.

Buchanan, James M., (1986), "The relevance of constitutional strategy", <u>Cato Journal</u>, vol. 6, pp. 513-517.

Bush, Winston C., and Arthur T. Denzau (1977), "The voting behavior of bureaucrats and public sector growth", Ch. 5 in: T.E. Borcherding (ed.), <u>Budgets and bureaucrats: The sources of government growth</u>, Duke University Press, Durham, pp. 90-99.

Cameron, D., (1978), "The expansion of the public economy; a comparative analysis", <u>American Political Science Review</u>, vol. 72, pp. 1243-1261.

Cavaco Silva, A.A., (1977), <u>Economic effects of public debt</u>, Robertson, London.

Chant, J.F., and K. Acheson (1973), "Mythology and central banking", <u>Kyklos</u>, vol. 26, pp. 362-379.

Chappell, Henry W. jr., (1983), "Presidential popularity and macroeconomic performance: are voters really so naive?", <u>Review of Economics and Statistics</u>, vol. 65, pp. 385-392.

Chappell, Henry W. jr., and William R. Keech (1985a), "A new view of political accountability for economic performance", <u>American Political Science Review</u>, vol. 79, pp. 10-27.

Chappell, Henry W. jr., and William R. Keech (1985b), "The political viability of rule-based monetary policy", <u>Public Choice</u>, vol. 46, pp. 125-140.

Chow, Gregory C., (1975), <u>Analysis and control of dynamic economic systems</u>, John Wiley and sons, New York.

Christ, C.F., (1967), "A short-run aggregate-demand model of the interdependence of monetary and fiscal policies with Keynesian and classical interest elasticities", <u>American Economic Review</u>, vol. 57, pp. 434-443.

Christ, C.F., (1979), "On fiscal and monetary policies and the government budget restraint", <u>American Economic Review</u>, vol. 69, pp. 526-538.

Chrystal, K. Alec, and James E. Alt (1981), "Some problems in formulating and testing a politico-economic model of the United Kingdom", <u>Economic Journal</u>, vol. 91, pp. 730-736.

Coleman, J.S., (1971), "Internal processes governing party positions in elections", <u>Public Choice</u>, vol. 11, pp. 35-60.

Council of Economic Experts (Commissie Economische Deskundigen) (1984), Rapport over het conjunctuurbeleid in de jaren tachtig, SER-rapport 84-13, 's-Gravenhage.

Courant, Paul N., Edward M. Gramlich and Daniel L. Rubinfeld (1980), "Why voters support tax limitation amendments: the Michigan case", National Tax Journal, vol. 33, pp. 1-20.

Cowart, Andrew T., (1978a), "The economic policies of European governments, part I: monetary policy", British Journal of Political Science, vol. 8, pp. 285-311.

Cowart, Andrew T., (1978b), "The economic policies of European governments, part II: fiscal policy", British Journal of Political Science, vol. 8, pp. 425-439.

Crain, W.M, and R.B. Ekelund jr. (1978), "Deficits and democracy", Southern Economic Journal, vol. 44, pp. 813-828.

Crotty, James R., (1973), "Specification error in macro-econometric models: the influence of policy goals", American Economic Review, vol. 63, pp. 1025-1030.

Davis, Otto A., M.A.H. Dempster and Aaron Wildavsky (1966), "A theory of the budgetary process", American Political Science Review, vol. 60, pp. 529-547.

De Grauwe, P., (1984), "Centrum-rechtse regeringen en belastingdruk", Economisch Statistische Berichten, vol. 69, p. 571.

De Grauwe, P., (1985), "Inflatie, werkloosheid en ideologie", Economisch Statistische Berichten, vol. 70, p. 1003.

De Meyer, Frank, and Charles R. Plott (1970), "The probability of a cyclical majority", Econometrica, vol. 38, pp. 345-354.

De Swaan, Abram, (1973), Coalition theories and cabinet formations, Elsevier, Amsterdam.

De Wolff, P., and W. Driehuis (1980), "A description of postwar economic developments and economic policy in the Netherlands", Ch. 2 in: R.T. Griffiths (ed.), The economy and politics of the Netherlands since 1945, Martinus Nijhoff, The Hague.

Den Butter, F.A.G., (1984), "Macro-economische modelbouw: een terugblik en enige recente ontwikkelingen", Economisch Statistische Berichten, vol. 69, pp. 1140-1148.

Denzau, Arthur T., and Michael C. Munger (1986), "Legislations and interest groups: how unorganized interests get represented", American Political Science Review, vol. 80, pp. 89-106.

Dewald, W.G., and H.G. Johnson (1963), "An objective analysis of the objectives of monetary policy", in: D. Carson (ed.), Banking and monetary studies, Irwin, Homewood Ill., pp. 171-189.

Domar, Evsey D., (1944), "The burden of the debt on the national income", American Economic Review, vol. 34, pp. 798-827.

Downs, Anthony, (1957), An economic theory of democracy, Harper and Row, New York.

Dunleavy, Patrick, (1985), "Bureaucrats, budgets and the growth of the state: reconstructing an instrumental model", British Journal of Political Science, vol. 15, pp. 299-328.

Enelow, James M., and Melvin J. Hinich (1984), The spatial theory of voting. An introduction, Cambridge University Press.

Esty, Daniel C., and Richard E. Caves (1983), "Market structure and political influence: new data on political expenditures, activity, and success", Economic Inquiry, vol. 21, pp. 24-38.

Fair, Ray C., (1978a), "The sensitivity of fiscal policy effects to assumptions about the behavior of the Federal Reserve", Econometrica, vol. 46, pp. 1165-1179.

Fair, Ray C., (1978b), "The effect of economic events on votes for president", Review of Economics and Statistics, vol. 60, pp. 159-173.

Farebrother, R.W., (1980), "The Durbin-Watson test for serial correlation when there is no intercept in the regression", Econometrica, vol. 48, pp. 1553-1563.

Fase, M.M.G., and F.A.G. den Butter (1977), "The endogeneity of monetary policy in the Netherlands: two reaction functions of the central bank", Cahiers Economiques et Monétaires, no. 6, pp. 177-204.

Fassbender, H., (1981), "From conventional IS-LM to political-economic models", Ch. 9 in: D.A. Hibbs jr. and H. Fassbender (eds.), Contemporary Political Economy, North-Holland PC, Amsterdam, pp. 153-167.

Fiorina, Morris, (1981), "Short- and long-term effects of economic conditions on individual voting decisions", Ch. 5 in: D.A. Hibbs jr. and H. Fassbender (eds.), Contemporary Political Economy, North Holland PC, Amsterdam, pp. 73-100.

Fiorina, Morris P., and Roger G. Noll (1978), "Voters, bureaucrats and legislators. A rational choice perspective on the growth of bureaucracy", Journal of Public Economics, vol. 9, pp. 239-254.

Fisher, Douglas, (1968), "The objectives of British monetary policy, 1951-1964", Journal of Finance, vol. 23, pp. 821-831.

Foley, Duncan K., (1978), "State expenditure from a Marxist perspective", Journal of Public Economics, vol. 9, pp. 221-238.

Fox, K.A., J.K. Sengupta, E. Thorbecke (1966), The theory of quantitative economic policy, North-Holland PC, Amsterdam.

Fratianni, Michele, and Franco Spinelli (1982), "The growth of government in Italy: Evidence from 1861 to 1979", Public Choice, vol. 39, pp. 221-243.

Freeman, Richard B., (1986), "Unionism comes to the public sector", Journal of Economic Literature, vol. 24, pp. 41-86.

Frey, Bruno S., (1978), "Politico-economic models and cycles", Journal of Public Economics, vol. 9, pp. 203-220.

Frey, Bruno S., (1983), Democratic Economic Policy, St. Martin's Press, New York.

Frey, Bruno S., (1984), International political economics, Basil Blackwell, Oxford.

Frey, Bruno S., and Lawrence J. Lau (1968), "Towards a mathematical model of government behaviour", Zeitschrift für Nationalökonomie, vol. 28, pp. 355-380..

Frey, Bruno S., and Werner W. Pommerehne (1982), "How powerful are public bureaucrats as voters?", Public Choice, vol. 38, pp. 253-262.

Frey, Bruno S., and Hans-Jürgen Ramser (1976), "The political business cycle: a comment", Review of Economic Studies, vol. 43, pp. 553-555.

Frey, Bruno S., and Friedrich Schneider (1975), "On the modelling of politico-economic interdependence", European Journal of Political Research, vol. 3, pp. 339-360.

Frey, Bruno S., and Friedrich Schneider (1978a), "An empirical study of politico-economic interaction in the United States", Review of Economics and Statistics, vol. 60, pp. 174-183.

Frey, Bruno S., and Friedrich Schneider (1978b), "A politico-economic model of the United Kingdom", Economic Journal, vol. 88, pp. 243-253.

Frey, Bruno S., and Friedrich Schneider (1979), "An econometric model with an endogenous government sector", Public Choice, vol. 34, pp. 29-43.

Frey, Bruno S., and Friedrich Schneider (1981a), "Recent research on empirical politico-economic models", Ch. 2 in: D.A. Hibbs jr. and H. Fassbender (eds.), Contemporary Political Economy, North Holland PC, Amsterdam, pp. 11-27.

Frey, Bruno S., and Friedrich Schneider (1981b), "A politico-economic model of the UK: new estimates and predictions", Economic Journal, vol. 91, pp. 737-740.

Frey, Bruno S., and Friedrich Schneider (1981c), "Central bank behaviour. A positive empirical analysis", Journal of Monetary Economics, vol. 7, pp. 291-315.

Frey, Bruno S., and Friedrich Schneider (1982), "Politico-economic models in competition with alternative models: which predict better?", European Journal of Political Research, vol. 10, pp. 241-254..

Frey, Bruno S., and Friedrich Schneider (1983), "Do governments respond to political incentives", European Journal of Political Research, vol. 11, pp. 125-126.

Friedlaender, Ann F., (1973), "Macro policy goals in the postwar period: a study in revealed preference", Quarterly Journal of Economics, vol. 87, pp. 25-43.

Friedman, Benjamin M., (1975), Economic stabilization policy: Methods in optimization, North-Holland PC, Amsterdam.

Froyen, Richard T., (1974), "A test of the endogeneity of monetary policy", Journal of Econometrics, Vol. 2, pp. 175-188.

Gandenberger, Otto, (1985), "On public debt and public choice", paper presented at the 1985 Congress of the European Public Choice Society, Alcalà de Henares.

Gandolfo, Giancarlo, (1980), Economic dynamics: methods and models, North-Holland PC, Amsterdam.

Gärtner, Manfred, (1981), "A politico-economic model of wage inflation", De Economist, vol. 129, pp. 183-205.

Gehrlein, William V., and Peter C. Fishburn (1976), "The probability of the paradox of voting: a computable solution", Journal of Economic Theory, vol. 13, pp. 14-25.

Ginsburgh, Victor, and Philippe Michel (1983), "Random timing of elections and the political business cycle", Public Choice, vol. 40, pp. 155-164.

Golden, David G., and James M. Poterba (1980), "The price of popularity: the political business cycle reexamined", American Journal of Political Science, vol. 24, pp. 696-714.

Goldscheid, Rudolf, (1967), "A sociological approach to problems of public finance", in: R.A. Musgrave and A.T. Peacock (eds.), Classics in the theory of public finance, Macmillan, London.

Goodhart, C.A.E., and R.J. Bhansali (1970), "Political economy", Political Studies, vol. 18, pp. 43-106.

Griffiths, Richard T., (1980), "The Netherlands Central Planning Bureau", Ch. 6 in: R.T. Griffiths (ed.), The economy and politics of the Netherlands since 1945, Martinus Nijhoff, The Hague.

Hafkamp, W.A., (1983), Triple layer model. A national-regional economic-environmental model for the Netherlands, Ph.D. dissertation, Free University Amsterdam.

Harsanyi, John C., (1963), "A simplified bargaining model for the n-person cooperative game", International Economic Review, vol. 4, pp. 194-220.

Hibbs, Douglas A. jr., (1977), "Political parties and macroeconomic policy", American Political Science Review, vol. 71, pp. 1467-1487.

Hibbs, Douglas A. jr., (1979), "The mass public and macroeconomic performance: the dynamics of public opinion toward unemployment and inflation", American Journal of Political Science, vol. 23, pp. 705-731.

Hibbs, Douglas A. jr., (1982a), "The dynamics of political support for American presidents among occupational and partisan groups", American Journal of Political Science, vol. 26, pp. 312-332.

Hibbs, Douglas A. jr., (1982b), "Economic outcomes and political support for British governments among occupational classes: a dynamic analysis", American Political Science Review, vol. 76, pp. 259-279.

Hibbs, Douglas A. jr., and Nicholas Vasilatos (1981), "Macroeconomic performance and mass political support in the United States and Great Brittain", Ch. 3 in: D.A. Hibbs jr. and H. Fassbender (eds.), Contemporary Political Economy, North Holland PC, Amsterdam, pp. 31-47.

Hu, Sheng Cheng, (1982), "Social security, majority-voting equilibrium and dynamic efficiency", International Economic Review, vol. 23, pp. 269-287.

Hughes Hallett, A.J., and H.J.B. Rees (1983), Quantitative economic policies and interactive planning, Cambridge University Press.

Jaarsma, Bert, Arthur Schram and Frans van Winden (1986), "On the voting participation of public bureaucrats", Public Choice, vol. 48, pp. 183-187.

Johansen, Leif, (1974), "Establishing preference functions for macro-economic decision models. Some observations on Ragnar Frisch's contributions", European Economic Review, vol. 5, pp. 41-66.

Kalecki, M., (1943), "Political aspects of full employment", Political Quarterly, vol. 14, pp. 322-331; reprinted in: M. Kalecki, Selected essays on the dynamics of the capitalist economy 1933-1970, Cambridge University Press, 1971.

Kane, E.J., (1980), "Politics and FED policy making. The more things change, the more they remain the same", Journal of Monetary Economics, vol. 6, pp. 199-211.

Keizer, P.K., and A.P. van Veen (1984), "Voter reaction as a welfare state stabilizer", Research Memorandum 84.010, Faculty of Economics, Limburg University.

Keizer, P., and T. van Veen (1986), "A behavioural-theoretic approach of voter behaviour, applied to the Dutch voters in the period 1970-1980", working paper, Limburg University.

Kiewiet, D. Roderick, and Douglas Rivers (1984), "A retrospective on retrospective voting", Political Behavior, vol. 6, pp. 369-393.

Kinder, Donald R., and D. Roderick Kiewiet (1979), "Economic discontent and political behavior: the role of personal grievances and collective economic judgments in congressional voting", American Journal of Political Science, vol. 23, pp. 495-527.

Kirchgässner, Gebhard, (1984), "On the theory of optimal government behaviour", Journal of Economic Dynamics and Control, vol. 8, pp. 167-195.

Kirchgässner, Gebhard, (1985), "Rationality, causality, and the relation between economic conditions and the popularity of parties. An empirical investigation for the Federal Republic of Germany, 1971-1982", European Economic Review, vol. 28, pp. 243-268.

Kirschen, E.S., et al. (1964), Economic policy in our time, 2 vols., North-Holland PC, Amsterdam.

Knegt, L., (1978), "Een endogene collectieve sector in een macro-economisch kader", Maandschrift Economie, vol. 42, pp. 289-312.

Knoester, A., (1983), "Stagnation and the inverted Haavelmo effect", De Economist, vol. 131, pp. 548-584..

Knoester, A., (1985), "Reply to Koefoed", De Economist, vol. 133, pp. 417-420.

Koefoed, O., (1985), "The forward shifting of taxes: a comment on a paper by A. Knoester", De Economist, vol. 133, pp. 415-417.

Kramer, Gerald H., (1971), "Short-term fluctuations in US voting behaviour, 1896-1964", American Political Science Review, vol. 65, pp. 131-143.

Kramer, Gerald H., (1983), "The ecological fallacy revisited: aggregate- versus individual-level findings on economics and elections, and sociotropic voting", American Political Science Review, vol. 77, pp. 92-111.

Kremers, J.J.M., (1983), "Public debt creation in the Netherlands, 1953-1980", De Economist, vol. 131, pp. 196-216.

Kristensen, Ole P., (1982), "Voter attitudes and public spending: is there a relationship?", European Journal of Political Research, vol. 10, pp. 35-52.

Kydland, Finn E., and Edward C. Prescott (1977), "Rules rather than discretion: the inconsistency of optimal plans", Journal of Political Economy, vol. 85, pp. 473-491.

Lächler, Ulrich, (1978), "The political business cycle: a complementary study", Review of Economic Studies, vol. 45, pp. 369-375.

Lächler, Ulrich, (1982), "On political business cycles with endogenous election dates", Journal of Public Economics, vol. 17, pp. 111-117.

Lächler, Ulrich, (1984), "The political business cycle under rational voting behavior", Public Choice, vol. 44, pp. 411-430.

Laney, Leroy O., and Thomas D. Willett (1983), "Presidential politics, budget deficits, and monetary policy in the United States; 1960-1976", Public Choice, vol. 40, pp. 53-69.

Larkey, P.D., C. Stolp and M. Winer (1981), "Theorizing about the growth of government: a research assessment", Journal of Public Policy, vol. 1, pp. 157-220.

Le Pen, Claude, (1985), "Public employment and economic theory of bureaucracy", paper presented at the 1985 Congress of the European Public Choice Society, Alcalá de Henares; discussion paper, Université de Paris IX Dauphine.

Lindbeck, Assar, (1975), "Business cycles, politics and international economic dependence", Skandinaviska Enskilda Banken Quarterly Review, pp. 53-68.

Lindbeck, Assar, (1976), "Stabilization policy in open economies with endogenous politicians", American Economic Review, vol. 66, papers and proceedings, pp. 1-19.

Lipsey, R.G., P.O. Steiner and D.D. Purvis (1987), Economics, 8th edition, Harper and Row, New York.

Lowery, David, (1985), "The Keynesian and political determinants of unbalanced budgets: U.S. fiscal policy from Eisenhower to Reagan", American Journal of Political Science, vol. 29, pp. 428-460.

Lowery, David, and William D. Berry (1983), "The growth of government in the United States: an empirical assessment of competing explanations", American Journal of Political Science, vol. 27, pp. 665-694.

Lucas, Robert E. jr., (1976), "Econometric policy evaluation: a critique", in: K. Brunner, A.H. Meltzer (eds.), The Phillips-curve and labor markets, Carnegie-Rochester Conferences on Public Policy, vol. 1, North-Holland PC, Amsterdam.

Lucas, Robert E. jr., (1987), Models of business cycles, Yrjö Jahnsson Lectures, Basil Blackwell, Oxford.

Lybeck, Johan A., (1986), "Long-run causes for the growth of government. A cross country study", paper presented at the 1986 Congress of the European Public Choice Society, Noordwijkerhout; published in his book The growth of government in developed economies, Gower, London.

MacRae, C. Duncan, (1977), "A political model of the business cycle", Journal of Political Economy, vol. 85, pp. 239-263.

MacRae, Duncan, (1981), "On the political business cycle", Ch. 10 in: D.A. Hibbs jr. and H. Fassbender (eds.), Contemporary Political Economy, North-Holland PC, Amsterdam, pp. 169-184.

Maddala, G.S., (1977), Econometrics, McGraw-Hill, New York.

Makin, John H., (1976), "Constraints on formulation of models for measuring revealed preferences of policy makers", Kyklos, vol. 29, pp. 709-732.

McKelvey, Richard D., (1979), "General conditions for global intransitivities in formal voting models", Econometrica, vol. 47, pp. 1085-1112.

Meijerink, M.H., (1974), "Een faktoranalyse van de Nederlandse schuldpolitiek, 1953-1971", De Economist, vol. 122, pp. 129-160.

Meltzer, Allan H., and Scott F. Richard (1981), "A rational theory of the size of government", Journal of Political Economy, vol. 89, pp. 914-927.

Meltzer, Allan H., and Scott F. Richard (1983), "Tests of a rational theory of the size of government", Public Choice, vol. 41, pp. 403-418.

Meltzer, Allan H., and Scott F. Richard (1985), "A positive theory of in-kind transfers and the negative income tax", Public Choice, vol. 47, pp. 231-265.

Merkies, A.H.Q.M., (1973), Van prognoses naar programma's, inaugural lecture, Free University Amsterdam.

Merkies, A.H.Q.M., and A.J. Vermaat (1981), "De onmacht van een kabinet. Een empirisch onderzoek naar sociaal- economische preferentiefuncties en hun gebruik als welvaartsindicator", Maandschrift Economie, vol. 45, pp. 101-118.

Merkies, A.H.Q.M., and M. Hofkes (1986), "Preferences and possibilities in the Dutch economy", paper presented at the 1986 Congress of the European Public Choice Society, Noordwijkerhout; discussion paper, Free University Amsterdam.

Michaels, Robert, (1986), "Reinterpreting the role of inflation in politico-economic models", Public Choice, vol. 48, pp. 113-124.

Migué, Jean-Luc, and Gérard Bélanger (1974), "Toward a general theory of managerial discretion", Public Choice, vol. 17, pp. 27-43.

Miliband, Ralph, (1973), The state in capitalist society, Quartet Books Ltd, London; first published in 1969 by Weidenfeld and Nicholson Ltd, London.

Miller, Garry J., (1977), "Bureaucratic compliance as a game on the unit square", Public Choice, vol. 29, pp. 37-51.

Miller, Garry J., and Terry M. Moe (1983), "Bureaucrats, legislators, and the size of government", American Political Science Review, vol. 77, pp. 297-322.

Minford, Patrick, and David Peel (1982), "The political theory of the business cycle", European Economic Review, vol. 17, pp. 253-270.

Moene, Karl O., (1985), "Types of bureaucratic interaction", paper presented at the 1985 Congress of the European Public Choice Society, Alcalá de Henares; memorandum no. 20, Department of Economics, University of Oslo.

Mosley, Paul, (1976), "Towards a 'satisficing' theory of economic policy", Economic Journal, vol. 86, pp. 59-72.

Mosley, Paul, (1984), The making of economic policy. Theory and evidence from Britain and the US since 1945, Wheatsheaf Books, Brighton.

Mosley, Paul, and Richard Cracknell (1984), "Endogenous government policy in a model of the UK economy", Applied Economics, vol. 16, pp. 633-645.

Mueller, Dennis C., (1986), "Rational egoism versus adaptive egoism as fundamental postulate for a descriptive theory of human behavior", Public Choice, vol. 51, pp. 3-23.

Mueller, Dennis C., and Peter Murrell (1986), "Interest groups and the size of government", Public Choice, vol. 48, pp. 125-145.

Mueller, John E., (1970), "Presidential popularity from Truman to Johnson", American Political Science Review, vol. 64, pp. 18-34.

Murrell, Peter, (1984), An examination of the factors affecting the formation of interest groups in OECD-countries", Public Choice, vol. 43, pp. 151-171.

Nash, John F., (1950), "The bargaining problem", Econometrica, vol. 18, pp. 155-162.

Nash, John F., (1953), "Two-person cooperative games", Econometrica vol. 21, pp. 128-140.

Neck, Reinhard, (1982), "Interactions between the political and the economic system in Austria", in: R. Trappl (ed.), Cybernetics and Systems Research, North-Holland PC, Amsterdam, pp. 513-520.

Nice, David C., (1984), "Interest groups and policymaking in the American states", Political Behavior, vol. 6, pp. 183-196.

Niskanen, William A. jr., (1971), Bureaucracy and representative government, Aldine, Chicago.

Niskanen, William A., (1975), "Bureaucrats and politicians", Journal of Law and Economics, vol. 18, pp. 617-643.

Nordhaus, William D., (1975), "The political business cycle", Review of Economic Studies, vol. 42, pp. 169-190.

Olson, Mancur, (1965), The logic of collective action. Public goods and the theory of groups, Harvard University Press, Cambridge Ma..

Olson, Mancur, (1982), The rise and decline of nations. Economic growth, stagflation and social rigidities, Yale University Press, New Haven and London.

Orzechowski, William, (1977), "Economic models of bureaucracy: Survey, extensions, and evidence", Ch. 13 in: T.E. Borcherding (ed.), Budgets and bureaucrats: The sources of government growth, Duke University Press, Durham, pp. 229-259.

Paldam, Martin, (1979), "Is there an electional cycle? A comparative study of national accounts", Scandinavian Journal of Economics, vol. 81, pp. 323-342.

Paldam, Martin, (1981), "A preliminary survey of the theories and findings on vote and popularity functions", European Journal of Political Research, vol. 9, pp. 181-199.

Parlement en Kiezer (1986), Jaarboek zittingsjaar 1984-1985, samengesteld door P. Goossen en drs G.G.J. Thissen, jaargang 68, Martinus Nijhoff, Leiden.

Peacock, A.T., and J. Wiseman (1961), The growth of public expenditure in the United Kingdom, Princeton University Press.

Peeperkorn, L.P.M., and T.B.M. Steenkamp (1986), "Regeringspopulariteit en economische omstandigheden", Maandschrift Economie, vol. 50, pp. 85-98.

Peltzman, Sam, (1976), "Toward a more general theory of regulation", Journal of Law and Economics, vol. 19, pp. 211-240.

Peltzman, Sam, (1980), "The growth of government", Journal of Law and Economics, vol. 23, pp. 209-287.

Pissarides, Christopher A., (1980), "British government popularity and economic performance", Economic Journal, vol. 90, pp. 569-581.

Pommer, Evert, Hans de Groot, Arthur Schram, and Frans van Winden (1987), "Individuele voorkeuren voor collectieve voorzieningen", Research Memorandum 8702, Department of Economics, University of Amsterdam.

Pommerehne, Werner W., (1978), "Institutional approaches to public expenditure. Empirical evidence from Swiss municipalities", Journal of Public Economics, vol. 9, pp. 255-280.

Pommerehne, Werner W., and Friedrich Schneider (1983), "Does government in a representative democracy follow a majority of voters' preferences? - An empirical examination", Ch. 5 in: H. Hanusch (ed.), Anatomy of government deficiencies, Springer-Verlag, Berlin, pp. 61-84.

Popper, Karl R., (1957), The poverty of historicism, Routledge and Kegan Paul, London .

Poulantzas, Nicos, (1973), Political power and social classes, New Left Books, London.

Preston A.J., and A.R. Pagan, (1982), The theory of economic policy, statics and dynamics, Cambridge University Press.

Przeworski, Adam, and Michael Wallerstein (1982), "The structure of class conflict in democratic capitalist societies", American Political Science Review, vol. 76, pp. 215-238.

Rau, Nicholas, (1985), "Simplifying the theory of the government budget restraint", Oxford Economic Papers, vol. 37, pp. 210-229.

Renaud, Paul S.A., Ben C.J. van Velthoven and Frans A.A.M. van Winden (1986), "A politico-economic analysis of the great depression. The United States and the Netherlands", paper presented at the European Meeting of the Econometric Society, Budapest .

Renaud, Paul S.A., and Frans A.A.M. van Winden (1987a), "Tax rate and government expenditure", Kyklos, pp. 349-367.

Renaud, Paul S.A., and Frans A.A.M. van Winden (1987b), "On the importance of elections and ideology for government policy in a multi-party system", in: M.J. Holler (ed.), The logic of multi-party systems, Physica Verlag, Würzburg.

Reuber, G.L., (1964), "The objectives of Canadian monetary policy, 1949-61. Empirical "trade-offs" and the reaction function of the authorities", Journal of Political Economy, vol. 72, pp. 109-132.

Riker, William H., (1980), "Implications from the disequilibrium of majority rule for the study of institutions", American Political Science Review, vol. 74, pp. 432-446.

Romer, Thomas, and Howard Rosenthal (1979), "The elusive median voter", Journal of Public Economics, vol. 12, pp. 143-170.

Roth, Alvin E., (1979), Axiomatic models of bargaining, Springer-Verlag, Berlin.

Rubinstein, Ariel, (1982), "Perfect equilibrium in a bargaining model", Econometrica, vol. 50, pp. 97-109.

Salamon, Lester M., and John J. Siegfried (1977), "Economic power and political influence; the impact of industry structure on public policy", American Political Science Review, vol. 71, pp. 1026-1043.

Samuelson, Paul A., (1980), Economics, 11th edition, McGraw-Hill, New York.

Sandee, J., (1977), "Optimum policy alternatives", in: C.A. van Bochove et al. (eds.), Modeling for government and business. Essays in honor of prof. dr P.J. Verdoorn, Martinus Nijhoff, Leiden, pp. 149-163.

Sargent, Thomas J., and Neil Wallace (1976), "Rational expectations and the theory of economic policy", Journal of Monetary Economics, vol. 2, pp. 169-183.

Saunders, Peter, and Friedrich Klau (1985), The role of the public sector. Causes and consequences of the growth of government, OECD Economic Studies nr. 4, Paris.

Scherer, F.M., (1970), Industrial market structure and economic performance, Rand McNally, Chicago.

Schneider, Friedrich, (1984), "Public attitudes toward economic conditions and their impact on government behaviour", Political Behavior, vol. 6, pp. 211-227.

Schneider, Friedrich, and Bruno S. Frey (1983), "An empirical study of politico-economic interaction in the United States: A reply", Review of Economics and Statistics, vol. 65, pp. 178-182.

Schneider, Friedrich, and Jörg Naumann (1982), "Interest groups in democracies - how influential are they? An empirical examination for Switzerland", Public Choice, vol. 38, pp. 281-303.

Schram, Arthur, and Frans van Winden (1986a), "An economic model of party choice in a multi-party system. An empirical application to the Netherlands", European Journal of Political Economy, vol. 2, pp. 465-497.

Schram, Arthur, and Frans van Winden (1986b), "Modelling voter behavior in a multi-party system", Research paper, Department of Economics, University of Amsterdam.

Seater, John J., (1985), "Does government debt matter? A review", Journal of Monetary Economics, vol. 16, pp. 121-131.

Sen, Amarty K., (1970), Collective choice and social welfare, North-Holland PC, Amsterdam.

Shubik, Martin, (1982), Game theory in the social sciences. Concepts and solutions, MIT press, Cambridge Ma..

Smyth, D.J., (1963), "Can 'automatic stabilizers' be destabilizing?", Public Finance, vol. 18, pp. 357-363.

Smyth, D.J., (1974), "Built-in flexibility of taxation and stability in a simple dynamic IS-LM model", Public Finance, vol. 29, pp. 111-114.

Snyder, W.W., (1970), "Measuring the stabilizing effects of social security programs in seven countries, 1955-1965", National Tax Journal, vol. 23, pp. 263-273.

Sociaal en Cultureel Planbureau (1986), Sociaal en Cultureel Rapport 1986, Staatsuitgeverij, 's-Gravenhage.

Söderström, Lars, (1982), "The life cycle hypothesis and aggregate household saving", American Economic Review, vol. 72, pp. 590-596.

Soh, Byung Hee, (1986), "Political business cycles in industrialized democratic countries", Kyklos, vol. 39, pp. 31-46.

Stigler, George J., (1972), "Economic competition and political competition", Public Choice, vol. 12, pp. 91-106.

Stigler, George J., (1973), "General economic conditions and national elections", American Economic Review, vol. 63, papers and proceedings, pp. 160-167.

Svejnar, Jan, (1986), "Bargaining power, fear of disagreement, and wage settlements: theory and evidence from U.S. industry", Econometrica, vol. 54, pp. 1055-1078.

Ten Raa, Thijs, (1984), "The interest function approach", De Economist, vol. 132, pp. 479-491.

Theil, Henri, (1958), Economic forecasts and policy, 2nd revised edition 1961, North-Holland PC, Amsterdam.

Thompson, William R., and Gary Zuk (1983), "American elections and the international-economic cycle: a test of the Tufte hypothesis", American Journal of Political Science, vol. 27, pp. 464-484.

Tinbergen, J., (1936), "Kan hier te lande, al dan niet na overheidsingrijpen, een verbetering van de binnenlandse conjunctuur intreden, ook zonder verbetering van onze export-positie?", in: Prae-adviezen van de Vereeniging voor de Staathuishoudkunde en de Statistiek, Martinus Nijhoff, The Hague.
An English translation under the titel "An economic policy for 1936", can be found in: J. Tinbergen (1959), Selected Papers, eds. L.H. Klaassen, L.M. Koyck, H.J. Witteveen, North-Holland PC, Amsterdam.

Tinbergen, J., (1952), On the theory of economic policy, North-Holland PC, Amsterdam.

Tufte, Edward R., (1978), Political control of the economy, Princeton University Press.

Van den Berg, J.Th.J., (1981), "Herkomst, ervaring en toekomstperspectief van kamerleden", Ch. 1 in: M.P.C.M. van Schendelen e.a. (eds.), "Leden van de Staten-Generaal,...", VUGA-uitgeverij, 's-Gravenhage.

Van der Geest, L., (1977), "Het vastleggen van economisch-politieke oordelen in een doelstellingsfunctie", Economisch Statistische Berichten, vol. 62, pp. 994-999.

Van der Ploeg, Frederick, (1984), "Government ideology and re-election efforts", Oxford Economic Papers, vol. 36, pp. 213-231.

Van Eijk, C.J., and J. Sandee (1959), "Quantitative determination of an optimum economic policy", Econometrica, vol. 27, pp. 1-13.

Van Praag, B.M.S., and H. Emanuel (1981), "On the concept of non-employability with respect to a non-homogeneous labour force", in: L. Söderström (ed.), Social insurance, North Holland PC, Amsterdam.

Van Praag, B.M.S., and V. Halberstadt (1980), "Towards an economic theory of non-employability: a first approach", in: Karl W. Roskamp (ed.), Public choice and public finance, Proceedings of the 34th Congress of the International Institute of Public Finance, Hamburg, 1978, Editions Cujas, Paris.

Van Velthoven, B.C.J., F.A.A.M. van Winden, and P.S.A. Renaud (1984), "Belastingdruk en overheidsbestedingen in Nederland, 1952-1977", Economisch Statistische Berichten, vol. 69, pp. 865-871.

Van Velthoven, Ben C.J., and Frans A.A.M. van Winden (1984), "Social classes and state behavior. An illustrative application to the US economy of the interest function approach to politico-economic modelling", Economics Letters, vol. 16, pp. 113-118.

Van Velthoven, Ben C.J., and Frans A.A.M. van Winden (1985), "Towards a politico-economic theory of social security", European Economic Review, vol. 27, pp. 263-289.

Van Velthoven, Ben C.J., and Frans A.A.M. van Winden (1986), "Social classes and state behaviour", Journal of Institutional and Theoretical Economics, vol. 142, pp. 542-570.

Van Wijngaarden, P., (1985), "Verzorgingsstaat en collectieve actie van uitkeringsgerechtigden", Sociaal Maandblad Arbeid, vol. 40, pp. 56-62.

Van Winden, Frans A.A.M., (1983), On the interaction between state and private sector. A study in political economics, North-Holland PC, Amsterdam (Ph.D. dissertation, Leyden University, 1981).

Van Winden, Frans A.A.M., (1984), "The interest function approach: a reply to Ten Raa", De Economist, vol. 132, pp. 491-496.

Van Winden, Frans A.A.M., (1987), "Man in the public sector", De Economist, vol. 135, pp. 1-28.

Verbon, H.A.A., and F.A.A.M. van Winden (1985), "Public pensions and political decision-making", De Economist, vol. 133, pp. 527-544.

Wagner, Richard E., and Warren E. Weber (1977), "Wagner's Law, fiscal institutions, and the growth of government", National Tax Journal, vol. 30, pp. 59-68.

Walters, A.A., (1967), "How to make a benefit of the burden of national debt", National Tax Journal, vol. 20, pp. 316-318.

White, Betsy B., (1978), "Empirical tests of the life cycle hypothesis", American Economic Review, vol. 68, pp. 547-560.

Wiebrens, C., (1982), "De uitkeringsgerechtigden", Beleid en Maatschappij, vol. 9, pp. 334-339.

Wolfinger, R.E., and S.J. Rosenstone (1980), Who votes?, Yale University Press.

Wood, J.H., (1967), "A model of Federal Reserve behaviour", in: G. Horwich (ed.), Monetary process and policy: A symposium, Irwin, Homewood Ill., pp. 135-166.

Zuidema, T., (1982), Een onderzoek naar de alternatieve kosten van overheidsprojecten: theorie en empirie, Ph.D. dissertation, University of Groningen.

AUTHOR INDEX

A
Aberbach, J.D., 80, 168
Abrams, R.K., 12, 303
Acheson, K., 332
Ahmad, K.U., 67, 68, 70, 72
Allen, S.D., 55, 324
Alt, J.E., 53, 60, 61, 62, 63, 71, 73, 75-77, 86, 130, 131, 157, 310, 311, 312
Amacher, R.C., 55
Andeweg, R.B., 156
Aranson, P.H., 251
Arrow, K., 36
Aubin, Ch., 22, 72

B
Bain, J.S., 315
Barro, R.J., 249, 250, 331, 332
Basu, K., 238, 325
Beck, N., 55, 56, 61, 68
Becker, G.S., 90
Bélanger, G., 82
Bendor, J., 312
Bennett, J.T., 79, 80
Berg, S., 38
Bernheim, B.D., 271, 333
Berry, W.D., 307
Bhansali, R.J., 43, 308
Binmore, K., 318
Black, D., 37
Blinder, A.S., 19, 250, 259
Boddy, R., 96, 97
Borooah, V.K., 48, 51, 59, 68, 70, 116, 117, 307, 308, 317
Boyes, W.J., 55
Brandsma, A.S., 320
Brennan, H.G., 296-299, 332, 336, 337
Breton, A., 83, 312
Brittain, J.A. 228
Brosio, G., 85
Browning, E.K., 203
Brunner, K., 304, 332
Buchanan, J.M., 250, 251, 268, 279, 282, 296-300, 332, 336, 337
Bush, W.C., 79

C
Cameron, D., 61, 307
Cavaco Silva, A.A., 332
Caves, R.E., 92
Centraal Bureau voor de Statistiek (CBS), 158, 159, 244, 245, 322, 323
Centraal Planbureau (CPB), 16-18, 181, 244, 303, 304, 322, 323
Chant, J.F., 332
Chappell, H.W. jr, 48, 49
Chow, G.C., 10
Christ, C.F., 249, 283
Chrystal, K.A., 53, 62, 71, 73, 75-77, 86, 130, 131, 311, 312
Coleman, J.S., 309
Commissie Economische Deskundigen, 335
Courant, P.N., 39, 80, 168
Cowart, A.T., 11, 12, 13, 62, 77, 157
Cracknell, R., 20
Crain, W.M., 250, 251, 252, 273
Crotty, J., 19, 96, 97

D
Davis, O.A., 86, 212, 312
De Grauwe, P., 157, 310
De Haan, R.J.A., 303
De Meyer, F., 38
De Swaan, A., 156, 165, 321, 323
De Wolff, P., 14
Den Butter, F.A.G., 12, 303, 304
Dempster, M.A.H., 86, 212, 312
Denzau, A.T., 79, 90, 314
Dewald, W.G., 12
Domar, E.D., 285
Don, F.J.M., 303
Downs, A., 37, 44, 60
Driehuis, W., 14, 303
Dunleavy, P., 168, 313

E
Ekelund, R.B. jr, 250, 251, 252, 273

Emanuel, H., 329, 331
Enelow, J.M., 38, 306
Esty, D.C., 92

F

Fair, R.C., 12, 20, 44, 48, 307, 308
Fase, M.M.G., 12, 303
Fassbender, H., 250
Fiorina, M., 44, 46, 83
Fishburn, P.C., 38
Fisher, D., 12
Foley, D.K., 95, 96
Fox, K.A., 10
Fratianni, M., 86, 92, 307
Freeman, R.B., 312
Frey, B.S., 22, 31, 42, 48, 50, 53, 58, 63-73, 76, 78, 79, 80, 86, 92, 131, 204, 250, 296, 308-311, 327, 328, 332
Friedlaender, A.F., 9, 12, 13, 29, 62, 303, 305
Friedman, B.M., 10
Froyen, R.T., 12, 13, 62, 303

G

Gandenberger, O., 320, 332
Gandolfo, G., 150, 327
Gärtner, M., 22, 90
Gehrlein, W.V., 38
Ginsburgh, V., 58
Golden, D.G., 56, 62, 68, 69, 72, 308
Goldscheid, R., 137
Goodhart, C.A.E., 43, 308
Gordon, D.F., 332
Goyeau, D., 22
Griffiths, R.T., 156, 304

H

Hafkamp, W.A., 304
Halberstadt, V., 329, 331
Harsanyi, J.C., 318
Hasselman, B.H., 303
Hibbs, D.A. Jr, 46, 48, 49, 50, 53, 60, 61, 131, 307, 308
Hinich, M.J., 38, 306
Hofkes, M., 305
Hu, S.C., 203
Hughes Hallett, A.J., 10

J

Jaarsma, B., 80
Johansen, L., 23, 25
Johnson, H.G., 12

K

Kalecki, M., 96, 97, 314
Kane, E.J., 332
Keech, W.R., 48, 49
Keizer, P.K., 51
Kiewiet, D.R., 43, 46, 308
Kinder, D.R., 46
Kirchgässner, G., 46, 49, 50, 58, 59, 308, 309, 310, 327
Kirschen, E.S., 14, 15, 60, 303
Klau, F., 1, 203, 249
Knegt, L., 304, 320
Knoester, A., 320
Koefoed, O., 320
Kramer, G.H., 43, 308
Kremers, J.J.M., 249, 250, 336
Kristensen, O.P., 39, 306
Kydland, F.E., 304

L

Lächler, U., 57, 58, 309
Laney, L.O., 56, 68
Larkey, P.D., 307
Lau, L.J., 63
Le Pen, Ch., 85
Lindbeck, A., 54, 59
Lipsey, R.G., 129, 319
Lowery, D., 56, 62, 307
Lucas, R.E. jr, 21, 306
Lybeck, J.A., 85, 93, 157

M

MacRae, C.D., 49, 54, 55, 308, 309
Makin, J.H., 29
Manzini, A., 85
McKelvey, R.D., 38
Meijerink, M.H., 336
Meltzer, A.H., 40, 41, 203, 304, 306, 307
Merkies, A.H.Q.M., 25, 26, 27, 305
Michaels, R., 49
Michel, Ph., 58
Migué, J.L., 82

Miliband, R., 95
Miller, G.J., 84, 313
Minford, P., 49, 62
Moe, T.M., 84, 312, 313
Moene, K.O., 84, 313
Mosley, P., 20, 31, 32, 46, 53, 56, 73-75, 305, 306, 307, 308, 311, 314
Mueller, D.C., 86, 89, 93, 316
Mueller, J.E., 43, 308
Munger, M.C., 90, 314
Murrell, P., 86, 89, 93

N
Nash, J.F., 123-126, 318
Naumann, J., 92
Neck, R., 67
Nice, D.C., 91
Niskanen, W.A. Jr, 81-87, 332
Noll, R.G., 83
Nordhaus, W.D., 53, 54, 55, 131, 308, 309, 319

O
Okker, V.R., 303
Olson, M., 88, 89
Orzechowski, W.P., 79, 80, 84

P
Pagan, A.R., 10
Paldam, M., 43, 55, 308
Peacock, A.T., 130, 212
Peel, D., 49, 62
Peeperkorn, L.P.M., 51
Peltzman, S., 90, 307
Pissarides, C.A., 48
Plott, Ch.R., 38
Pommer, E., 168
Pommerehne, W.W., 39, 40, 78, 79, 80
Popper, K.R., 300
Poterba, J.M., 56, 62, 68, 69, 72, 308
Poulantzas, N., 95
Prescott, E.C., 304
Preston, A.J., 10
Przeworski, A., 95
Purvis, D.D., 129, 319

R
Radner, R., 316
Ramser, H.J., 58
Rau, N., 283
Rees, H.J.B., 10
Renaud, P.S.A., 51, 67, 77, 157, 161, 185, 321, 323
Reuber, G.L., 12
Richard, S.F., 40, 41, 203, 306, 307
Riker, W.H., 38, 306
Rivers, D., 43, 46, 308
Roberts, P.C., 332
Rockman, B.A., 80, 168
Romer, Th., 39, 41, 306
Rosenstone, S.J., 80
Rosenthal, H., 39, 41, 306
Roth, A.E., 318
Rubinstein, A., 318

S
Sabo, W.A., 55, 324
Salamon, L.M., 91, 315
Samuelson, P.A., 129, 319
Sandee, J., 24, 303, 305
Sargent, Th.J., 21, 304
Saunders, P., 1, 203, 249
Scherer, F.M., 315
Schneider, F., 31, 40, 42, 43, 48, 50, 53, 63-73, 76, 86, 92, 131, 156, 157, 161, 179, 204, 250, 308-311, 327, 328, 332
Schram, A., 80, 156, 325
Seater, J.J., 332
Sen, A.K., 23, 36, 306
Sengupta, J.K., 10
Shleifer, A., 271, 333
Shubik, M., 123
Siegfried, J.F., 91, 315
Smyth, D.J., 145, 151
Snyder, W.W., 228
Sociaal en Cultureel Planbureau (SCP), 39, 328
Söderström, L., 332
Solow, R.M., 19, 250, 259
Soh, B.H., 55, 77, 308
Spinelli, F., 86, 92, 307
Steenkamp, T.B.M., 51
Steiner, P.O., 129, 319
Stigler, G.J., 47, 58

Stolp, C., 307
Sulock, J.M., 55, 324
Summers, L.A., 271, 333
Svejnar, J., 318

T

Ten Raa, Th., 105, 117, 121, 126
Theil, H., 8, 10, 305
Thompson, W.R., 55, 308
Thorbecke, E., 10
Tinbergen, J., 7, 16
Tobin, J., 324
Tufte, E.R., 55, 61, 77, 308
Tullock, G., 296

V

Van de Beld, C.A., 303
Van den Berg, J.Th.J., 79, 324
Van den Berg, P.J.C.M., 303
Van der Geest, L., 25, 27
Van der Ploeg, F., 48, 51, 57, 58, 59, 68, 70, 116, 117, 307, 308, 309, 317
Van der Windt, N., 320
Van Eijk, C.J., 24
Van Praag, B.M.S., 329, 331
Van Veen, A.P., 51
Van Velthoven, B.C.J., 101, 161, 179, 185, 194, 315, 319, 321, 323, 324, 327, 328, 330
Van Wijngaarden, P., 204

Van Winden, F.A.A.M., 51, 67, 77, 80, 100, 101-128, 185, 194, 204, 315, 316, 317, 319, 321-325, 327, 328, 330, 331
Vasilatos, N., 48, 307, 308
Verbon, H.A.A., 204
Verdoorn, P.J., 303
Vermaat, A.J., 26, 27, 305

W

Wagner, R.E., 130, 250, 251, 268, 279, 282
Wallace, N., 21, 304
Wallerstein, M., 95
Walters, A.A., 249
Waud, R.N., 12, 303
Weber, W.E., 131
White, B.B., 332
Wiebrens, C., 204
Wildavsky, A., 86, 212, 312
Willett, Th.D., 56, 68
Winer, M., 307
Wintrobe, R., 83, 312
Wiseman, J., 130, 212
Wolfinger, R.E., 80
Wolinsky, A., 318
Wood, J.H., 12

Z

Zuidema, T., 273
Zuk, G., 55, 308

SUBJECT INDEX

A
Abstention, 37, 41
Accelerator mechanism, 151
Acknowledged power, 112, 120, 167
Action, collective
  see Collective action
Altruism, 105, 106
Automatic stabilization 145, 150-152

B
Behavioural equations of the state 136, 210, 261
Bonds, 253, 260
Budget
  along business cycle, 286
  along steady growth path, 284
  balanced, 145, 147
  constraint, 65, 135, 136, 211, 260
  constraint, intertemporal, 254, 261
  countercyclical behavior of the, 278, 279, 287
  deficit/surplus, 134, 249, 253, 262-263, 279
  deficit parameter, 136, 160, 264
  discretionary, 82
  maximization, 82
  procyclical behaviour of the, 278, 279, 287
Budget-output function, 81
Bureaucracy, 6, 65, 69, 78-87, 108
  interaction with politicians, 81
Bureaucrats, 6, 99, 108, 114, 168
  as voters, 79
  positive agency effect on, 80, 168
  voting turnout of, 79, 80
Business cycle, 286
  see also Political business cycle

C
Capital, 95
  human, 250, 271
  market imperfections, 249, 255
  non-human, 250, 271
Capitalist(s), 94, 103, 137, 206, 271-272
Central bank (behaviour), 20, 68, 254, 310, 332
Christian-democrats (CDA), 25-27, 51, 155, 273, 305, 321
Class(es), 60, 94, 101, 103, 132, 206, 253, 258
Coalition government, 50, 58, 77, 155
Collective action, 299, 313, 315
  logic of, 88-89
Computer simulation, 187, 310, 327
Constitutional choice, positive theory of, 300
Constitutional political economy, 297-300
Consumption, 19, 142, 218
Contractarian approach, 298
Core constituency, 53, 59, 60
Crisis management, 32, 73
Criterion function, 8, 35
Cycling, 36, 41

D
Democracy, 6, 35
  direct, 40
  representative, 6, 40
Demographic developments, 228-229
Dependant(s), 103, 132-133, 206, 237, 258, 270
Displacement effects, 130, 212
Disposable income, growth of real, 43, 45-46, 63
Dynamic analysis, 148-152, 185-202, 283-290

E
Economic policy, 7, 33
  advice, 148, 296
  adviser, 296, 304
  instruments of, 7, 14, 56, 62
  targets of, 7, 13
  theory of, 3, 7, 297, 300
  time lags in, 15, 30
Economic positions
  see Positions

Effective interest structure, 136, 212, 223, 229
Effective interest weight, 139, 230, 261
Effective time preference schedule, 262, 269
Election(s), 42, 155
  date, 57
  outcome, 43, 79
Electoral
  cycle, 43, 73
  period, 57, 58, 155
Elementary economic position, 103, 132, 206
Employment, 222
  private sector, 143, 147, 189, 197
  rate, 163, 165
  state (sector), 133, 144, 145, 189
Exports, 218

F
Fiscal policy, 12-13, 20
  reaction functions, 13
Flexible target model, 9
Free-rider (problem), 83, 88, 336

G
Goods
  collective, 132, 142
  market, 103, 132
  non-marketed, 103, 132
  state, 133, 137
Government, 6, 53
Growth, 277-279, 284-286
  rate of, 277
  of real disposable income, 43, 45, 63
  steady state, 284

H
Heterogeneous membership, 105, 107

I
Ideology, 53, 59, 64, 70, 105, 106, 111, 311
Imports, 218
Income-expenditure model, 19, 129, 153, 187, 218
Income tax, 139, 263, 274
  differentiated, 140, 263
  uniform, 139, 264
Income transfers, 133, 203, 258
Incremental budgeting behaviour, 86, 212
Industrial organization, 100, 119
Inflation, 43, 46, 49, 54, 63, 279-280
Institutional equations, 17
Interactive optimization, 304
Interest(s), 102, 127
  class, 103, 120
  diffuse, 89
  elementary, 103
  representation, 102
  specialized, 89
  tree, 109
  vested, 112, 120, 167
Interest blocs, 107
  level specific, 107, 108, 109
  representative, 107, 108, 109
Interest function
  augmented, 111-114
  complex, 106, 109, 111-113, 164, 207
  elementary, 104, 106, 113, 116, 133, 208, 253, 256, 259, 332
  nested complex, 107, 109, 110, 112-114
  state, 116, 127, 133, 208, 259
Interest function approach, 4, 101, 131
  discussion of the, 113-126
  outline of the, 101-113
Interest groups, 73, 79, 88-94, 111, 122
  influence of, 89-93
  number of, 89, 93
Interest payments, 260, 275
Interest rate, 254, 259, 275
Interest weight
  effective, 139, 230, 261
  influence weighted, 261
Intransitivity, 36, 41
Investment, 19, 129, 142, 151, 218

K
Keynesian income-expenditure model
  see Income-expenditure model

L

Labour force, 208
Labour market, 135, 209
Labour productivity, 134, 146, 200, 209
Lagrangean multiplier approach, 121-123
Liberal-conservatives (VVD), 26, 51, 155, 273, 321
Life-cycle model, 254, 332
Lucas' critique, 20-22

M

Macroeconometric models, 16-18
  critique of, 18-23
  in the Netherlands, 16-18
  specification errors in, 19
Market power, 142
Marxist approach, 35, 94-97, 99
Median income, 40, 307
Median voter, 37, 203, 306
Median voter model, 36-41, 79, 312
  empirical tests, 39-41
  multi-dimensional issue, 38
  one-dimensional issue, 37
Mobility (anticipated social), 105, 106, 111, 115, 164, 206
Monetary policy, 12, 20, 295
  reaction functions, 12
Multi-party system(s)
  ideology in, 60
  in the Netherlands, 77, 156
  voting- and popularity-functions in case of, 45, 50, 69, 77
Multiple positions, 105, 106, 111
Multiplier, 19-20, 34, 143, 144, 220

N

Nash bargaining solution, 123-126, 318
  asymmetric, 318
Nash product, 124

P

Paradox of voting, 36, 38
Pareto frontier, 118, 122, 124
Pareto optimal outcome, 117
Partial adjustment process, 174, 232, 325

Partisan effect, 60, 310
  sustained, 60
  transitory, 60
Party allegiance, 59, 60
Party identification, 45, 52
Permanent income theory, 73, 76-77, 130, 138
Perpetuities, 258
Phase-diagram, 189, 191, 196
Phillips-curve, 48, 54-55, 58
Policy-ineffectiveness proposition, 46, 304, 308
Policy reaction functions, 10, 64, 72, 74, 130, 204, 249, 250
  derivation of, 10
  and the electoral calendar, 56
  empirical evidence, 11-13
  impact of politics on, 13
Political business cycle, 53-59
  discussion, 56
  empirical tests, 55-56
  Marxist version of the, 96, 97
Political parties, 37, 44-45, 59, 77
  in the Netherlands, 25-27, 51, 155, 273, 305, 321
Political power, 142
Politicians, 6, 42, 59, 77, 98, 108, 114
  interaction with bureaucracy, 81
Politico-economic interdependence, 43
  closed model of, 71, 296
Politico-economic model(s), 142
  closed, 186, 296
  dynamic, 148
  including social security, 218
  static Keynesian, 142
Popularity deficit, 64
Popularity function(s), 42, 56, 63
  differences from voting functions, 43
  discussion, 45
  empirical evidence, 45
  empirical findings for the Netherlands, 51
Popularity surplus, 64
Positions
  elementary economic, 103, 132, 206
  multiple, 105, 106, 111
Power
  coefficient, 136, 144-146, 161, 173, 212

distribution, 137, 140, 173
  market, 142
  political, 142
  structure of society, 185, 186
  weights, 119, 120, 162, 229, 232
Preference function of the policy maker, 8, 23
  establishing the, 23-31
Preference weights, 137, 161, 174, 229, 232, 267
Pressure, 102, 111, 113, 114, 162
Pressure groups, 111, 204
Private sector, 134, 135, 142, 218
  worker, see Worker(s)
Production, 142, 222
Profit tax, 134, 209, 260, 274
Public choice approach, 3, 35, 94
Public sector, 6, 108

R
Rate of growth, 277
Rate of growth of real disposable income, 43, 45, 46, 63
Rate of inflation, 43, 45, 46, 63
Rate of interest
  see Interest rate
Rate of time preference, 268, 272
Rate of unemployment, 43, 45, 46, 63
Reaction functions
  see Policy reaction functions
Re-election, 54, 58, 64
  activities, 56, 165
  efforts, 66, 69
  prospects, 53
Relative numerical strength, 104, 132, 162, 167, 232
Representation, see Interest(s)
Representative agent, 102, 104, 108, 133, 316
Revealed preference, 28, 120, 177, 238
Ricardian equivalence, 249, 255, 331, 332

S
Satisficing, 31, 64, 74
Selective incentives, 89
Self-employed, 163, 180, 243
Simultaneity bias, 34, 68, 322, 324
Social classes, see Class(es)

Social-democrats (PvdA), 25-27, 51, 155, 273, 321
Social security, 133, 203
  labour market related, 206, 215, 224, 226
  labour market unrelated, 206, 213, 222, 225
Social welfare functions, 23, 36
Specification errors, 19
Stability problems, 47, 145, 149-152, 186-199, 225-228
State, 6
  behaviour, 133, 136, 137, 210, 261
  debt, level of, 260, 275
  employment, 133
  expenditure, 134, 138
  expenditure, non-wage material, 134, 148, 218
  interest function, 116, 127, 133, 208, 259
  sector worker, see Worker(s)
Strategic bequest motive, 257, 271
Structural coercion, 102, 113, 117, 135
Structure-conduct-performance approach, 100, 315
Supernumerary tax capacity, 211

T
Tax
  base, 139, 147, 260, 277
  income, see Income tax
  profit, see Profit tax
  rate, 134, 139, 209, 254, 260
  shifting, 134, 139, 209, 266, 274, 320, 322
Tax capacity, 211, 220, 223
  intertemporal discretionary, 261, 275
  supernumerary, 211
Threat point, 124-126
Time discount rate of voters, 48
Time horizon, 254
  of the social classes, 257, 268, 276
  of the state, 257, 268, 276, 280
Time preference
  effective .. schedule, 262, 269
  rate of, 268, 272
  schedule, 254, 269, 270

U

Unemployed, 163, 206
Unemployment, 43, 49-50, 54, 63, 75
Unemployment benefit, 206, 209, 214, 224

V

Veil of uncertainty, 299
Voter(s)
  different groups of, 49
  median, see Median voter model
  swing, 45
  time discount rate of, 48
  turnout, 79, 80
Voting, 42-52
  aggregation problem, 307
  equilibrium, 37
  functions, 42, 43
  myopic, 48
  personal financial conditions and, 46
  rational, 48, 57
  retrospective, 44
  sophisticated, 48
  strategic, 48, 57

W

Wage rate(s), 135, 209
Wagner's law, 130, 138, 206
Welfare function, 8, 23, 74, 305
Worker(s), 94, 103
  private sector, 103, 132, 206, 270
  state sector, 103, 108, 132, 206, 270

D. Bös, M. Rose, C. Seidl (Eds.)

Welfare and Efficiency in Public Economics

1988. 28 figures. XVI, 424 pages.
ISBN 3-540-18824-X

Contents: Introduction. - Welfare and Efficiency Measures - General Aspects. - Computing Welfare Effects of Fiscal Policy Programmes in an Applied General Equilibrium Setting. - Welfare and Efficiency of Selected Fiscal Policy Measures. - Addresses of Authors.

This book contains 15 selected and revised papers presented at a conference in Neresheim, West Germany, in June 1986.

R. Pethig, U. Schlieper (Eds.)

Efficiency, Institutions, and Economic Policy

Proceedings of a Workshop held by the Sonderforschungsbereich 5 at the University of Mannheim, June 1986

1987. 21 figures. IX, 225 pages.
ISBN 3-540-18450-3

Contents: Economic Order and Public Policy-Market, Constitution and the Welfare State. - Macroeconomic Policy, Rent Seeking and Economic Order. - The Growth of Government and the Rise of Pressure Groups. - Family Structure and Intergenerational Transfers in Social Health Insurance: A Public Choice Model. - The Demsetz Hypothesis on the Emergence of Property Rights Reconsidered. - The Efficiency of the Common Law: A New Institutional Economics Perspective. - Specific Human Capital and Collective Codetermination Rights. - Free Riders and Voluntary Contributions Reconsidered. - Competition versus Monopoly in the Supply of Public Goods.

Springer-Verlag
Berlin Heidelberg New York
London Paris Tokyo Hong Kong

W. Weidlich, G. Haag (Eds.)

Interregional Migration

Dynamic Theory and Comparative Analysis

With contributions by Å. E. Andersson, G. Haag, I. Holmberg, J. Ledent, M. Munz, D. Pumain, G. Rabino, R. Reiner, N. Sarafoglou, M. Sonis, W. Weidlich

1988. 129 figures, 64 tables. XIV, 387 pages.
ISBN 3-540-18441-4

Contents: Introduction. - General Theory: Concepts of the Dynamic Migration Model. The Migratory Equations of Motion. The Estimation of Parameters. - Interregional Migration in Individual Countries: Federal Republic of Germany. Canada. France. Israel. Italy. Sweden. - Comparative Studies: Comparative Analysis of Population Evolution Models. Comparative Analysis of Interregional Migration. - Mathematical Methods: Derivation of the Master Equation. Solutions of the Master Equation. Tests of Significance in the Ranking Regression Analysis. Ranking Regression Analysis of the Global Mobility. A Compter Program for the Estimation of Utilities and Mobilities. - References.

G. Fels, G. M. von Furstenberg (Eds.)

A Supply-Side Agenda for Germany

Sparks from: the United States; Great Britain; European Integration

1989. 7 figures. VI, 439 pages.
ISBN 3-540-50544-X

This book deals with supply-side economics and the needed reorientation it would bring to West German policy. The Change, recommended after searching analysis, would add up to an overall strategy for freeing markets, for removing government-imposed distortions, and for using free-market approaches to correct distortions imposed by pressure groups. The strategy would pierce Germany's state-supported encrustations and corporatism. It would equip the country to follow the lead of the United States and Great Britain in starting to escape from the tangle in which taxes, regulations, and unemployment have grown in step. The impending completion of the European internal market in 1992 adds urgency to this task.

The objective of this series is to report new developments in the broad field of modern economics. Special emphasis is to be given to the publication of new research results, be it in the classical areas of economics or in newly developed ones. Surveys are also to be published.

The type of material considered for publication therefore includes:

1. Monographs on the afore mentioned fields
2. Working and discussion papers
3. Lectures on a new field or presentation of a new angle in a classical field
4. Seminar work-outs
5. Translations
6. Reports of meetings, provided they are
    a) of exceptional interest and
    b) devoted to a single topic

Texts which are out of print but still in demand may also be considered if they fall within these categories.

Manuscripts

Manuscripts should be no less than 100 and preferably no more than 500 pages in length. On request, the publisher will supply special paper with the typing area outlined and essentials for the preparation of camera-ready manuscripts. Manuscripts should be sent directly to Springer-Verlag Heidelberg or Springer-Verlag New York.

Springer-Verlag, Heidelberger Platz 3, D-1000 Berlin 33
Springer-Verlag, Tiergartenstraße 17, D-6900 Heidelberg 1
Springer-Verlag, 175 Fifth Avenue, New York, NY 10010/USA
Springer-Verlag, 37-3, Hongo 3-chome, Bunkyo-ku, Tokyo 113, Japan

H.L GRANT	DATE DUE	
	JUN 1 6 1997	